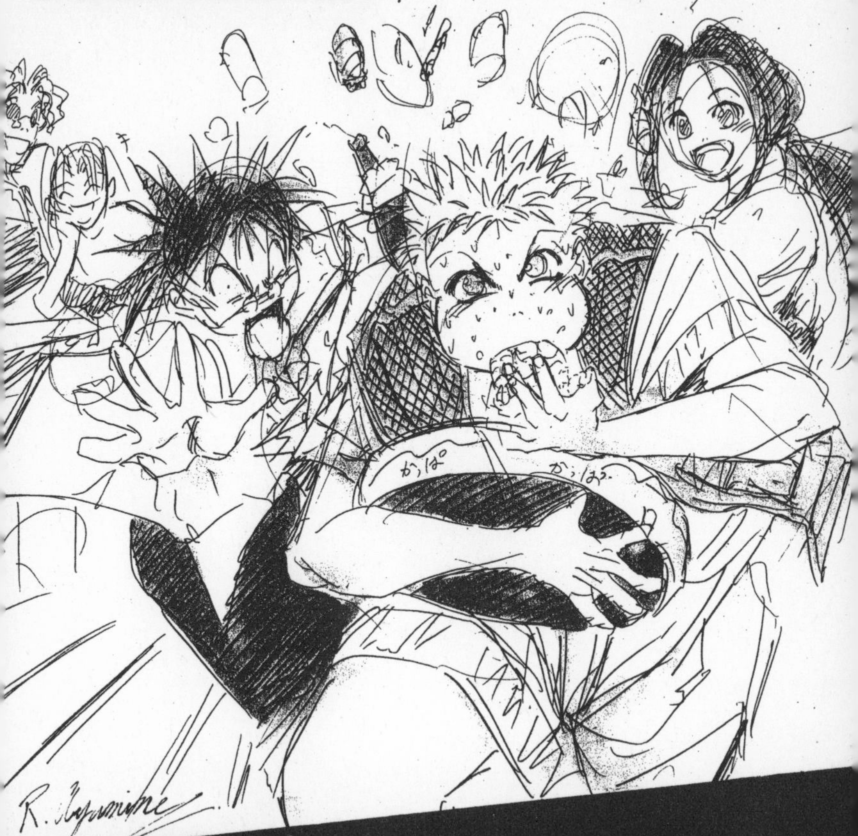
かっぱ

2

GETBACKERS™

GETBACKERS

Volume 2

Art by Rando Ayamine
Story by Yuya Aoki

Los Angeles • Tokyo • London

Translator - James Cohen
English Adaptation - Ryan Shankel
Associate Editor - Arthur Milliken
Retouch and Lettering - Vincente Rivera, Jr.
Cover Layout - Patrick Hook

Editor - Luis Reyes
Digital Imaging Manager - Chris Buford
Pre-Press Manager - Antonio DePietro
Production Managers - Jennifer Miller, Mutsumi Miyazaki
Art Director - Matt Alford
Managing Editor - Jill Freshney
VP of Production - Ron Klamert
President & C.O.O. - John Parker
Publisher & C.E.O. - Stuart Levy

E-mail: info@TOKYOPOP.com
Come visit us online at www.TOKYOPOP.com

A  Manga

TOKYOPOP Inc.
5900 Wilshire Blvd. Suite 2000
Los Angeles, CA 90036

Get Backers Vol. 2

ISBN: 1-59182-634-9

First TOKYOPOP printing: April 2004

10 9 8 7 6 5 4 3 2 1

Printed in the USA

Story Thus Far:

Ginji Amano can amplify the electrical currents in his body. Ban Mido has the power to create illusions in people's minds for one minute. Together they are the GetBackers, a retrieval agency whose motto is, "We get back what shouldn't be gone." For the right price, they'll return anything that's been taken.

Well, recently the duo has fallen on hard times, and would have crapped out entirely if it wasn't for the work of the well-buxomed HEVN, who has a knack for getting them work, even if the work often gets them in way over their heads.

Their current client is a young lady who implores them to return a family heirloom—a giant Chinese statue of a cat that is supposed to bring good luck. But little do they know that the lady is working for a crooked doctor who actually wants a disk that's hidden in the statue...a disk, unluckily enough, that has fallen out of the statue and into Ginji's backpack. Now the doctor has sent his goons to get it back...and pick up a few more bodies to harvest for organs to sell on the black market.

Ya caught up? Then here we go.

Table of Contents

Act II: The Case of the Lucky Cat

Act III: Givers and Takers

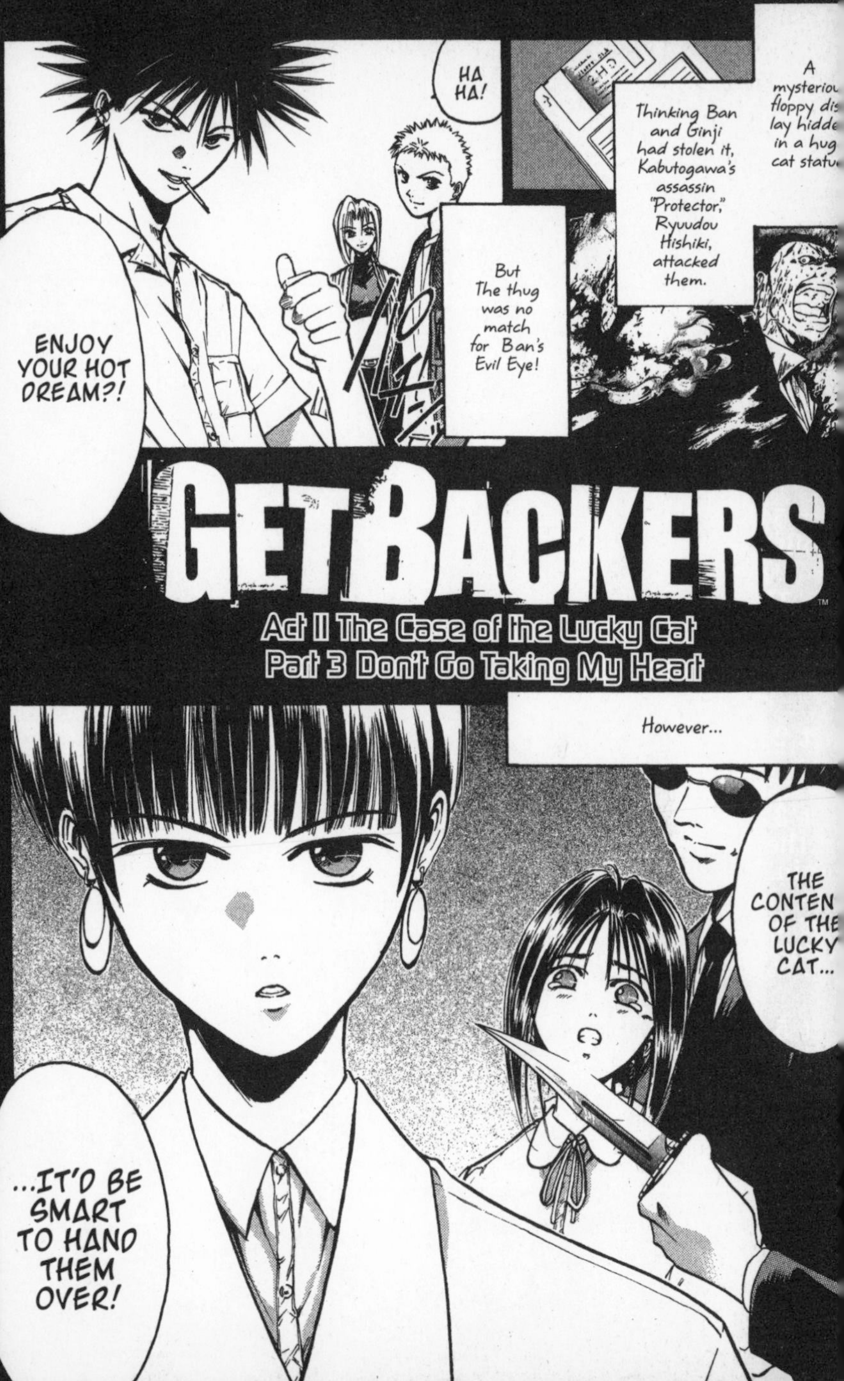
A mysteriou floppy dis lay hidde in a hug cat statu
Thinking Ban and Ginji had stolen it, Kabutogawa's assassin "Protector," Ryuudou Hishiki, attacked them.
But The thug was no match for Ban's Evil Eye!
HA HA!
ENJOY YOUR HOT DREAM?!
GETBACKERS
Act II The Case of the Lucky Cat
Part 3 Don't Go Taking My Heart
However...
THE CONTEN OF THE LUCKY CAT...
...IT'D BE SMART TO HAND THEM OVER!

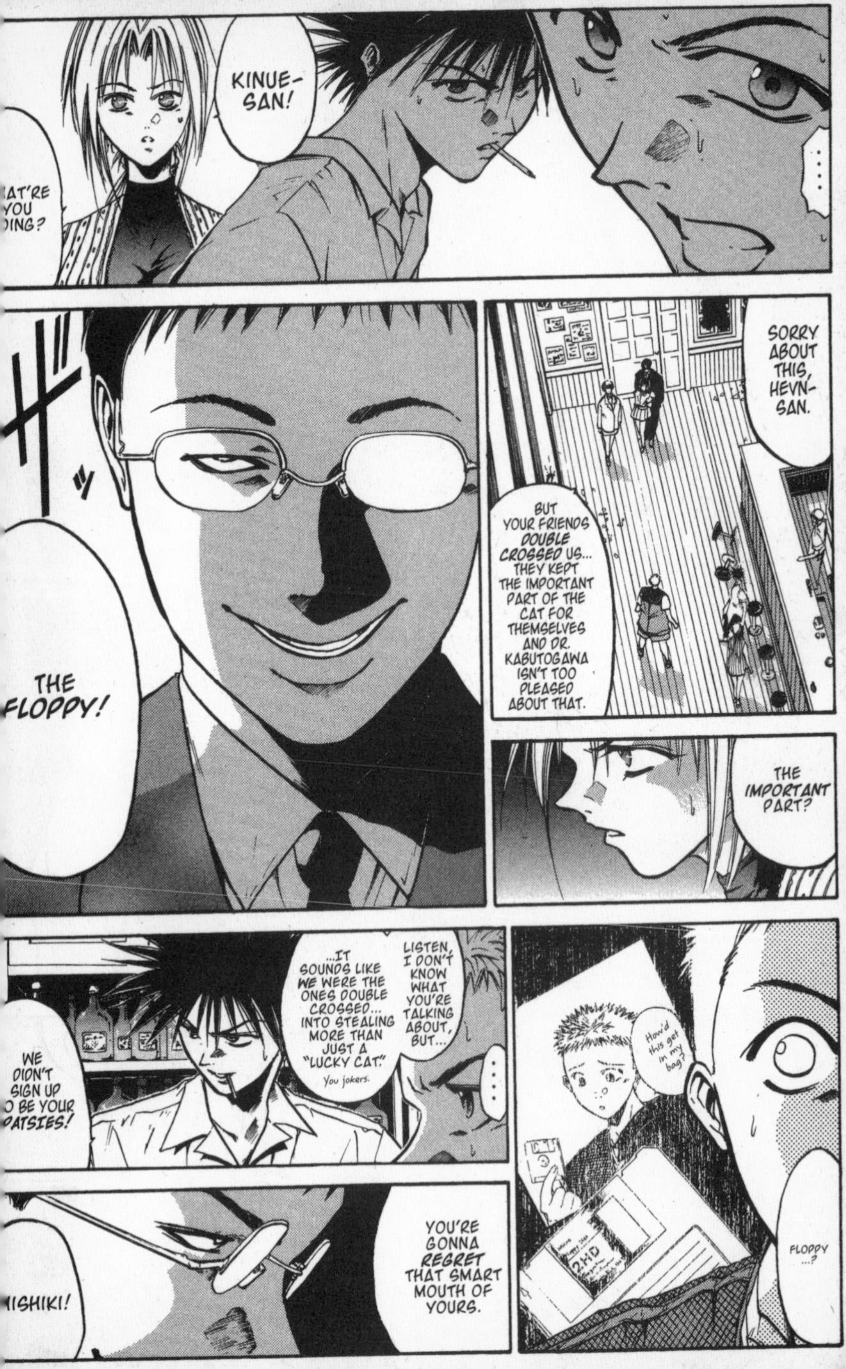
....
KINUE-SAN!
AT'RE YOU DING?
SORRY ABOUT THIS, HEVN-SAN.
BUT YOUR FRIENDS DOUBLE CROSSED US... THEY KEPT THE IMPORTANT PART OF THE CAT FOR THEMSELVES AND DR. KABUTOGAWA ISN'T TOO PLEASED ABOUT THAT.
THE IMPORTANT PART?
THE FLOPPY!
How'd this get in my bag?
FLOPPY ...?
....
LISTEN, I DON'T KNOW WHAT YOU'RE TALKING ABOUT, BUT...
...IT SOUNDS LIKE WE WERE THE ONES DOUBLE CROSSED... INTO STEALING MORE THAN JUST A "LUCKY CAT."
You jokers.
WE DIDN'T SIGN UP O BE YOUR PATSIES!
YOU'RE GONNA REGRET THAT SMART MOUTH OF YOURS.
ISHIKI!

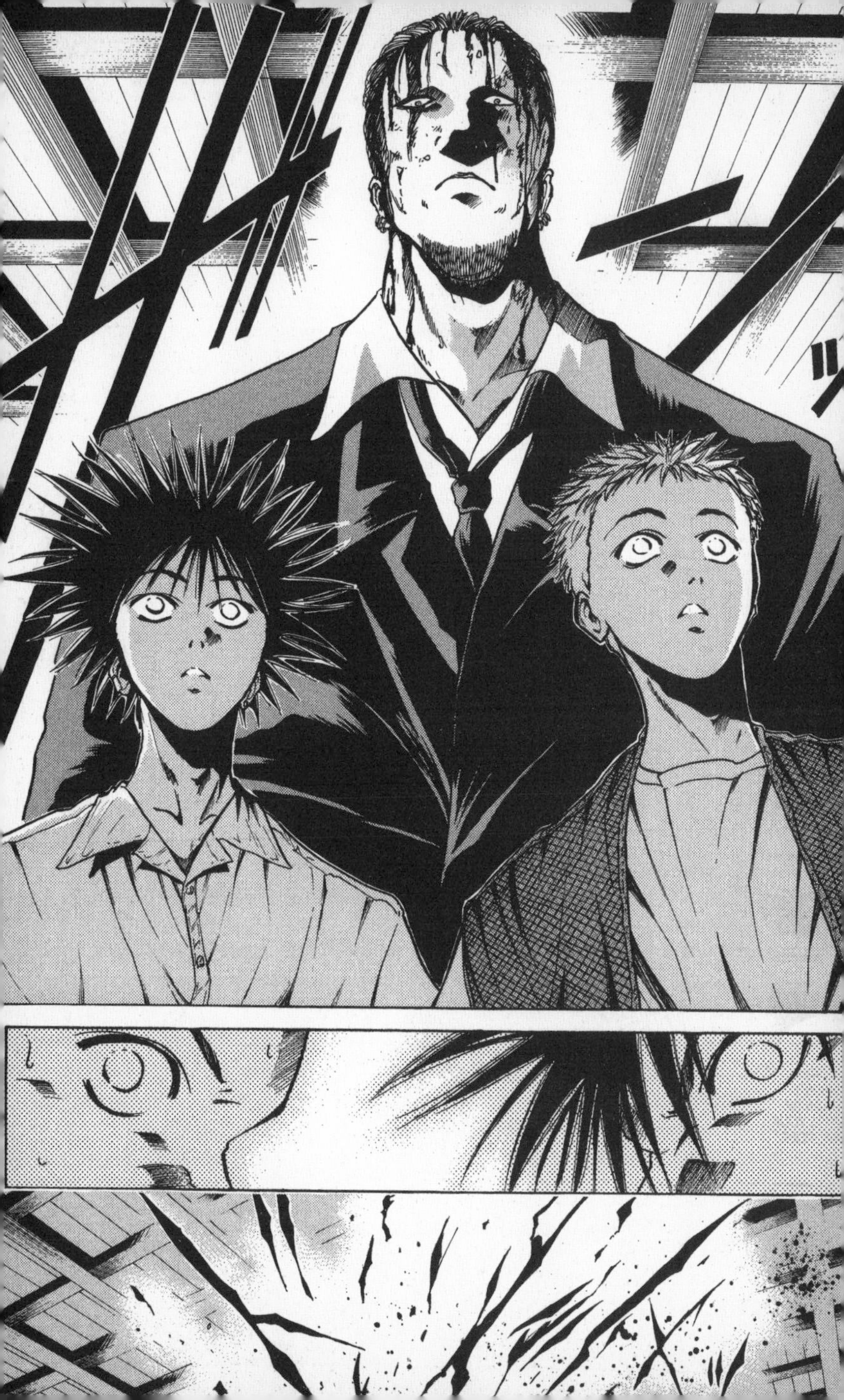

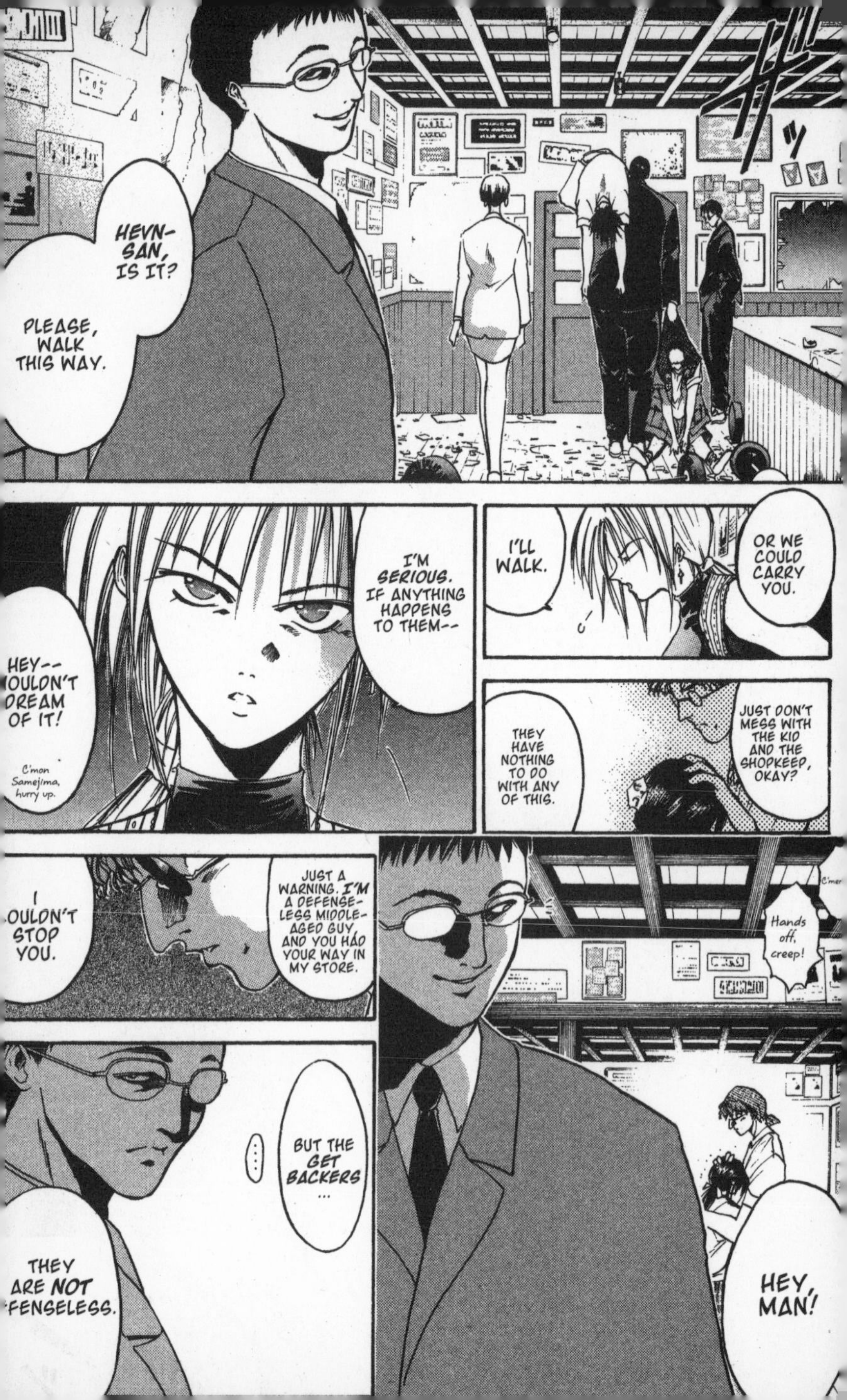
HEVN-SAN, IS IT?
PLEASE, WALK THIS WAY.
OR WE COULD CARRY YOU.
I'LL WALK.
JUST DON'T MESS WITH THE KID AND THE SHOPKEEP, OKAY?
THEY HAVE NOTHING TO DO WITH ANY OF THIS.
I'M SERIOUS. IF ANYTHING HAPPENS TO THEM--
HEY-- OULDN'T DREAM OF IT!
C'mon Samejima, hurry up.
C'mer
Hands off, creep!
HEY, MAN!
JUST A WARNING. I'M A DEFENSELESS MIDDLE-AGED GUY, AND YOU HAD YOUR WAY IN MY STORE.
I OULDN'T STOP YOU.
...
BUT THE GET BACKERS...
THEY ARE NOT FENSELESS.

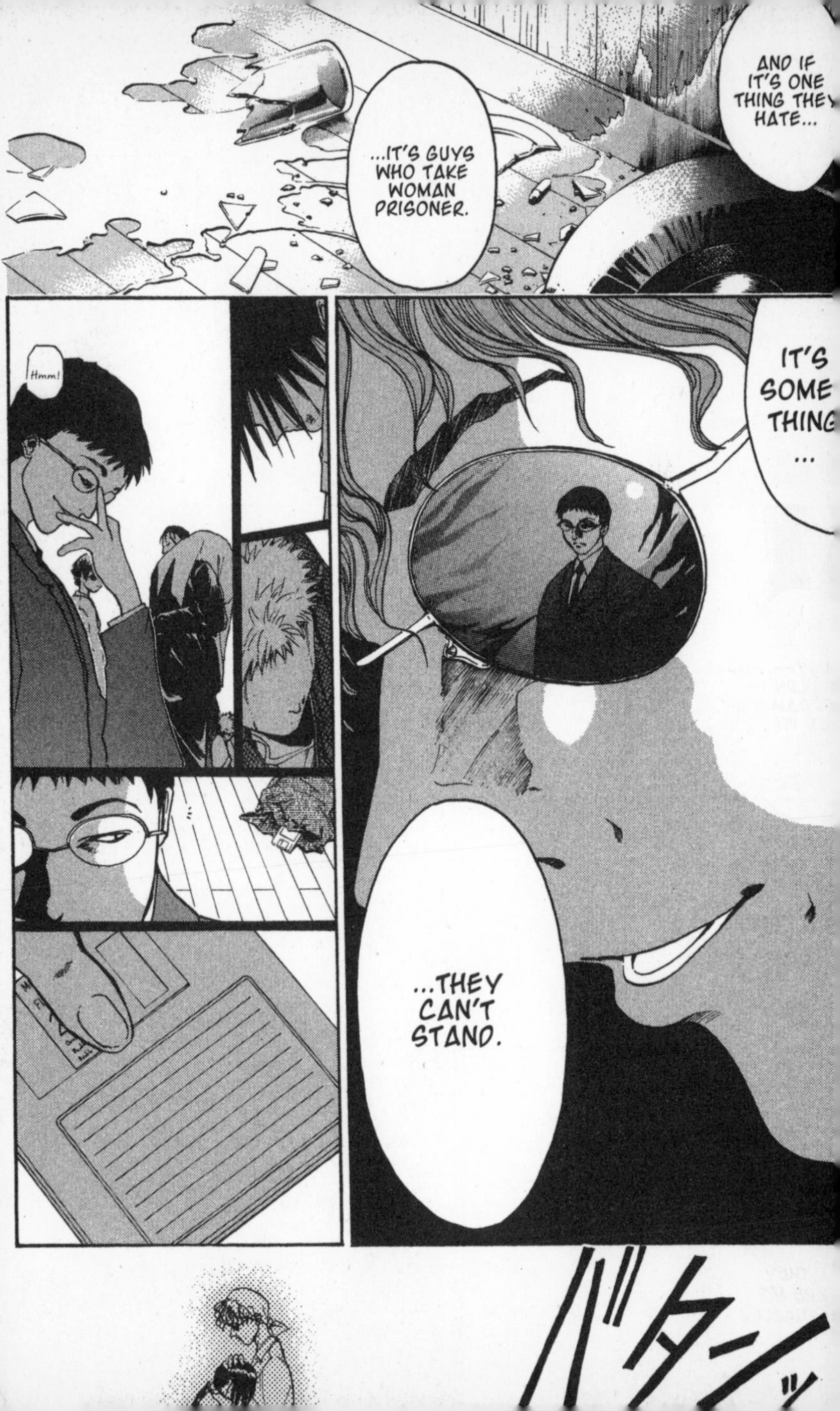
AND IF IT'S ONE THING THEY HATE...
...IT'S GUYS WHO TAKE WOMAN PRISONER.
IT'S SOME THING ...
...THEY CAN'T STAND.
Hmm!
バタンッ

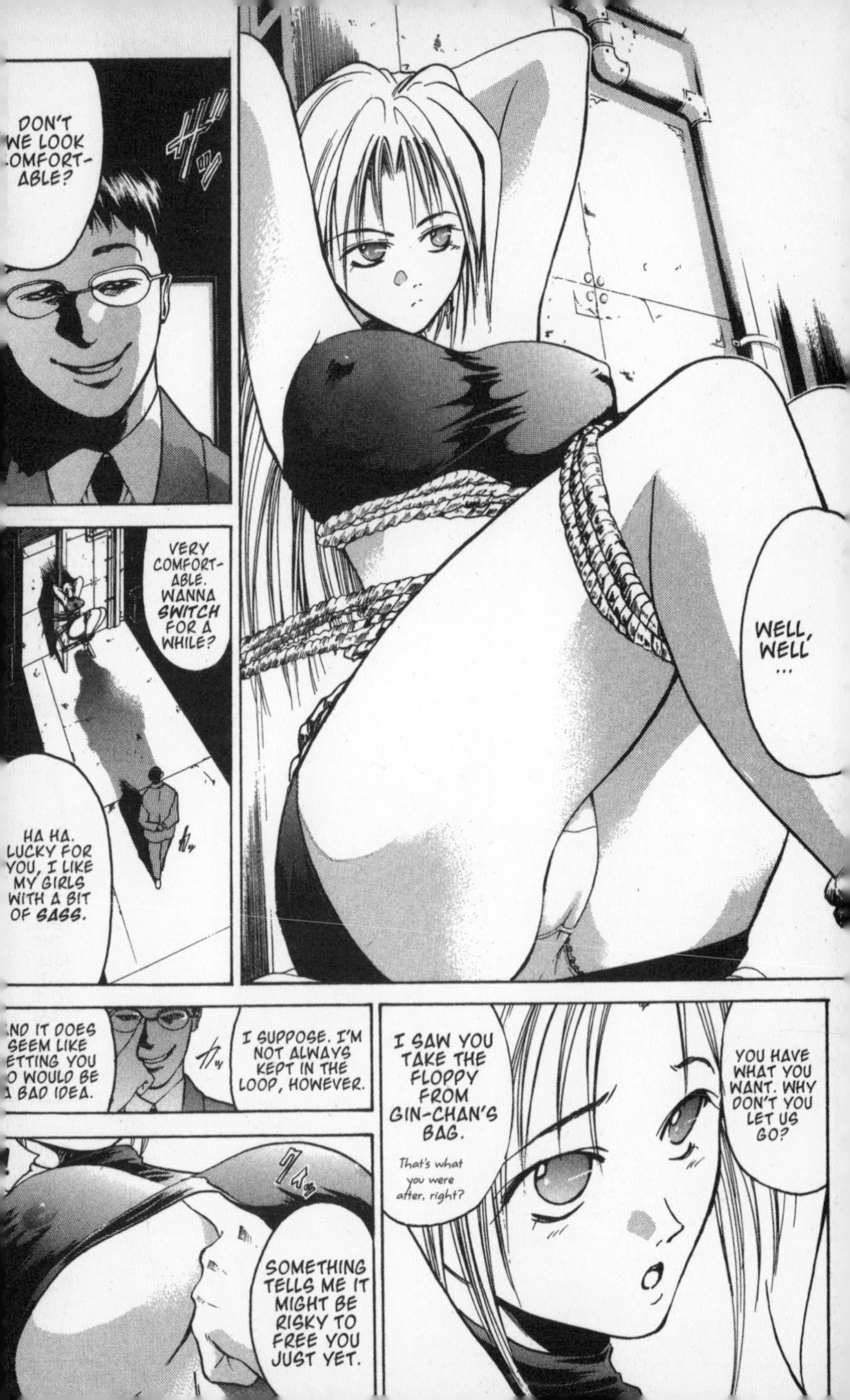
WELL, WELL...
DON'T WE LOOK COMFORTABLE?
VERY COMFORTABLE. WANNA SWITCH FOR A WHILE?
HA HA. LUCKY FOR YOU, I LIKE MY GIRLS WITH A BIT OF SASS.
YOU HAVE WHAT YOU WANT. WHY DON'T YOU LET US GO?
I SAW YOU TAKE THE FLOPPY FROM GIN-CHAN'S BAG.
That's what you were after, right?
I SUPPOSE. I'M NOT ALWAYS KEPT IN THE LOOP, HOWEVER.
AND IT DOES SEEM LIKE LETTING YOU GO WOULD BE A BAD IDEA.
SOMETHING TELLS ME IT MIGHT BE RISKY TO FREE YOU JUST YET.

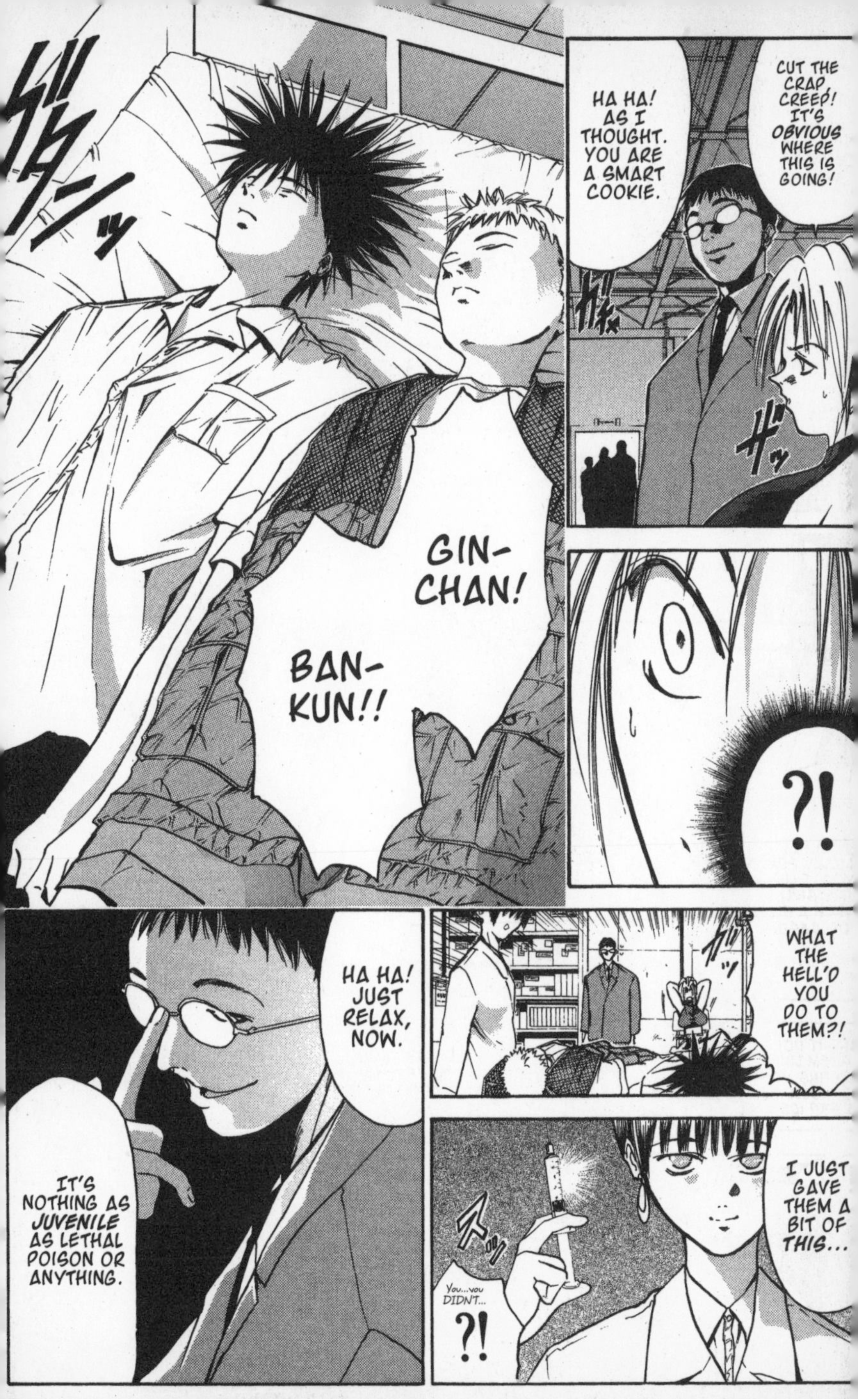
CUT THE CRAP, CREEP! IT'S OBVIOUS WHERE THIS IS GOING!
HA HA! AS I THOUGHT. YOU ARE A SMART COOKIE.
?!
GIN-CHAN!
BAN-KUN!!
WHAT THE HELL'D YOU DO TO THEM?!
I JUST GAVE THEM A BIT OF THIS...
You...you DIDN'T...
?!
HA HA! JUST RELAX, NOW.
IT'S NOTHING AS JUVENILE AS LETHAL POISON OR ANYTHING.

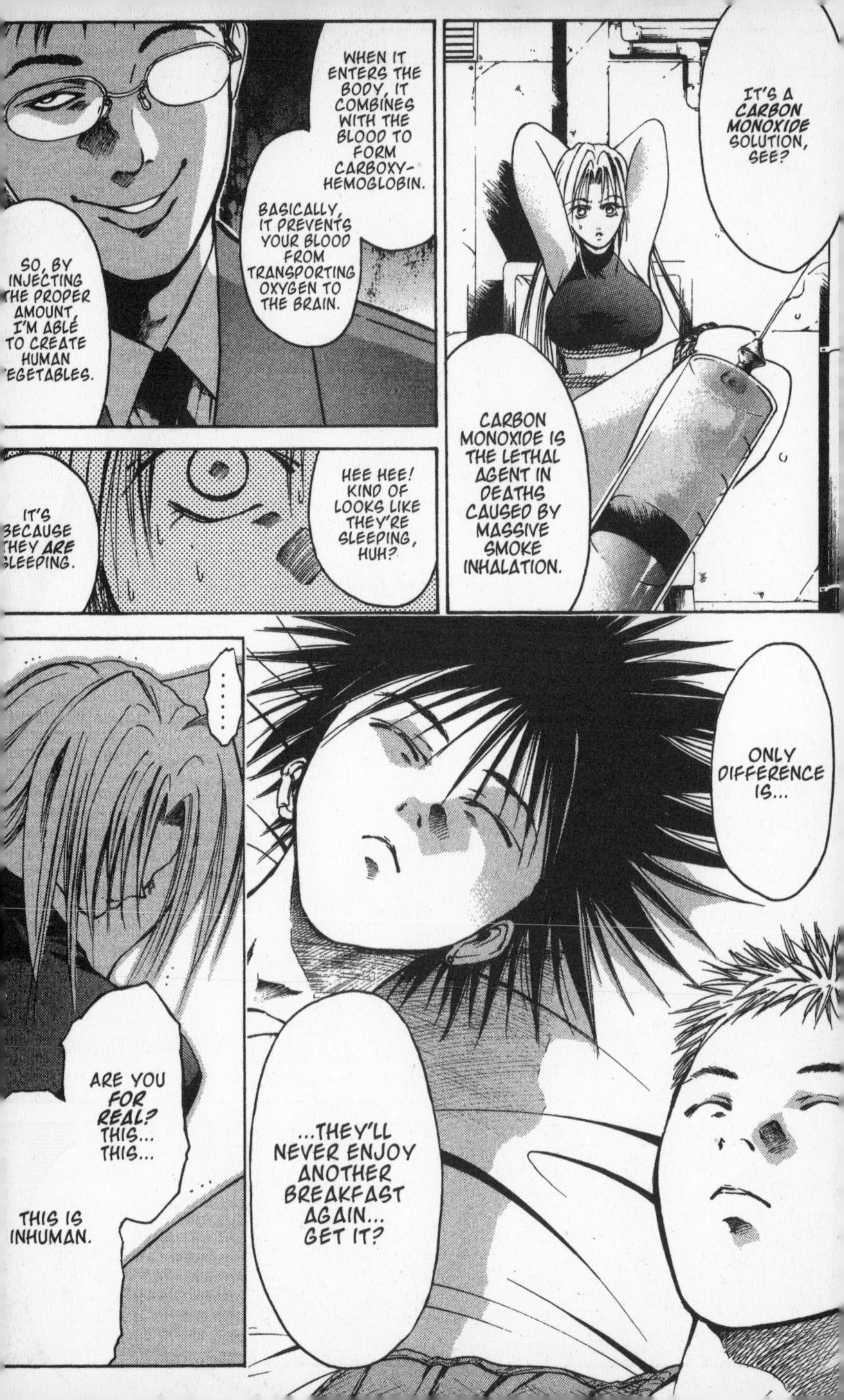
IT'S A CARBON MONOXIDE SOLUTION, SEE?
CARBON MONOXIDE IS THE LETHAL AGENT IN DEATHS CAUSED BY MASSIVE SMOKE INHALATION.
WHEN IT ENTERS THE BODY, IT COMBINES WITH THE BLOOD TO FORM CARBOXY-HEMOGLOBIN.
BASICALLY, IT PREVENTS YOUR BLOOD FROM TRANSPORTING OXYGEN TO THE BRAIN.
SO, BY INJECTING THE PROPER AMOUNT, I'M ABLE TO CREATE HUMAN VEGETABLES.
HEE HEE! KIND OF LOOKS LIKE THEY'RE SLEEPING, HUH?
IT'S BECAUSE THEY *ARE* SLEEPING.
ONLY DIFFERENCE IS...
...THEY'LL NEVER ENJOY ANOTHER BREAKFAST AGAIN... GET IT?
......
ARE YOU *FOR REAL?* THIS... THIS...
THIS IS INHUMAN.

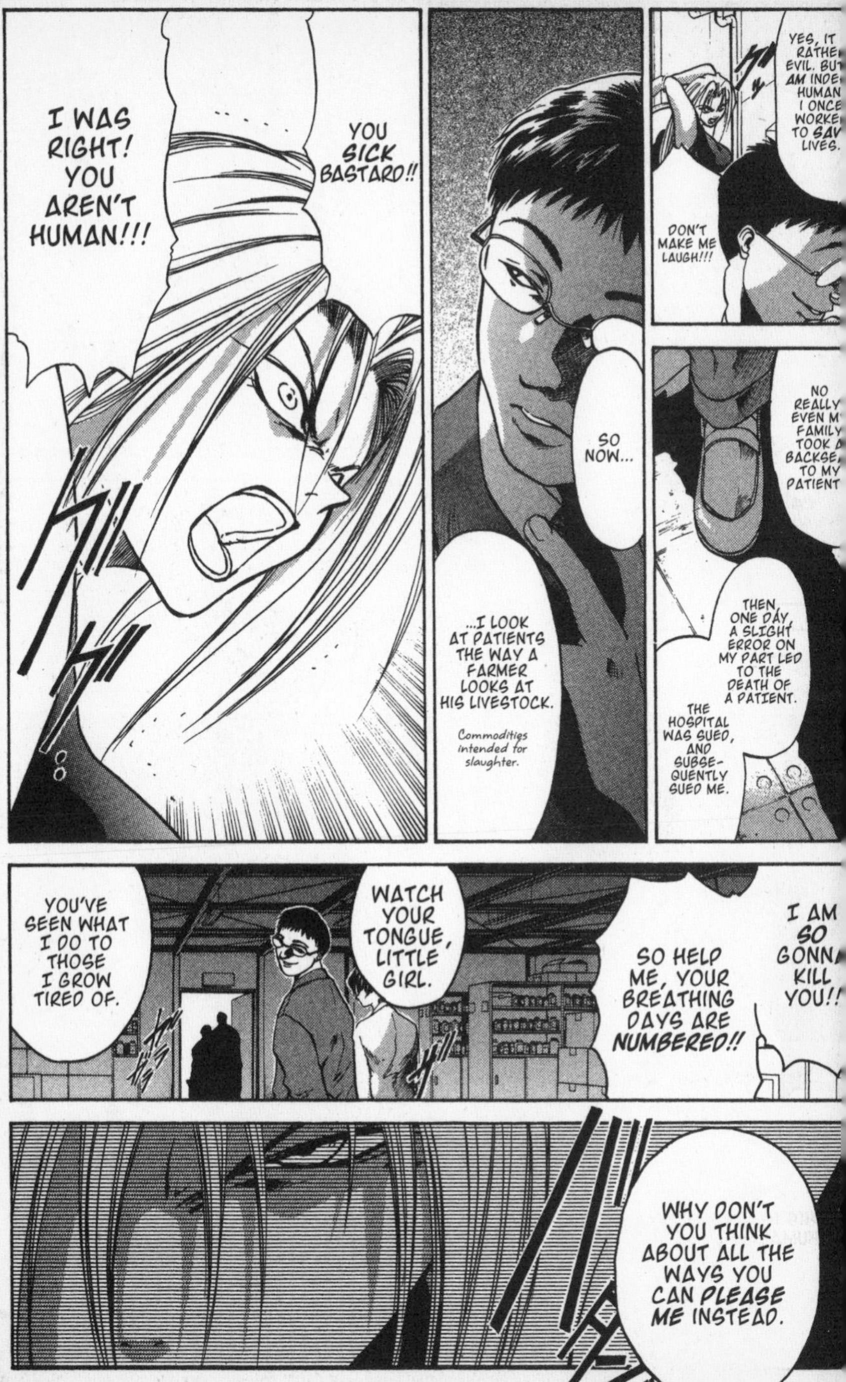
YES, IT RATHE EVIL. BU AM INDE HUMAN I ONCE WORKE TO SAV LIVES.
DON'T MAKE ME LAUGH!!!
NO REALLY EVEN M FAMILY TOOK A BACKSE TO MY PATIENT
THEN, ONE DAY, A SLIGHT ERROR ON MY PART LED TO THE DEATH OF A PATIENT.
THE HOSPITAL WAS SUED, AND SUBSE-QUENTLY SUED ME.
SO NOW...
...I LOOK AT PATIENTS THE WAY A FARMER LOOKS AT HIS LIVESTOCK.
Commodities intended for slaughter.
YOU SICK BASTARD!!
...
I WAS RIGHT! YOU AREN'T HUMAN!!!
I AM SO GONN KILL YOU!!
SO HELP ME, YOUR BREATHING DAYS ARE NUMBERED!!
WATCH YOUR TONGUE, LITTLE GIRL.
YOU'VE SEEN WHAT I DO TO THOSE I GROW TIRED OF.
WHY DON'T YOU THINK ABOUT ALL THE WAYS YOU CAN PLEASE ME INSTEAD.

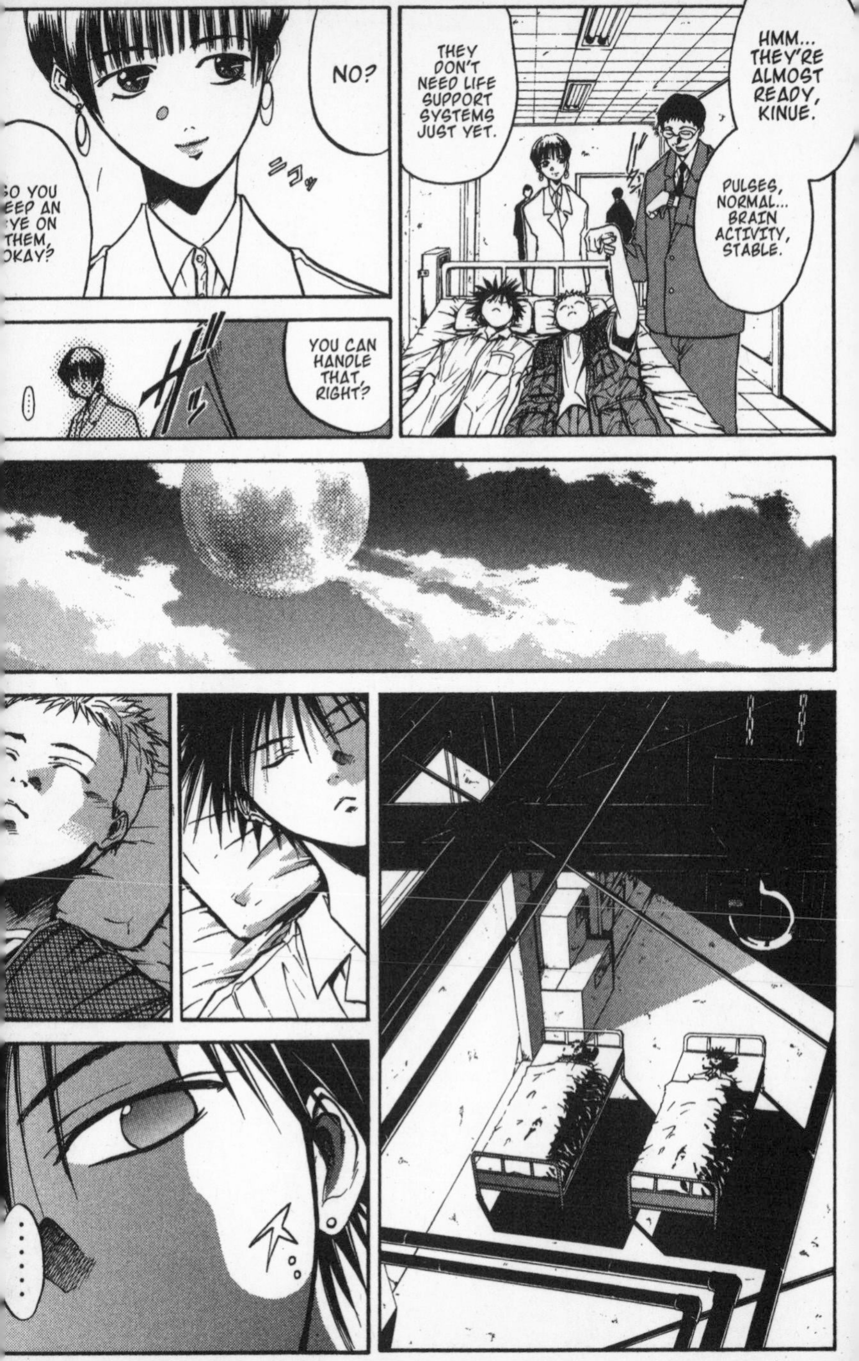

HMM... THEY'RE ALMOST READY, KINUE.
PULSES, NORMAL... BRAIN ACTIVITY, STABLE.
THEY DON'T NEED LIFE SUPPORT SYSTEMS JUST YET.
NO?
O YOU EEP AN YE ON THEM, OKAY?
YOU CAN HANDLE THAT, RIGHT?
...
......

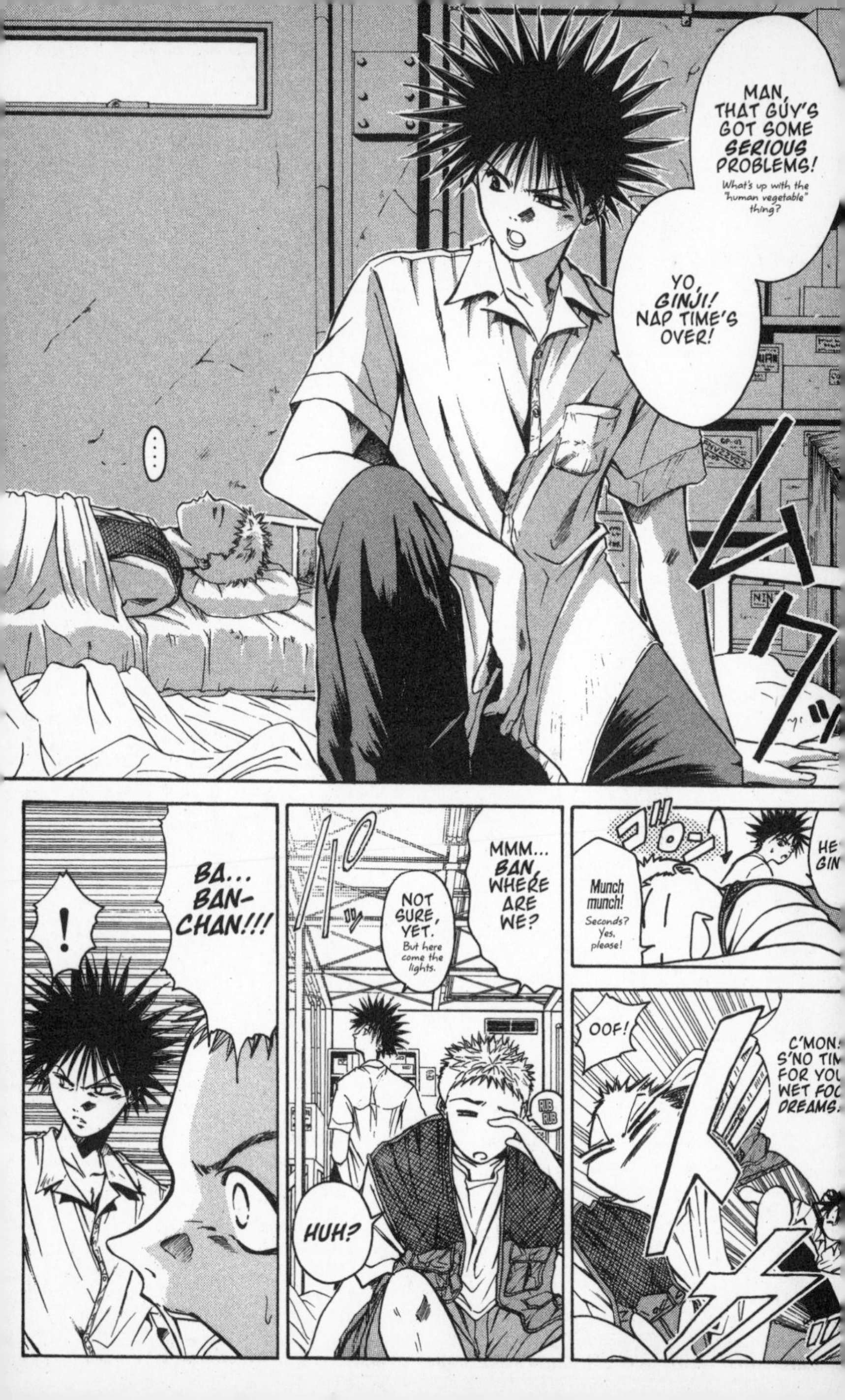

MAN, THAT GUY'S GOT SOME SERIOUS PROBLEMS!
What's up with the "human vegetable" thing?
YO, GINJI! NAP TIME'S OVER!
...
HE GIN
Munch munch!
Seconds? Yes, please!
OOF!
C'MON! S'NO TIM FOR YOU WET FOO DREAMS.
MMM... BAN, WHERE ARE WE?
NOT SURE, YET.
But here come the lights.
RUB RUB
HUH?
BA... BAN-CHAN!!!
!

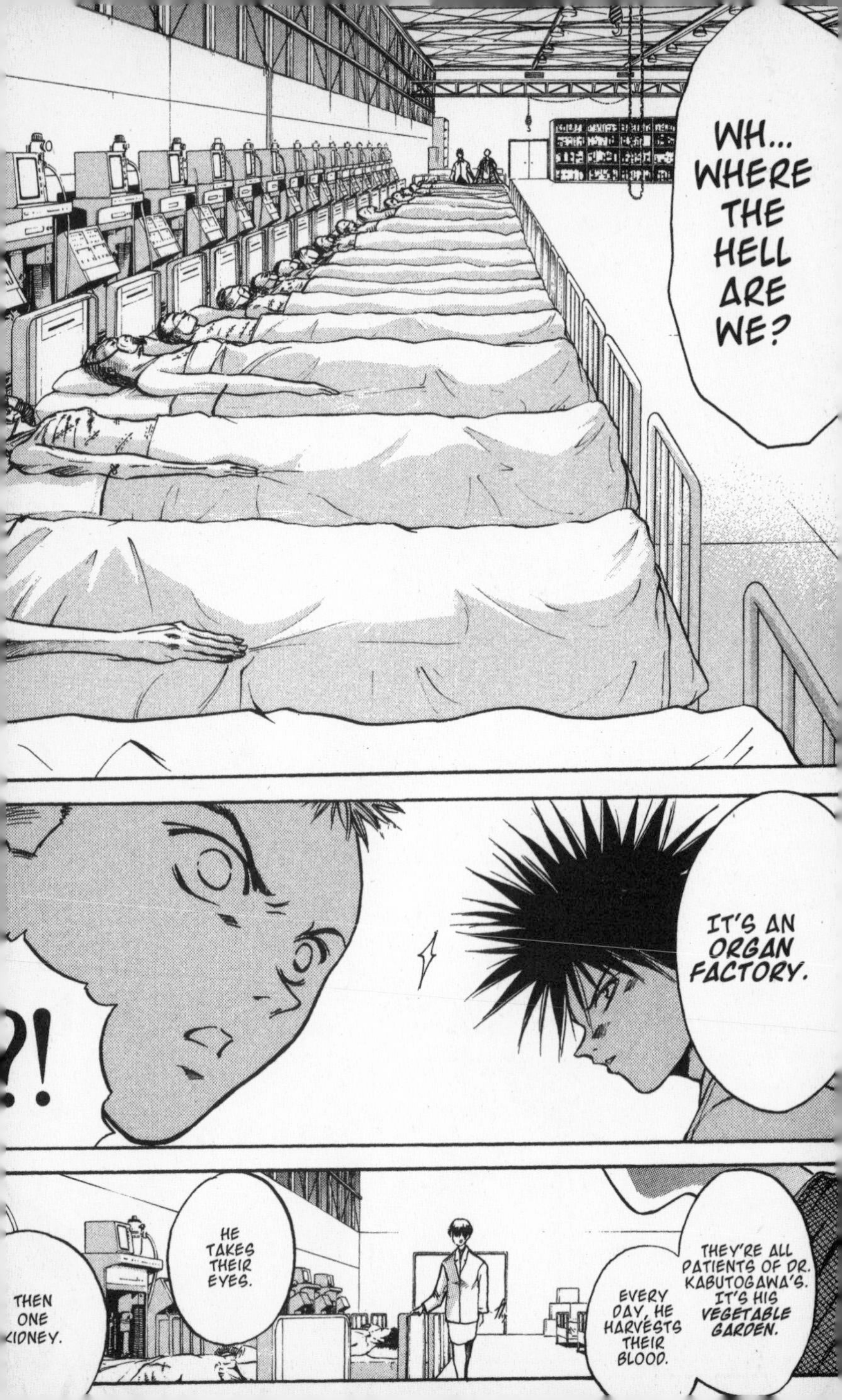
WH... WHERE THE HELL ARE WE?
IT'S AN ORGAN FACTORY.
?!
THEY'RE ALL PATIENTS OF DR. KABUTOGAWA'S. IT'S HIS VEGETABLE GARDEN.
EVERY DAY, HE HARVESTS THEIR BLOOD.
HE TAKES THEIR EYES.
THEN ONE KIDNEY.

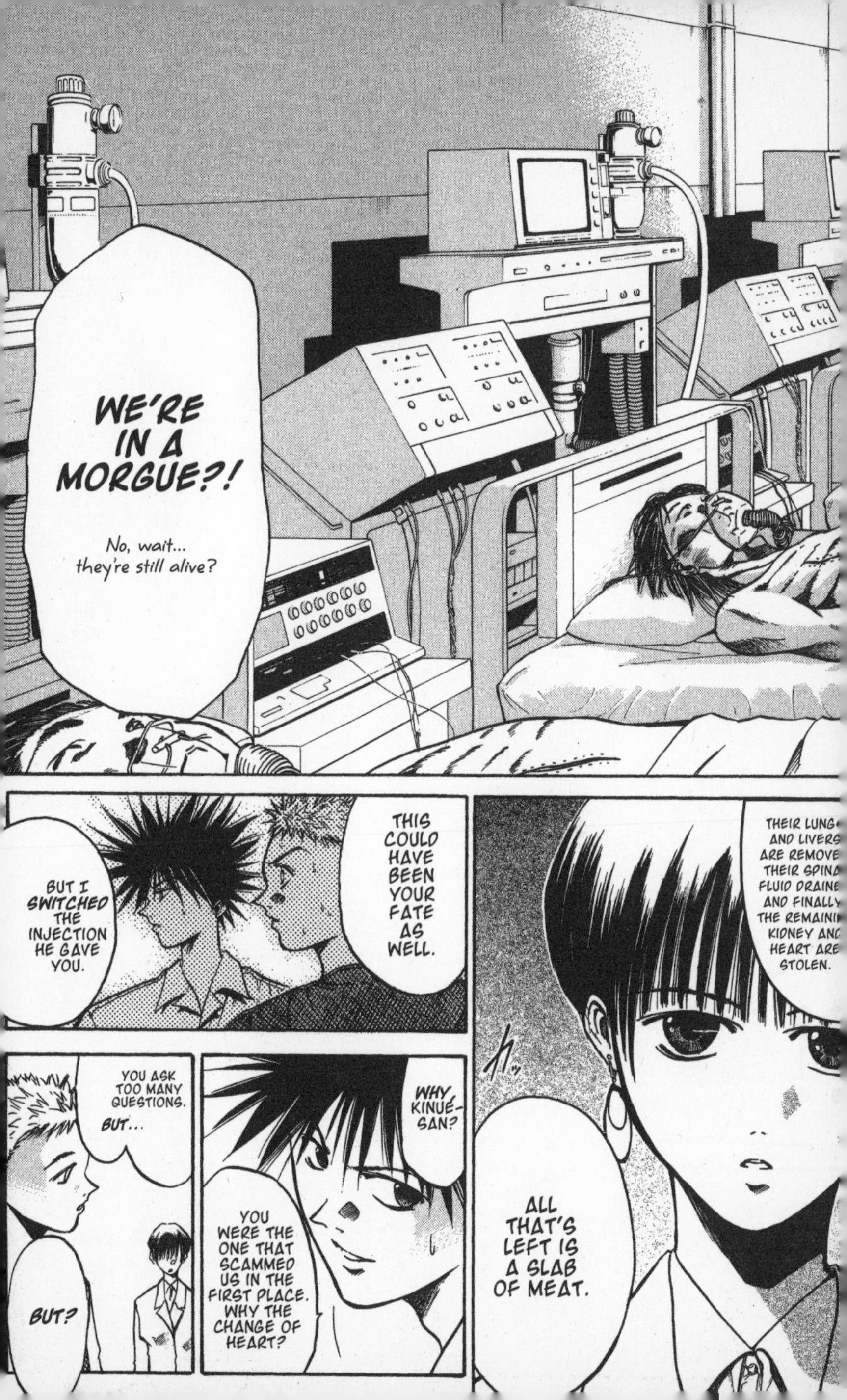
WE'RE IN A MORGUE?!
No, wait... they're still alive?
THEIR LUNG AND LIVERS ARE REMOVE THEIR SPINA FLUID DRAINE AND FINALLY THE REMAINI KIDNEY AND HEART ARE STOLEN.
ALL THAT'S LEFT IS A SLAB OF MEAT.
THIS COULD HAVE BEEN YOUR FATE AS WELL.
BUT I SWITCHED THE INJECTION HE GAVE YOU.
WHY, KINUÉ-SAN?
YOU WERE THE ONE THAT SCAMMED US IN THE FIRST PLACE. WHY THE CHANGE OF HEART?
YOU ASK TOO MANY QUESTIONS.
BUT...
BUT?

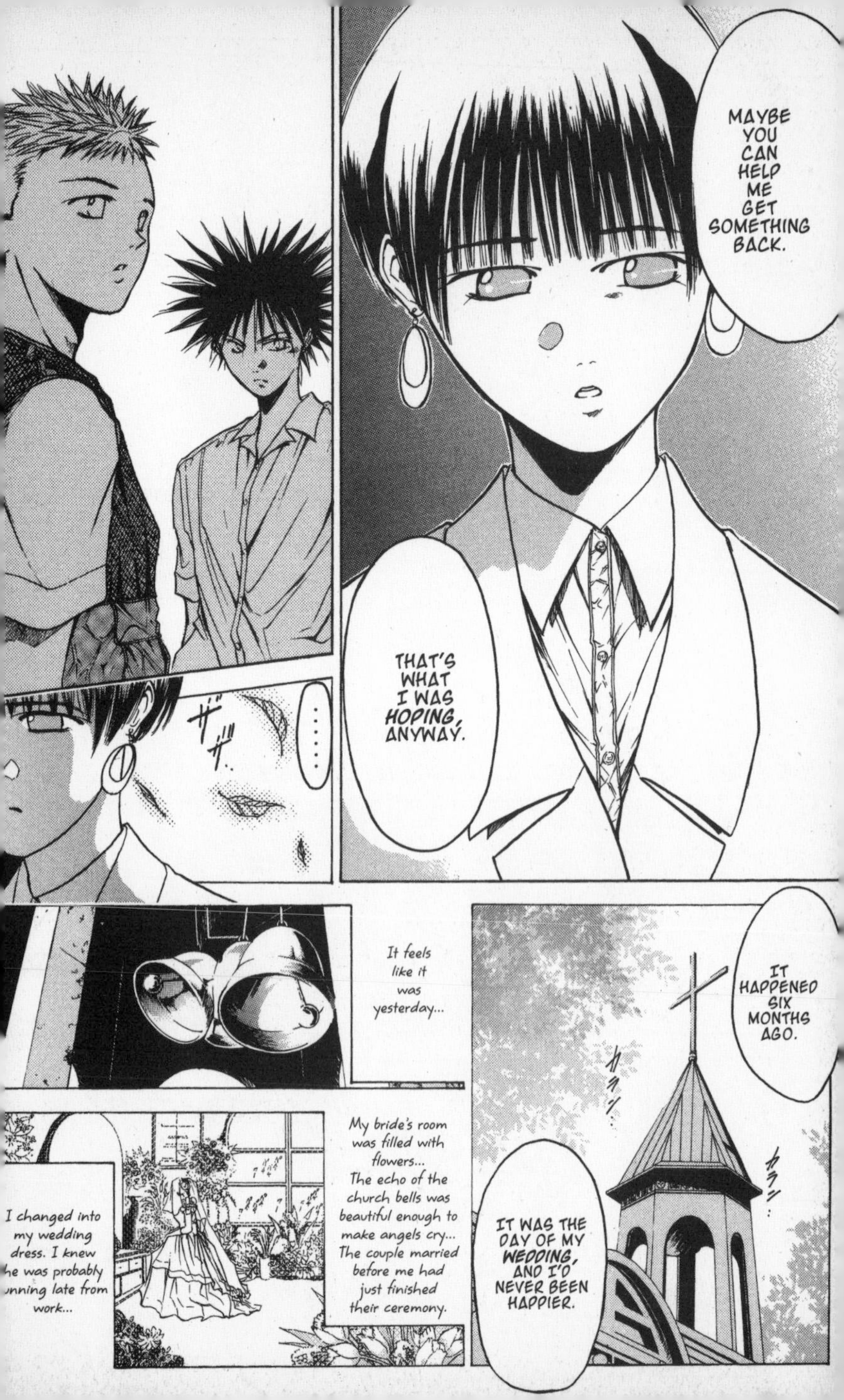

MAYBE YOU CAN HELP ME GET SOMETHING BACK.
THAT'S WHAT I WAS *HOPING*, ANYWAY.
......
ザザ..
IT HAPPENED SIX MONTHS AGO.
カラン
カラン
IT WAS THE DAY OF MY *WEDDING*, AND I'D NEVER BEEN HAPPIER.
It feels like it was yesterday...
My bride's room was filled with flowers... The echo of the church bells was beautiful enough to make angels cry... The couple married before me had just finished their ceremony.
I changed into my wedding dress. I knew he was probably unning late from work...

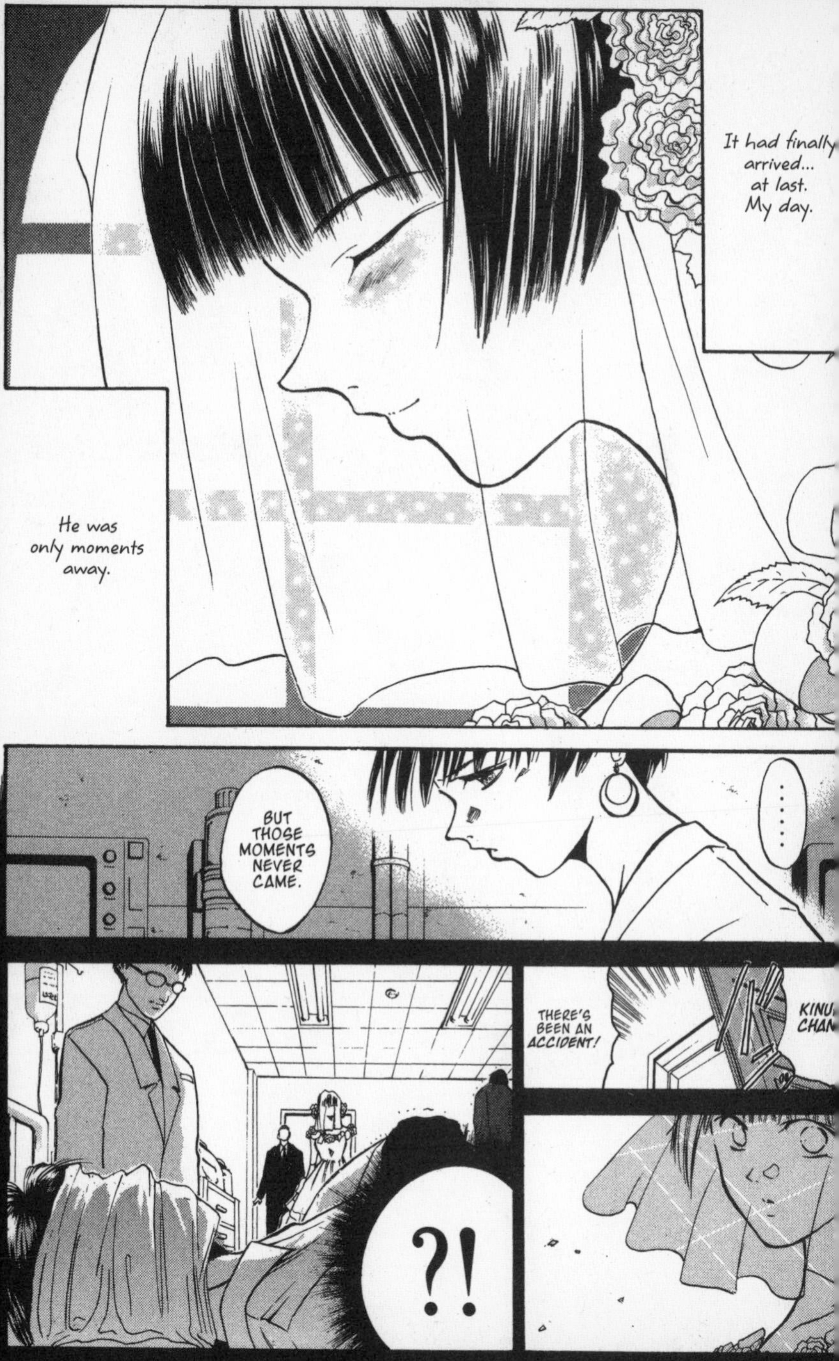
It had finally arrived... at last. My day.
He was only moments away.
......
BUT THOSE MOMENTS NEVER CAME.
KINU CHAN
THERE'S BEEN AN ACCIDENT!
?!

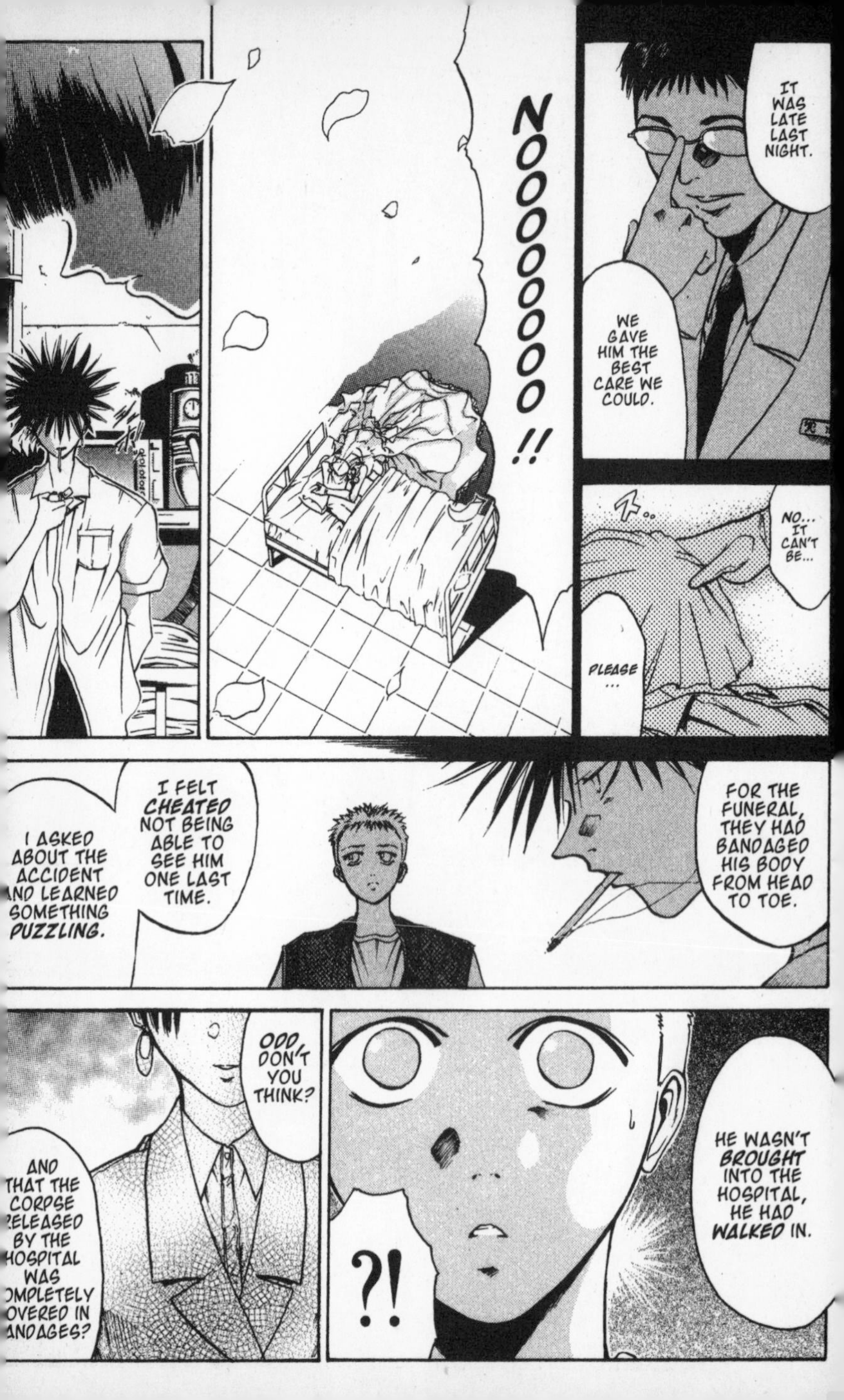
IT WAS LATE LAST NIGHT.
WE GAVE HIM THE BEST CARE WE COULD.
NO... IT CAN'T BE...
PLEASE...
NOOOOOOOOOO!!
FOR THE FUNERAL, THEY HAD BANDAGED HIS BODY FROM HEAD TO TOE.
I FELT CHEATED NOT BEING ABLE TO SEE HIM ONE LAST TIME.
I ASKED ABOUT THE ACCIDENT AND LEARNED SOMETHING PUZZLING.
HE WASN'T BROUGHT INTO THE HOSPITAL, HE HAD WALKED IN.
?!
ODD, DON'T YOU THINK?
AND THAT THE CORPSE RELEASED BY THE HOSPITAL WAS COMPLETELY COVERED IN BANDAGES?

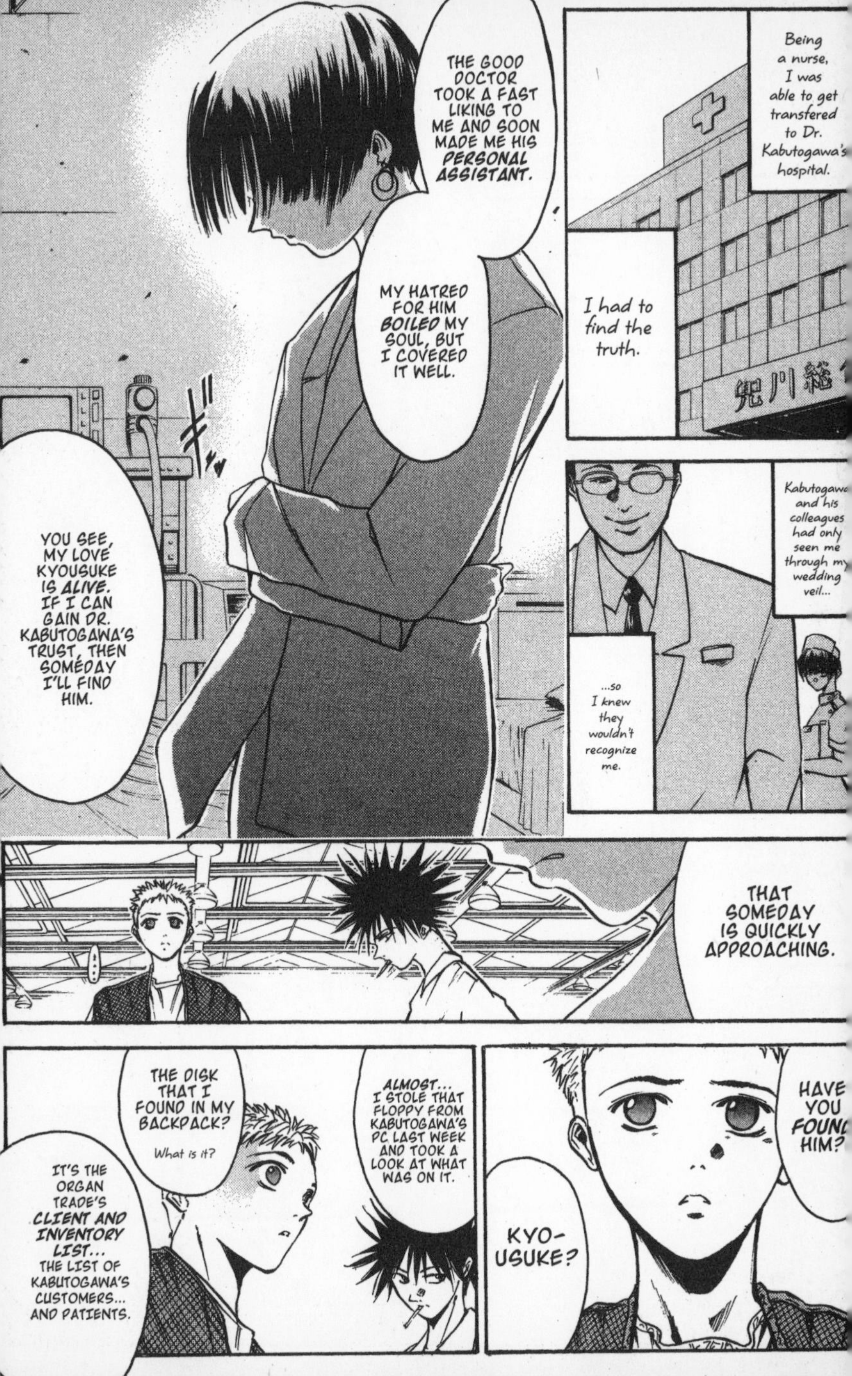
Being a nurse, I was able to get transfered to Dr. Kabutogawa's hospital.
I had to find the truth.
Kabutogawa and his colleagues had only seen me through my wedding veil...
...so I knew they wouldn't recognize me.
THE GOOD DOCTOR TOOK A FAST LIKING TO ME AND SOON MADE ME HIS PERSONAL ASSISTANT.
MY HATRED FOR HIM BOILED MY SOUL, BUT I COVERED IT WELL.
YOU SEE, MY LOVE KYOUSUKE IS ALIVE. IF I CAN GAIN DR. KABUTOGAWA'S TRUST, THEN SOMEDAY I'LL FIND HIM.
THAT SOMEDAY IS QUICKLY APPROACHING.
...
HAVE YOU FOUND HIM?
KYO-USUKE?
ALMOST... I STOLE THAT FLOPPY FROM KABUTOGAWA'S PC LAST WEEK AND TOOK A LOOK AT WHAT WAS ON IT.
THE DISK THAT I FOUND IN MY BACKPACK?
What is it?
IT'S THE ORGAN TRADE'S CLIENT AND INVENTORY LIST... THE LIST OF KABUTOGAWA'S CUSTOMERS... AND PATIENTS.

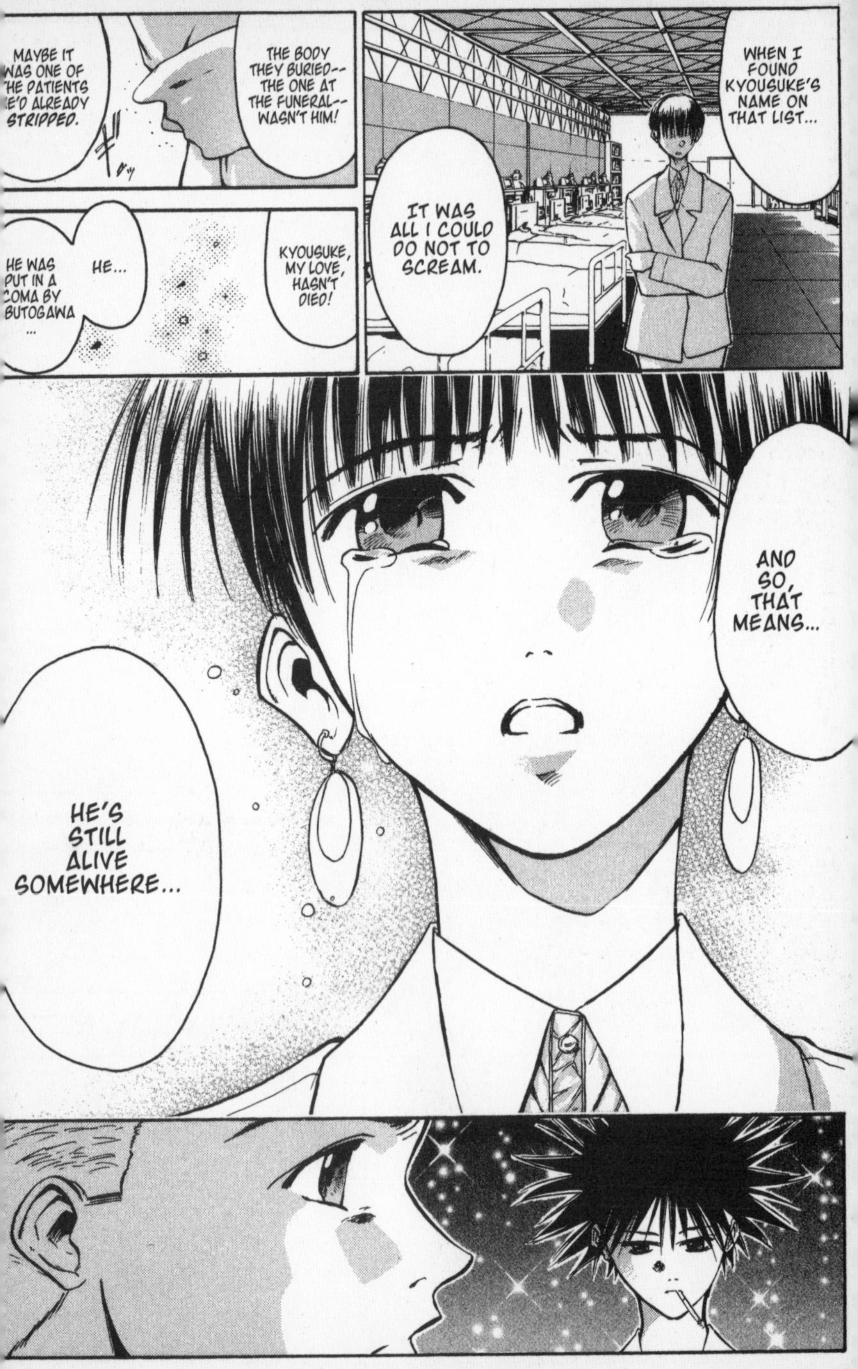
WHEN I FOUND KYOUSUKE'S NAME ON THAT LIST...
IT WAS ALL I COULD DO NOT TO SCREAM.
THE BODY THEY BURIED-- THE ONE AT THE FUNERAL-- WASN'T HIM!
MAYBE IT WAS ONE OF THE PATIENTS HE'D ALREADY STRIPPED.
KYOUSUKE, MY LOVE, HASN'T DIED!
HE...
HE WAS PUT IN A COMA BY BUTOGAWA ...
AND SO, THAT MEANS...
HE'S STILL ALIVE SOMEWHERE...

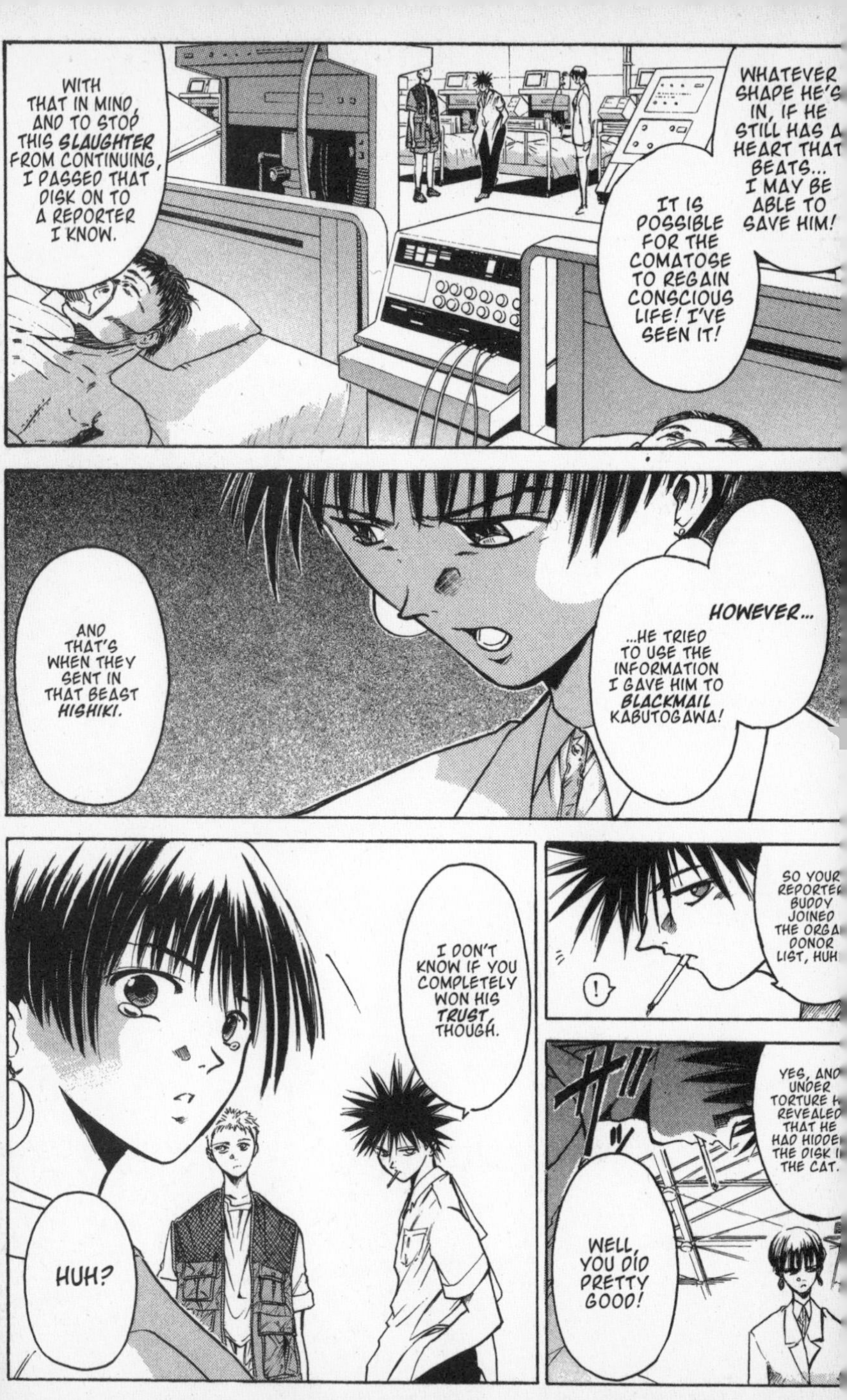
WHATEVER SHAPE HE'S IN, IF HE STILL HAS A HEART THAT BEATS... I MAY BE ABLE TO SAVE HIM!
IT IS POSSIBLE FOR THE COMATOSE TO REGAIN CONSCIOUS LIFE! I'VE SEEN IT!
WITH THAT IN MIND, AND TO STOP THIS SLAUGHTER FROM CONTINUING, I PASSED THAT DISK ON TO A REPORTER I KNOW.
HOWEVER...
...HE TRIED TO USE THE INFORMATION I GAVE HIM TO BLACKMAIL KABUTOGAWA!
AND THAT'S WHEN THEY SENT IN THAT BEAST HISHIKI.
SO YOUR REPORTER BUDDY JOINED THE ORGA DONOR LIST, HUH
!
YES, AND UNDER TORTURE H REVEALED THAT HE HAD HIDDE THE DISK I THE CAT.
WELL, YOU DID PRETTY GOOD!
I DON'T KNOW IF YOU COMPLETELY WON HIS TRUST, THOUGH.
HUH?

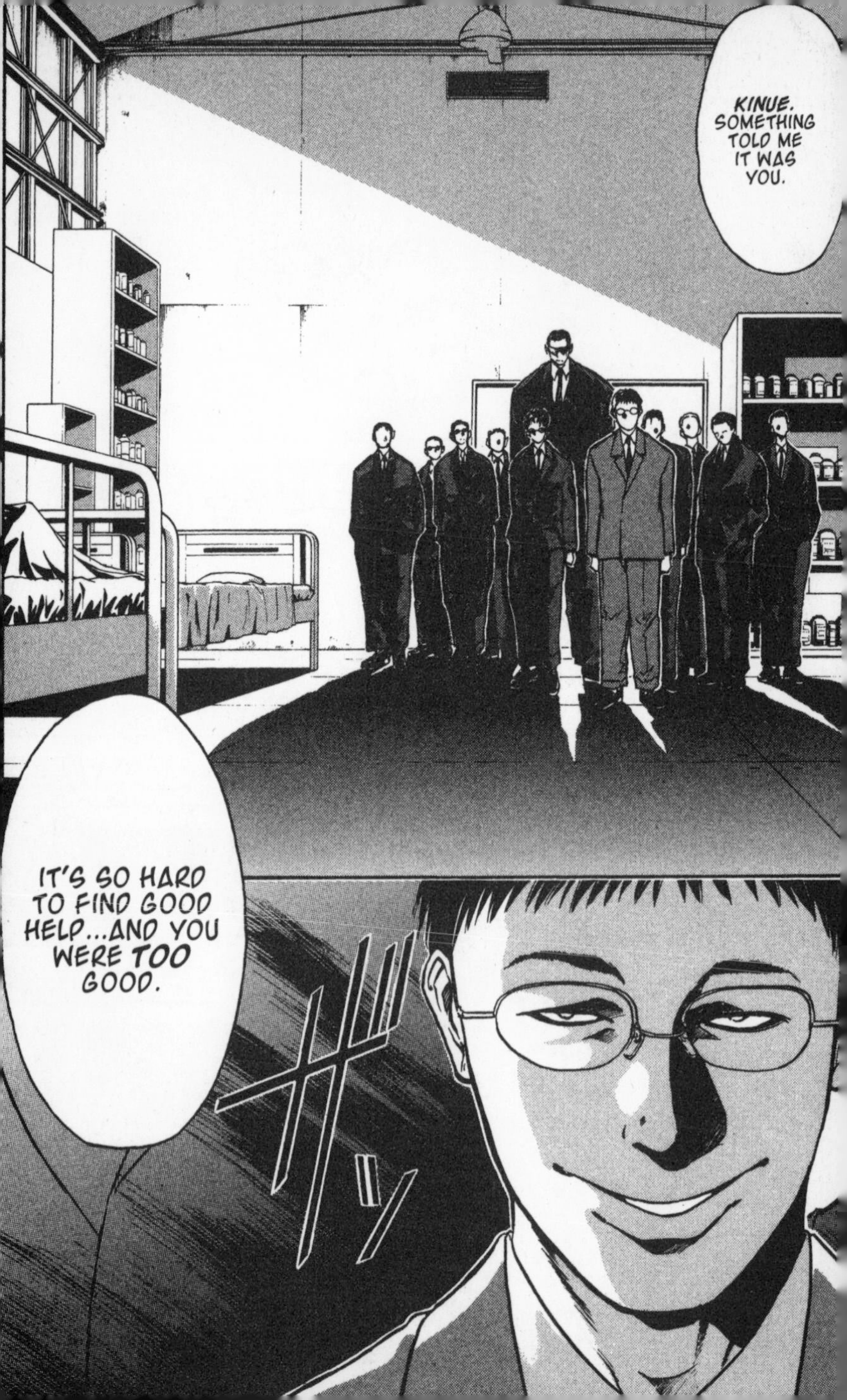
KINUE. SOMETHING TOLD ME IT WAS YOU.
IT'S SO HARD TO FIND GOOD HELP...AND YOU WERE TOO GOOD.

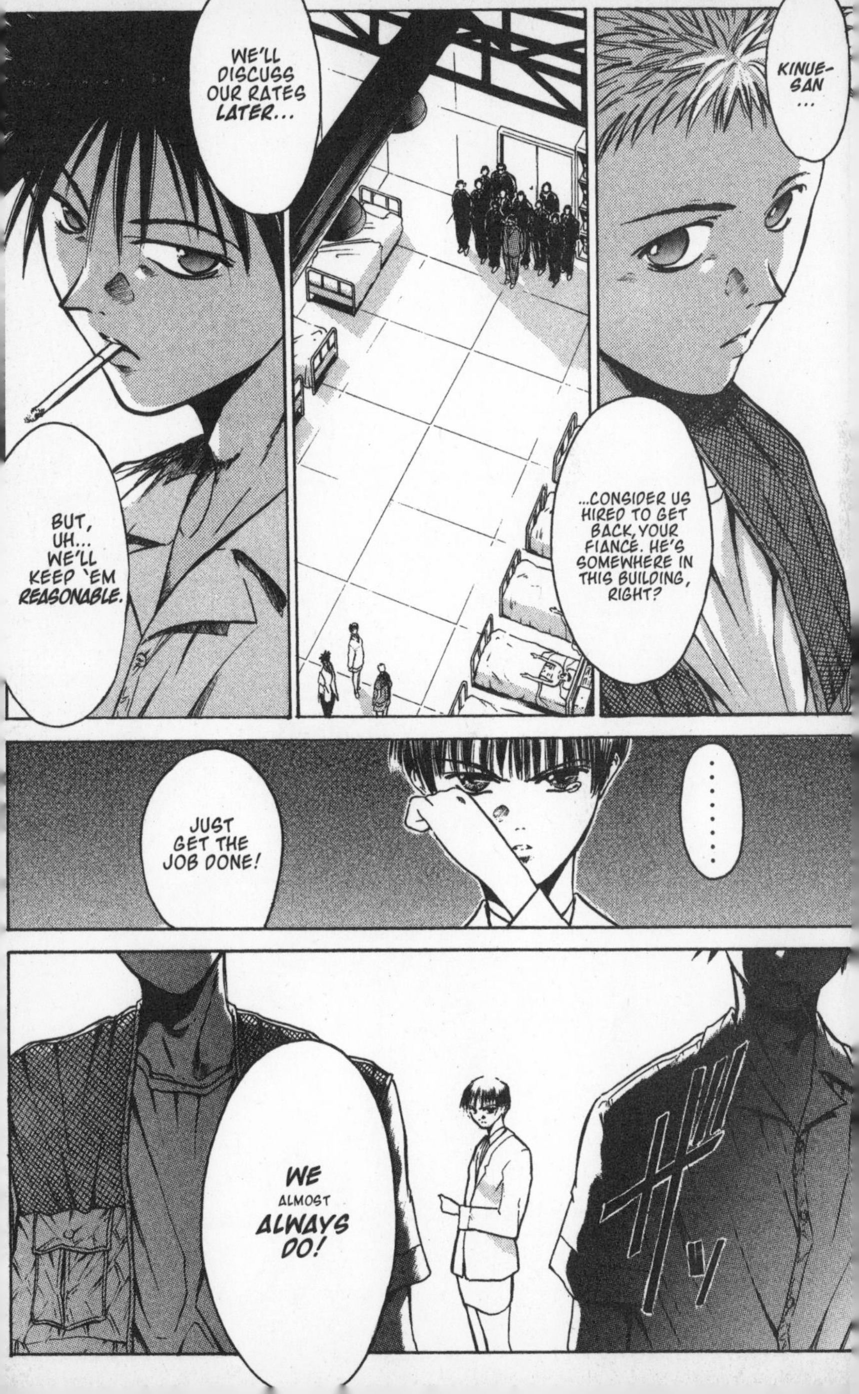
KINUE-SAN...
...CONSIDER US HIRED TO GET BACK, YOUR FIANCE. HE'S SOMEWHERE IN THIS BUILDING, RIGHT?
WE'LL DISCUSS OUR RATES LATER...
BUT, UH... WE'LL KEEP 'EM REASONABLE.
....
JUST GET THE JOB DONE!
WE ALMOST ALWAYS DO!

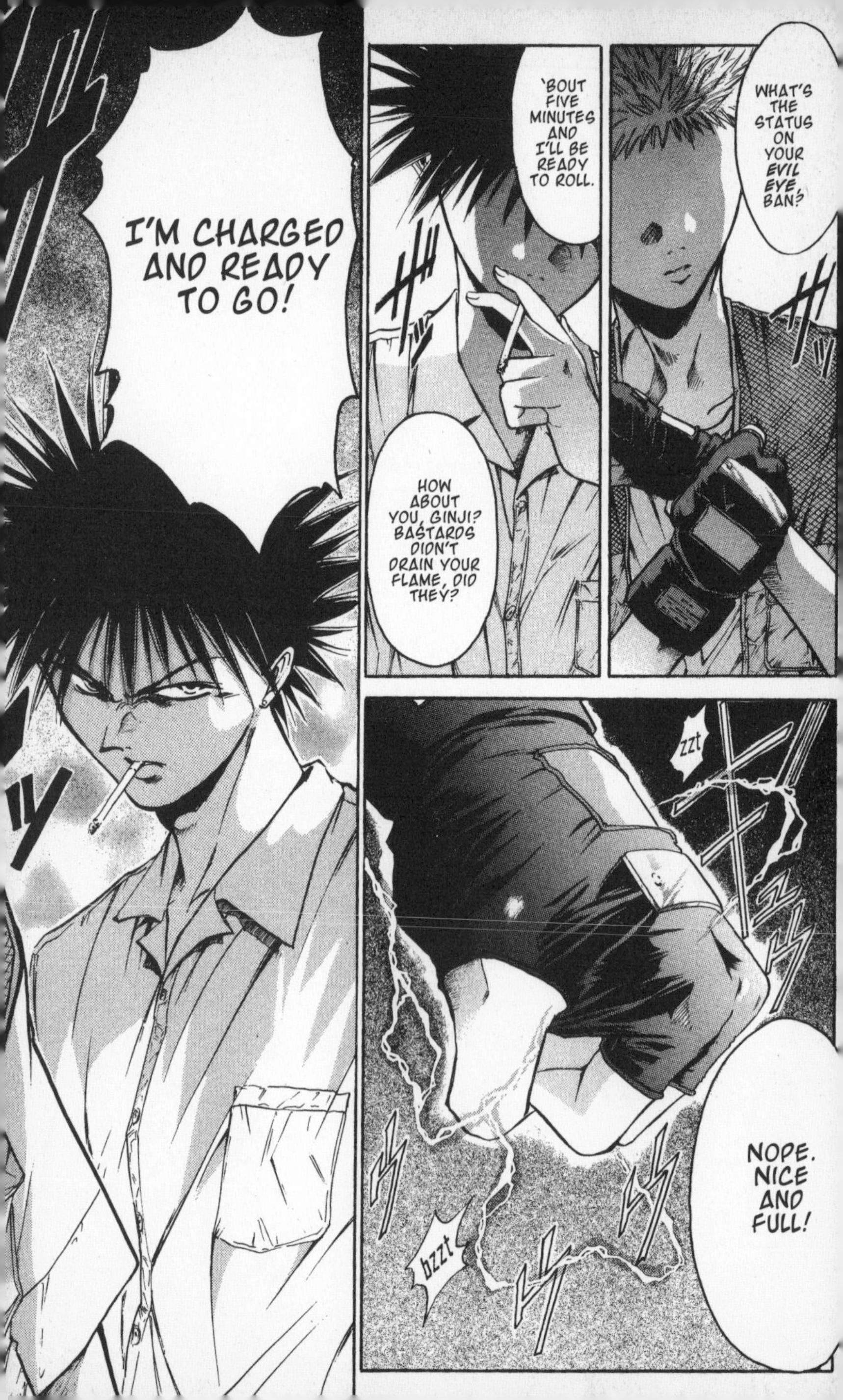
WHAT'S THE STATUS ON YOUR EVIL EYE, BAN?
'BOUT FIVE MINUTES AND I'LL BE READY TO ROLL.
HOW ABOUT YOU, GINJI? BASTARDS DIDN'T DRAIN YOUR FLAME, DID THEY?
zzt
NOPE. NICE AND FULL!
bzzt
I'M CHARGED AND READY TO GO!

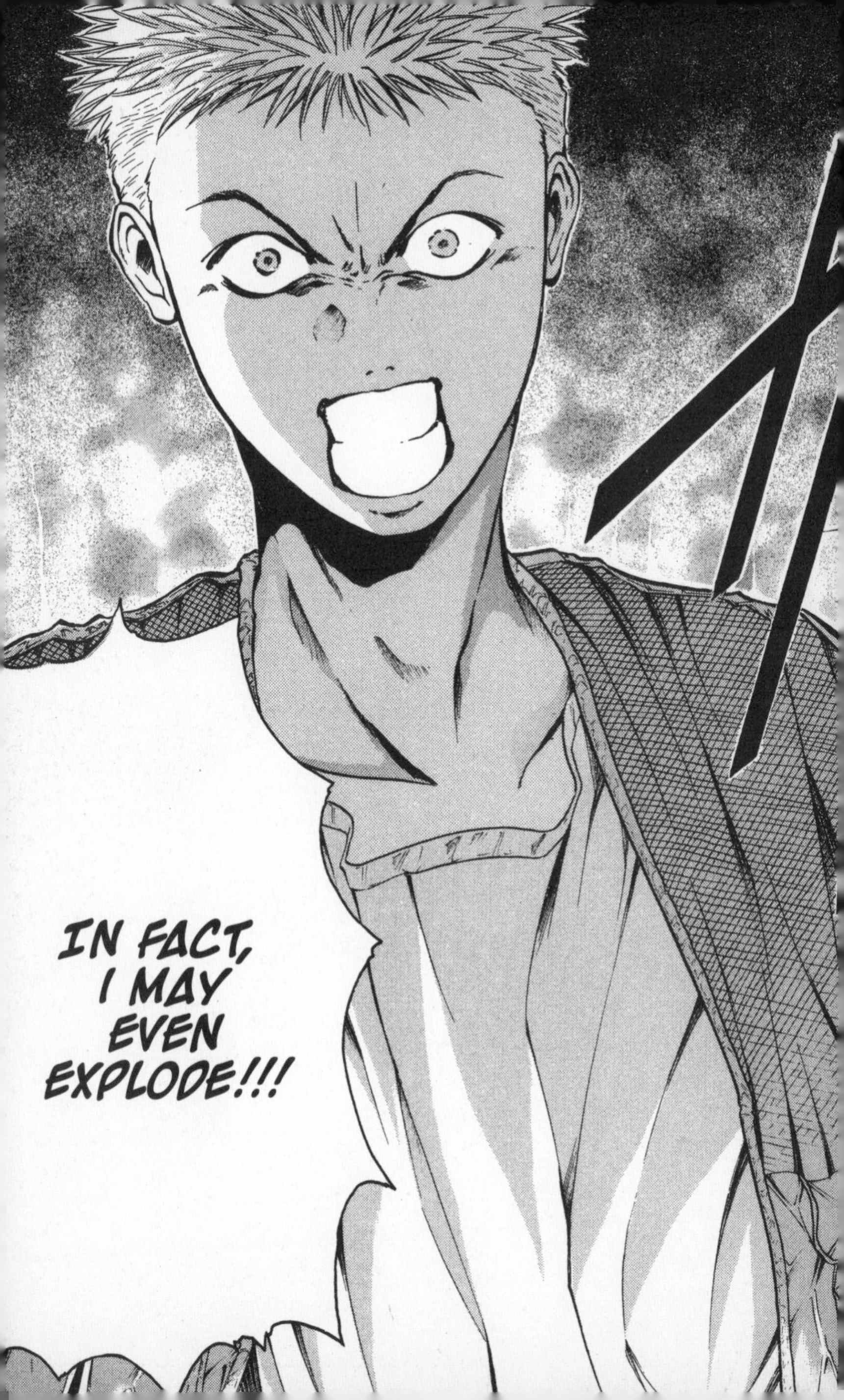
IN FACT, I MAY EVEN EXPLODE!!!

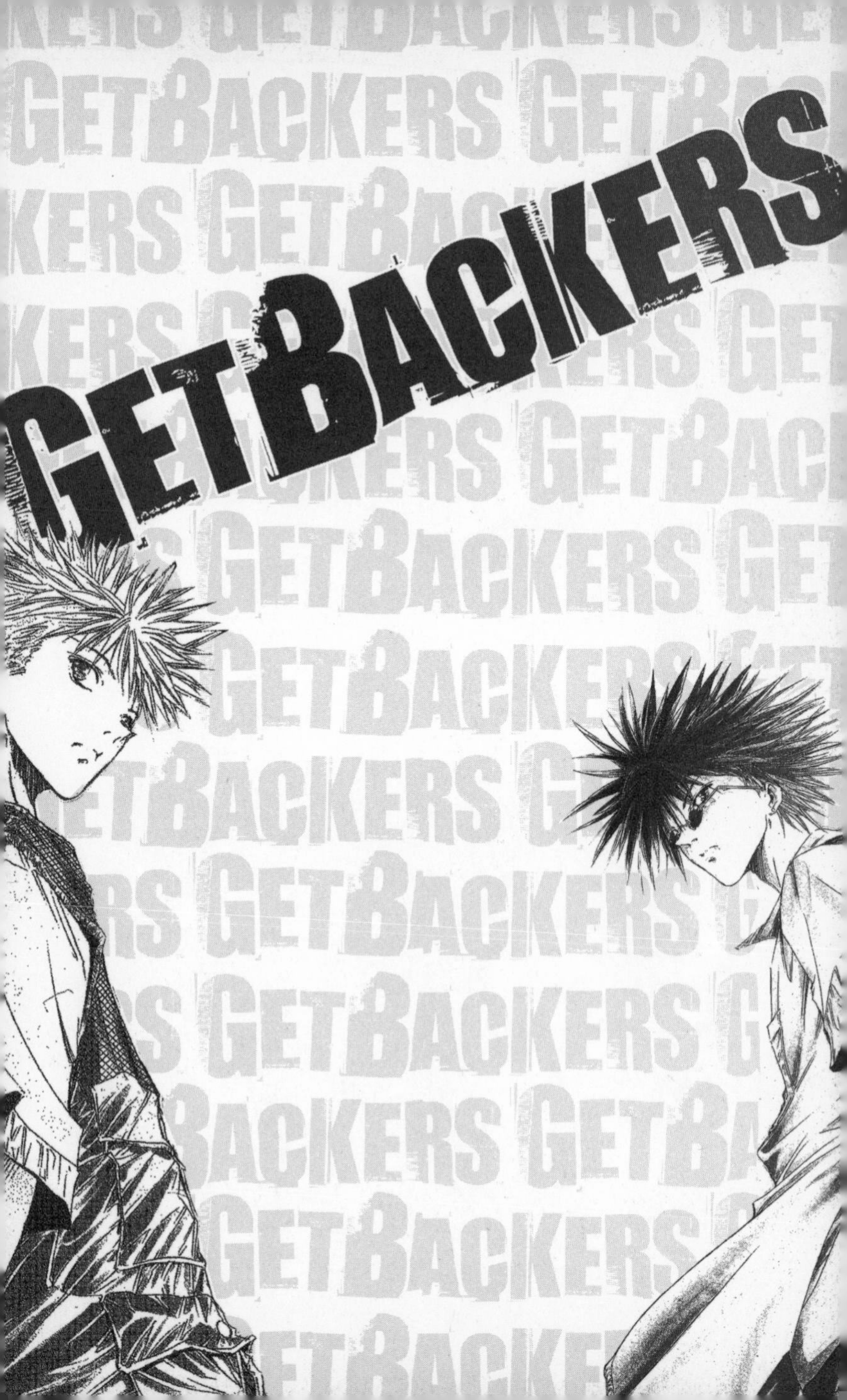
GETBACKERS

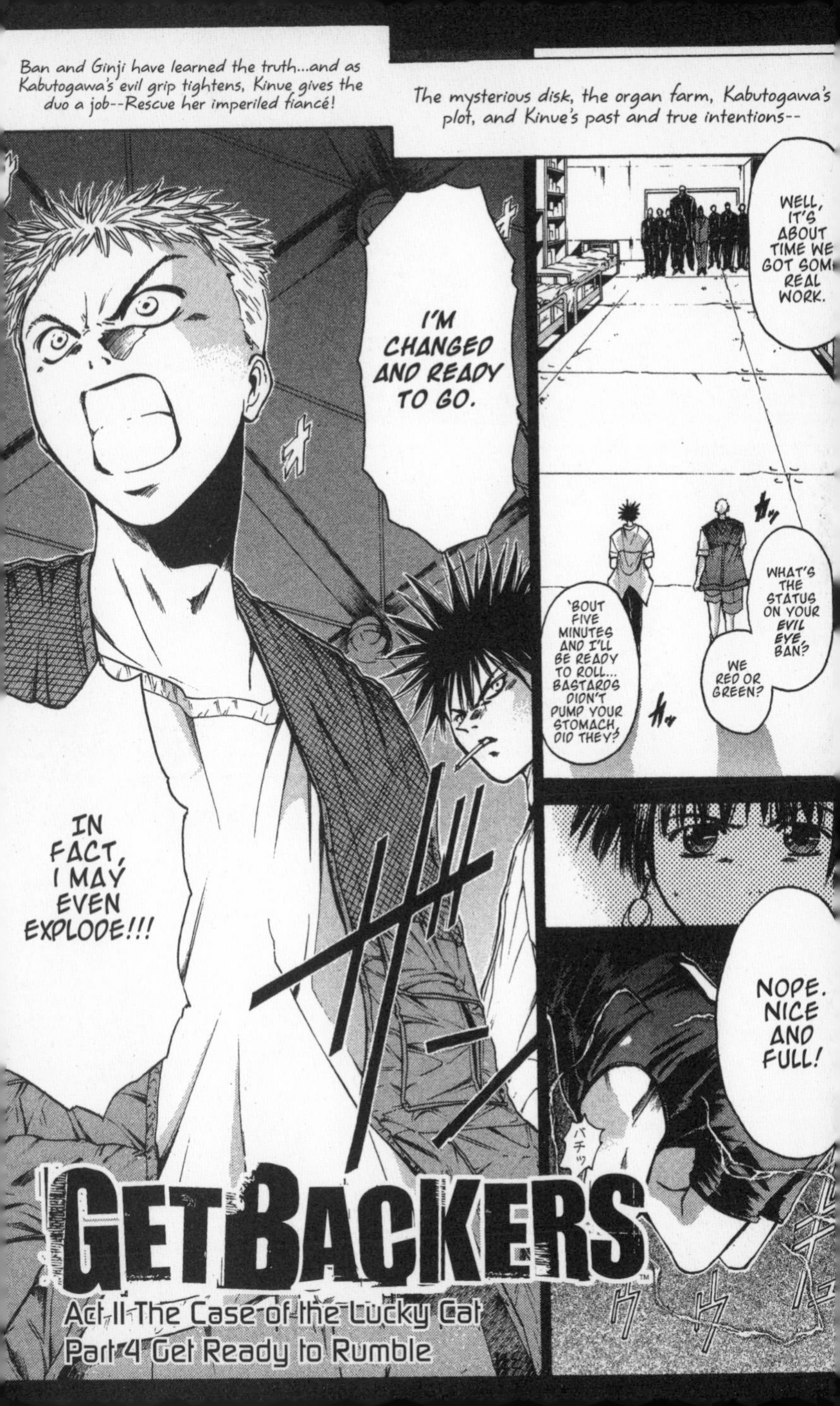

The mysterious disk, the organ farm, Kabutogawa's plot, and Kinue's past and true intentions--
Ban and Ginji have learned the truth...and as Kabutogawa's evil grip tightens, Kinue gives the duo a job--Rescue her imperiled fiancé!
WELL, IT'S ABOUT TIME WE GOT SOM REAL WORK.
WHAT'S THE STATUS ON YOUR EVIL EYE, BAN?
WE RED OR GREEN?
'BOUT FIVE MINUTES AND I'LL BE READY TO ROLL... BASTARDS DIDN'T PUMP YOUR STOMACH, DID THEY?
NOPE. NICE AND FULL!
バチッ
I'M CHANGED AND READY TO GO.
IN FACT, I MAY EVEN EXPLODE!!!
GETBACKERS™
Act II The Case of the Lucky Cat
Part 4 Get Ready to Rumble

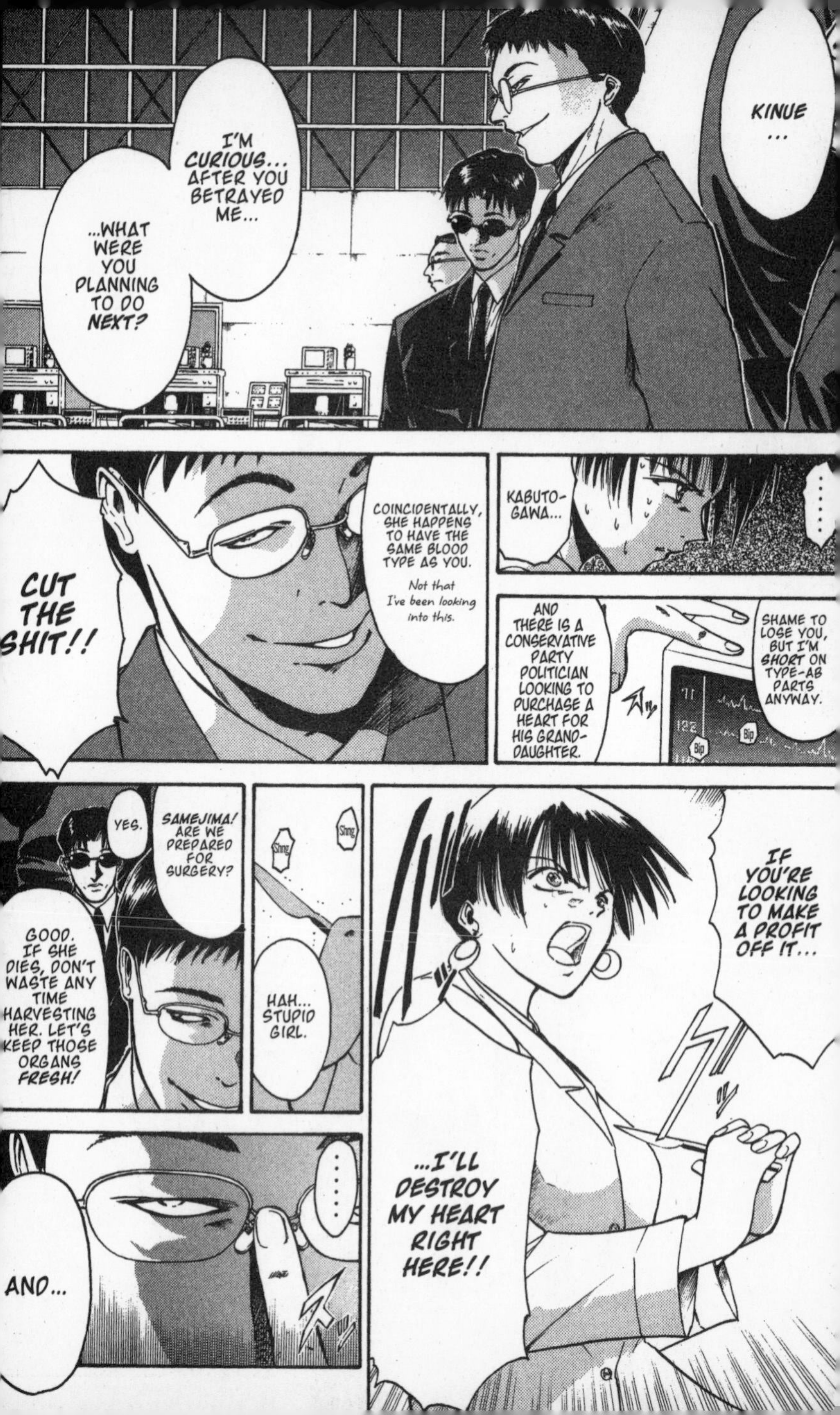
KINUE ...
I'M CURIOUS... AFTER YOU BETRAYED ME...
...WHAT WERE YOU PLANNING TO DO NEXT?
......
KABUTO-GAWA...
SHAME TO LOSE YOU, BUT I'M SHORT ON TYPE-AB PARTS ANYWAY.
Bip
Bip
AND THERE IS A CONSERVATIVE PARTY POLITICIAN LOOKING TO PURCHASE A HEART FOR HIS GRAND-DAUGHTER.
COINCIDENTALLY, SHE HAPPENS TO HAVE THE SAME BLOOD TYPE AS YOU.
Not that I've been looking into this.
CUT THE SHIT!!
IF YOU'RE LOOKING TO MAKE A PROFIT OFF IT...
...I'LL DESTROY MY HEART RIGHT HERE!!
Shing
Shing
HAH... STUPID GIRL.
SAMEJIMA! ARE WE PREPARED FOR SURGERY?
YES.
GOOD. IF SHE DIES, DON'T WASTE ANY TIME HARVESTING HER. LET'S KEEP THOSE ORGANS FRESH!
......
AND...

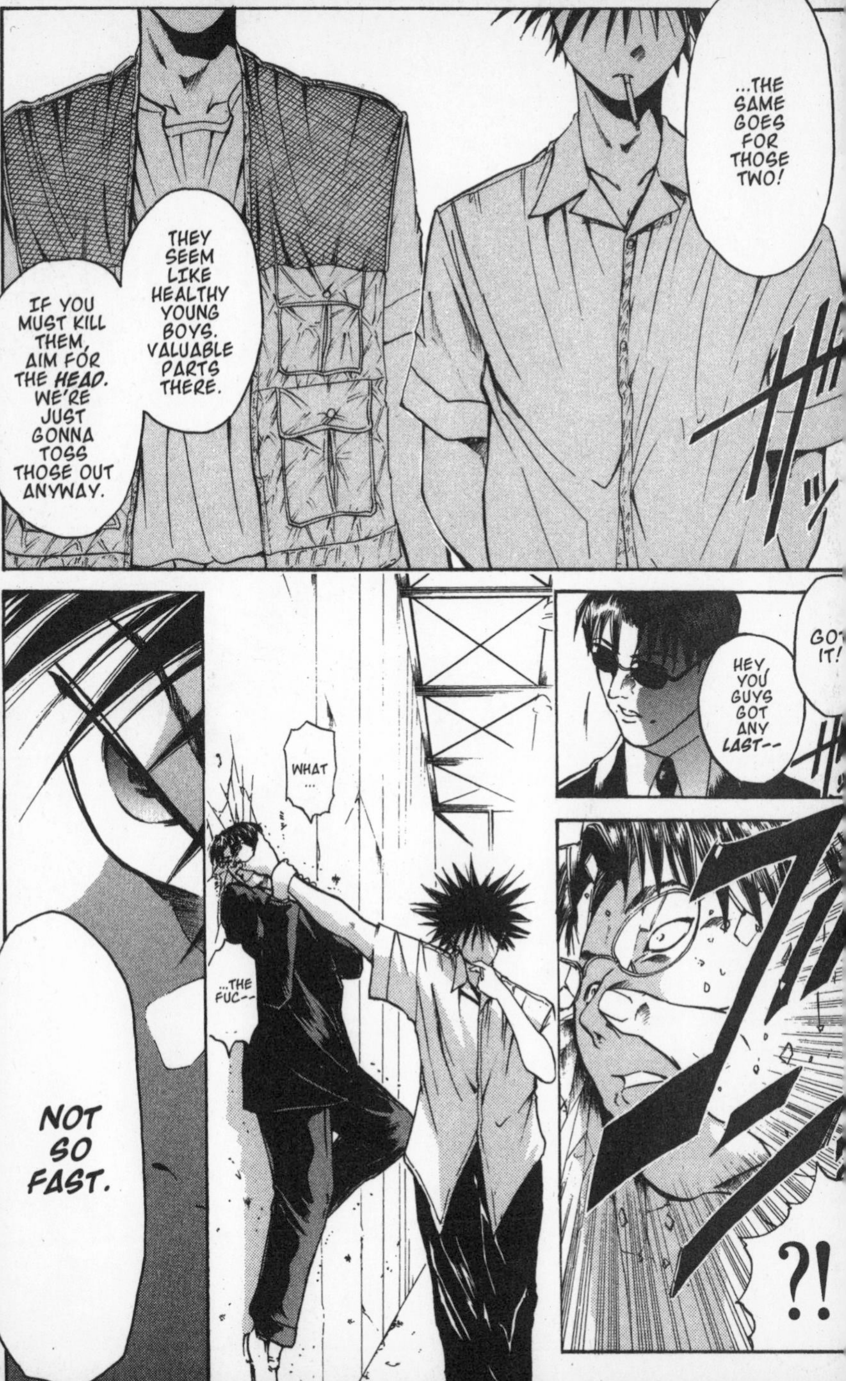
...THE SAME GOES FOR THOSE TWO!
THEY SEEM LIKE HEALTHY YOUNG BOYS. VALUABLE PARTS THERE.
IF YOU MUST KILL THEM, AIM FOR THE HEAD. WE'RE JUST GONNA TOSS THOSE OUT ANYWAY.
GOT IT!
HEY, YOU GUYS GOT ANY LAST--
?!
WHAT ...
...THE FUC--
NOT SO FAST.

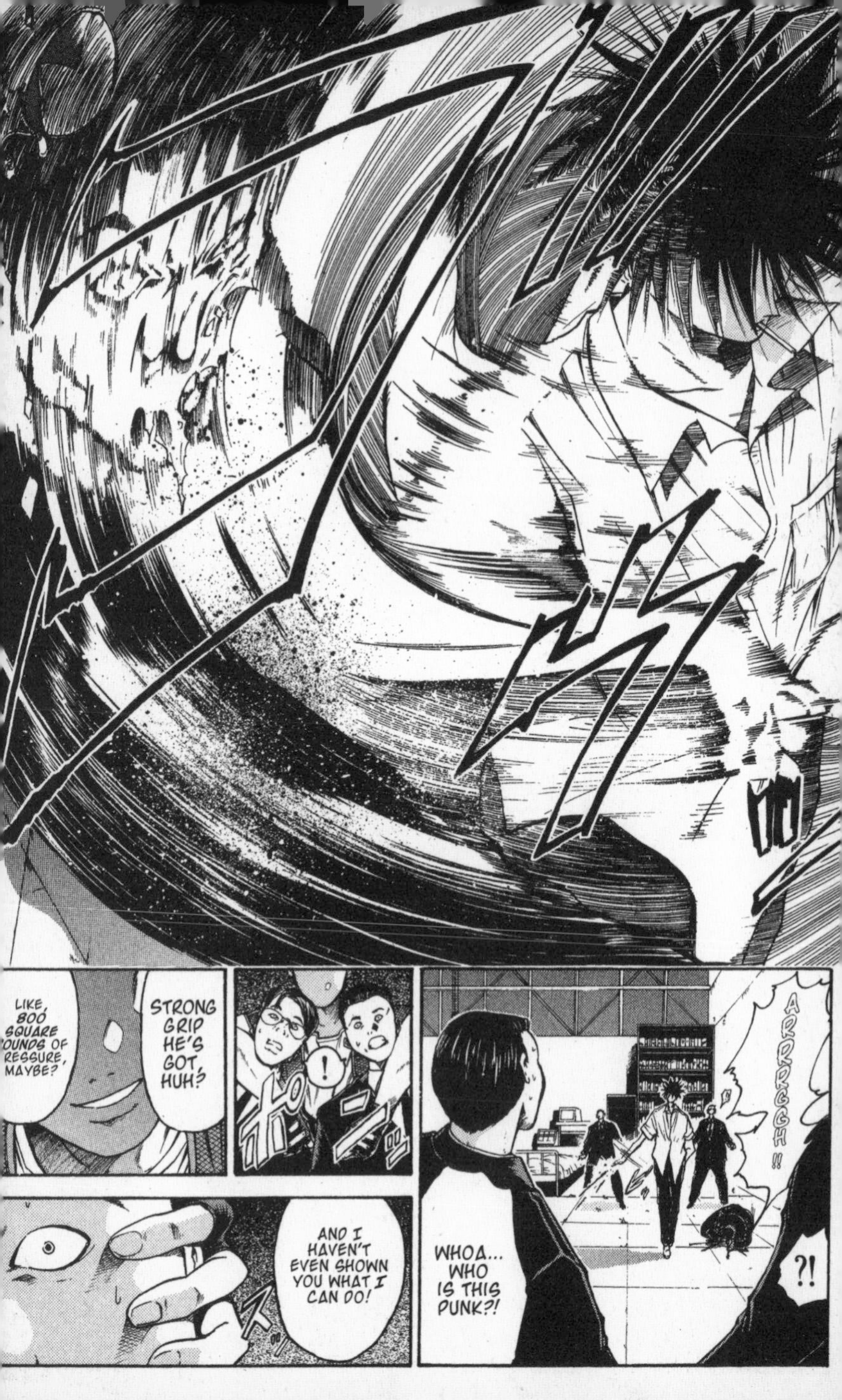
ARRRRGGH!!
?!
WHOA... WHO IS THIS PUNK?!
!
STRONG GRIP HE'S GOT, HUH?
LIKE, 800 SQUARE OUNDS OF RESSURE, MAYBE?
AND I HAVEN'T EVEN SHOWN YOU WHAT I CAN DO!

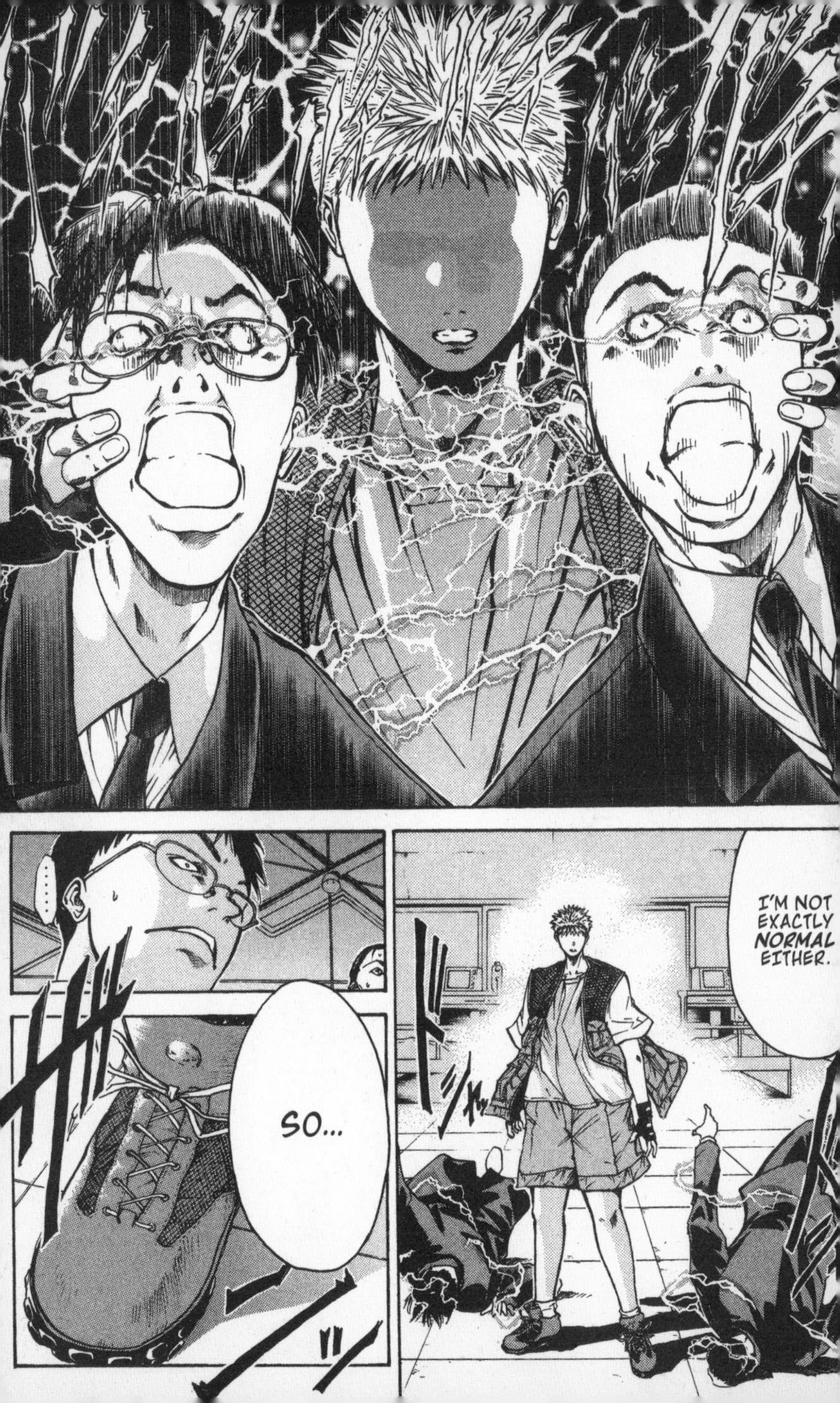
I'M NOT EXACTLY NORMAL EITHER.
SO...

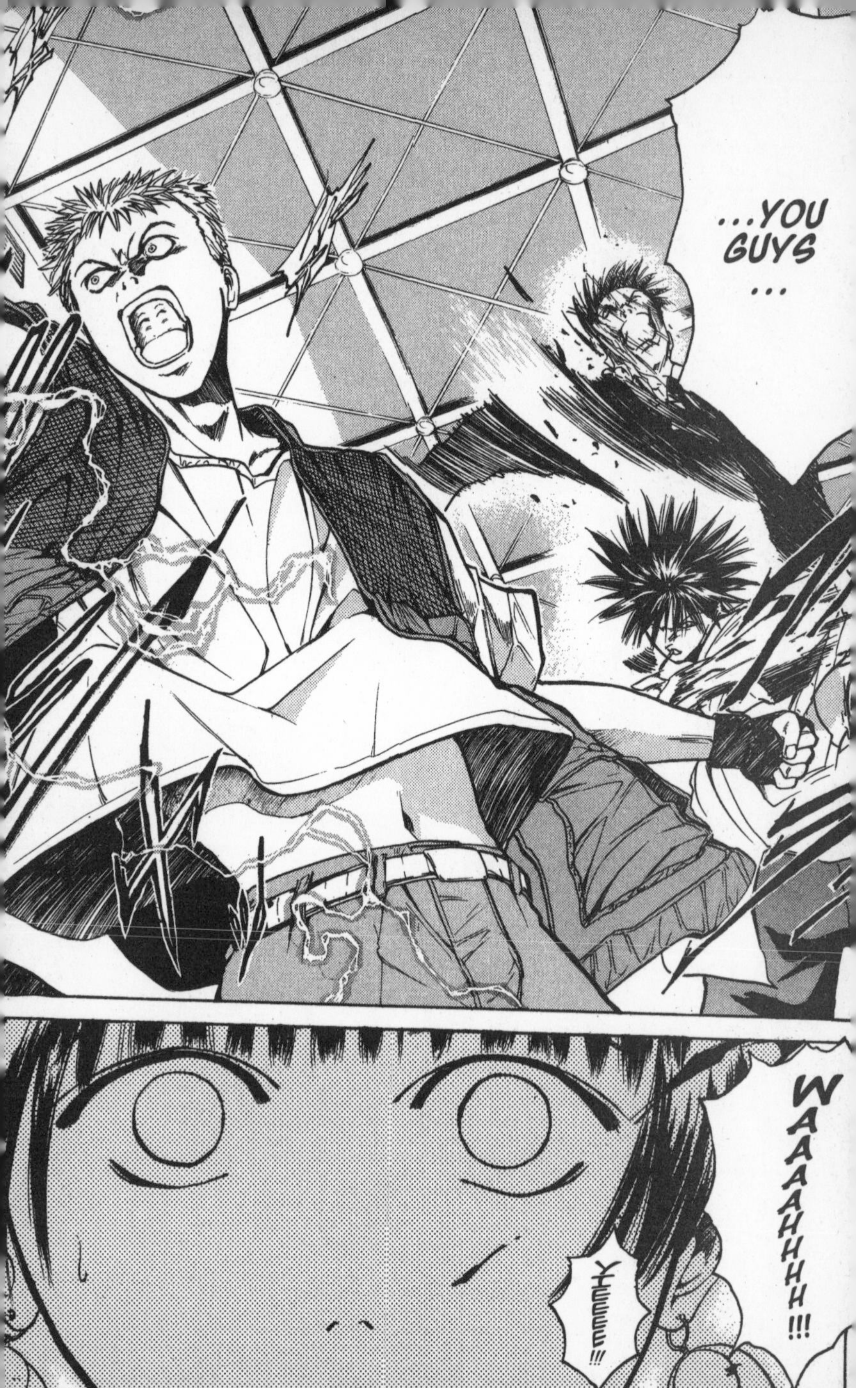
...YOU GUYS ...
WAAAAHHHH!!!
YIEEEE!!!

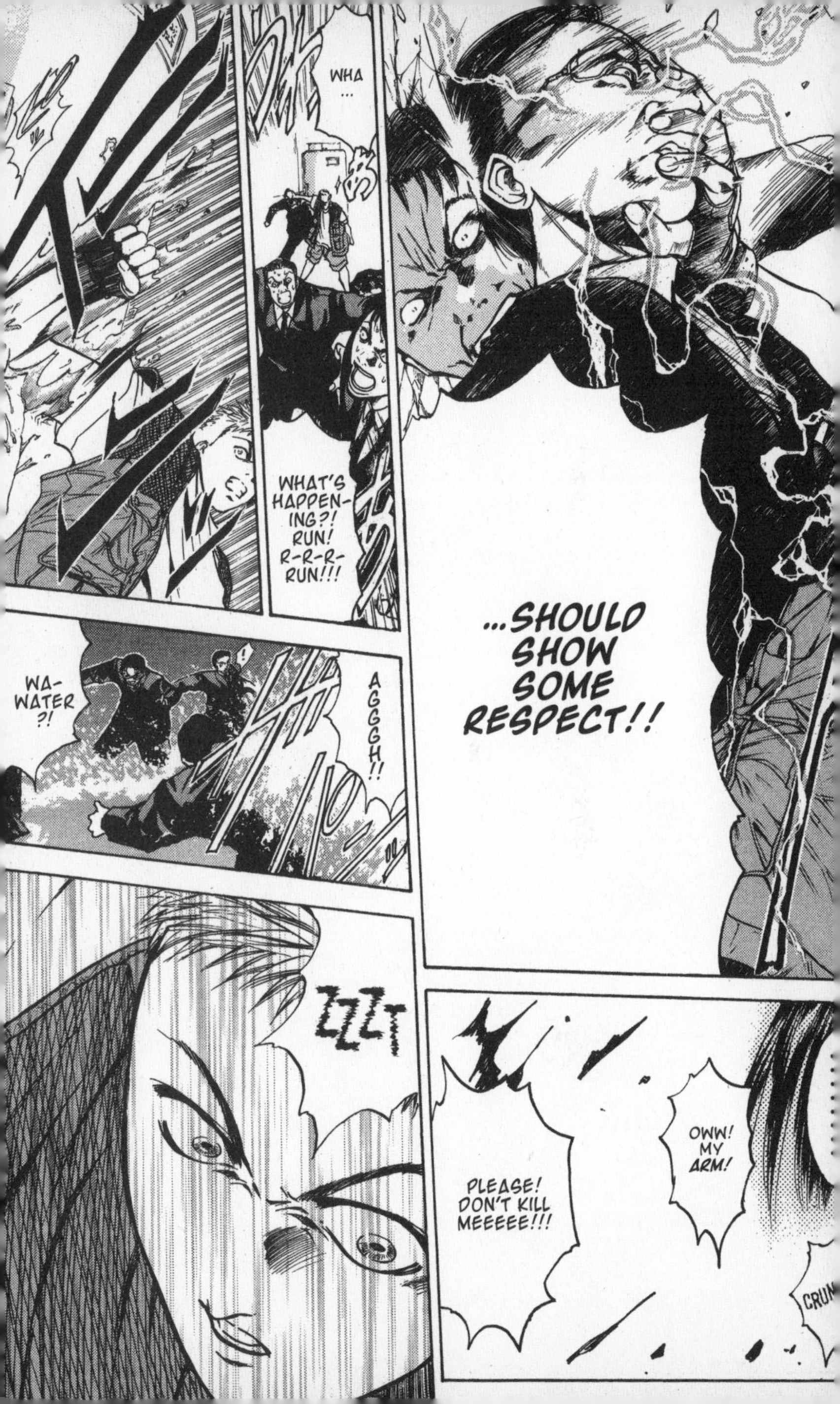
...SHOULD SHOW SOME RESPECT!!
WHA ...
WHAT'S HAPPENING?! RUN! R-R-R-RUN!!!
AGGGH!!
WA-WATER ?!
OWW! MY ARM!
PLEASE! DON'T KILL MEEEEE!!!
CRUN
ZZZT

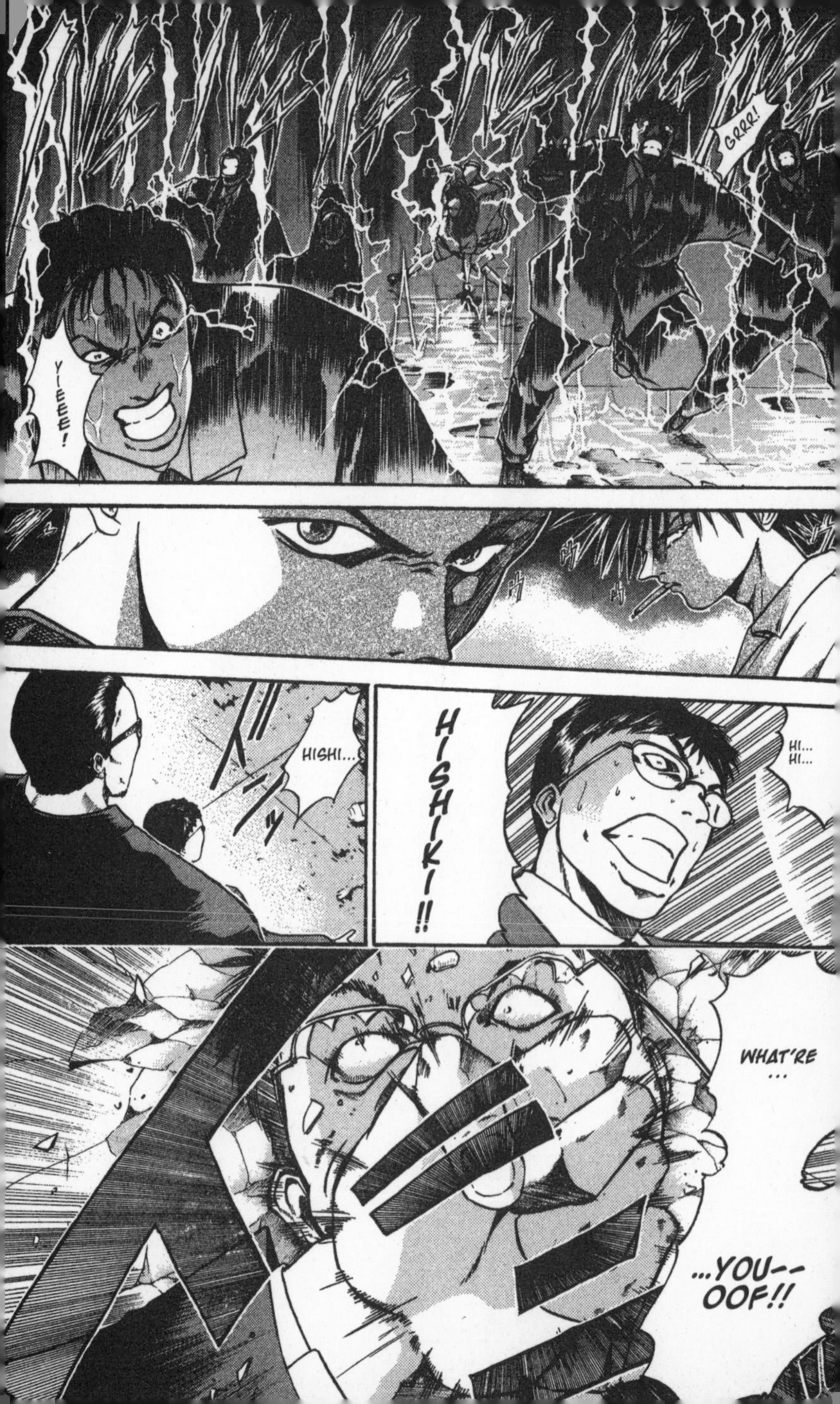
GRRR!
YIEEE!
HI... HI...
HISHIKI!!
HISHI...
WHAT'RE ...
...YOU--OOF!!

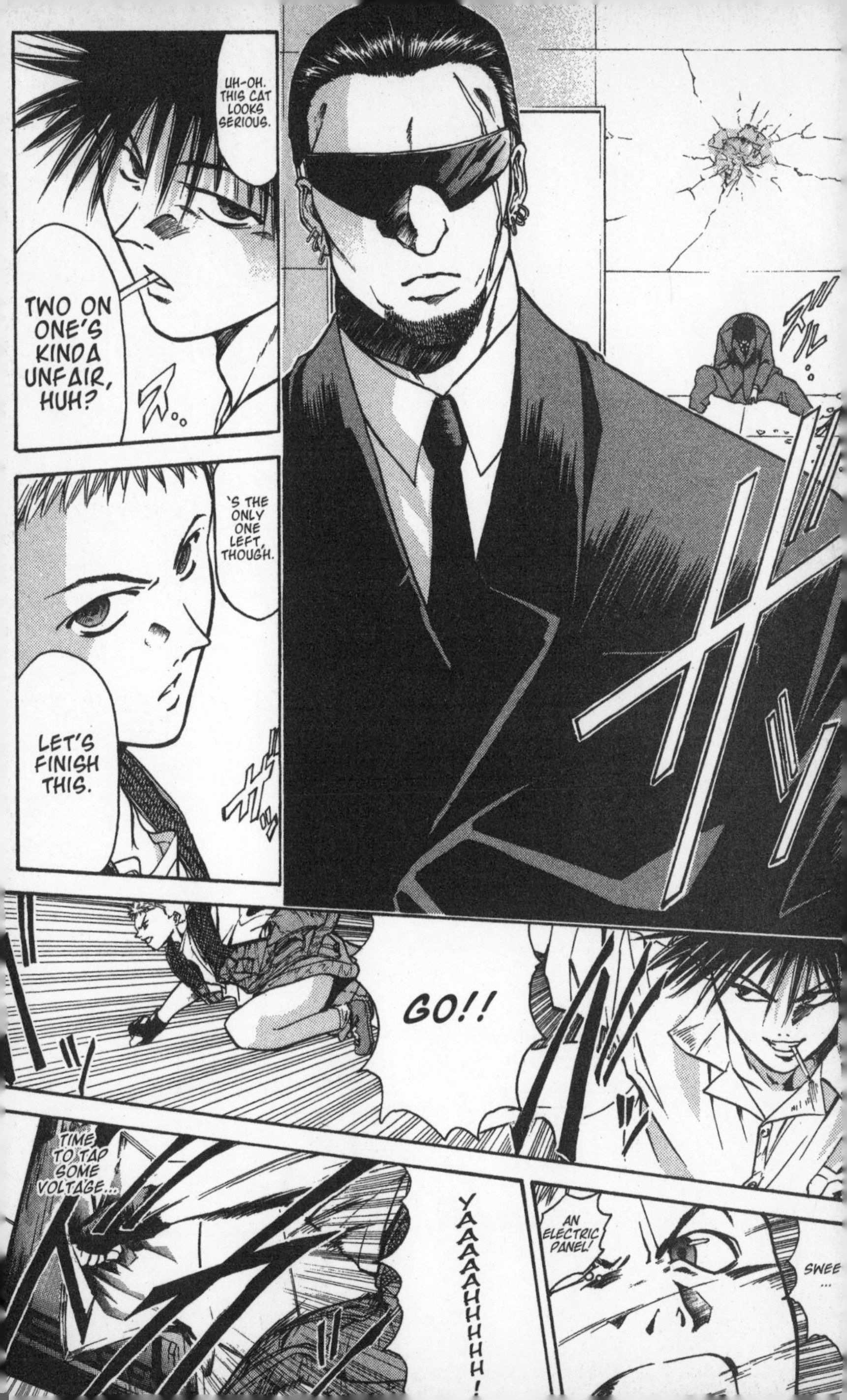
UH-OH. THIS CAT LOOKS SERIOUS.
TWO ON ONE'S KINDA UNFAIR, HUH?
'S THE ONLY ONE LEFT, THOUGH.
LET'S FINISH THIS.
GO!!
AN ELECTRIC PANEL!
SWEE...
YAAAAAHHHHHH!
TIME TO TAP SOME VOLTAGE...

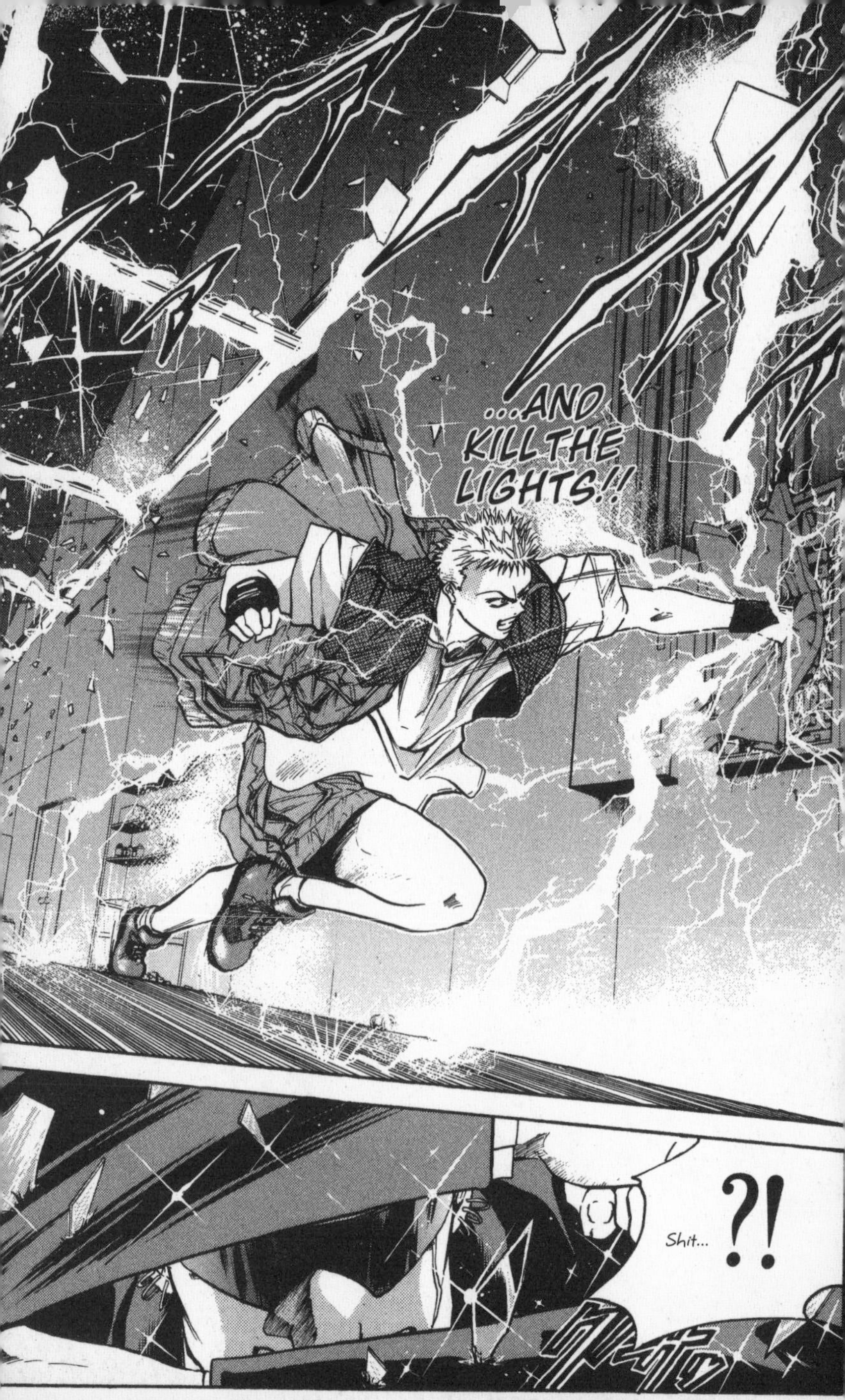
...AND KILL THE LIGHTS!!
Shit...
?!

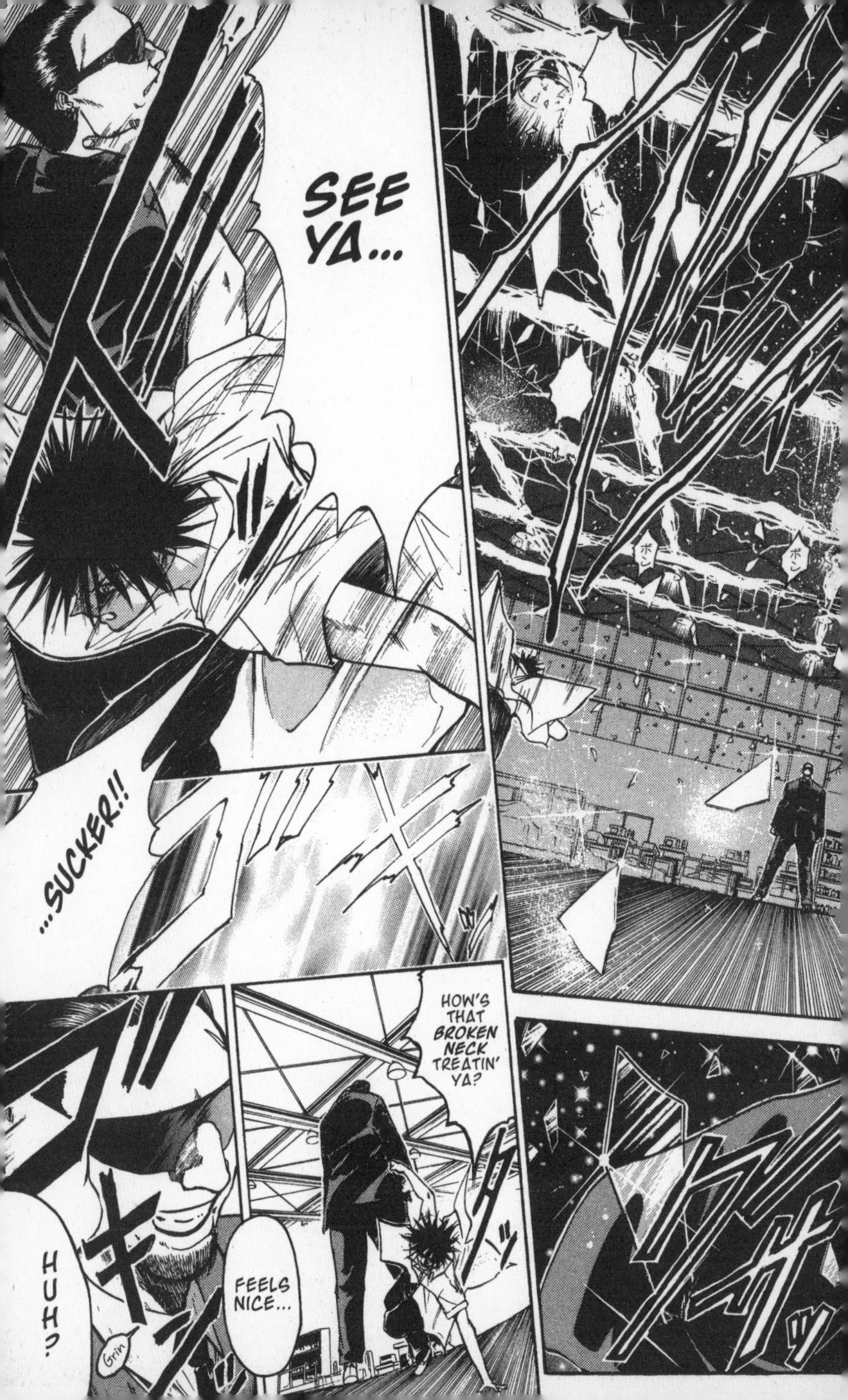
ボン
ボン
SEE YA...
...SUCKER!!
HOW'S THAT BROKEN NECK TREATIN' YA?
FEELS NICE...
HUH?
Grin

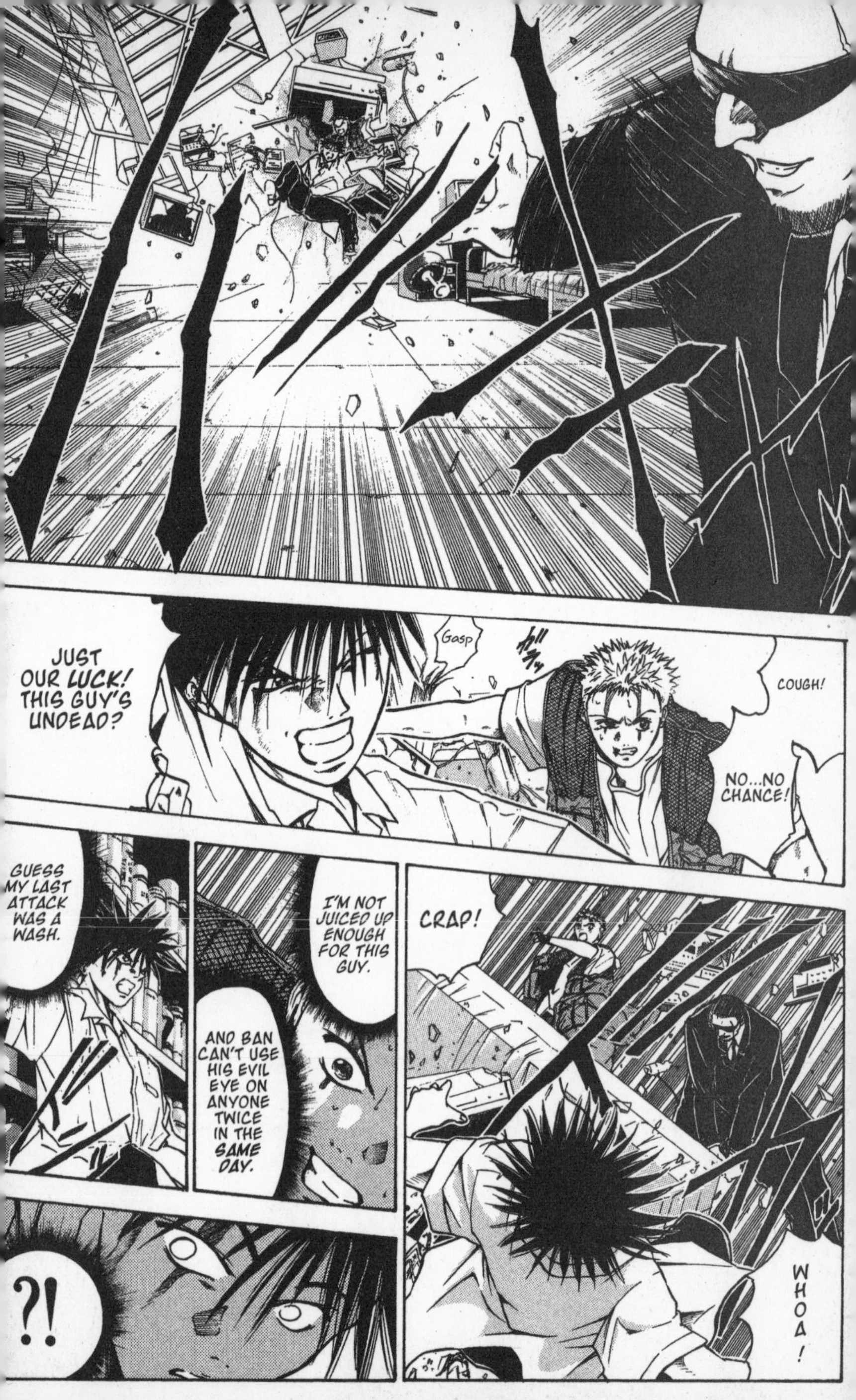
COUGH!
Gasp
JUST OUR LUCK! THIS GUY'S UNDEAD?
NO...NO CHANCE!
CRAP!
WHOA!
I'M NOT JUICED UP ENOUGH FOR THIS GUY.
AND BAN CAN'T USE HIS EVIL EYE ON ANYONE TWICE IN THE SAME DAY.
GUESS MY LAST ATTACK WAS A WASH.
?!

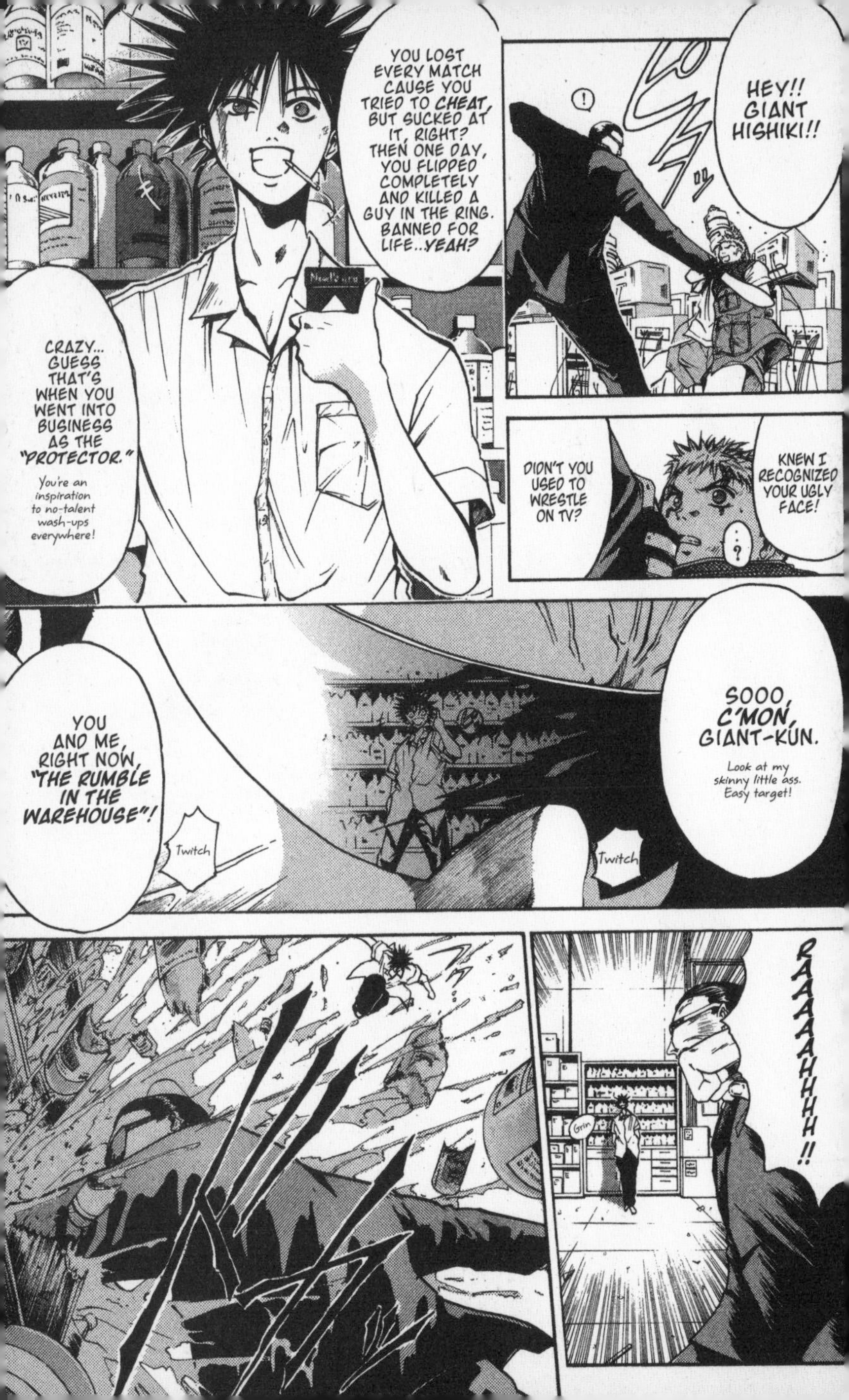
HEY!! GIANT HISHIKI!!
!
KNEW I RECOGNIZED YOUR UGLY FACE!
DIDN'T YOU USED TO WRESTLE ON TV?
...?
YOU LOST EVERY MATCH CAUSE YOU TRIED TO *CHEAT*, BUT SUCKED AT IT, RIGHT? THEN ONE DAY, YOU FLIPPED COMPLETELY AND KILLED A GUY IN THE RING. BANNED FOR LIFE...*YEAH?*
CRAZY... GUESS THAT'S WHEN YOU WENT INTO BUSINESS AS THE *"PROTECTOR."*
You're an inspiration to no-talent wash-ups everywhere!
SOOO, *C'MON*, GIANT-KUN.
Look at my skinny little ass. Easy target!
Twitch
YOU AND ME, RIGHT NOW, *"THE RUMBLE IN THE WAREHOUSE"*!
Twitch
RAAAAAHHHH!!
Grin

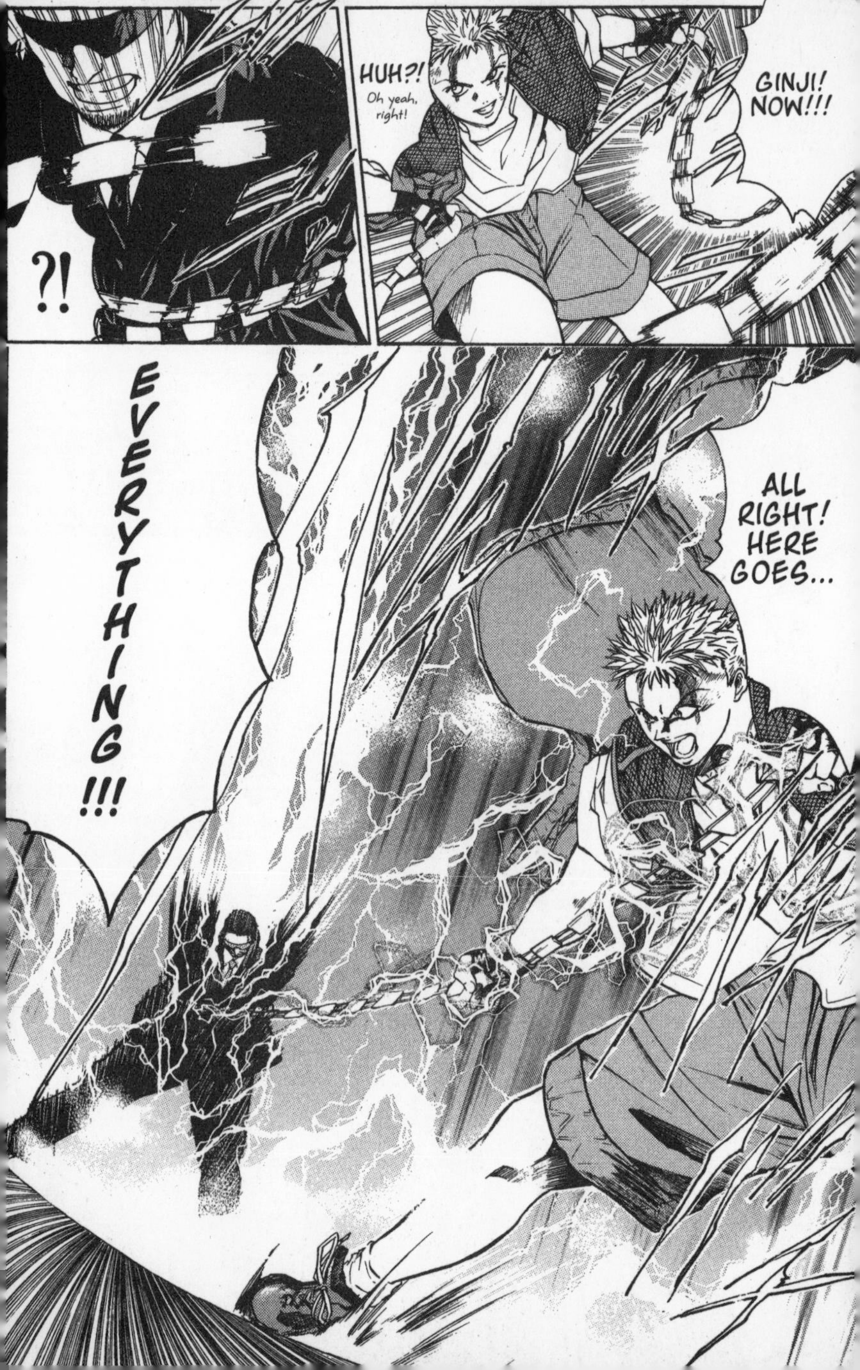
GINJI! NOW!!!
HUH?!
Oh yeah, right!
?!
ALL RIGHT! HERE GOES...
EVERYTHING!!!

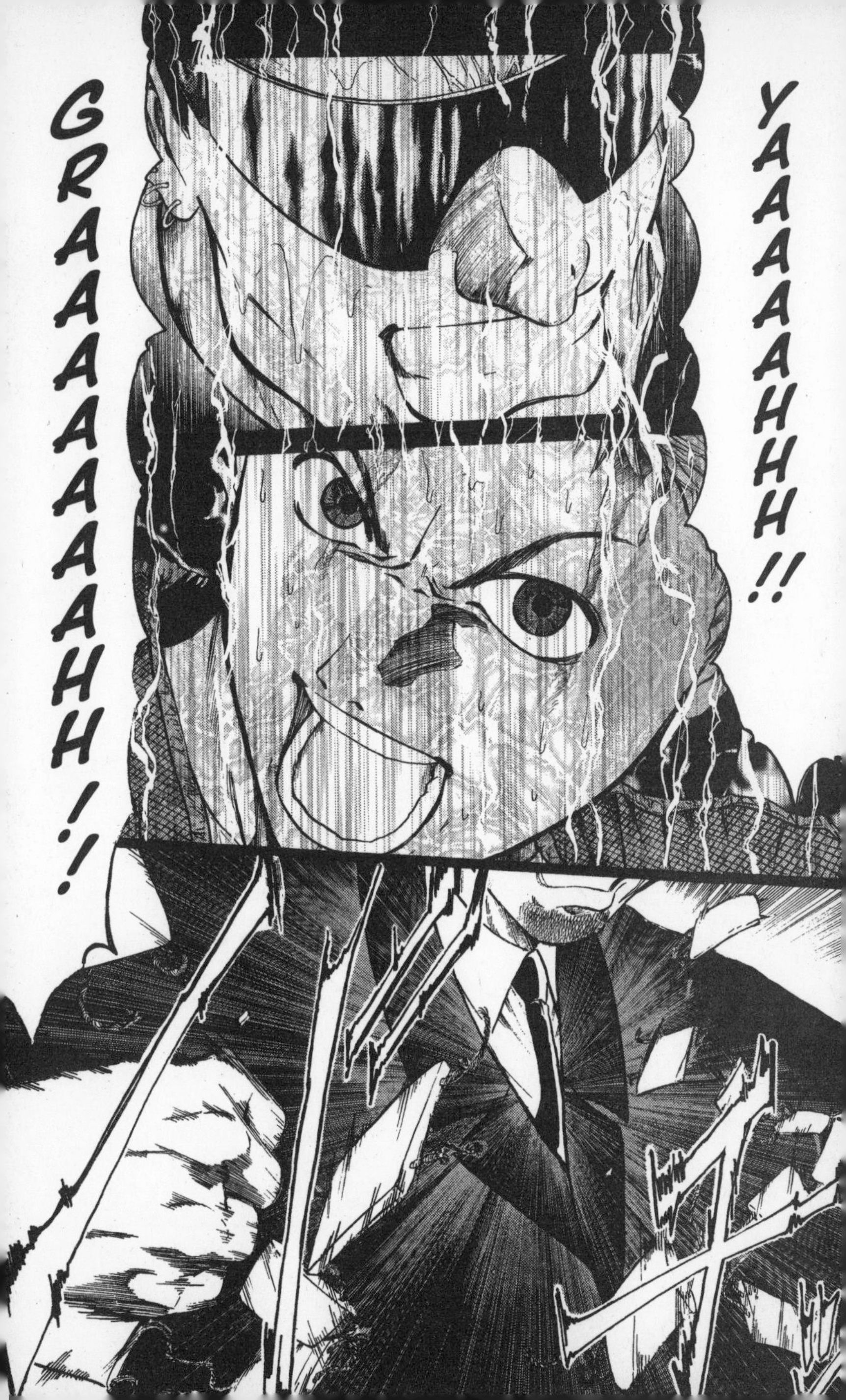
YAAAAAHHH!!
GRAAAAAAAAHH!!

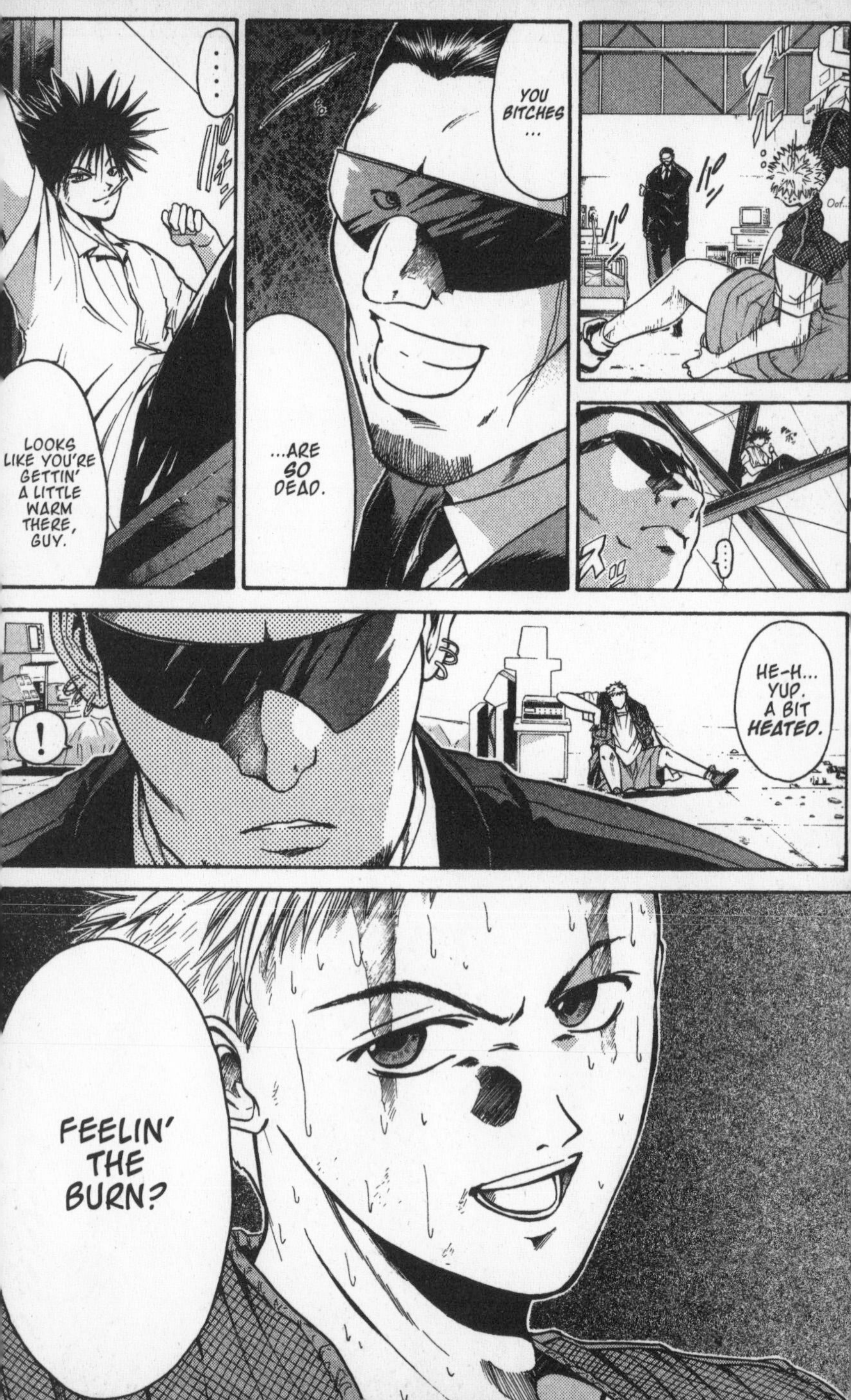
Oof...
...
YOU BITCHES...
...ARE SO DEAD.
...
LOOKS LIKE YOU'RE GETTIN' A LITTLE WARM THERE, GUY.
HE-H... YUP. A BIT HEATED.
!
FEELIN' THE BURN?

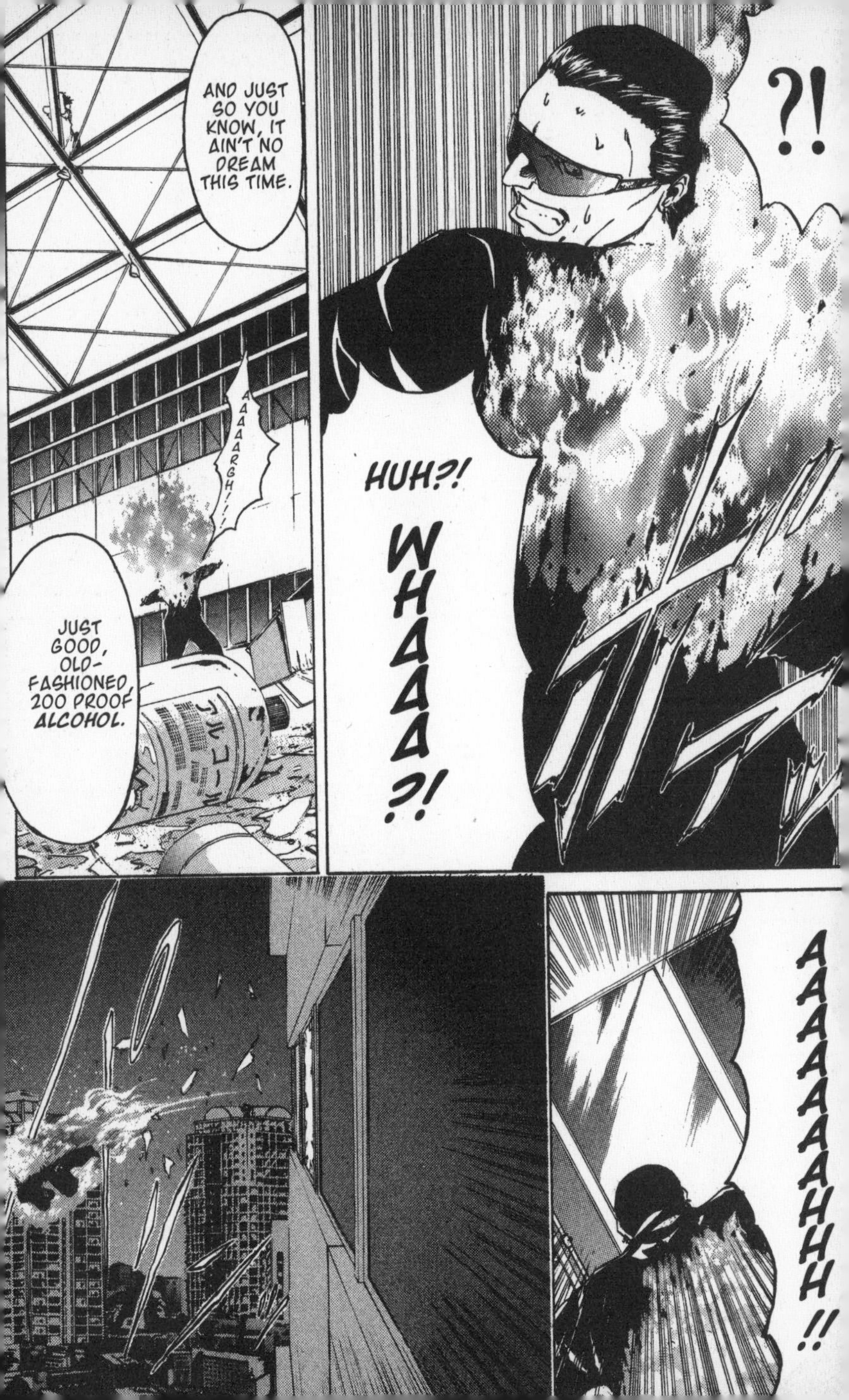
?!
HUH?!
WHAAAA?!
AND JUST SO YOU KNOW, IT AIN'T NO DREAM THIS TIME.
AAAAARGH!!!
JUST GOOD, OLD-FASHIONED 200 PROOF ALCOHOL.
AAAAAAAHHH!!

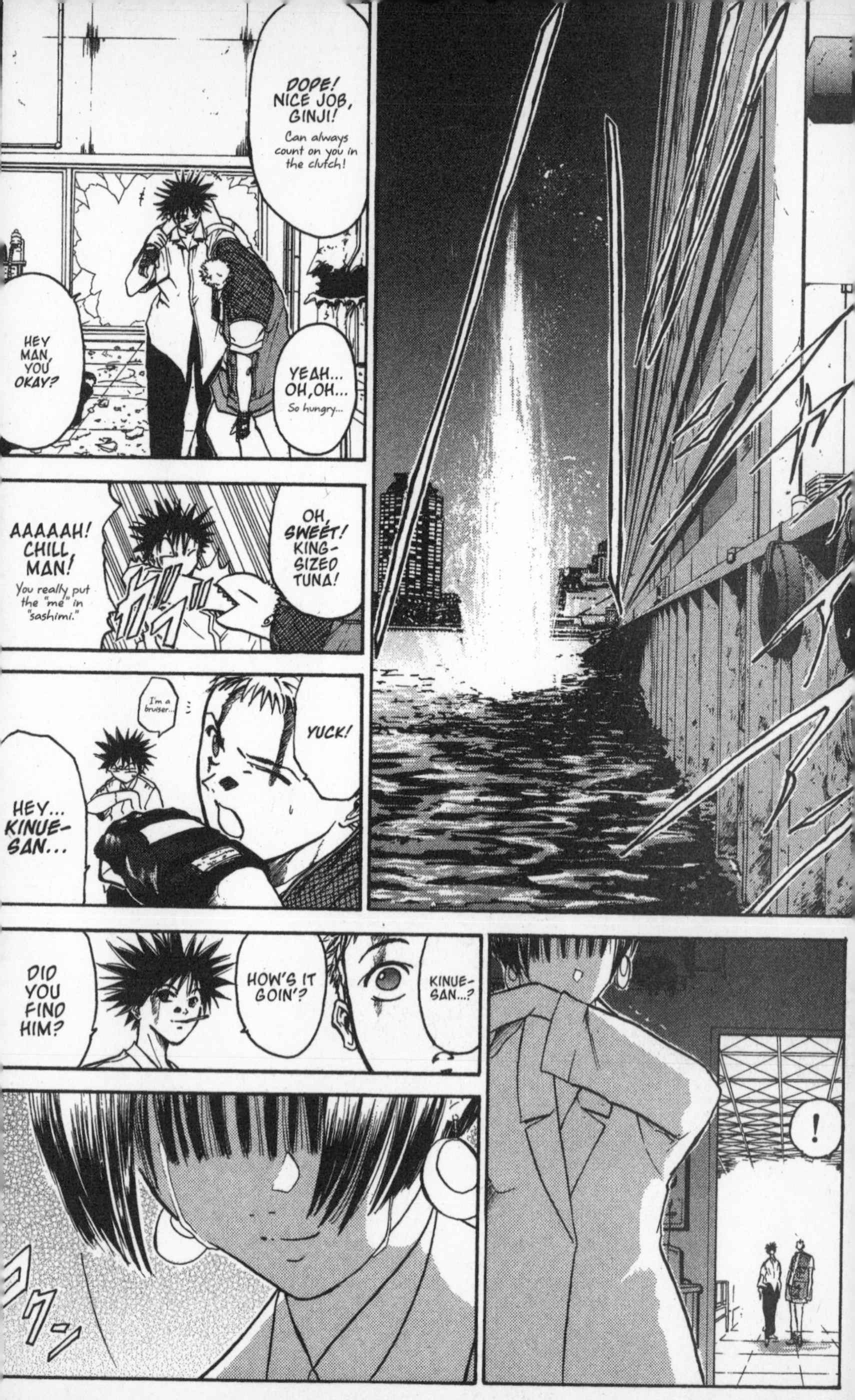
DOPE! NICE JOB, GINJI!
Can always count on you in the clutch!
HEY MAN, YOU OKAY?
YEAH... OH,OH...
So hungry...
OH, SWEET! KING-SIZED TUNA!
AAAAAH! CHILL MAN!
You really put the "me" in "sashimi."
YUCK!
I'm a bruiser...
HEY... KINUE-SAN...
!
KINUE-SAN...?
HOW'S IT GOIN'?
DID YOU FIND HIM?

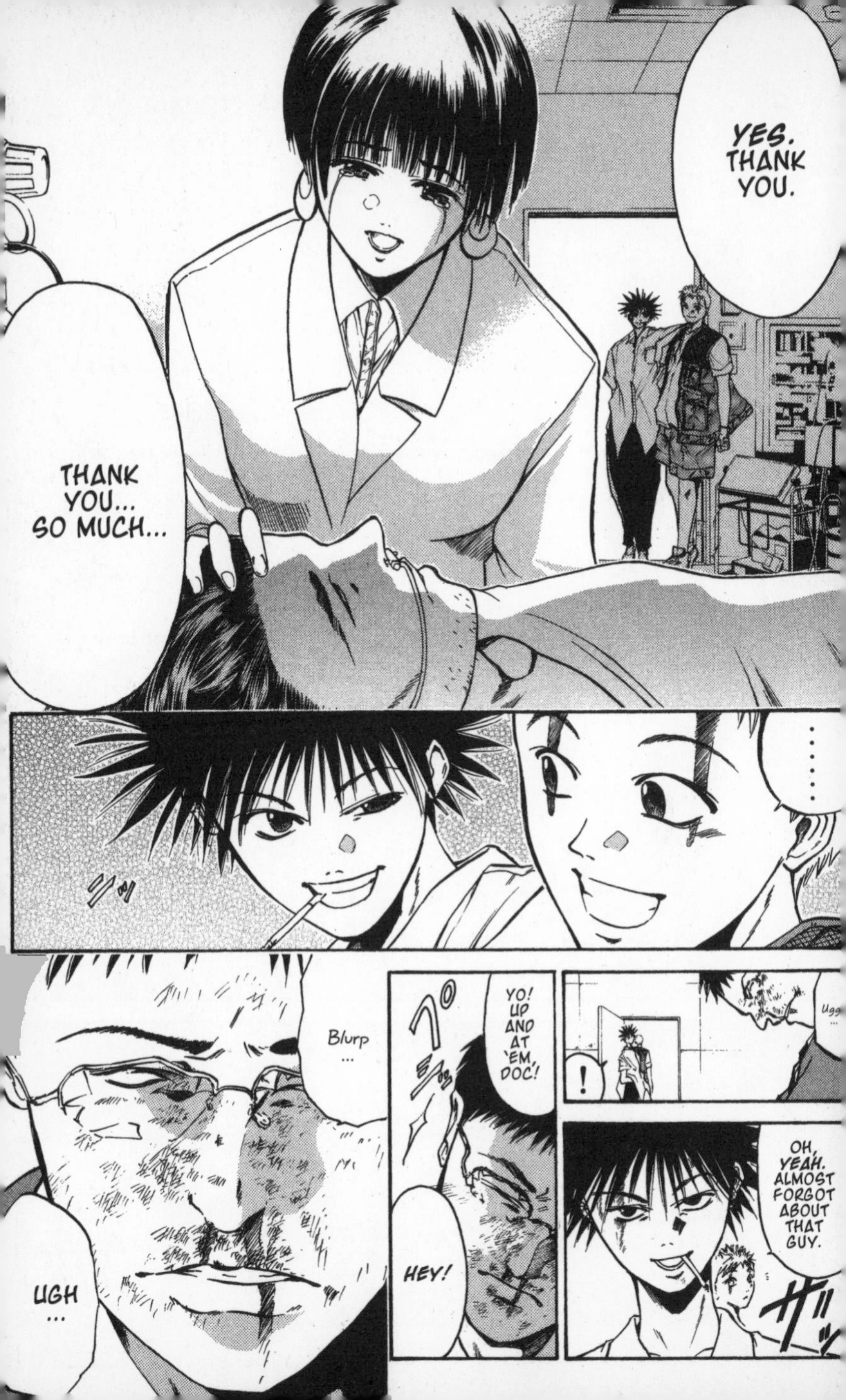
YES. THANK YOU.
THANK YOU... SO MUCH...
......
Ugg...
!
OH, YEAH. ALMOST FORGOT ABOUT THAT GUY.
YO! UP AND AT 'EM, DOC!
HEY!
Blurp...
UGH...

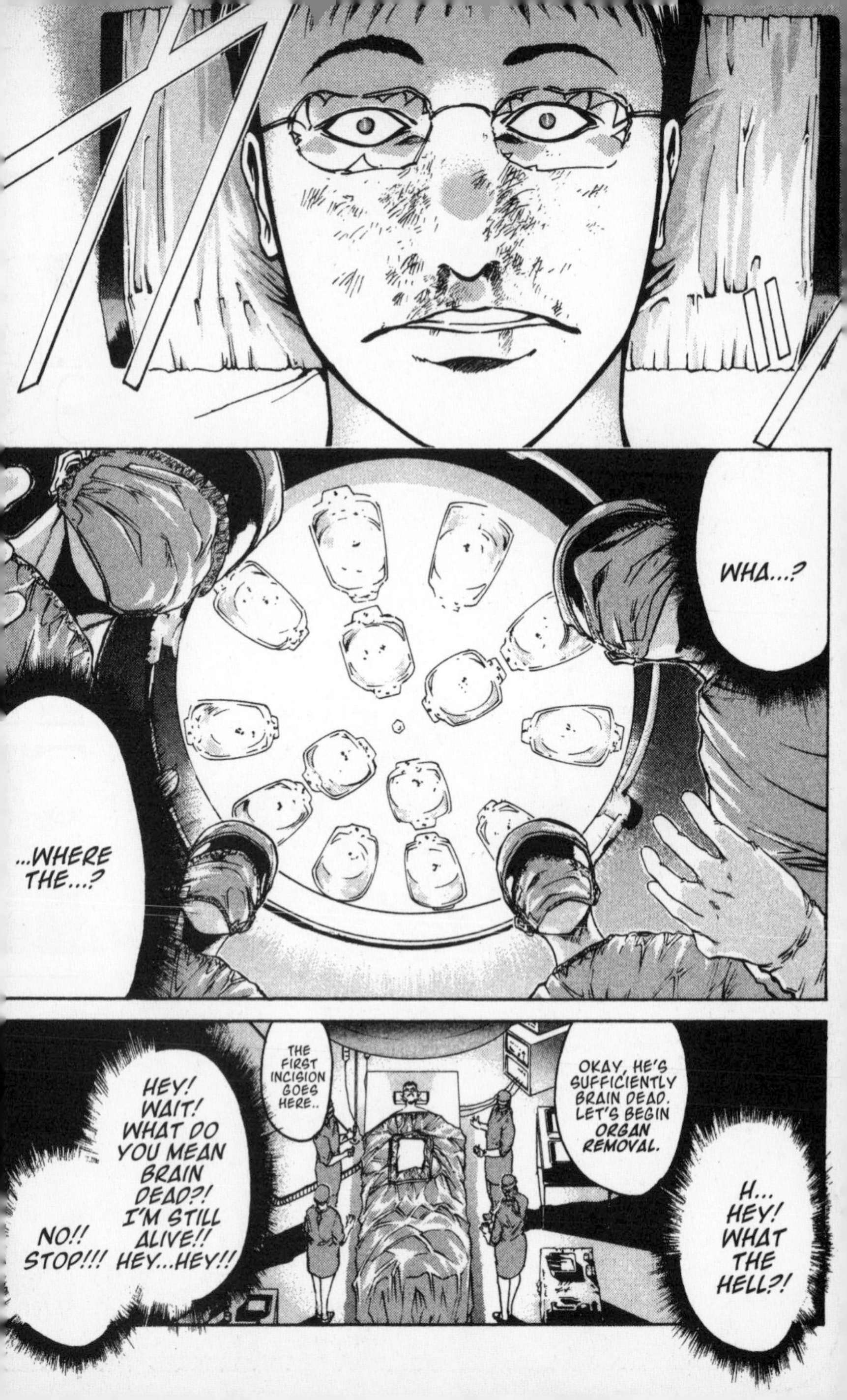
WHA...?
...WHERE THE...?
OKAY, HE'S SUFFICIENTLY BRAIN DEAD. LET'S BEGIN ORGAN REMOVAL.
THE FIRST INCISION GOES HERE..
H... HEY! WHAT THE HELL?!
HEY! WAIT! WHAT DO YOU MEAN BRAIN DEAD?! I'M STILL ALIVE!! HEY...HEY!!
NO!! STOP!!!

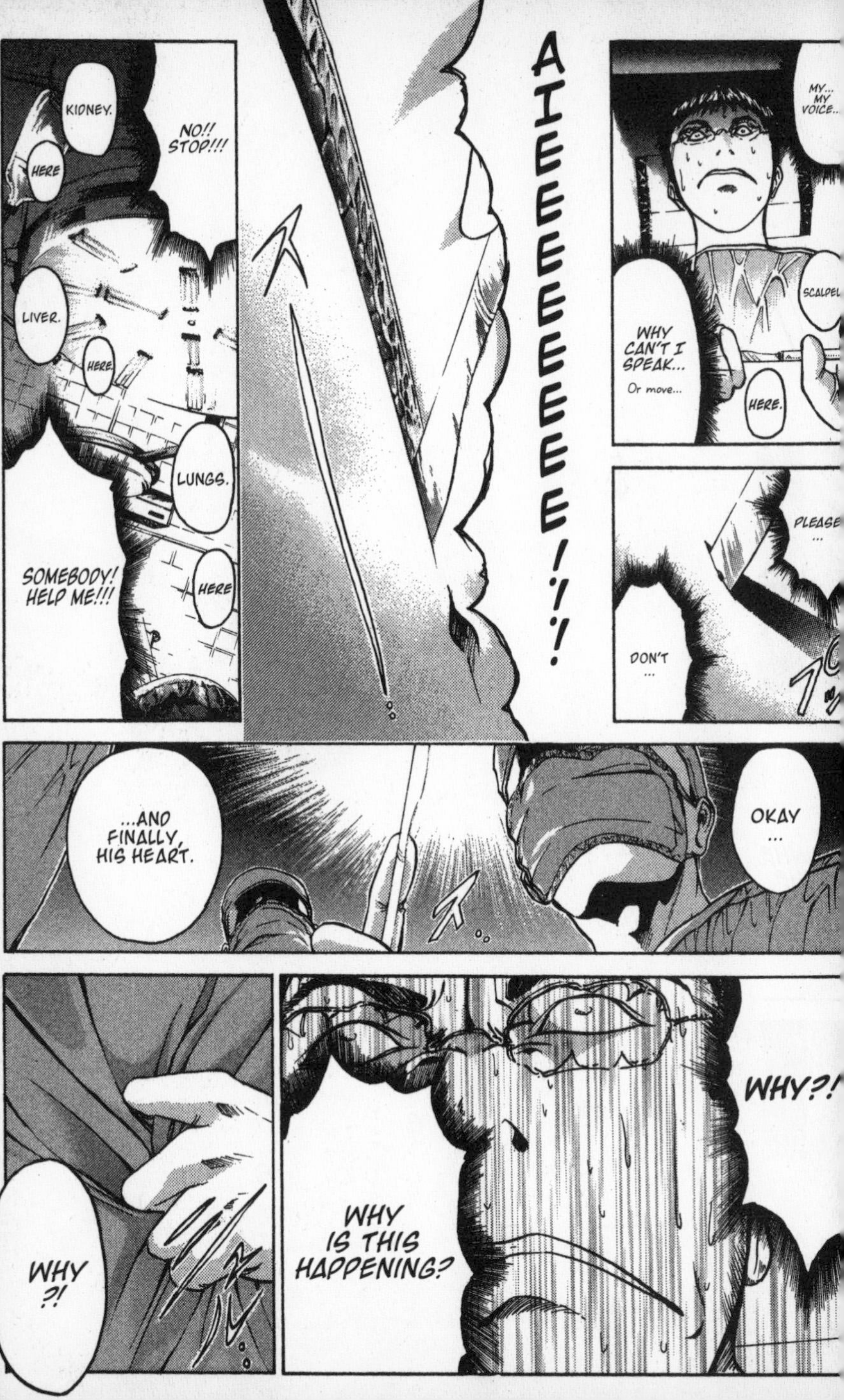
MY... MY VOICE...
SCALPEL
WHY CAN'T I SPEAK...
Or move...
HERE.
PLEASE...
DON'T...
AIEEEEEEEEEE!!!
NO!! STOP!!!
KIDNEY.
HERE
LIVER.
HERE
LUNGS.
HERE
SOMEBODY! HELP ME!!!
OKAY...
...AND FINALLY, HIS HEART.
WHY?!
WHY IS THIS HAPPENING?
WHY?!

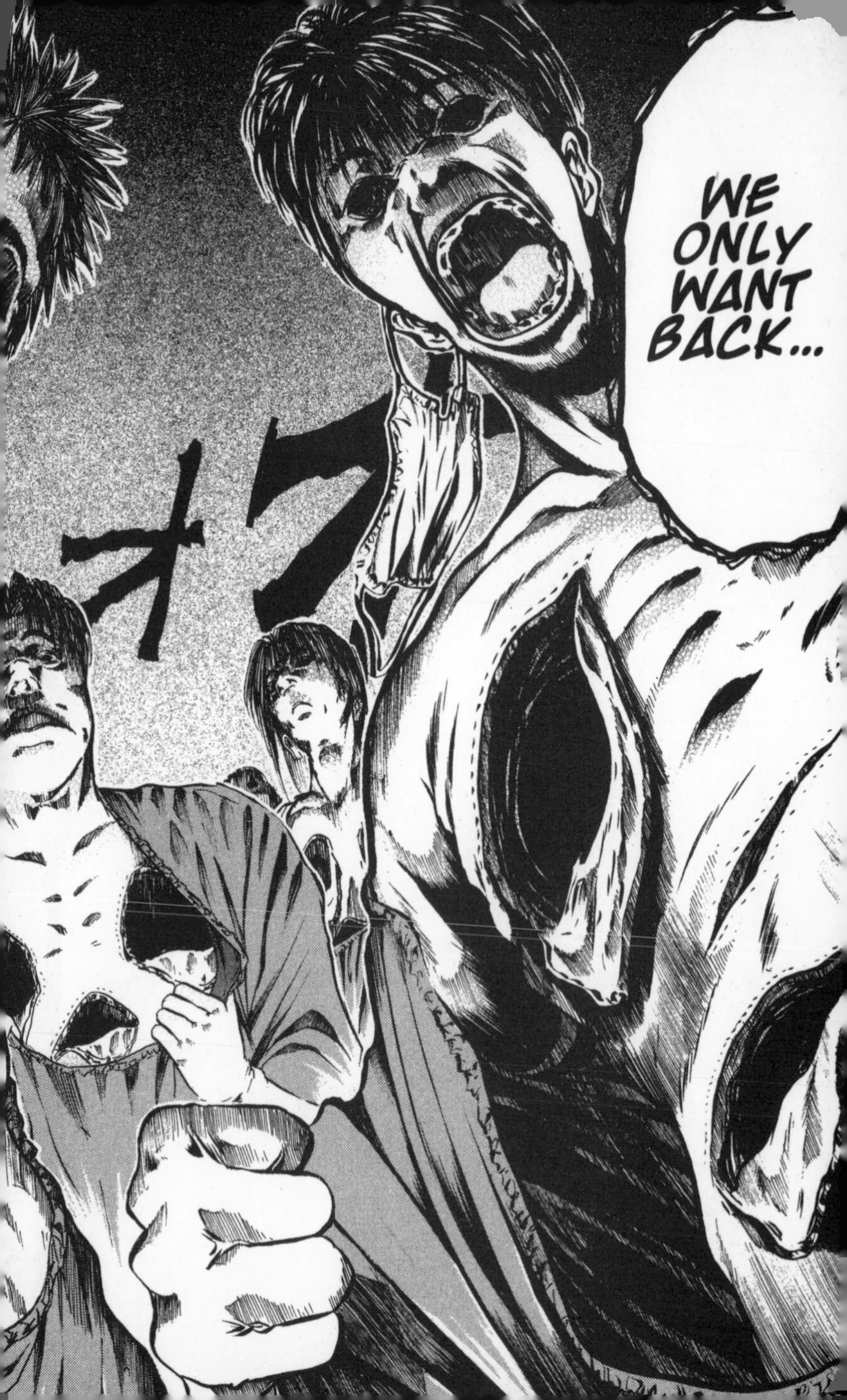
WE ONLY WANT BACK...

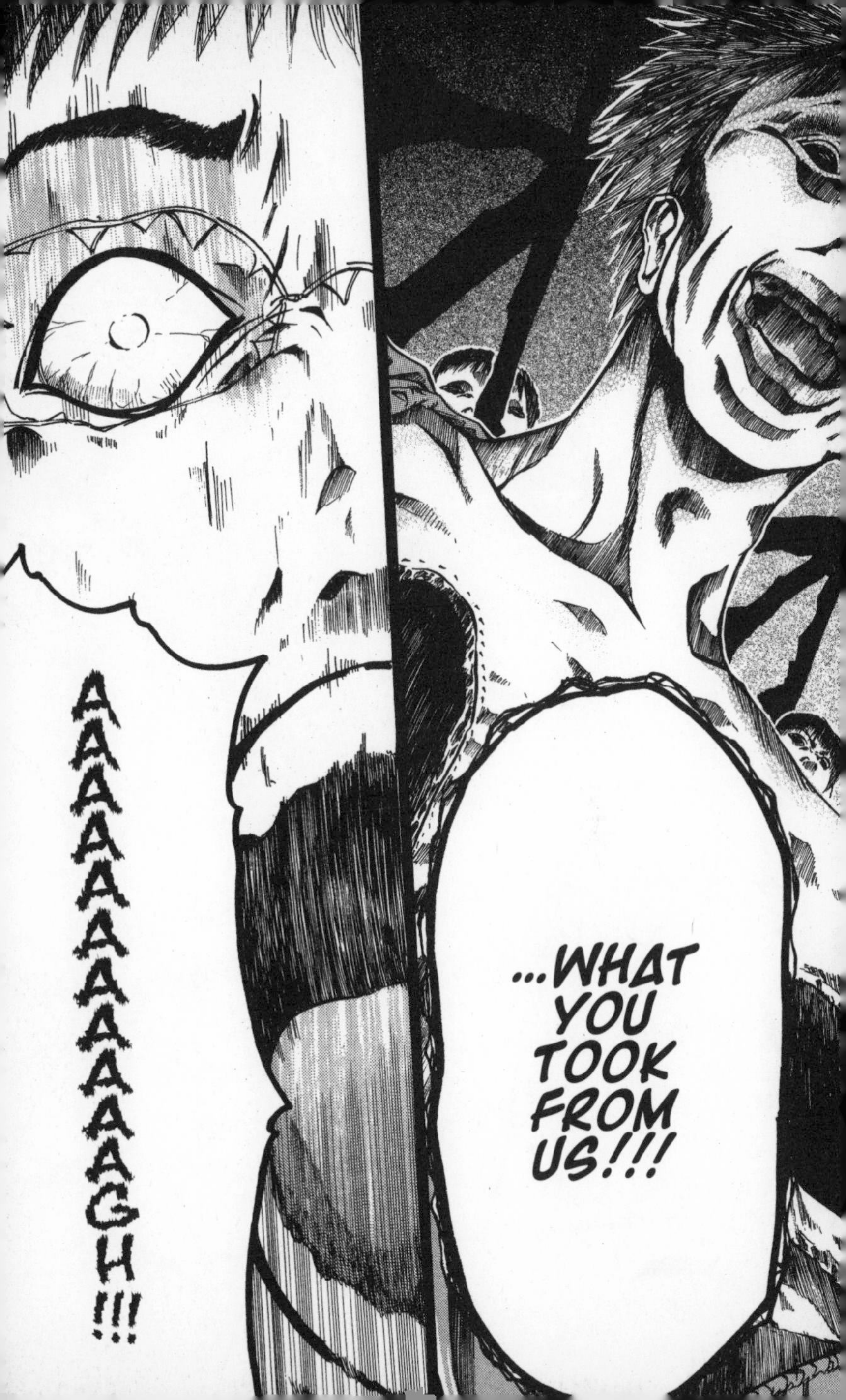
...WHAT YOU TOOK FROM US!!!
AAAAAAAAAAAGH!!!

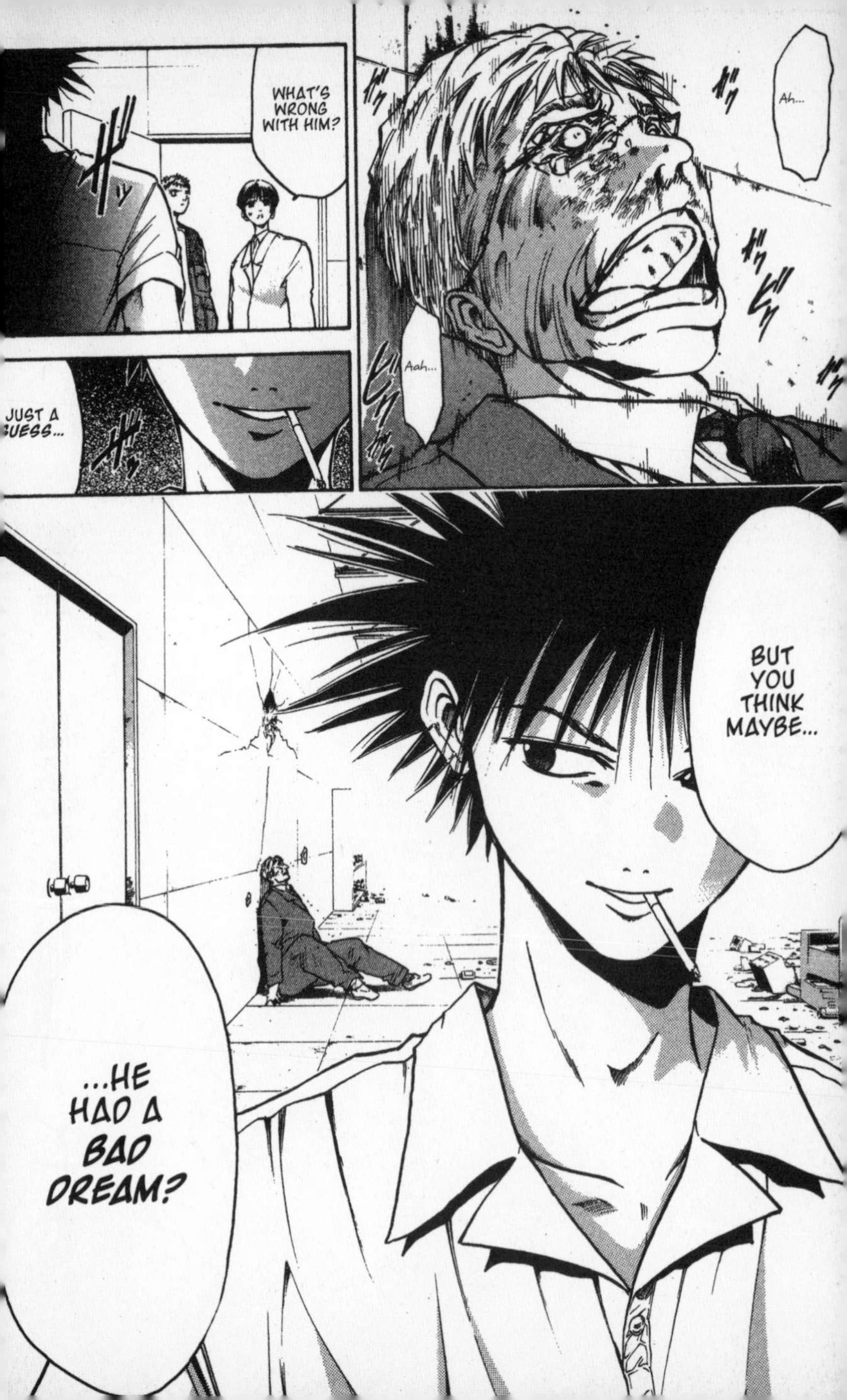

Ah...
Aah...
WHAT'S WRONG WITH HIM?
JUST A GUESS...
BUT YOU THINK MAYBE...
...HE HAD A BAD DREAM?

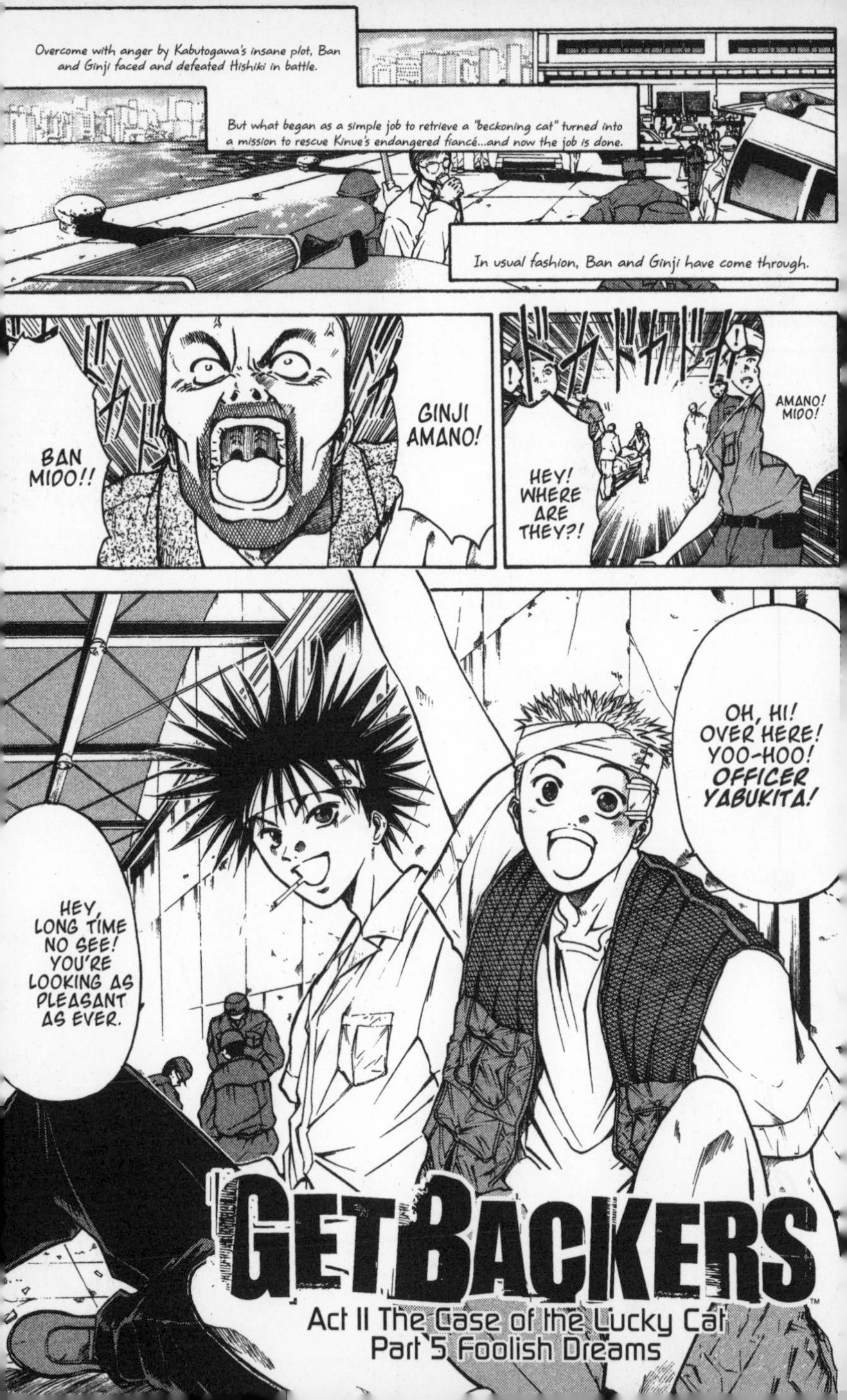

Overcome with anger by Kabutogawa's insane plot, Ban and Ginji faced and defeated Hishiki in battle.
But what began as a simple job to retrieve a "beckoning cat" turned into a mission to rescue Kinue's endangered fiancé...and now the job is done.
In usual fashion, Ban and Ginji have come through.
AMANO! MIDO!
HEY! WHERE ARE THEY?!
GINJI AMANO!
BAN MIDO!!
OH, HI! OVER HERE! YOO-HOO! OFFICER YABUKITA!
HEY, LONG TIME NO SEE! YOU'RE LOOKING AS PLEASANT AS EVER.
GETBACKERS™
Act II The Case of the Lucky Cat
Part 5 Foolish Dreams

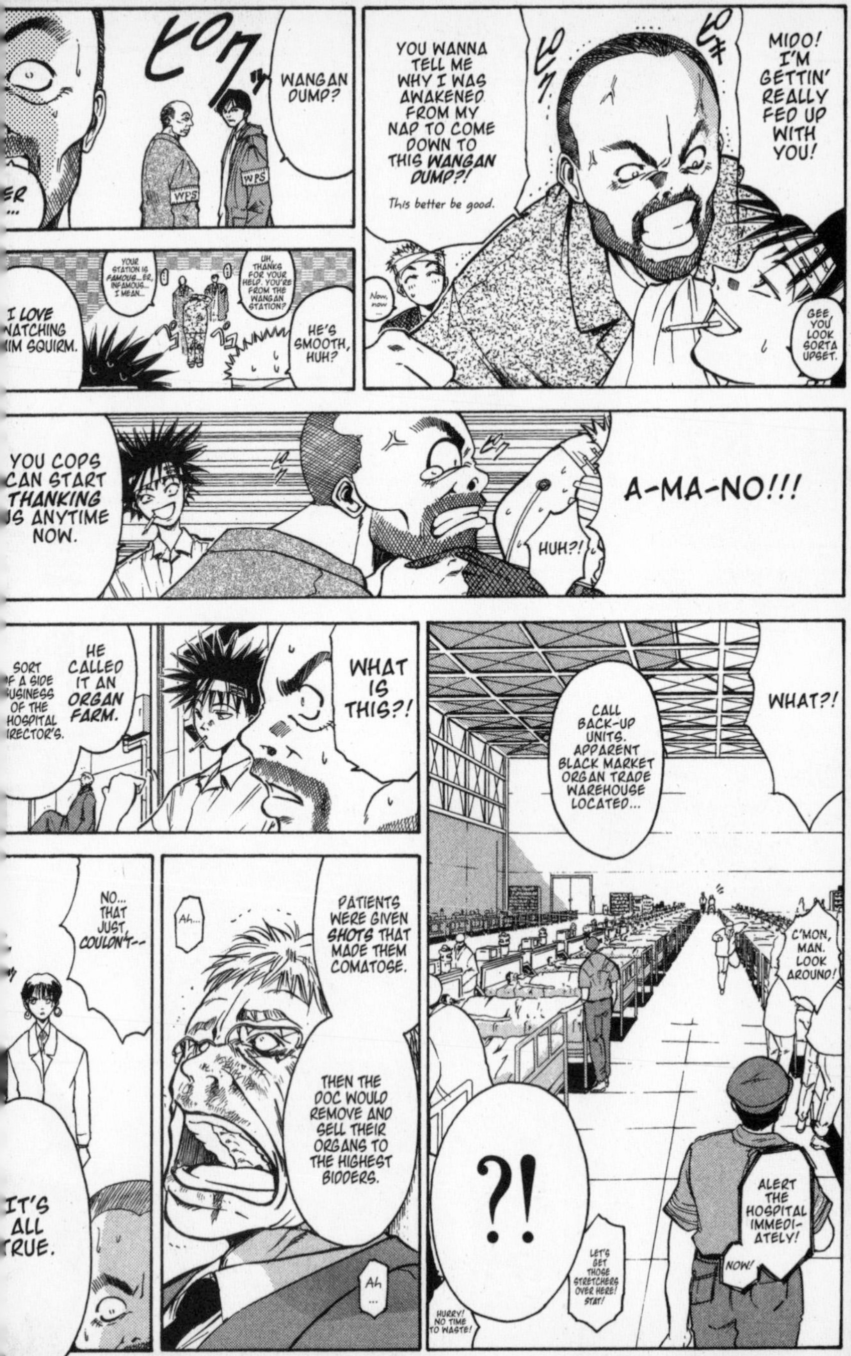
MIDO! I'M GETTIN' REALLY FED UP WITH YOU!
YOU WANNA TELL ME WHY I WAS AWAKENED FROM MY NAP TO COME DOWN TO THIS WANGAN DUMP?!
This better be good.
GEE, YOU LOOK SORTA UPSET.
Now, now ...
WANGAN DUMP?
ER ...
HE'S SMOOTH, HUH?
UH, THANKS FOR YOUR HELP. YOU'RE FROM THE WANGAN STATION?
YOUR STATION IS FAMOUS... ER, INFAMOUS... I MEAN...
I LOVE WATCHING HIM SQUIRM.
A-MA-NO!!!
HUH?!
YOU COPS CAN START THANKING US ANYTIME NOW.
WHAT?!
CALL BACK-UP UNITS. APPARENT BLACK MARKET ORGAN TRADE WAREHOUSE LOCATED...
C'MON, MAN. LOOK AROUND!
ALERT THE HOSPITAL IMMEDIATELY!
NOW!
?!
LET'S GET THOSE STRETCHERS OVER HERE! STAT!
HURRY! NO TIME TO WASTE!
WHAT IS THIS?!
HE CALLED IT AN ORGAN FARM.
SORT OF A SIDE BUSINESS OF THE HOSPITAL DIRECTOR'S.
PATIENTS WERE GIVEN SHOTS THAT MADE THEM COMATOSE.
Ah...
THEN THE DOC WOULD REMOVE AND SELL THEIR ORGANS TO THE HIGHEST BIDDERS.
Ah ...
NO... THAT JUST COULDN'T--
IT'S ALL TRUE.

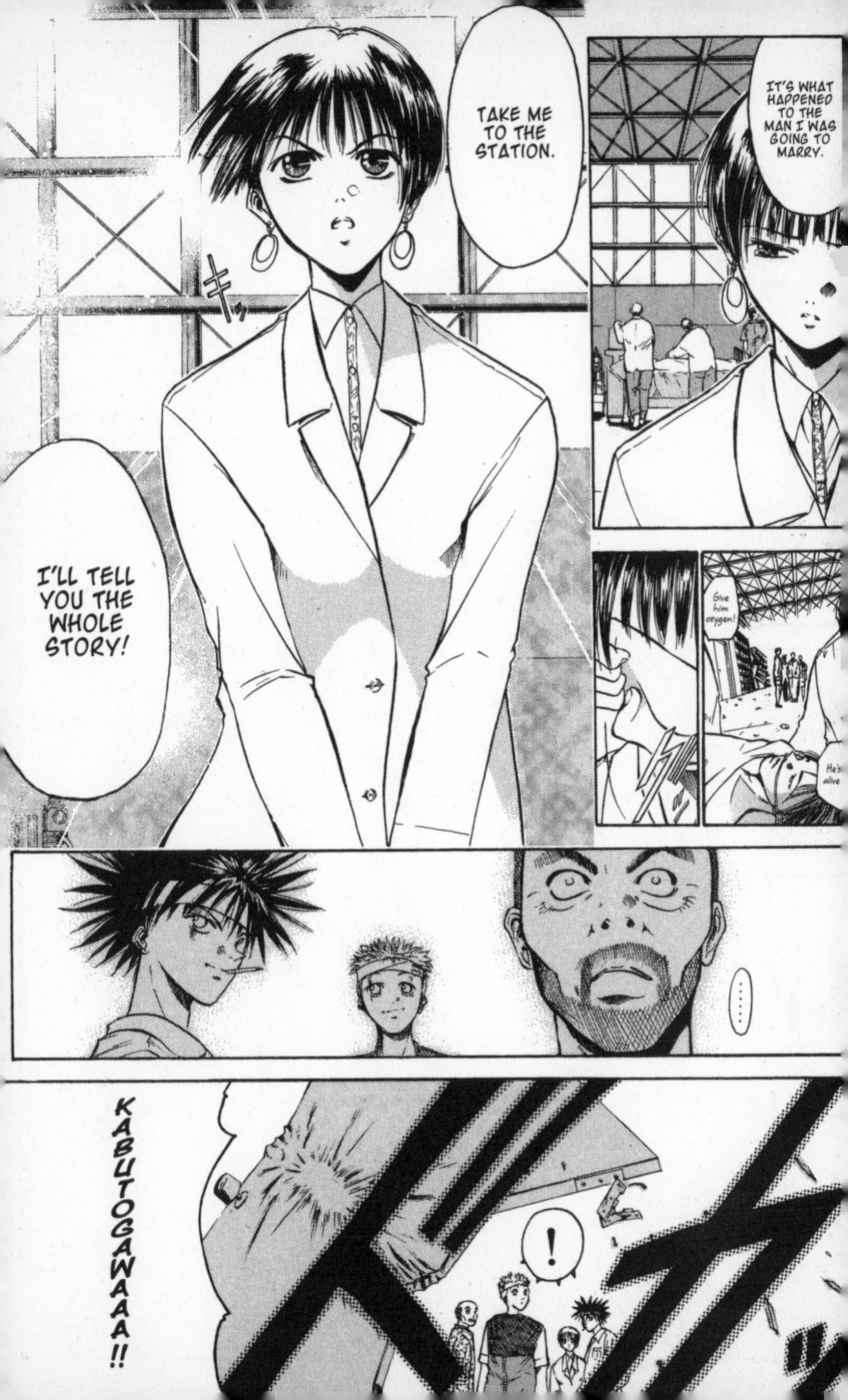
IT'S WHAT HAPPENED TO THE MAN I WAS GOING TO MARRY.
Give him oxygen!
He's alive
TAKE ME TO THE STATION.
ギッ
I'LL TELL YOU THE WHOLE STORY!
......
!
KABUTOGAWAAAA!!

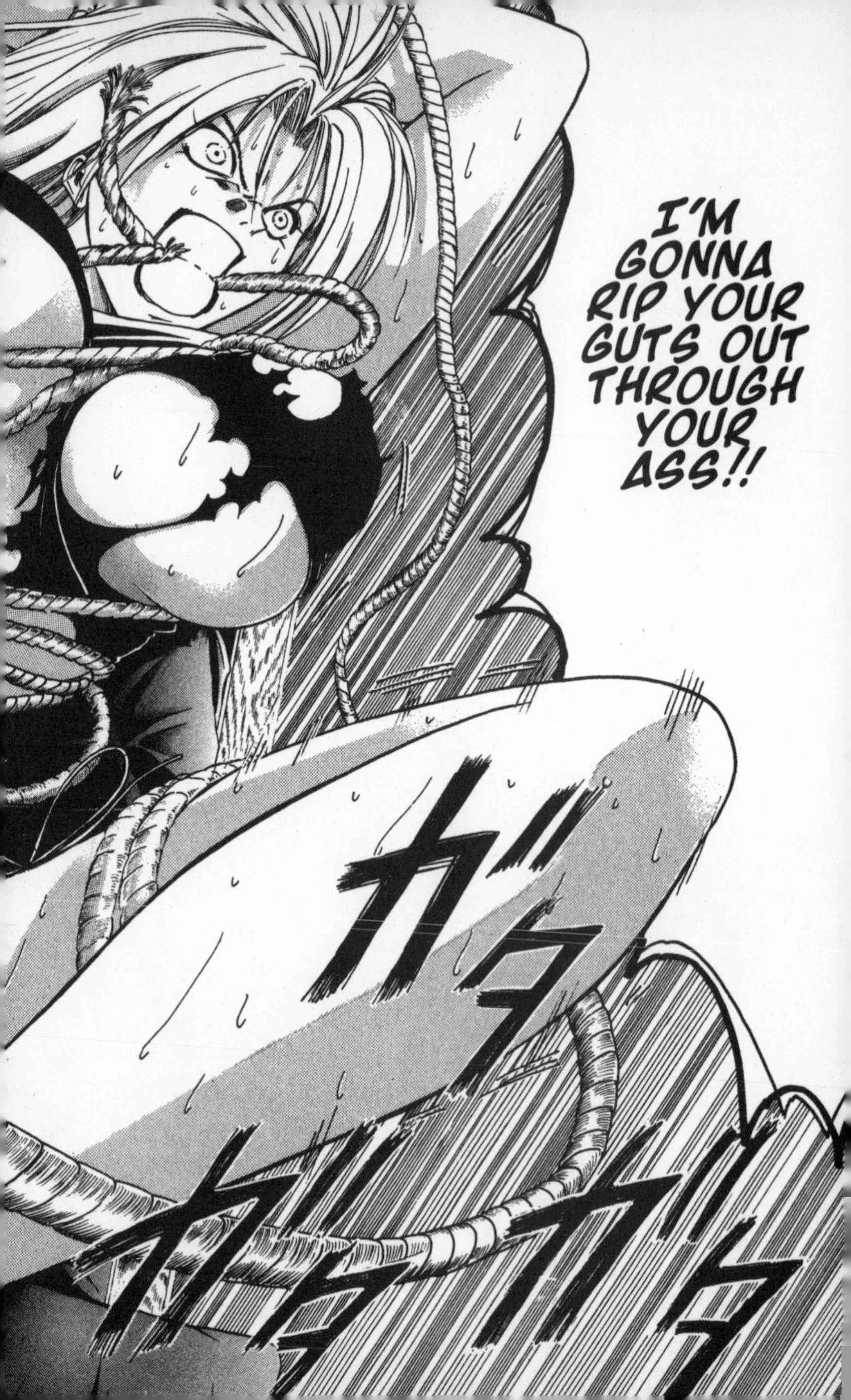
I'M GONNA RIP YOUR GUTS OUT THROUGH YOUR ASS!!

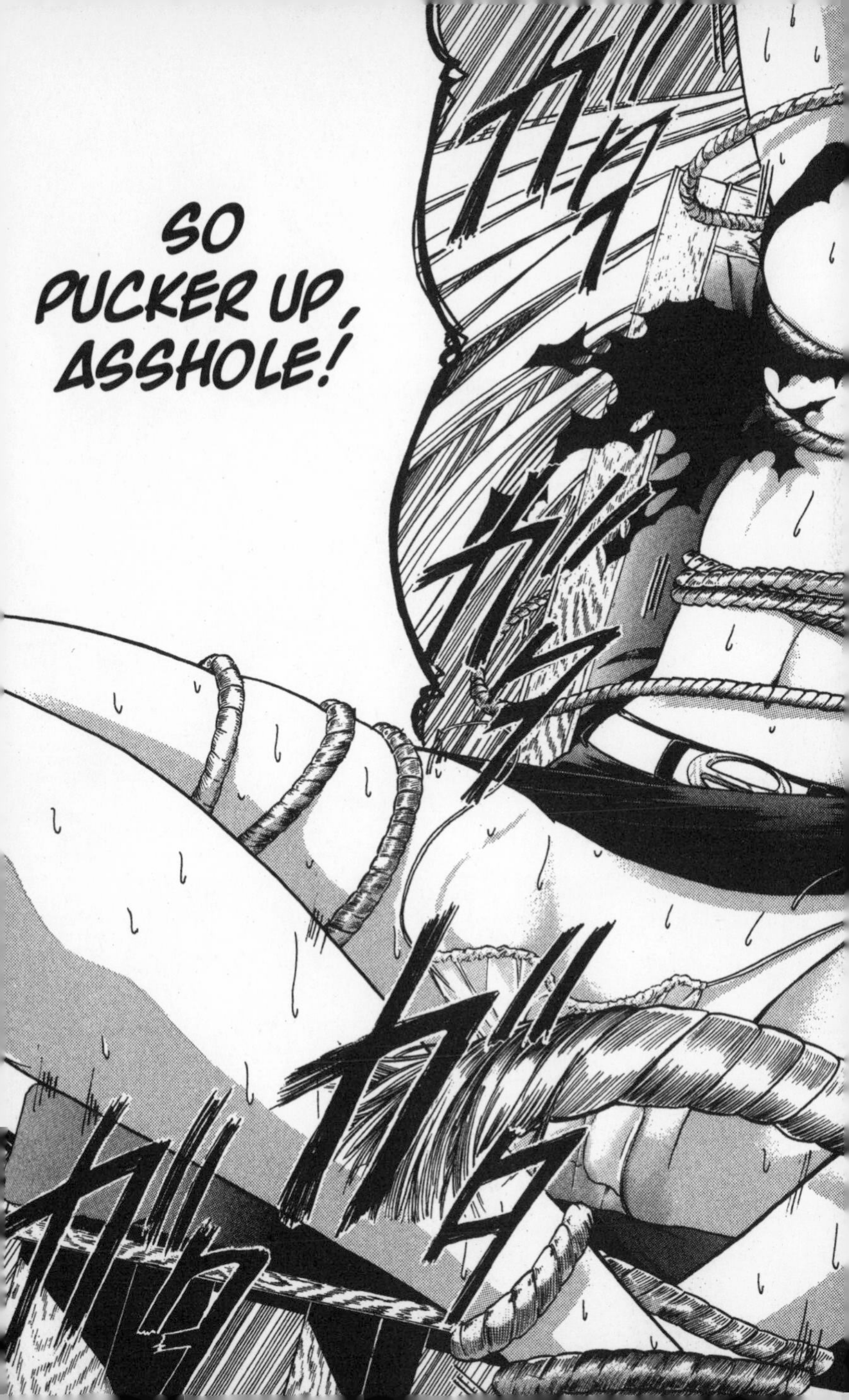
SO PUCKER UP, ASSHOLE!

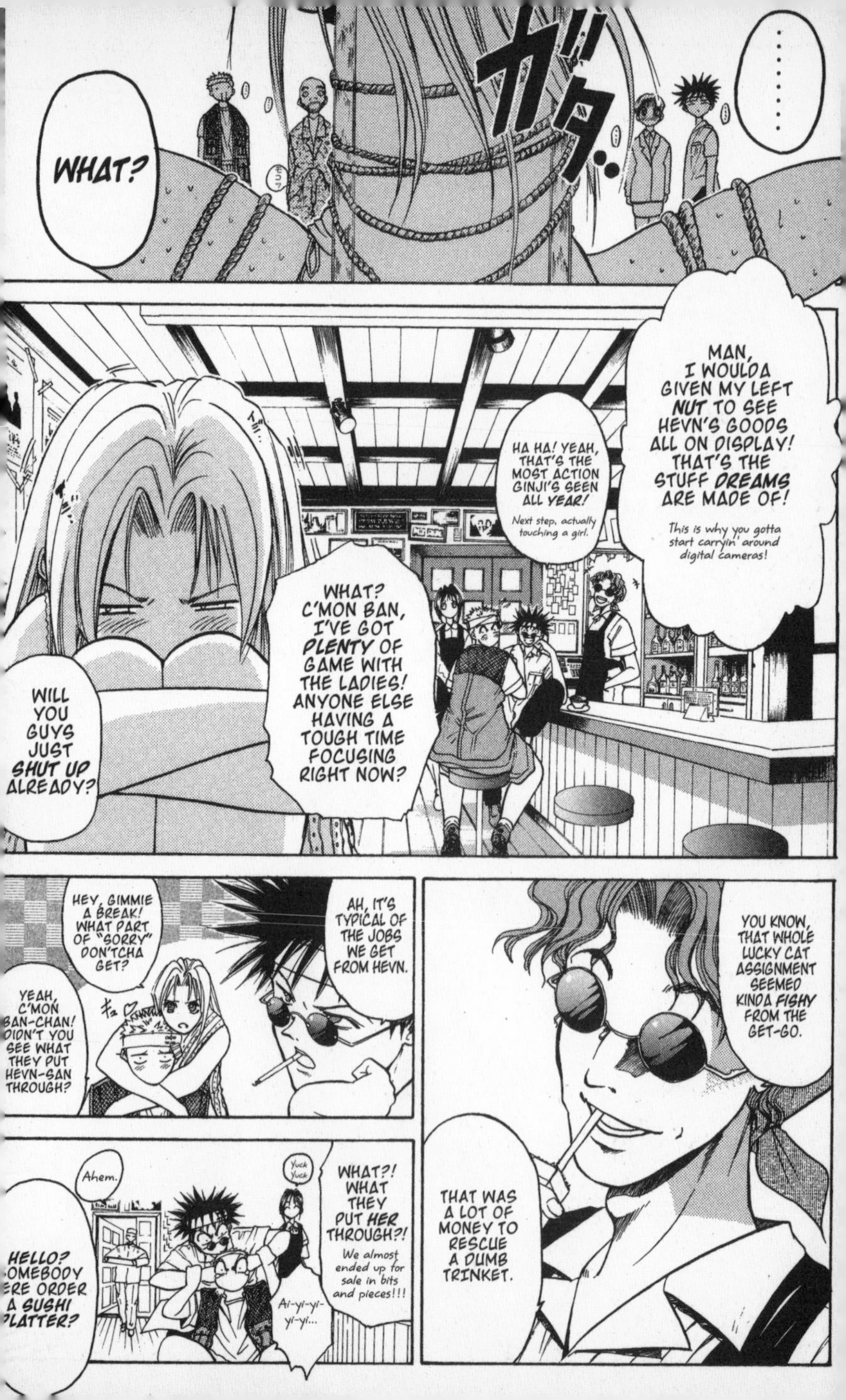
.....
ガタ..
WHAT?
MAN, I WOULDA GIVEN MY LEFT NUT TO SEE HEVN'S GOODS ALL ON DISPLAY! THAT'S THE STUFF DREAMS ARE MADE OF!
This is why you gotta start carryin' around digital cameras!
HA HA! YEAH, THAT'S THE MOST ACTION GINJI'S SEEN ALL YEAR!
Next step, actually touching a girl.
WHAT? C'MON BAN, I'VE GOT PLENTY OF GAME WITH THE LADIES! ANYONE ELSE HAVING A TOUGH TIME FOCUSING RIGHT NOW?
WILL YOU GUYS JUST SHUT UP ALREADY?
YOU KNOW, THAT WHOLE LUCKY CAT ASSIGNMENT SEEMED KINDA FISHY FROM THE GET-GO.
THAT WAS A LOT OF MONEY TO RESCUE A DUMB TRINKET.
AH, IT'S TYPICAL OF THE JOBS WE GET FROM HEVN.
HEY, GIMMIE A BREAK! WHAT PART OF "SORRY" DON'TCHA GET?
YEAH, C'MON BAN-CHAN! DIDN'T YOU SEE WHAT THEY PUT HEVN-SAN THROUGH?
WHAT?! WHAT THEY PUT HER THROUGH?!
We almost ended up for sale in bits and pieces!!!
Yuck Yuck
Ahem.
Ai-yi-yi-yi-yi...
HELLO? OMEBODY ERE ORDER A SUSHI LATTER?

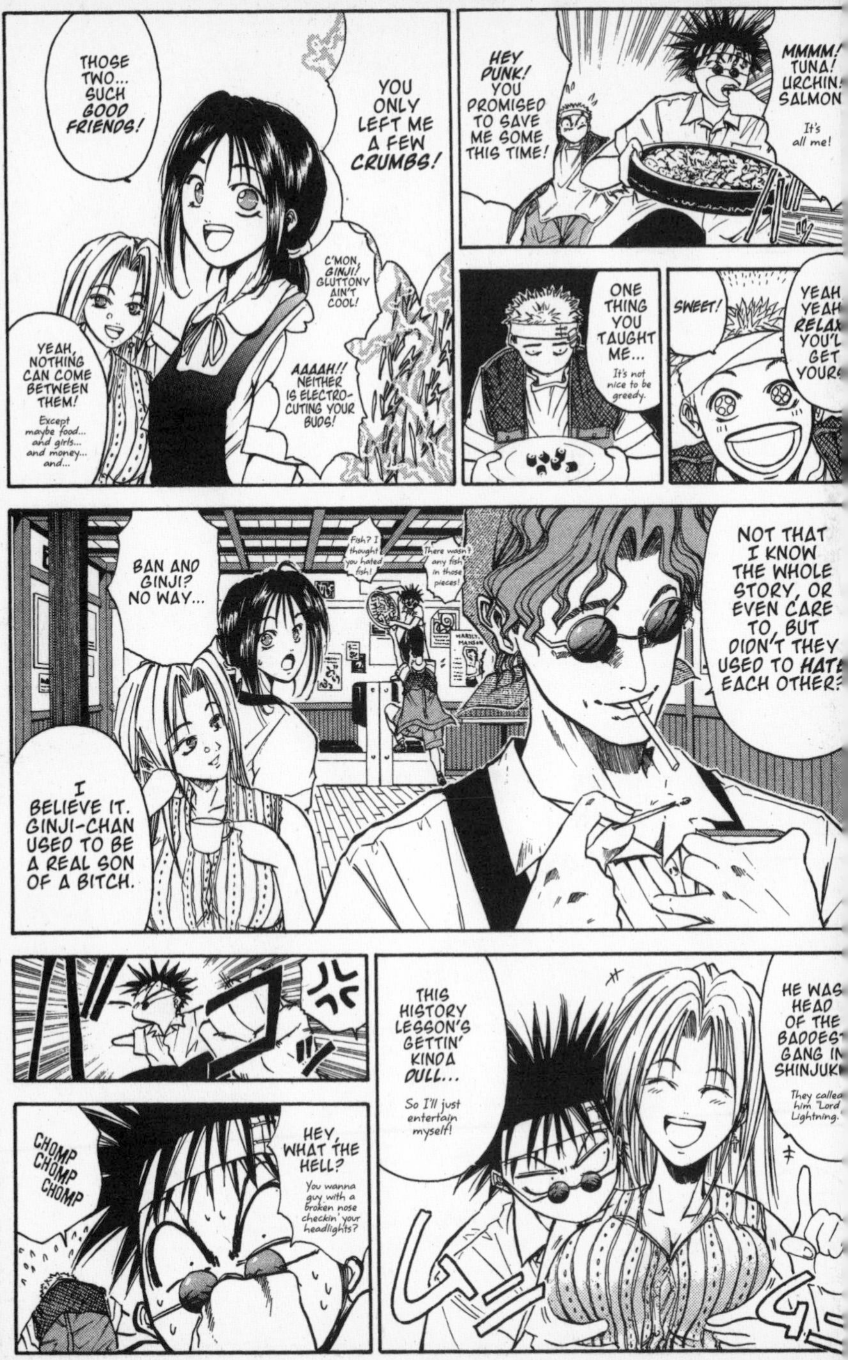
MMMM! TUNA! URCHIN! SALMON!
It's all me!
HEY PUNK! YOU PROMISED TO SAVE ME SOME THIS TIME!
YEAH YEAH RELAX YOU'L GET YOURS
SWEET!
ONE THING YOU TAUGHT ME...
It's not nice to be greedy.
YOU ONLY LEFT ME A FEW CRUMBS!
THOSE TWO... SUCH GOOD FRIENDS!
C'MON, GINJI! GLUTTONY AIN'T COOL!
AAAAH!! NEITHER IS ELECTROCUTING YOUR BUDS!
YEAH, NOTHING CAN COME BETWEEN THEM!
Except maybe food... and girls... and money... and...
NOT THAT I KNOW THE WHOLE STORY, OR EVEN CARE TO, BUT DIDN'T THEY USED TO HATE EACH OTHER?
There wasn't any fish in those pieces!
Fish? I thought you hated fish!
BAN AND GINJI? NO WAY...
I BELIEVE IT. GINJI-CHAN USED TO BE A REAL SON OF A BITCH.
HE WAS HEAD OF THE BADDEST GANG IN SHINJUKU
They called him "Lord Lightning."
THIS HISTORY LESSON'S GETTIN' KINDA DULL...
So I'll just entertain myself!
HEY, WHAT THE HELL?
You wanna guy with a broken nose checkin' your headlights?
CHOMP CHOMP CHOMP

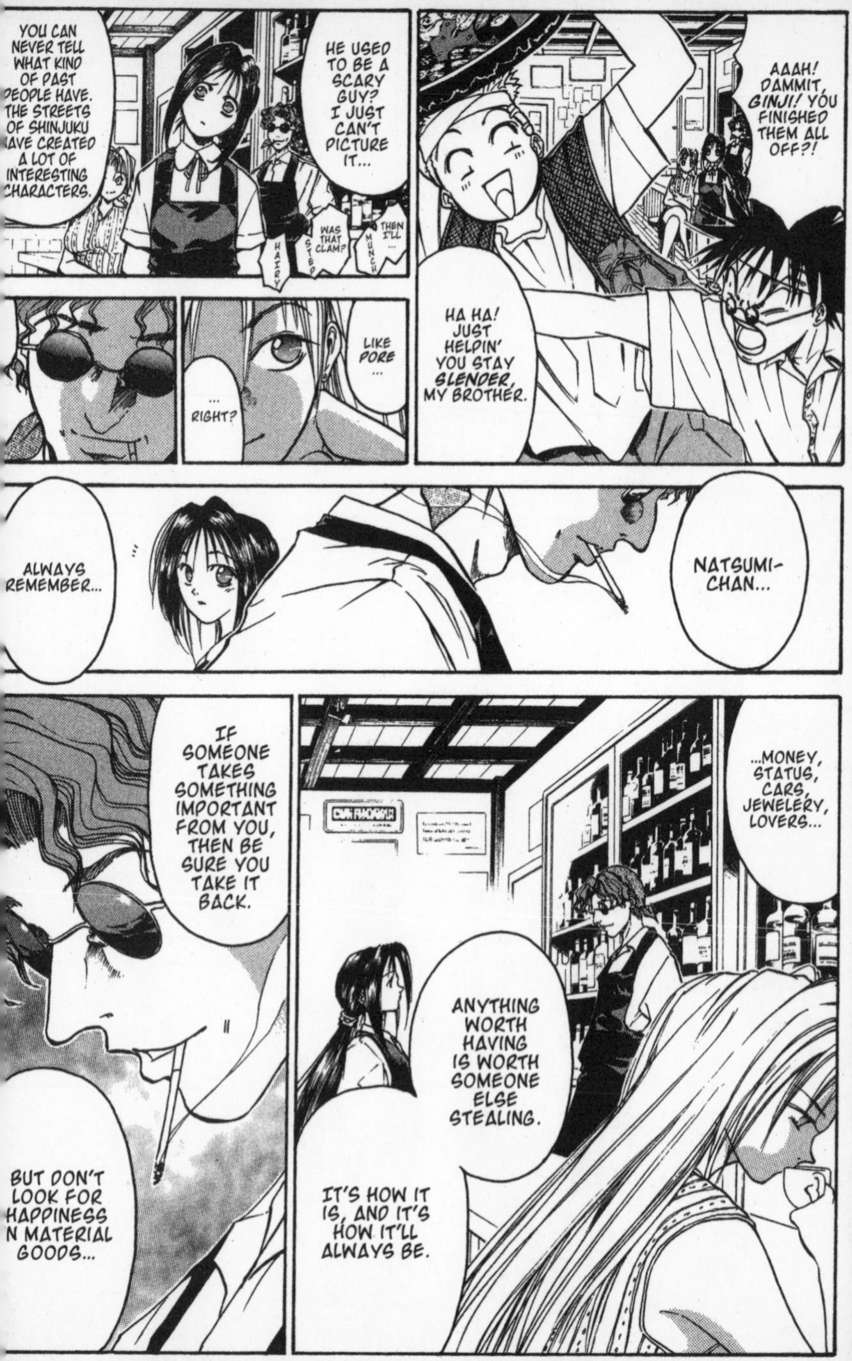
AAAH! DAMMIT, GINJI! YOU FINISHED THEM ALL OFF?!
HA HA! JUST HELPIN' YOU STAY SLENDER, MY BROTHER.
HE USED TO BE A SCARY GUY? I JUST CAN'T PICTURE IT...
THEN I'LL ...
MUNCH
WAS THAT CLAM?
STEP
HAIRY
YOU CAN NEVER TELL WHAT KIND OF PAST PEOPLE HAVE. THE STREETS OF SHINJUKU HAVE CREATED A LOT OF INTERESTING CHARACTERS.
LIKE PORE ...
... RIGHT?
NATSUMI-CHAN...
...
ALWAYS REMEMBER...
...MONEY, STATUS, CARS, JEWELERY, LOVERS...
ANYTHING WORTH HAVING IS WORTH SOMEONE ELSE STEALING.
IT'S HOW IT IS, AND IT'S HOW IT'LL ALWAYS BE.
IF SOMEONE TAKES SOMETHING IMPORTANT FROM YOU, THEN BE SURE YOU TAKE IT BACK.
BUT DON'T LOOK FOR HAPPINESS IN MATERIAL GOODS...

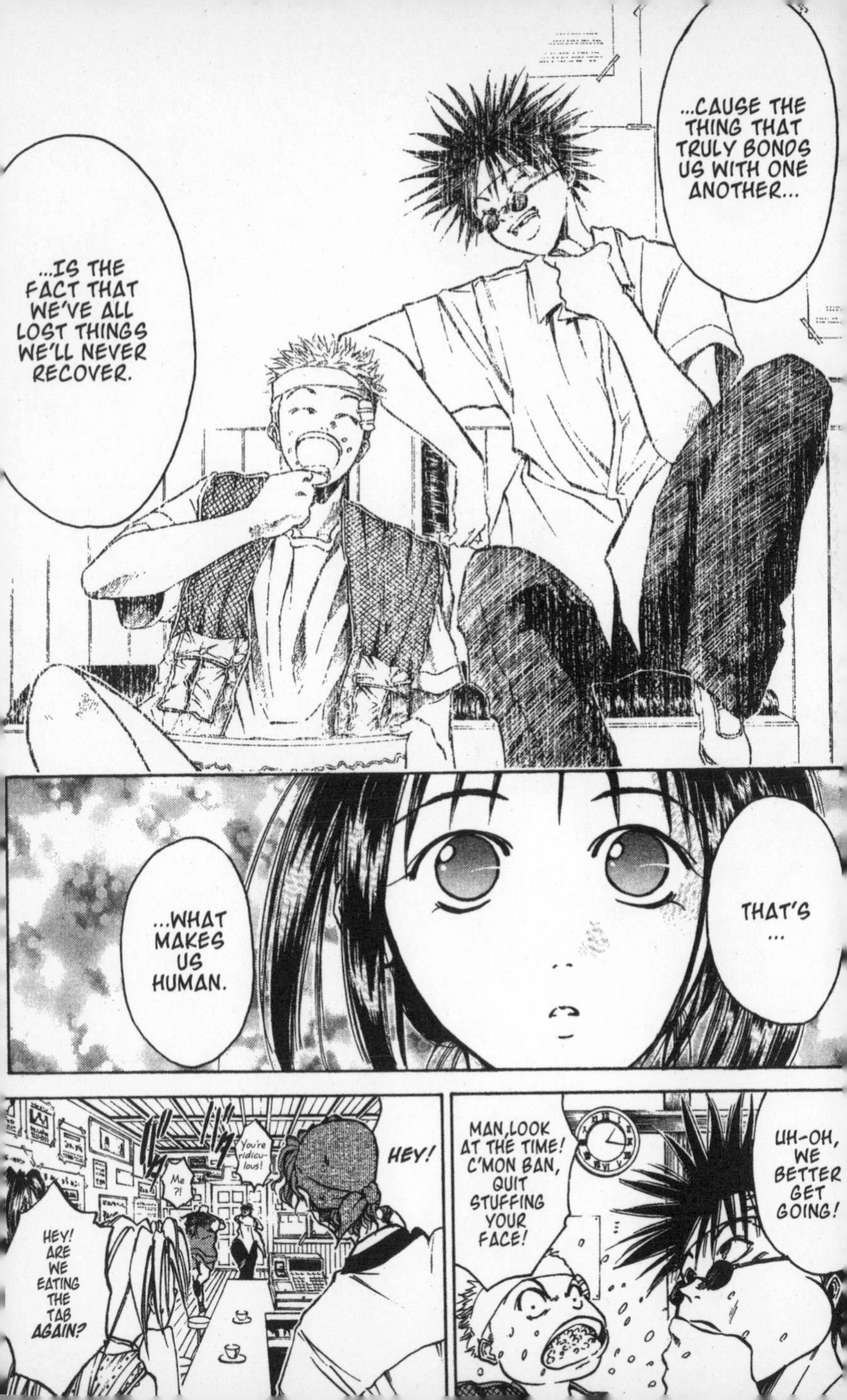
...CAUSE THE THING THAT TRULY BONDS US WITH ONE ANOTHER...
...IS THE FACT THAT WE'VE ALL LOST THINGS WE'LL NEVER RECOVER.
THAT'S ...
...WHAT MAKES US HUMAN.
UH-OH, WE BETTER GET GOING!
MAN,LOOK AT THE TIME! C'MON BAN, QUIT STUFFING YOUR FACE!
HEY!
You're ridicu-lous!
Me ?!
HEY! ARE WE EATING THE TAB AGAIN?

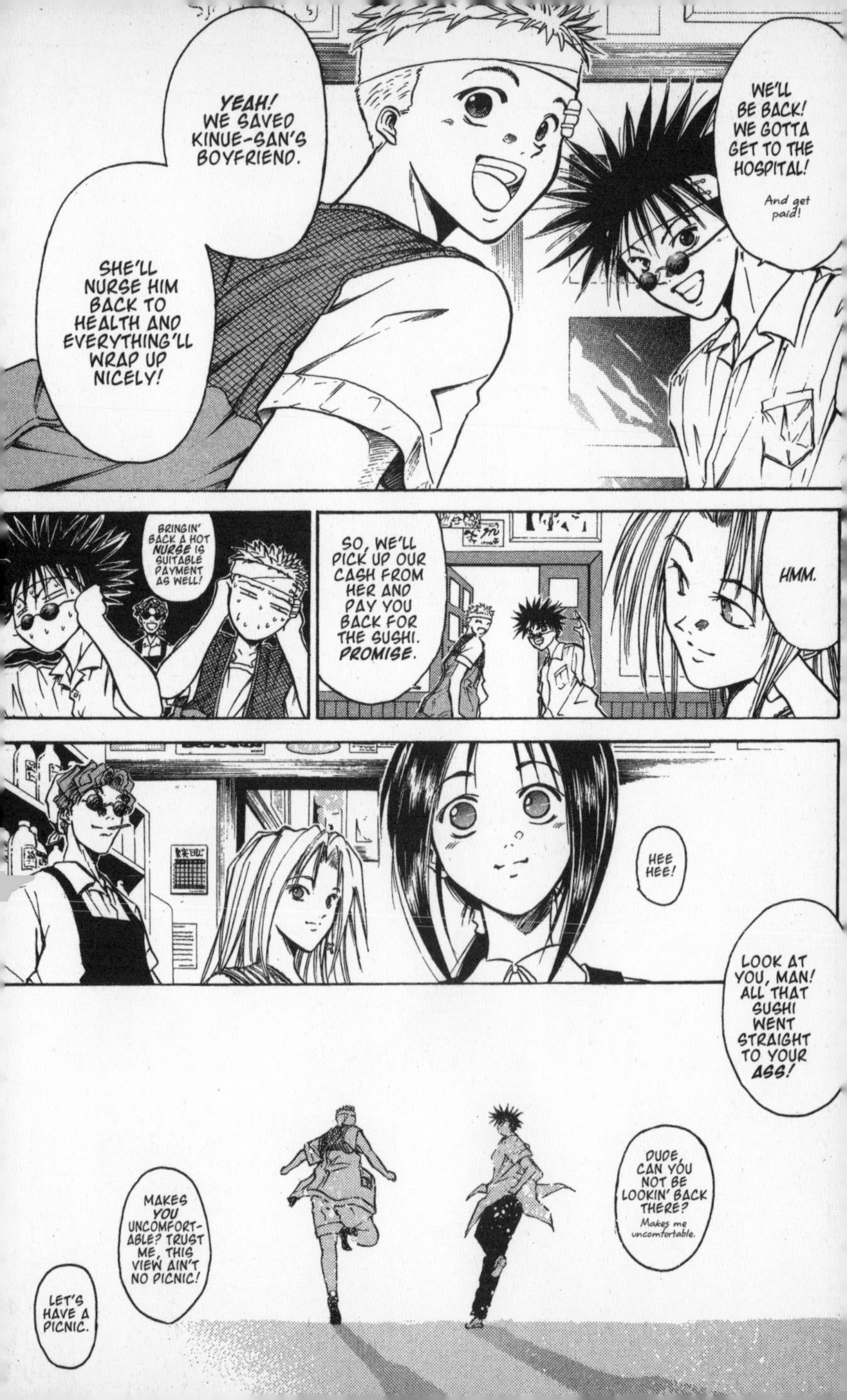
WE'LL BE BACK! WE GOTTA GET TO THE HOSPITAL!
And get paid!
YEAH! WE SAVED KINUE-SAN'S BOYFRIEND.
SHE'LL NURSE HIM BACK TO HEALTH AND EVERYTHING'LL WRAP UP NICELY!
HMM.
SO, WE'LL PICK UP OUR CASH FROM HER AND PAY YOU BACK FOR THE SUSHI. PROMISE.
BRINGIN' BACK A HOT NURSE IS SUITABLE PAYMENT AS WELL!
HEE HEE!
LOOK AT YOU, MAN! ALL THAT SUSHI WENT STRAIGHT TO YOUR ASS!
DUDE, CAN YOU NOT BE LOOKIN' BACK THERE?
Makes me uncomfortable.
MAKES YOU UNCOMFORT-ABLE? TRUST ME, THIS VIEW AIN'T NO PICNIC!
LET'S HAVE A PICNIC.

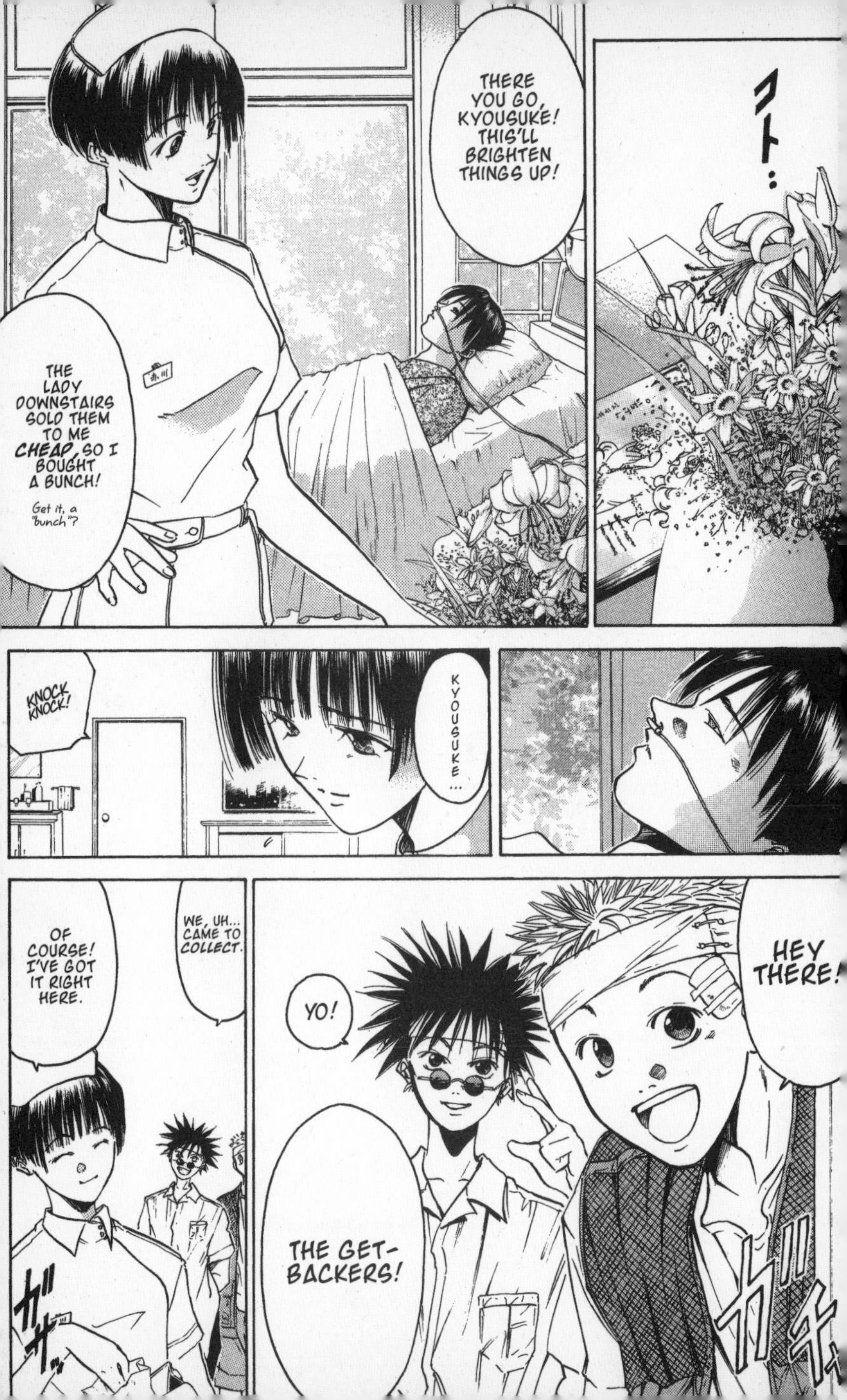
コト…
THERE YOU GO, KYOUSUKE! THIS'LL BRIGHTEN THINGS UP!
THE LADY DOWNSTAIRS SOLD THEM TO ME CHEAP, SO I BOUGHT A BUNCH!
Get it, a "bunch"?
KYOUSUKE...
KNOCK KNOCK!
HEY THERE!
YO!
THE GET-BACKERS!
WE, UH... CAME TO COLLECT.
OF COURSE! I'VE GOT IT RIGHT HERE.
ガサ

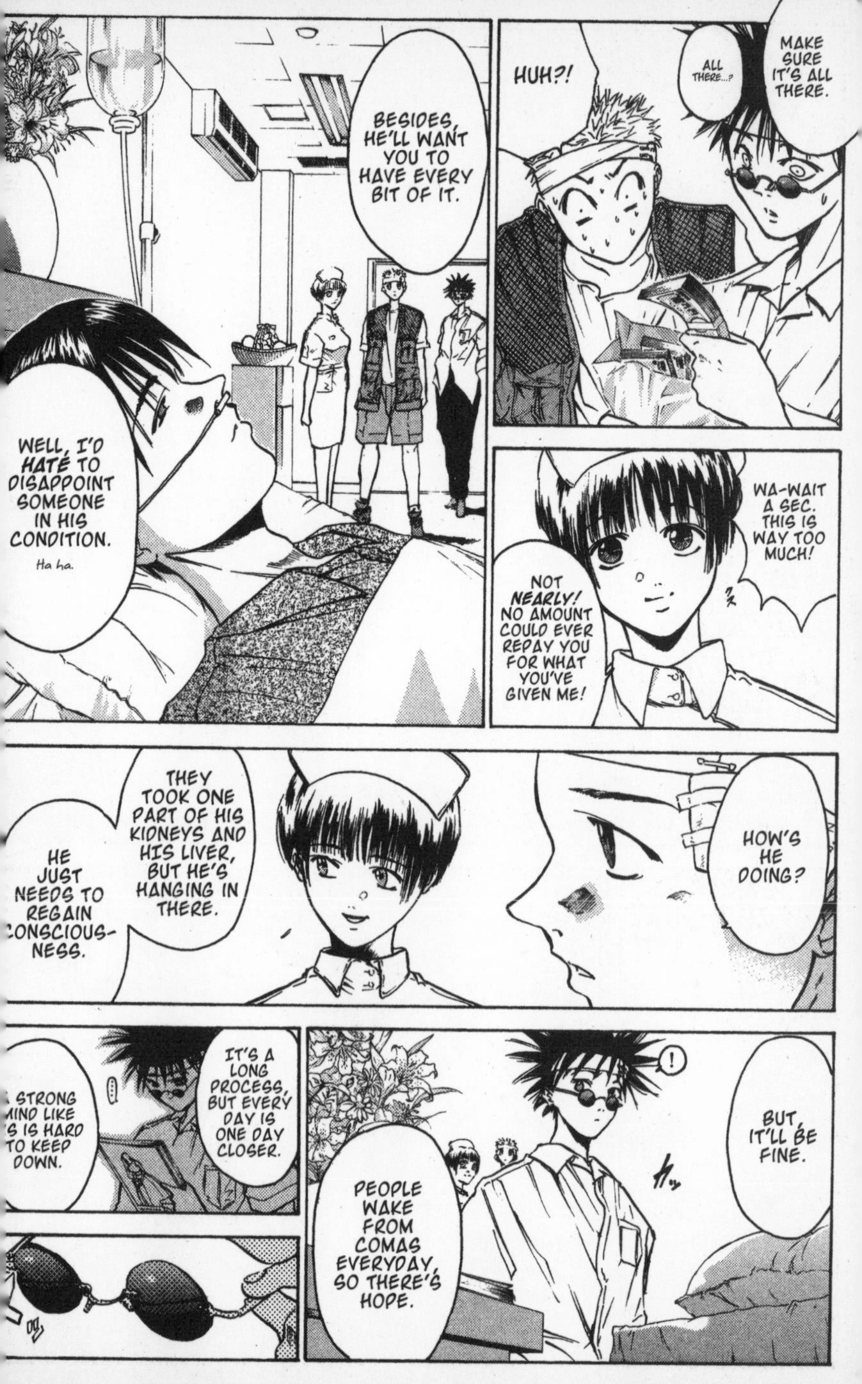
MAKE SURE IT'S ALL THERE.
ALL THERE...?
HUH?!
WA-WAIT A SEC. THIS IS WAY TOO MUCH!
NOT NEARLY! NO AMOUNT COULD EVER REPAY YOU FOR WHAT YOU'VE GIVEN ME!
BESIDES, HE'LL WANT YOU TO HAVE EVERY BIT OF IT.
WELL, I'D HATE TO DISAPPOINT SOMEONE IN HIS CONDITION.
Ha ha.
HOW'S HE DOING?
THEY TOOK ONE PART OF HIS KIDNEYS AND HIS LIVER, BUT HE'S HANGING IN THERE.
HE JUST NEEDS TO REGAIN CONSCIOUS-NESS.
!
BUT, IT'LL BE FINE.
PEOPLE WAKE FROM COMAS EVERYDAY, SO THERE'S HOPE.
IT'S A LONG PROCESS, BUT EVERY DAY IS ONE DAY CLOSER.
STRONG MIND LIKE S IS HARD TO KEEP DOWN.
...

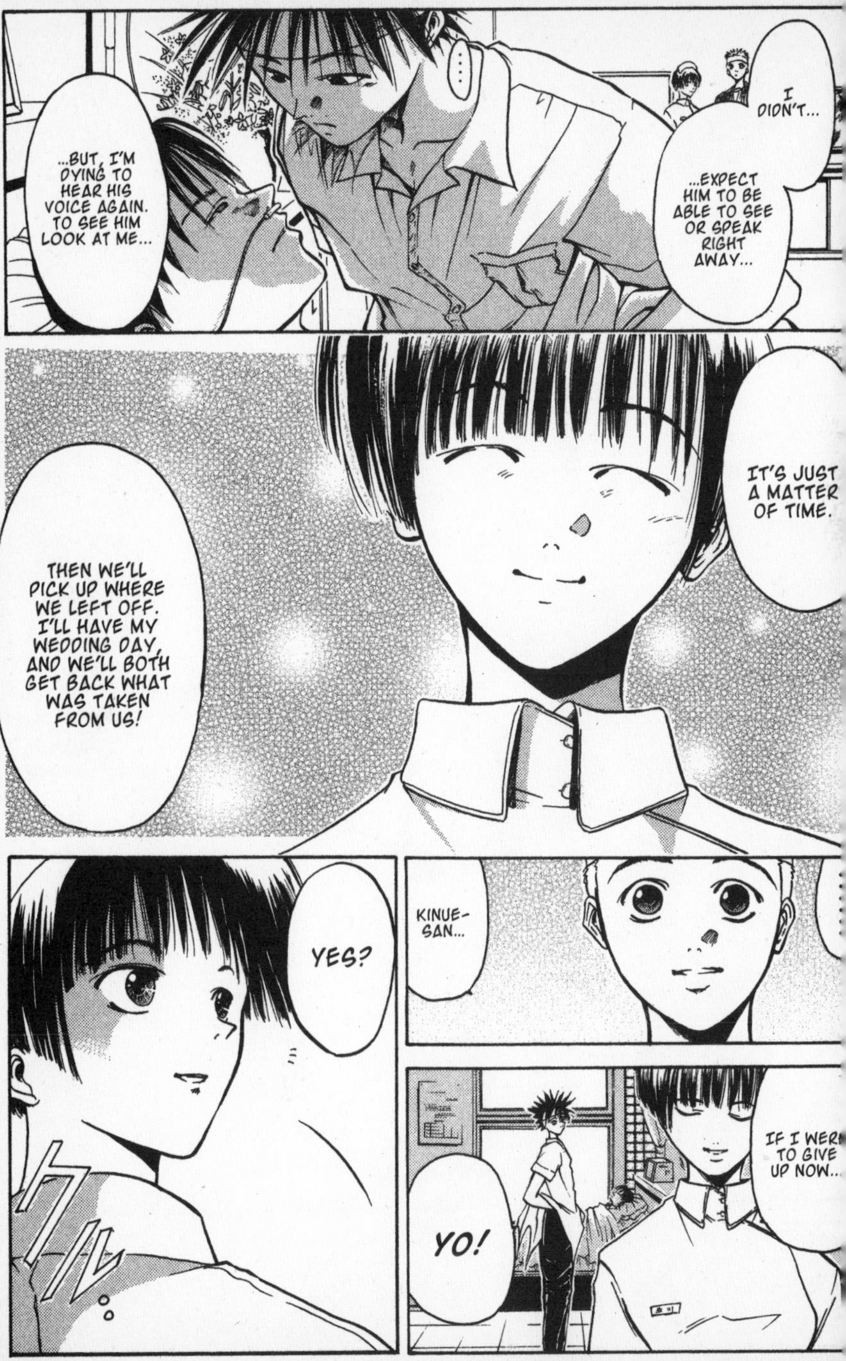
I DIDN'T...
...EXPECT HIM TO BE ABLE TO SEE OR SPEAK RIGHT AWAY...
....
...BUT, I'M DYING TO HEAR HIS VOICE AGAIN. TO SEE HIM LOOK AT ME...
IT'S JUST A MATTER OF TIME.
THEN WE'LL PICK UP WHERE WE LEFT OFF. I'LL HAVE MY WEDDING DAY, AND WE'LL BOTH GET BACK WHAT WAS TAKEN FROM US!
KINUE-SAN...
IF I WER TO GIVE UP NOW...
YO!
YES?
クル。

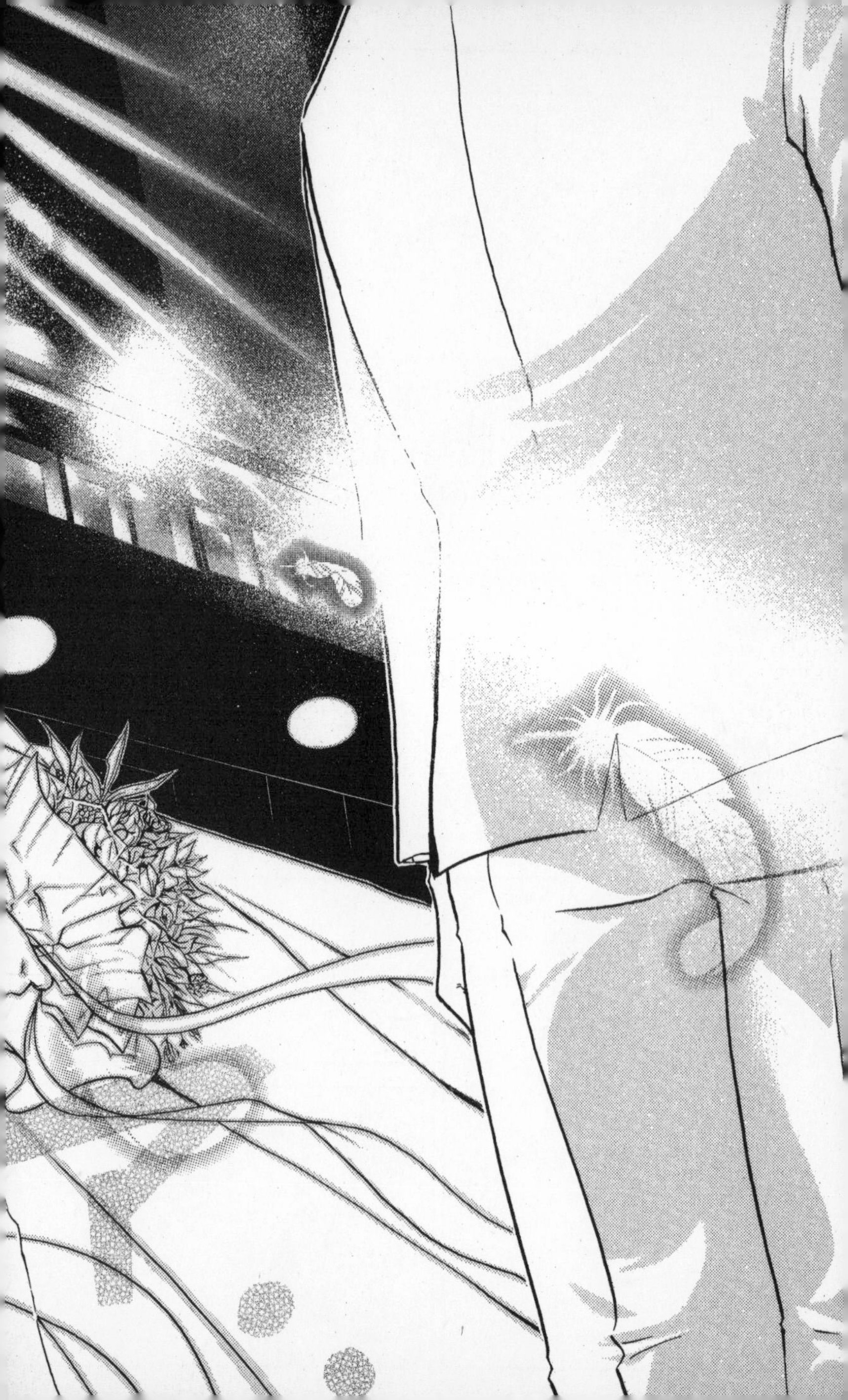

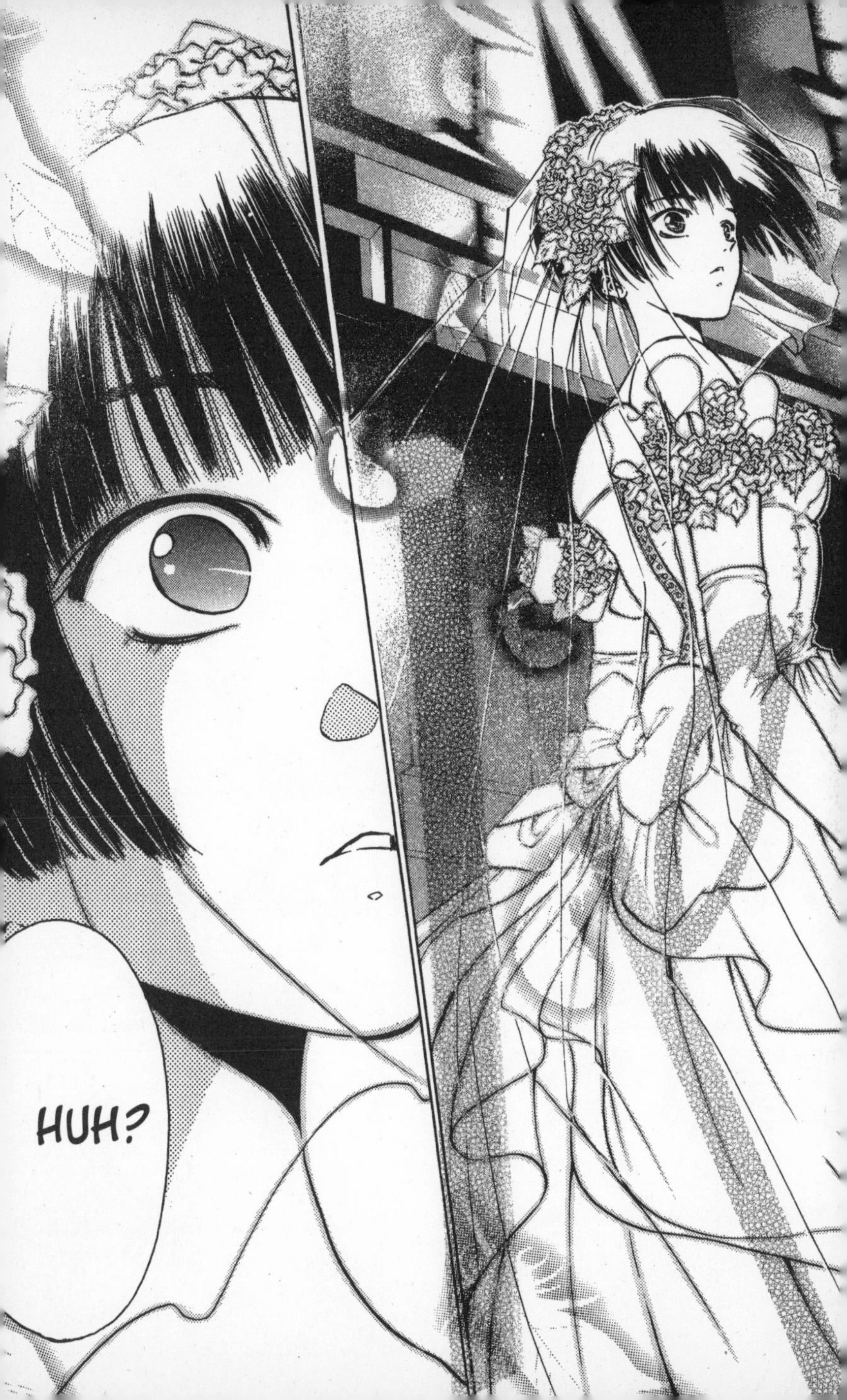
HUH?

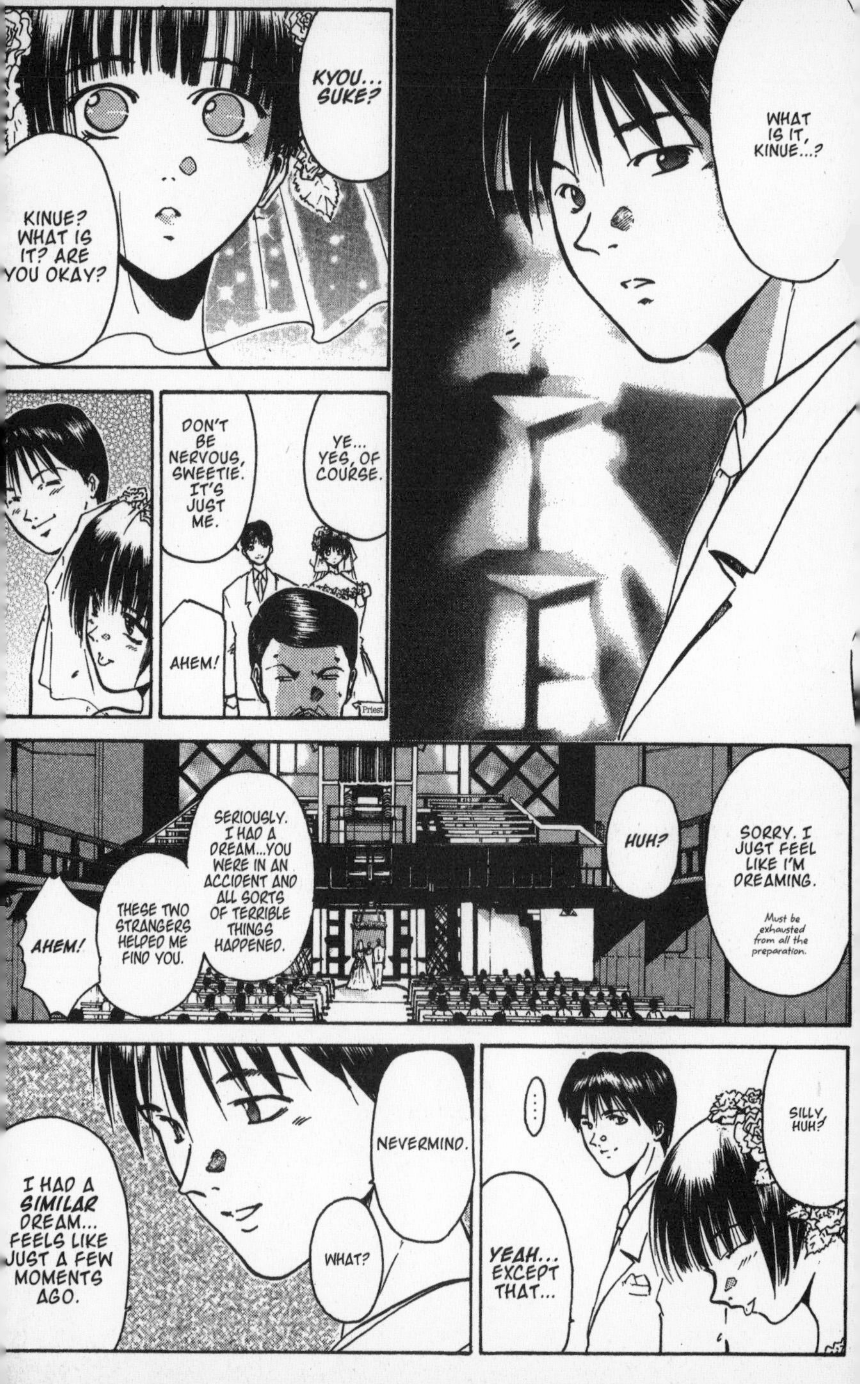
WHAT IS IT, KINUE...?
KYOU... SUKE?
KINUE? WHAT IS IT? ARE YOU OKAY?
YE... YES, OF COURSE.
DON'T BE NERVOUS, SWEETIE. IT'S JUST ME.
AHEM!
Priest
SORRY. I JUST FEEL LIKE I'M DREAMING.
Must be exhausted from all the preparation.
HUH?
SERIOUSLY. I HAD A DREAM...YOU WERE IN AN ACCIDENT AND ALL SORTS OF TERRIBLE THINGS HAPPENED.
THESE TWO STRANGERS HELPED ME FIND YOU.
AHEM!
SILLY, HUH?
...
YEAH... EXCEPT THAT...
NEVERMIND.
WHAT?
I HAD A SIMILAR DREAM... FEELS LIKE JUST A FEW MOMENTS AGO.

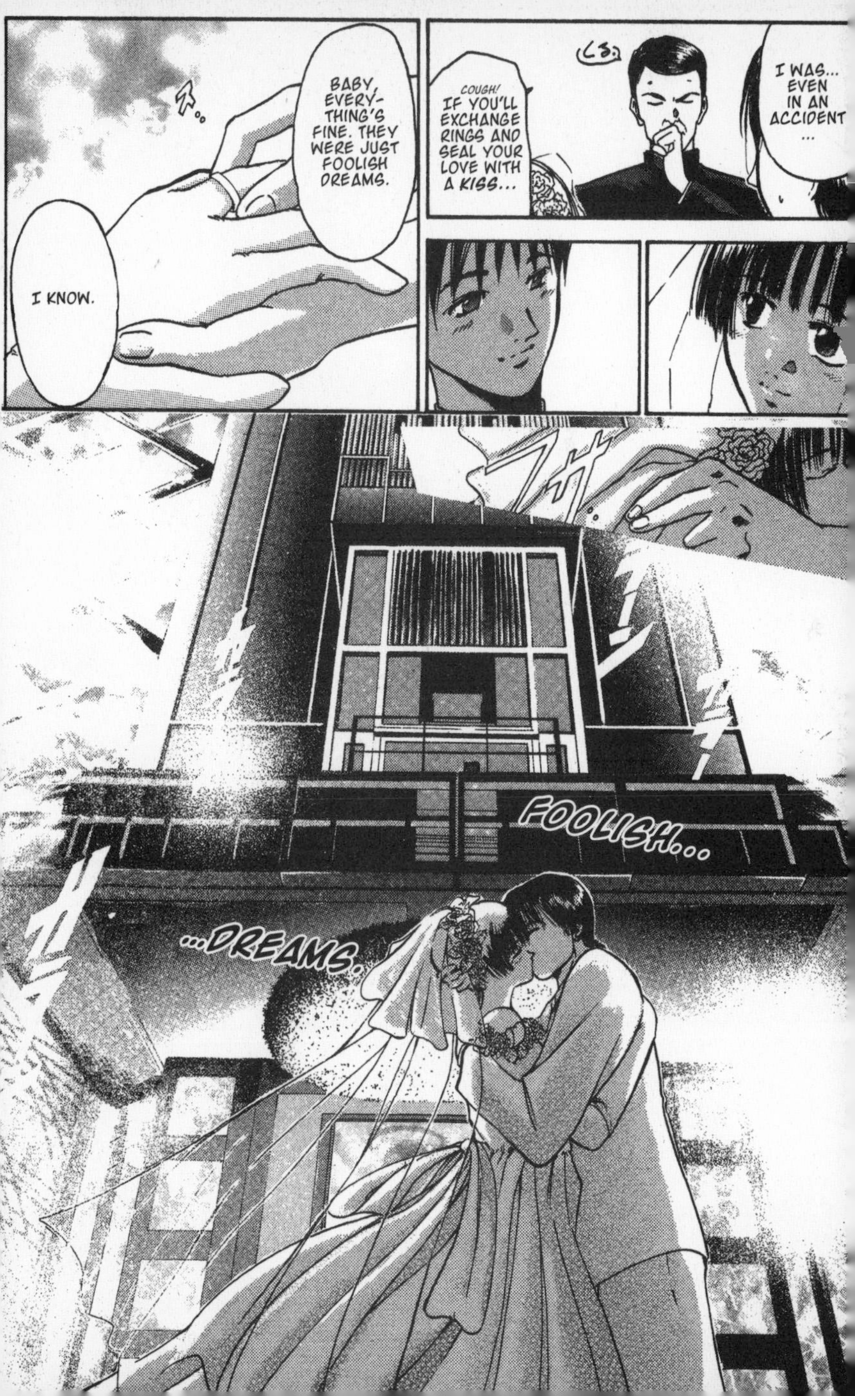
I WAS... EVEN IN AN ACCIDENT...
COUGH! IF YOU'LL EXCHANGE RINGS AND SEAL YOUR LOVE WITH A KISS...
BABY, EVERY-THING'S FINE. THEY WERE JUST FOOLISH DREAMS.
I KNOW.
FOOLISH...
...DREAMS.

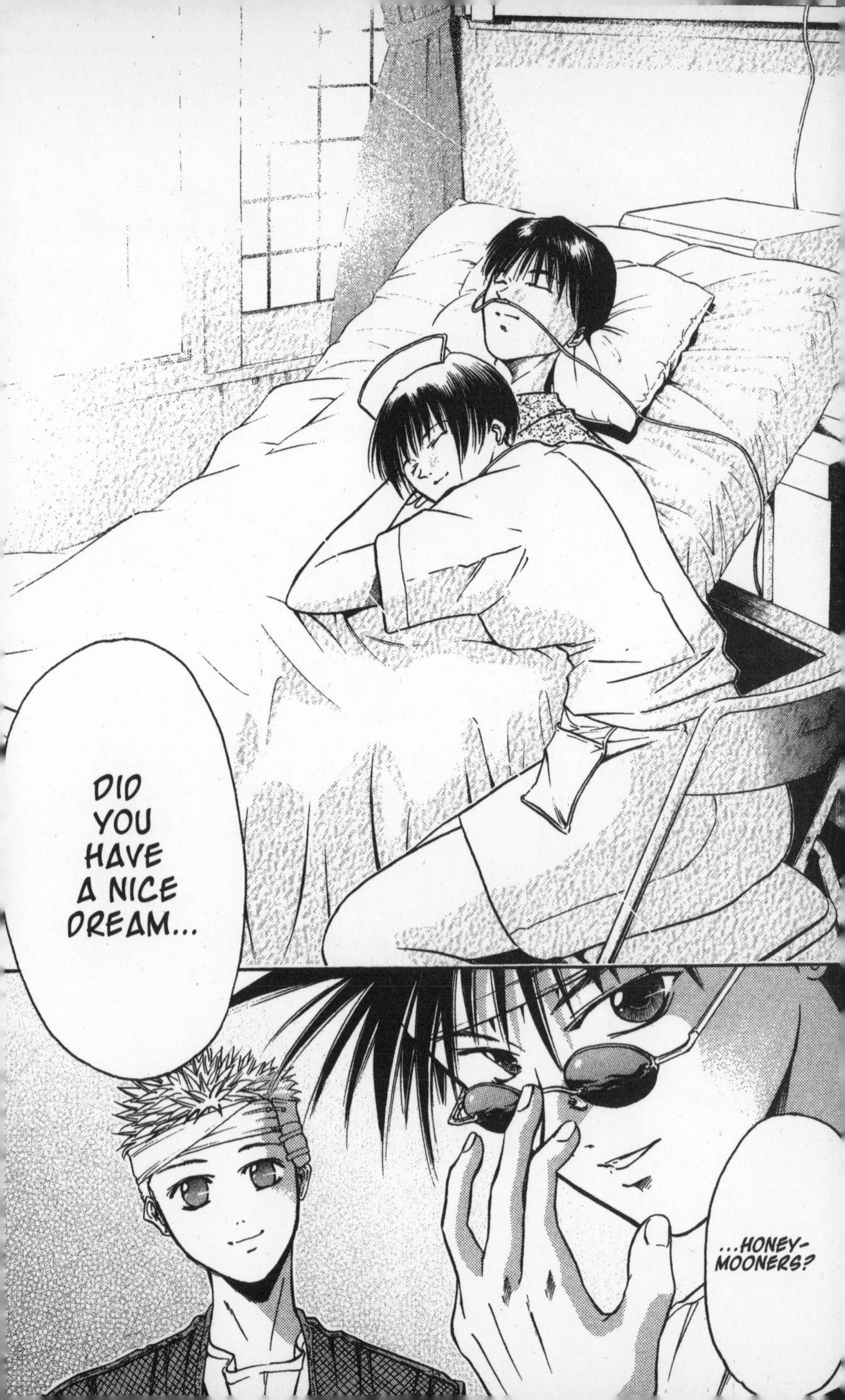
DID YOU HAVE A NICE DREAM...
...HONEY-MOONERS?

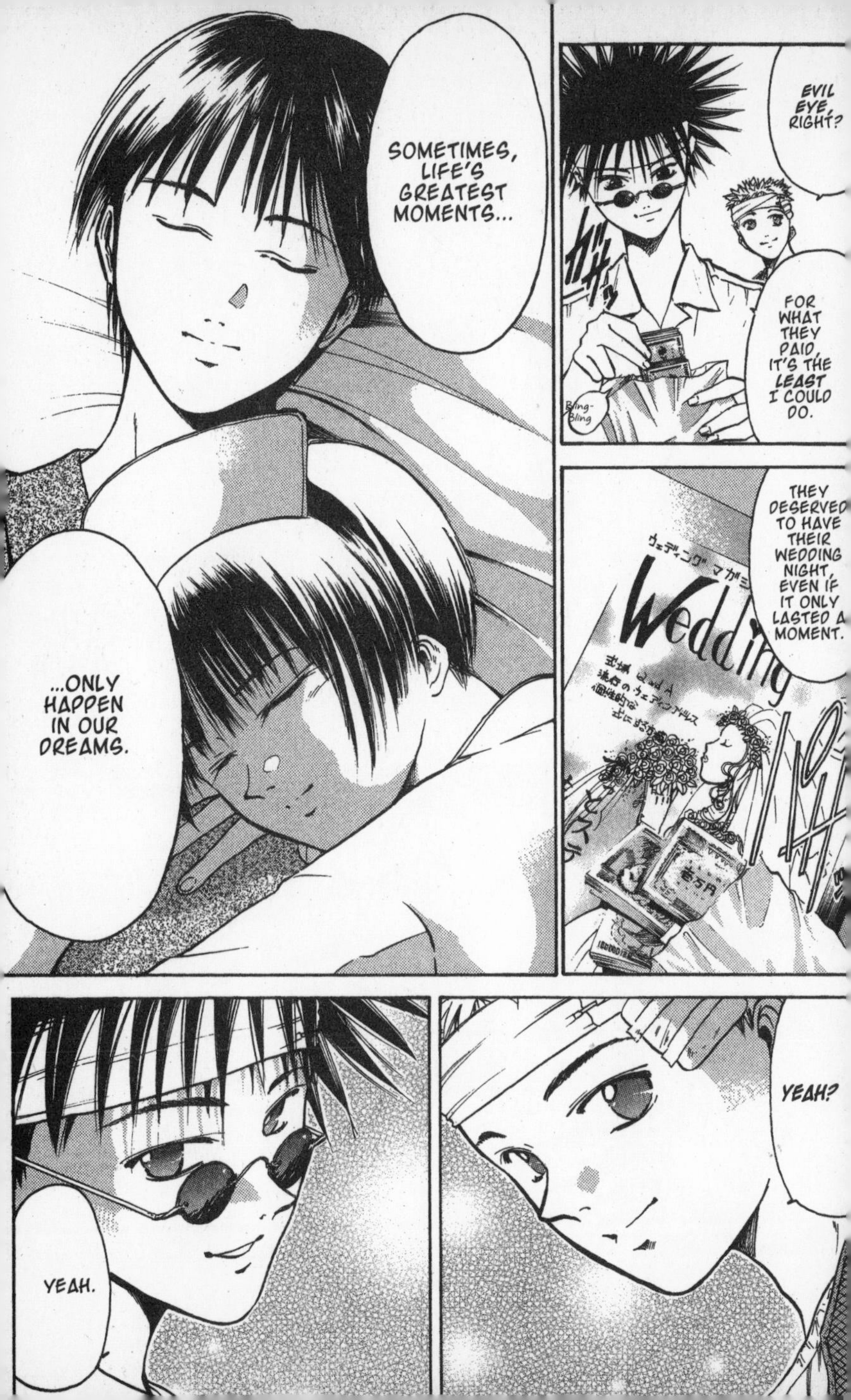
EVIL EYE, RIGHT?
FOR WHAT THEY PAID, IT'S THE LEAST I COULD DO.
Bling-Bling
THEY DESERVED TO HAVE THEIR WEDDING NIGHT, EVEN IF IT ONLY LASTED A MOMENT.
Wedding
SOMETIMES, LIFE'S GREATEST MOMENTS...
...ONLY HAPPEN IN OUR DREAMS.
YEAH?
YEAH.

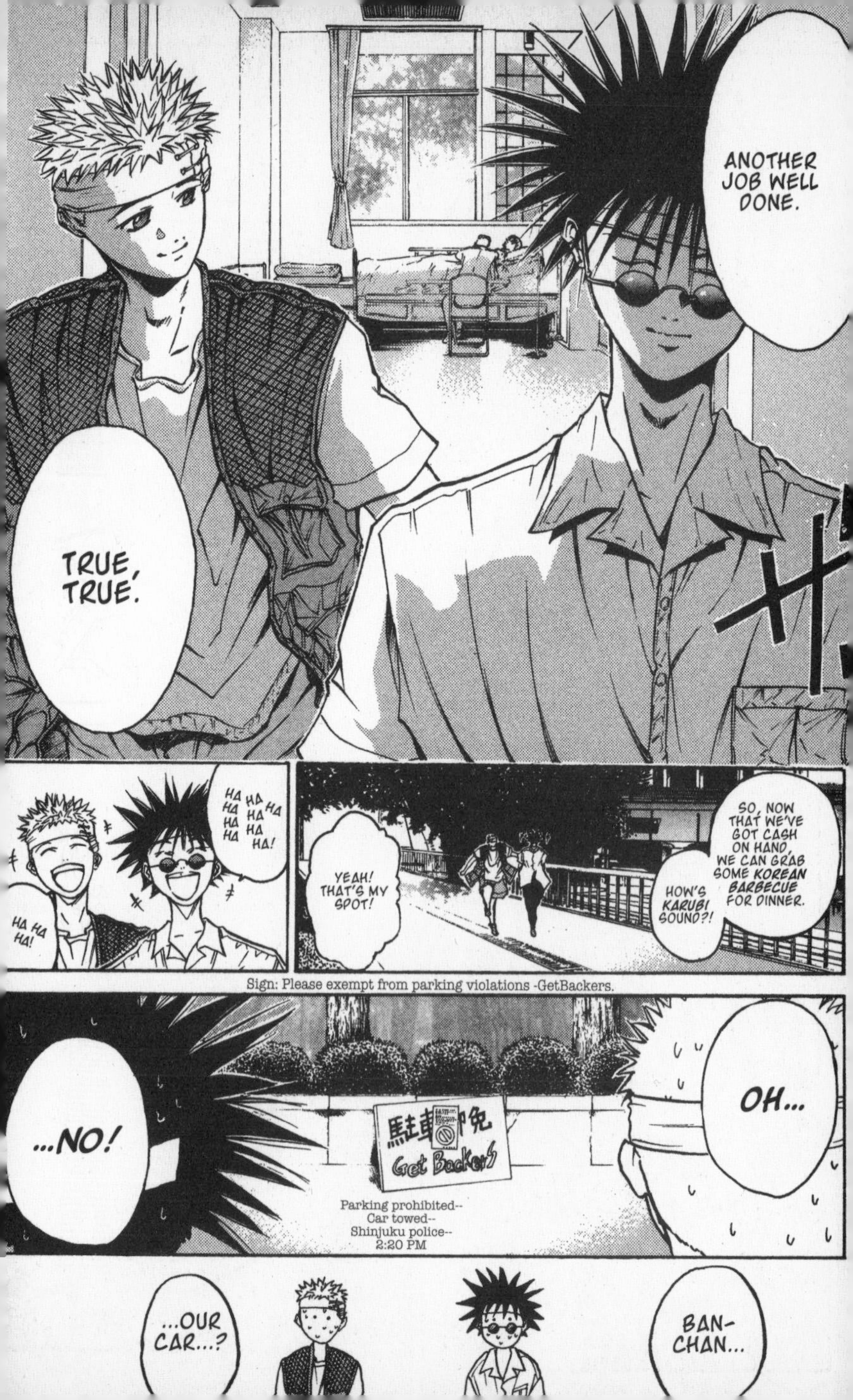
ANOTHER JOB WELL DONE.
TRUE, TRUE.
SO, NOW THAT WE'VE GOT CASH ON HAND, WE CAN GRAB SOME KOREAN BARBECUE FOR DINNER.
HOW'S KARUBI SOUND?!
YEAH! THAT'S MY SPOT!
HA HA HA HA HA HA HA HA HA HA!
HA HA HA!
Sign: Please exempt from parking violations -GetBackers.
OH...
...NO!
Get BackerS
Parking prohibited-- Car towed-- Shinjuku police-- 2:20 PM
BAN-CHAN...
...OUR CAR...?

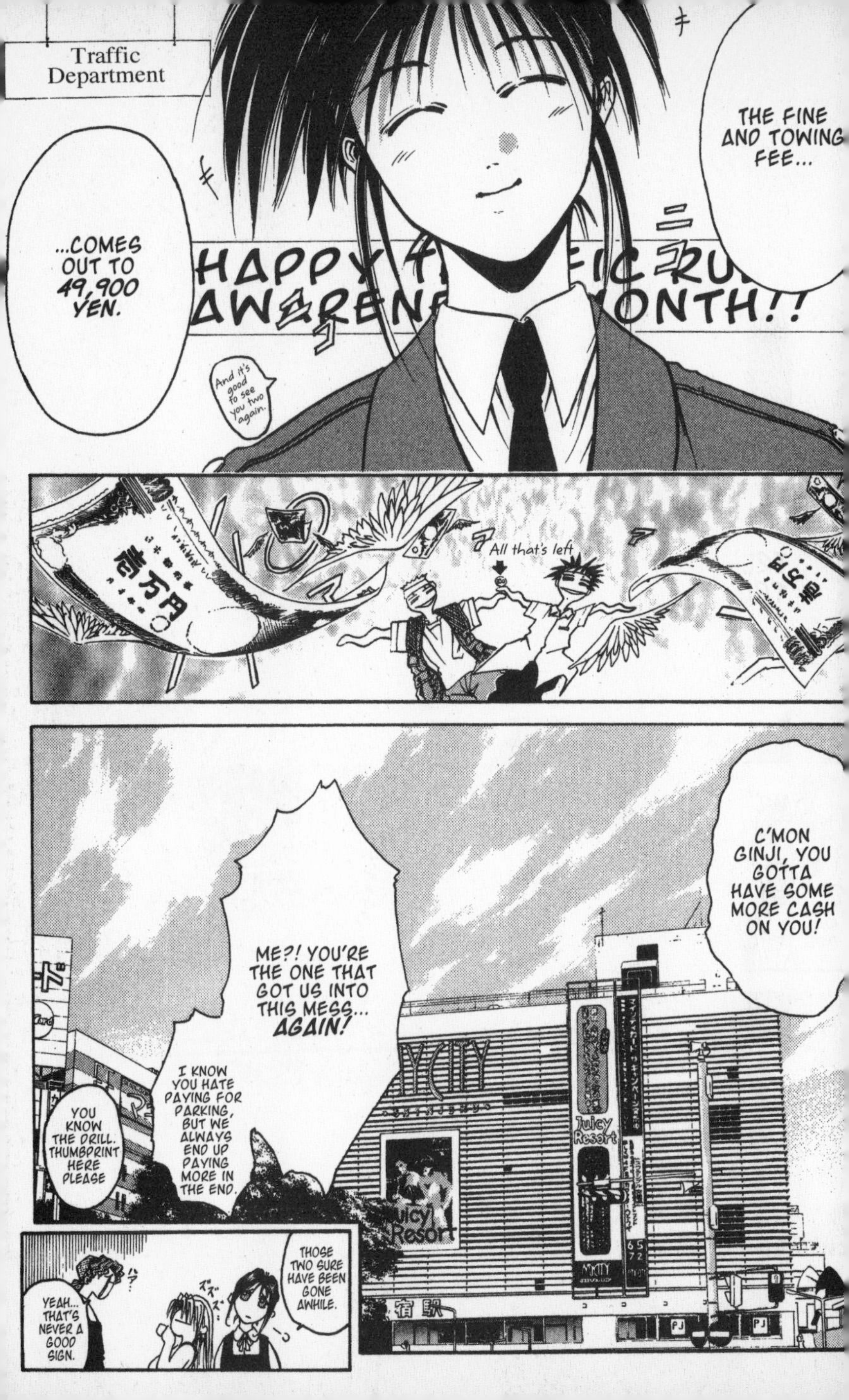
Traffic Department
THE FINE AND TOWING FEE...
...COMES OUT TO 49,900 YEN.
HAPPY
And it's good to see you two again.
All that's left
C'MON GINJI, YOU GOTTA HAVE SOME MORE CASH ON YOU!
ME?! YOU'RE THE ONE THAT GOT US INTO THIS MESS... AGAIN!
I KNOW YOU HATE PAYING FOR PARKING, BUT WE ALWAYS END UP PAYING MORE IN THE END.
YOU KNOW THE DRILL. THUMBPRINT HERE PLEASE
Juicy Resort
Juicy Resort
THOSE TWO SURE HAVE BEEN GONE AWHILE.
YEAH... THAT'S NEVER A GOOD SIGN.

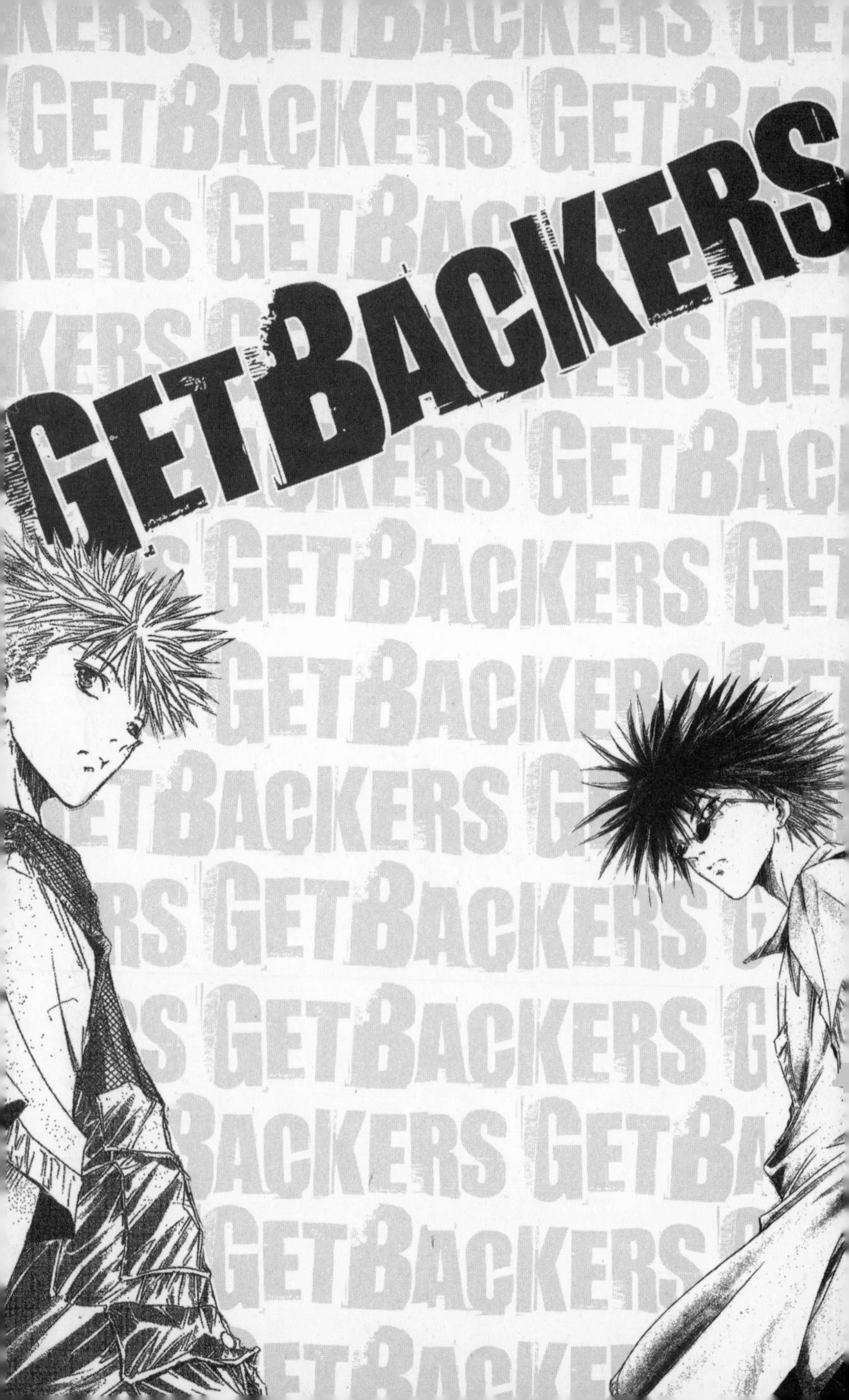
GETBACKERS

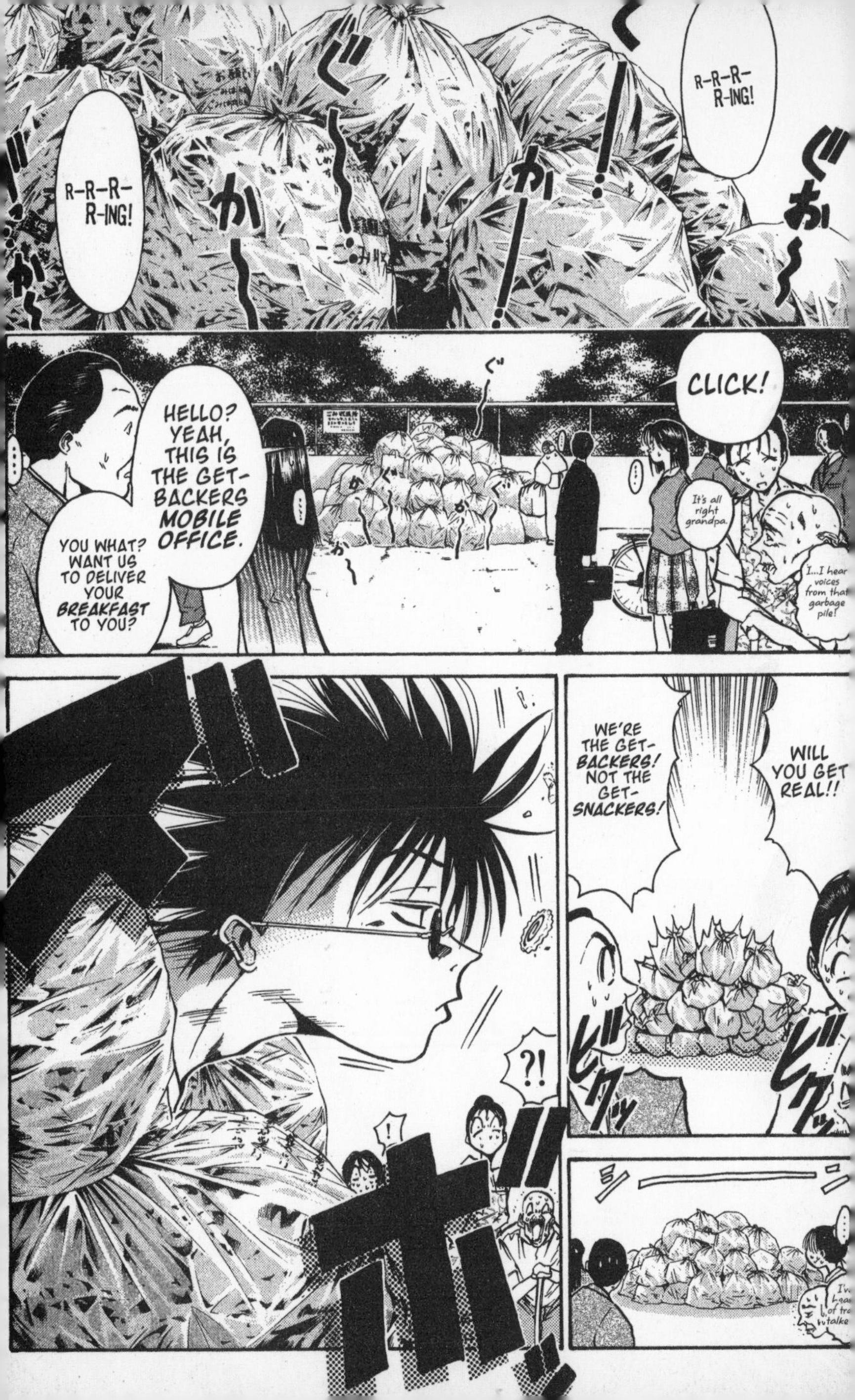
R-R-R-R-ING!
R-R-R-R-ING!
CLICK!
It's all right grandpa.
I...I hear voices from that garbage pile!
HELLO? YEAH, THIS IS THE GET-BACKERS MOBILE OFFICE.
YOU WHAT? WANT US TO DELIVER YOUR BREAKFAST TO YOU?
WILL YOU GET REAL!!
WE'RE THE GET-BACKERS! NOT THE GET-SNACKERS!
?!
!

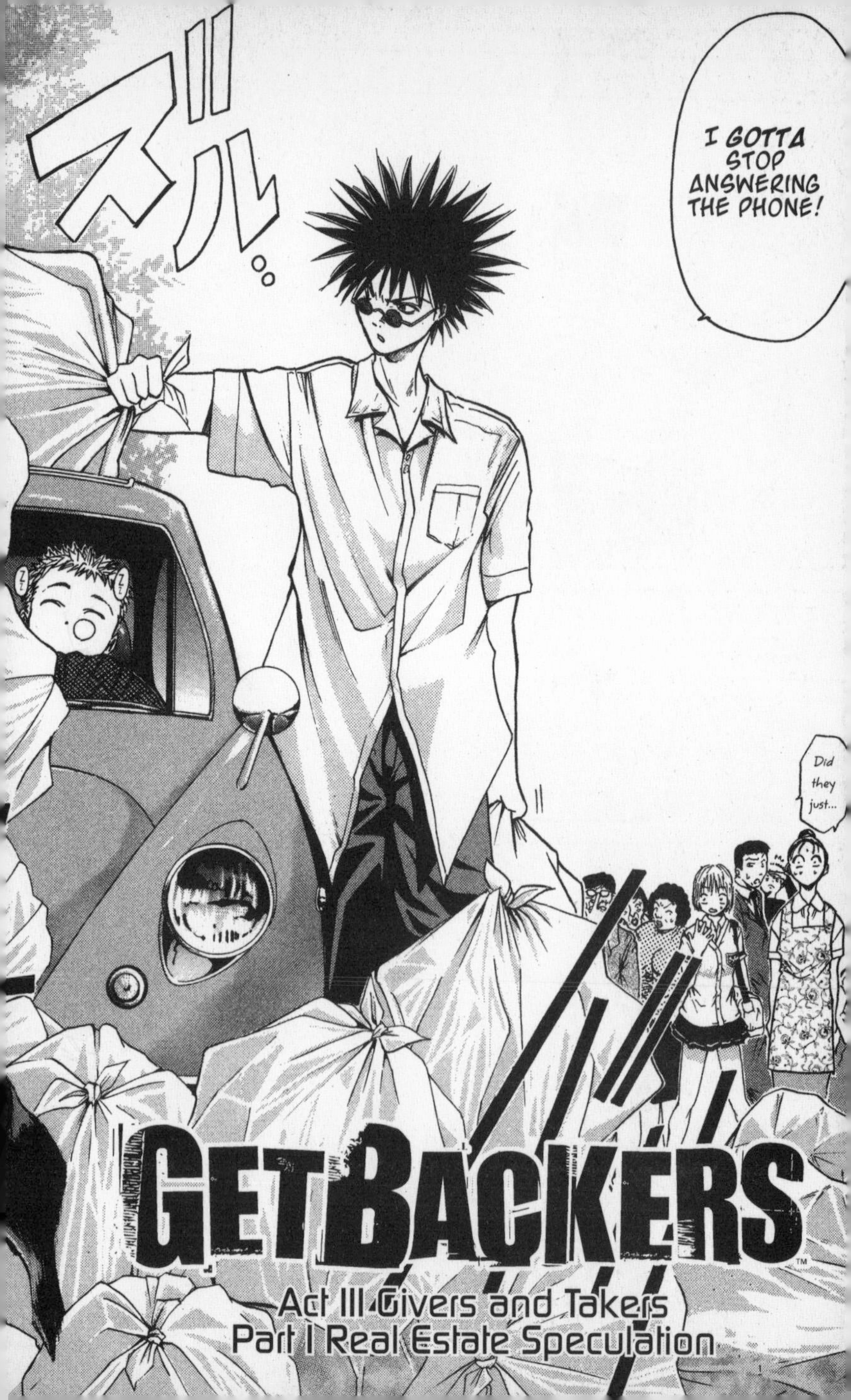
I GOTTA STOP ANSWERING THE PHONE!
ズル
Did they just...
GETBACKERS™
Act III Givers and Takers
Part I Real Estate Speculation

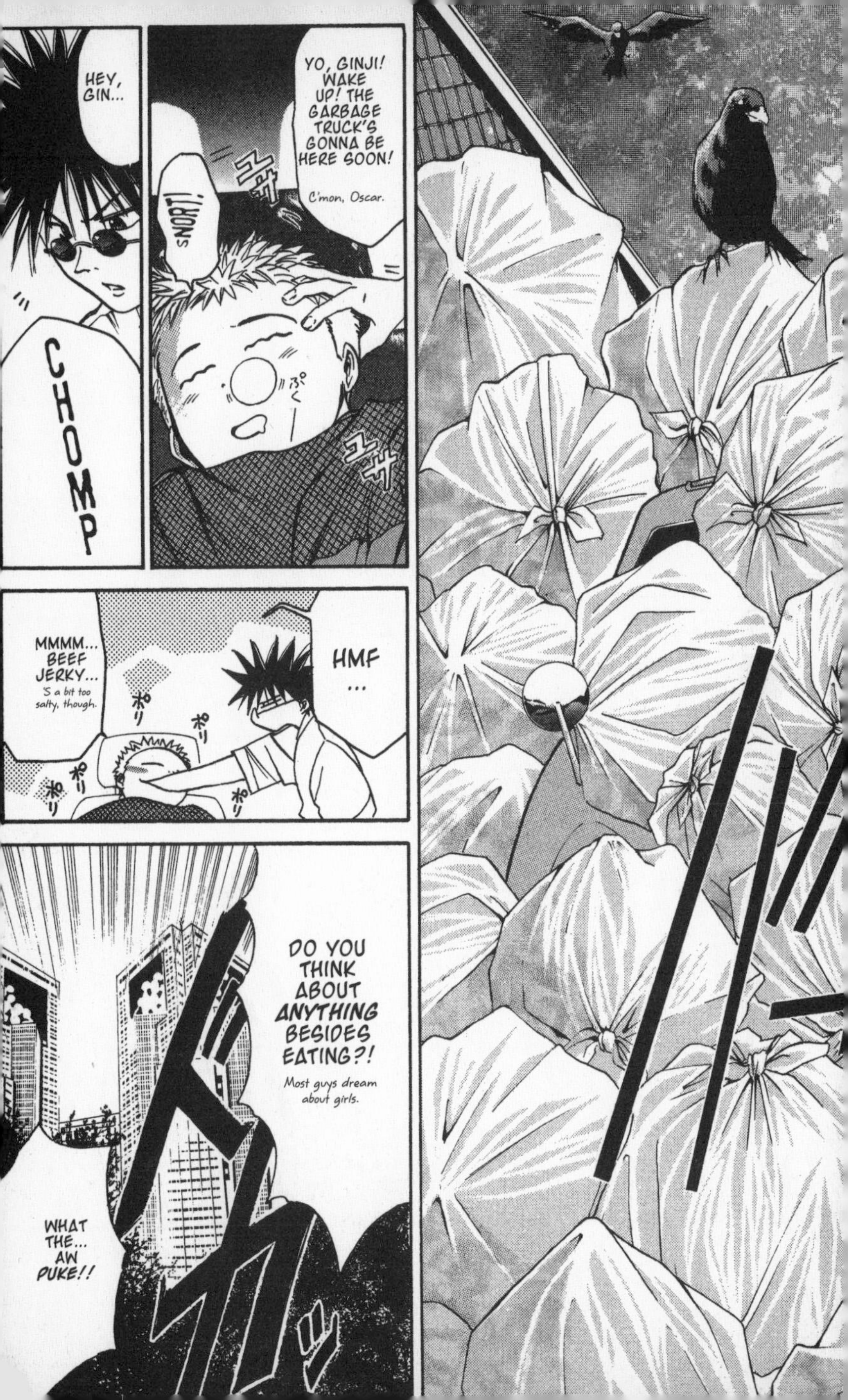
YO, GINJI! WAKE UP! THE GARBAGE TRUCK'S GONNA BE HERE SOON!
C'mon, Oscar.
SNORT!
HEY, GIN...
CHOMP
HMF ...
MMMM... BEEF JERKY...
'S a bit too salty, though.
DO YOU THINK ABOUT ANYTHING BESIDES EATING?!
Most guys dream about girls.
WHAT THE... AW PUKE!!

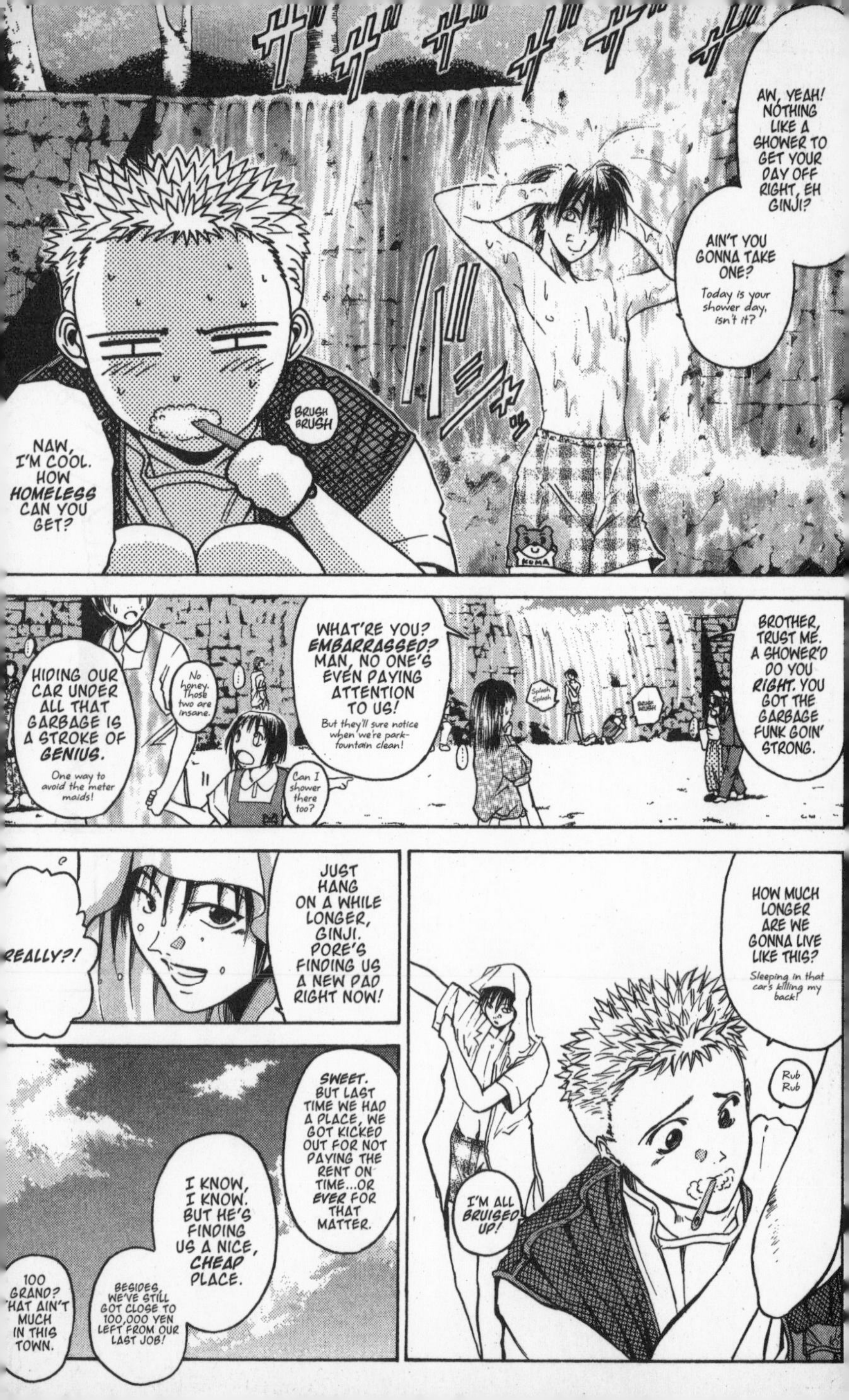
AW, YEAH! NOTHING LIKE A SHOWER TO GET YOUR DAY OFF RIGHT, EH GINJI?
AIN'T YOU GONNA TAKE ONE? Today is your shower day, isn't it?
BRUSH BRUSH
NAW, I'M COOL. HOW HOMELESS CAN YOU GET?
KUMA
BROTHER, TRUST ME. A SHOWER'D DO YOU RIGHT. YOU GOT THE GARBAGE FUNK GOIN' STRONG.
WHAT'RE YOU? EMBARRASSED? MAN, NO ONE'S EVEN PAYING ATTENTION TO US! But they'll sure notice when we're park-fountain clean!
Splash Splash
BRUSH BRUSH
...
Can I shower there too?
No honey. Those two are insane.
...
HIDING OUR CAR UNDER ALL THAT GARBAGE IS A STROKE OF GENIUS. One way to avoid the meter maids!
HOW MUCH LONGER ARE WE GONNA LIVE LIKE THIS? Sleeping in that car's killing my back!
Rub Rub
I'M ALL BRUISED UP!
JUST HANG ON A WHILE LONGER, GINJI. PORE'S FINDING US A NEW PAD RIGHT NOW!
REALLY?!
SWEET. BUT LAST TIME WE HAD A PLACE, WE GOT KICKED OUT FOR NOT PAYING THE RENT ON TIME...OR EVER FOR THAT MATTER.
I KNOW, I KNOW. BUT HE'S FINDING US A NICE, CHEAP PLACE.
BESIDES, WE'VE STILL GOT CLOSE TO 100,000 YEN LEFT FROM OUR LAST JOB!
100 GRAND? THAT AIN'T MUCH IN THIS TOWN.

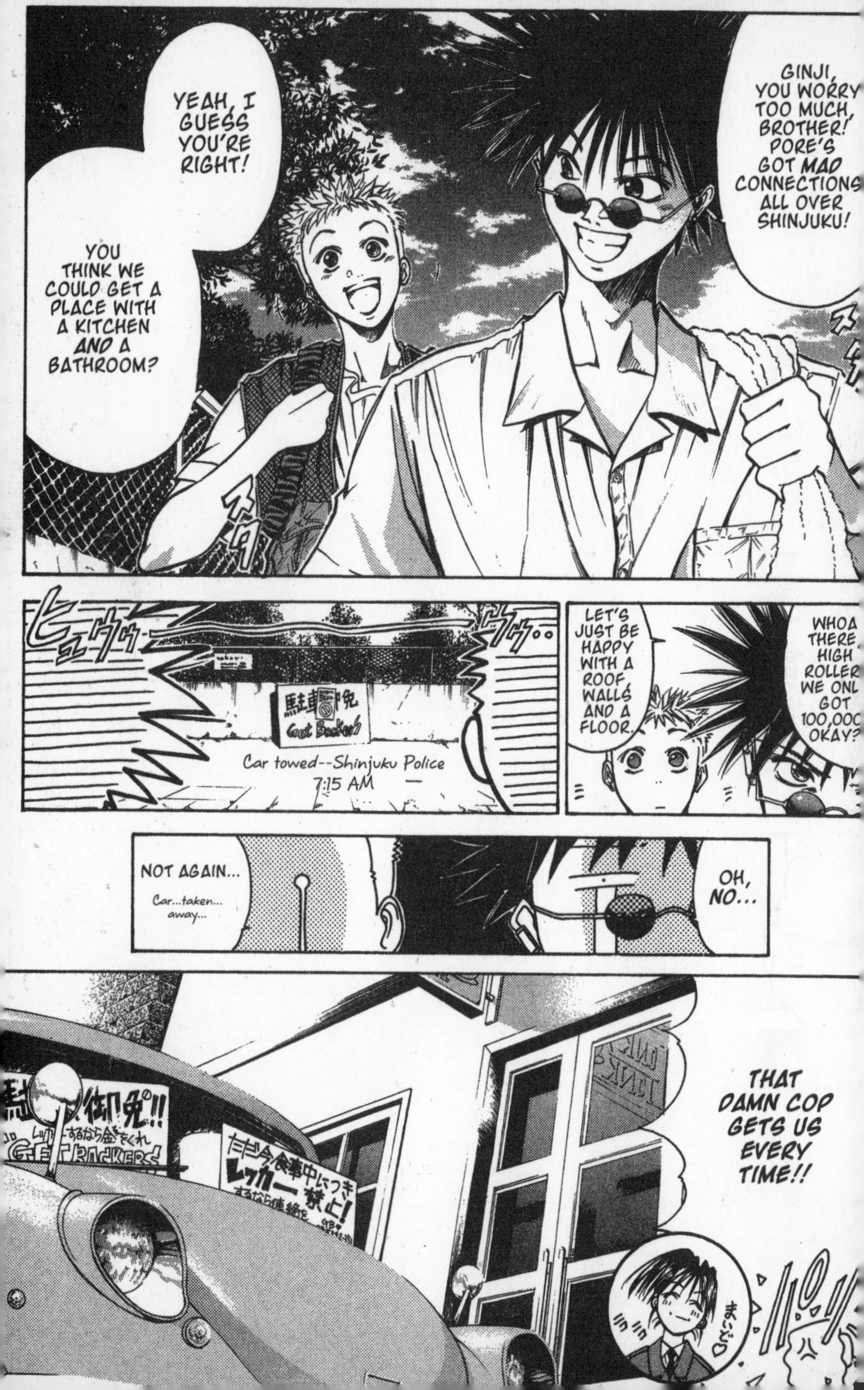
GINJI, YOU WORRY TOO MUCH, BROTHER! PORE'S GOT MAD CONNECTIONS ALL OVER SHINJUKU!
YEAH, I GUESS YOU'RE RIGHT!
YOU THINK WE COULD GET A PLACE WITH A KITCHEN AND A BATHROOM?
WHOA THERE, HIGH ROLLER WE ONL GOT 100,000 OKAY?
LET'S JUST BE HAPPY WITH A ROOF, WALLS AND A FLOOR.
Get Backers
Car towed--Shinjuku Police 7:15 AM
OH, NO...
NOT AGAIN...
Car...taken... away...
THAT DAMN COP GETS US EVERY TIME!!
ただ今食事中につき
レッカー禁止!

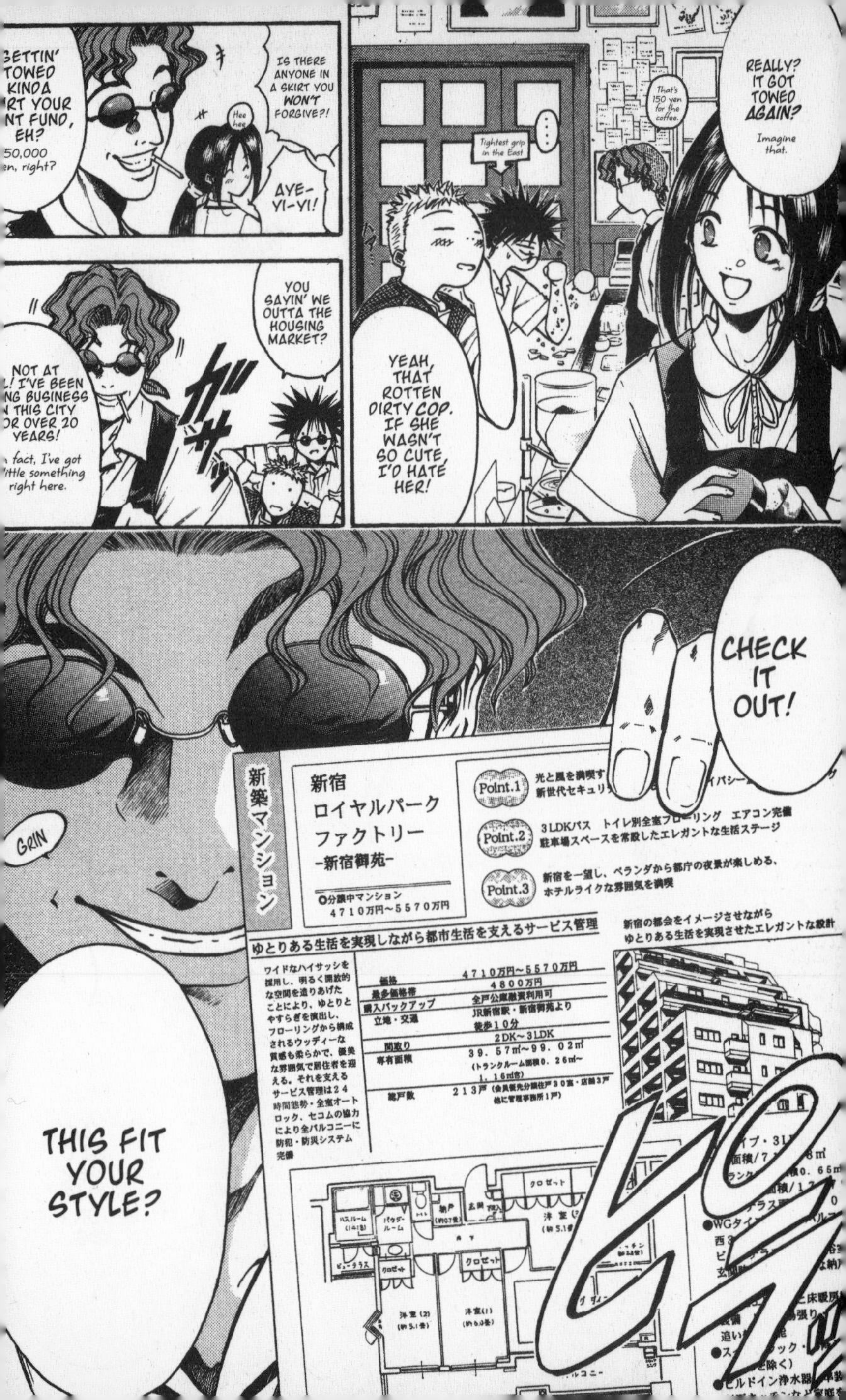
REALLY? IT GOT TOWED AGAIN?
Imagine that.
That's 150 yen for the coffee.
...
Tightest grip in the East
YEAH, THAT ROTTEN DIRTY COP. IF SHE WASN'T SO CUTE, I'D HATE HER!
IS THERE ANYONE IN A SKIRT YOU WON'T FORGIVE?!
AYE-YI-YI!
Hee hee
GETTIN' TOWED KINDA RT YOUR NT FUND, EH?
50,000 en, right?
YOU SAYIN' WE OUTTA THE HOUSING MARKET?
NOT AT ! I'VE BEEN NG BUSINESS N THIS CITY OR OVER 20 YEARS!
n fact, I've got little something right here.
ガサッ
CHECK IT OUT!
GRIN
THIS FIT YOUR STYLE?
新築マンション
新宿 ロイヤルパークファクトリー -新宿御苑-
○分譲中マンション 4710万円～5570万円
Point.1 光と風を満喫す 新世代セキュリ
Point.2 3LDKバス トイレ別全室フローリング エアコン完備 駐車場スペースを常設したエレガントな生活ステージ
Point.3 新宿を一望し、ベランダから都庁の夜景が楽しめる、ホテルライクな雰囲気を満喫
ゆとりある生活を実現しながら都市生活を支えるサービス管理
新宿の都会をイメージさせながらゆとりある生活を実現させたエレガントな設計
ワイドなハイサッシを採用し、明るく開放的な空間を造りあげたことにより、ゆとりとやすらぎを演出し、フローリングから構成されるウッディーな質感も柔らかで、優美な雰囲気で居住者を迎える。それを支えるサービス管理は24時間態勢・全室オートロック、セコムの協力により全バルコニーに防犯・防災システム完備
価格 4710万円～5570万円
最多価格帯 4800万円
購入バックアップ 全戸公庫融資利用可
立地・交通 JR新宿駅・新宿御苑より徒歩10分
間取り 2DK～3LDK
専有面積 39.57㎡～99.02㎡ (トランクルーム面積0.26㎡～1.16㎡含)
総戸数 213戸

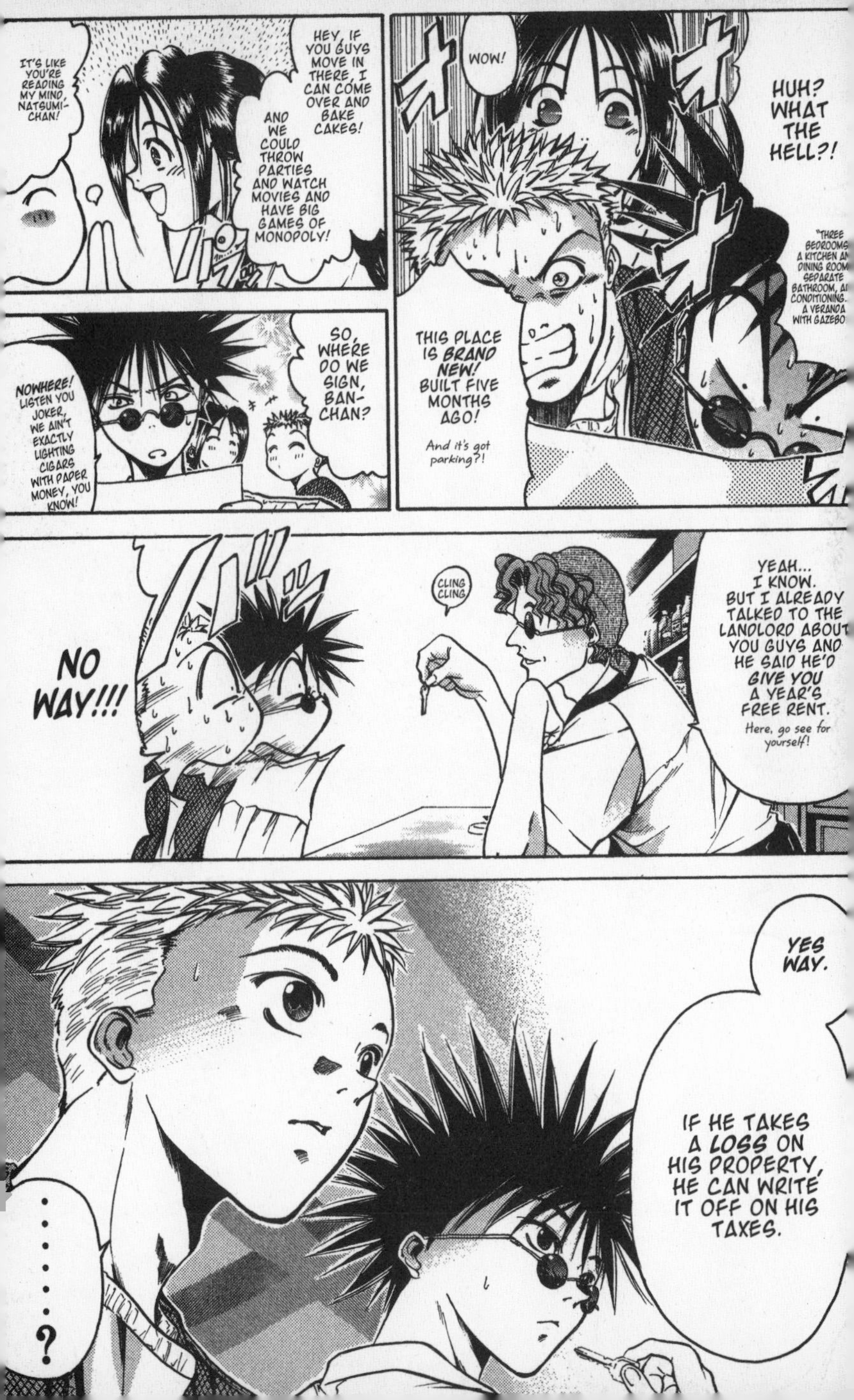
WOW!
HUH? WHAT THE HELL?!
"THREE BEDROOMS A KITCHEN AN DINING ROOM SEPARATE BATHROOM, AI CONDITIONING... A VERANDA WITH GAZEBO
THIS PLACE IS BRAND NEW! BUILT FIVE MONTHS AGO!
And it's got parking?!
HEY, IF YOU GUYS MOVE IN THERE, I CAN COME OVER AND BAKE CAKES!
AND WE COULD THROW PARTIES AND WATCH MOVIES AND HAVE BIG GAMES OF MONOPOLY!
IT'S LIKE YOU'RE READING MY MIND, NATSUMI-CHAN!
SO, WHERE DO WE SIGN, BAN-CHAN?
NOWHERE! LISTEN YOU JOKER, WE AIN'T EXACTLY LIGHTING CIGARS WITH PAPER MONEY, YOU KNOW!
YEAH... I KNOW. BUT I ALREADY TALKED TO THE LANDLORD ABOUT YOU GUYS AND HE SAID HE'D GIVE YOU A YEAR'S FREE RENT.
Here, go see for yourself!
CLING CLING
NO WAY!!!
YES WAY.
IF HE TAKES A LOSS ON HIS PROPERTY, HE CAN WRITE IT OFF ON HIS TAXES.
......?

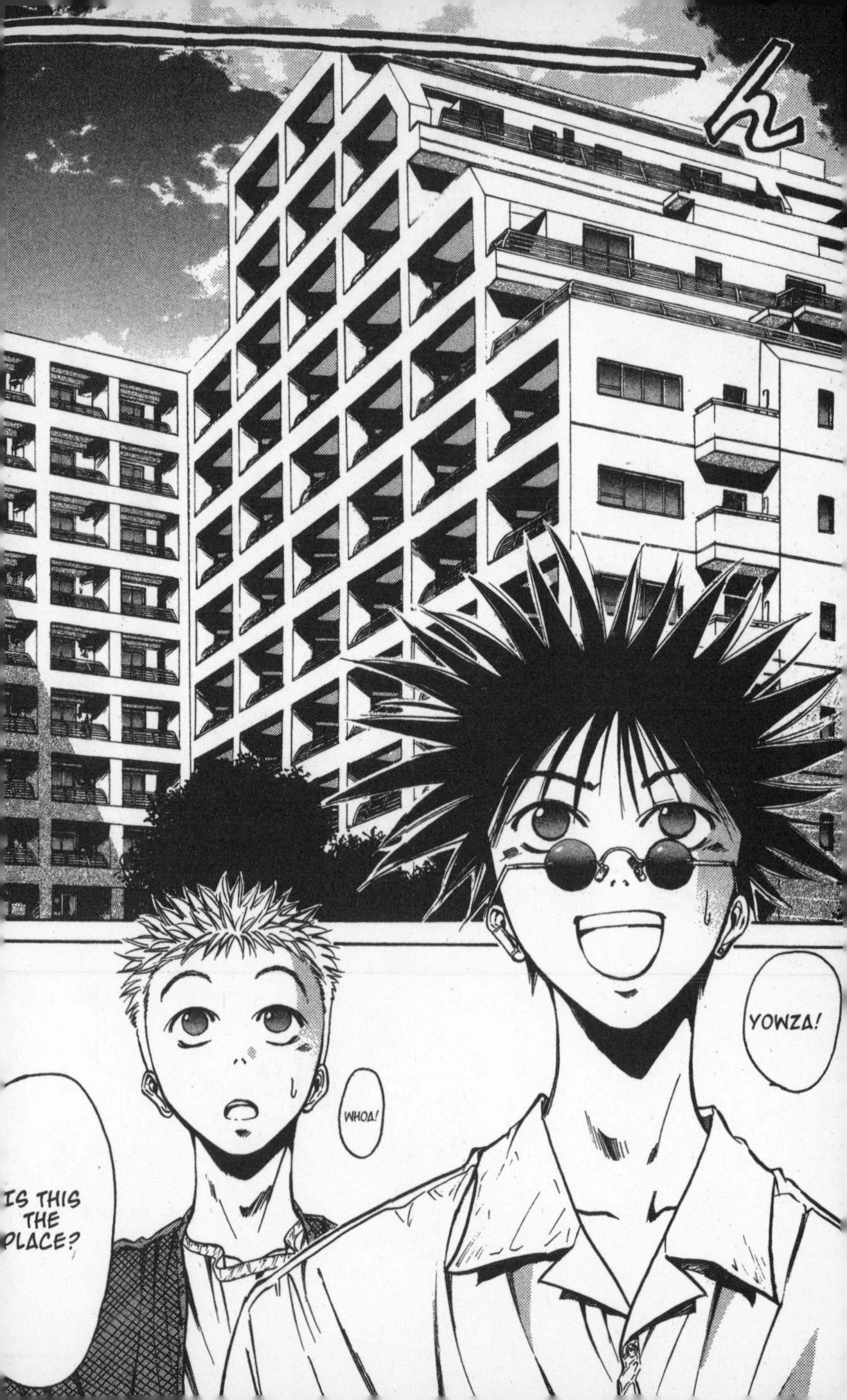
YOWZA!
WHOA!
IS THIS THE PLACE?

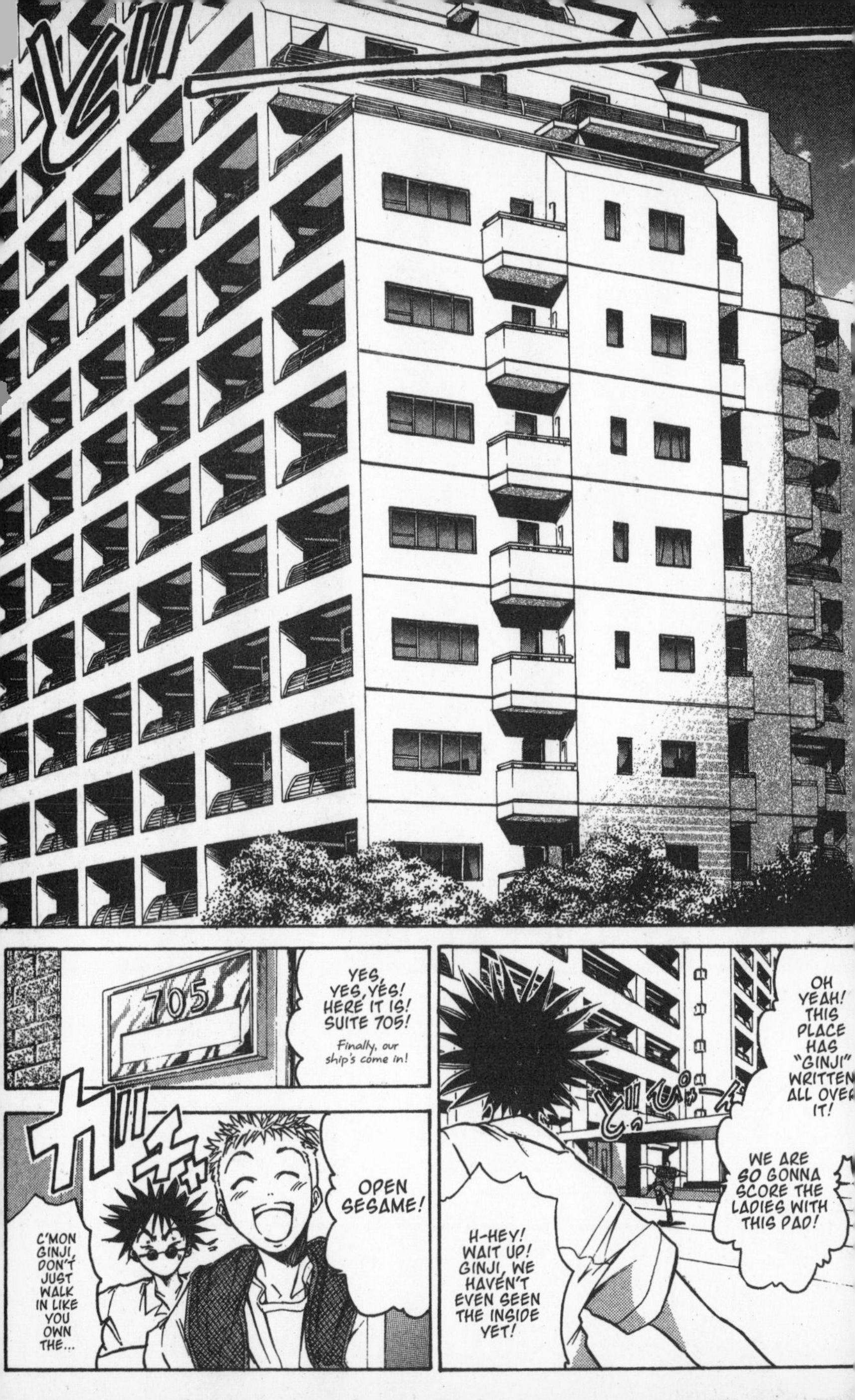

OH YEAH! THIS PLACE HAS "GINJI" WRITTEN ALL OVER IT!
WE ARE SO GONNA SCORE THE LADIES WITH THIS PAD!
H-HEY! WAIT UP! GINJI, WE HAVEN'T EVEN SEEN THE INSIDE YET!
705
YES, YES, YES! HERE IT IS! SUITE 705!
Finally, our ship's come in!
OPEN SESAME!
C'MON GINJI, DON'T JUST WALK IN LIKE YOU OWN THE...

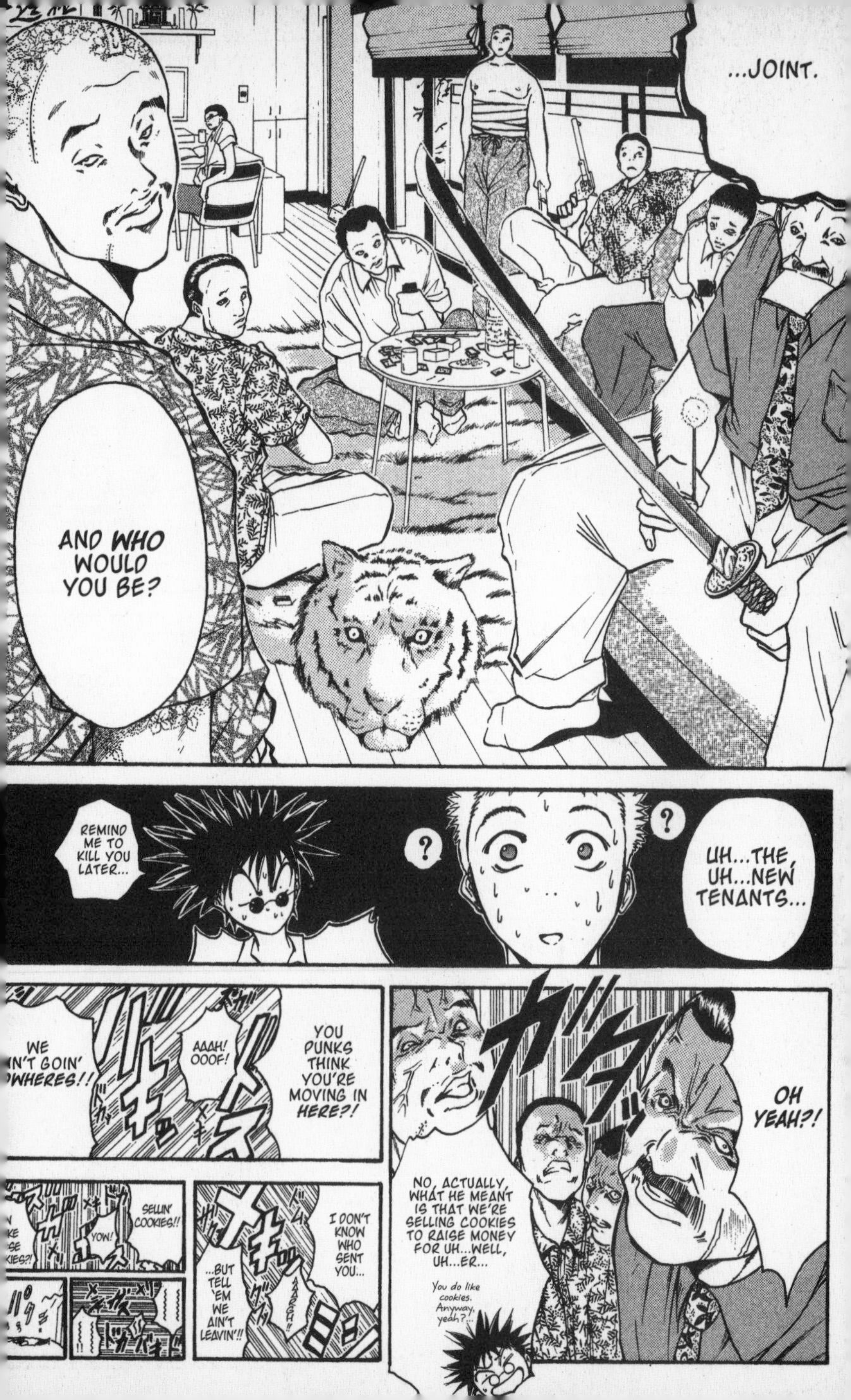
...JOINT.
AND WHO WOULD YOU BE?
UH...THE, UH...NEW TENANTS...
REMIND ME TO KILL YOU LATER...
OH YEAH?!
NO, ACTUALLY, WHAT HE MEANT IS THAT WE'RE SELLING COOKIES TO RAISE MONEY FOR UH...WELL, UH...ER...
You do like cookies. Anyway, yeah?...
YOU PUNKS THINK YOU'RE MOVING IN HERE?!
AAAH! OOOF!
WE N'T GOIN' OWHERES!!
I DON'T KNOW WHO SENT YOU...
...BUT TELL 'EM WE AIN'T LEAVIN'!!
AAARGH!!
SELLIN' COOKIES!!
YOW!

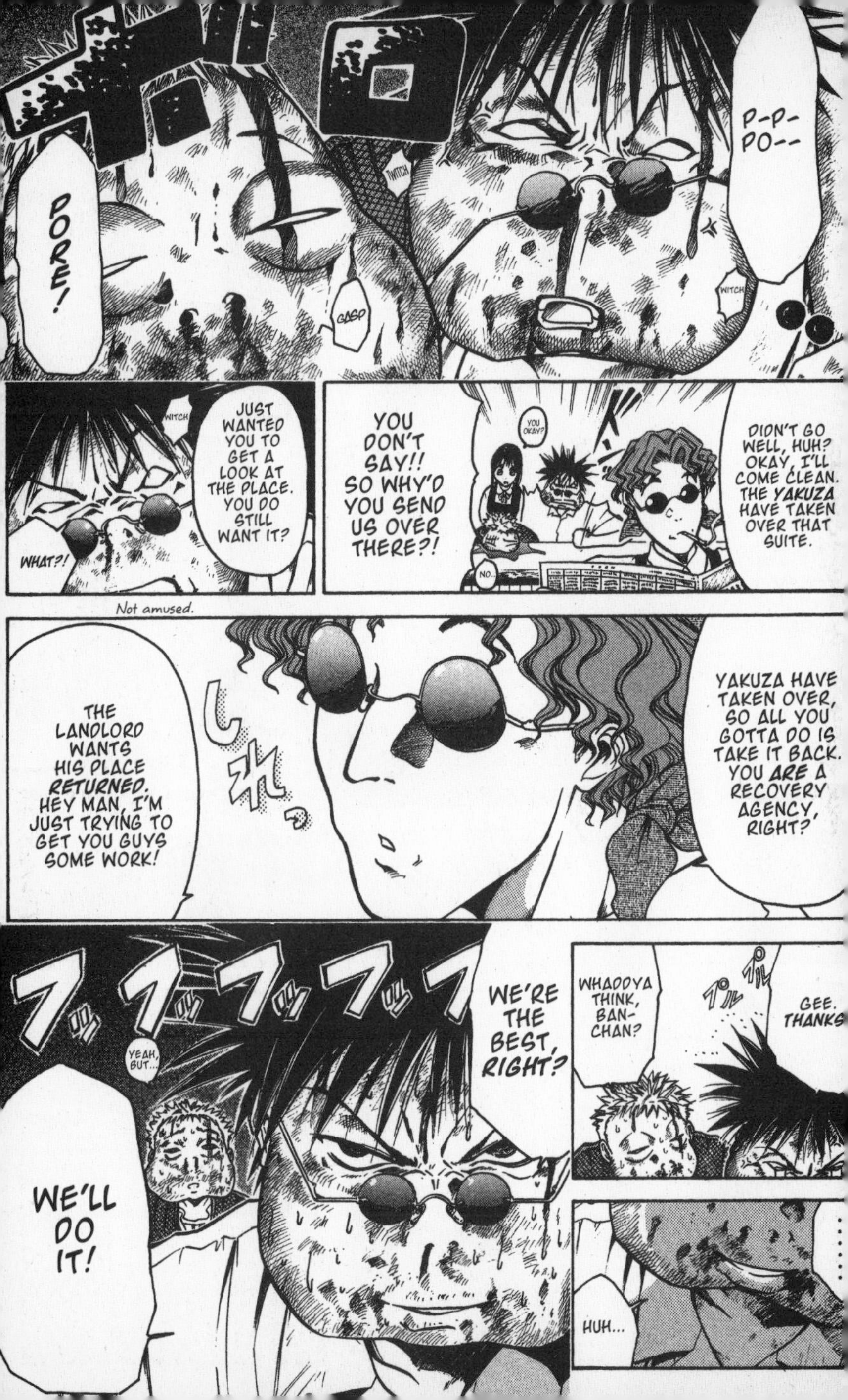
P-P-PO--
TWITCH
WITCH
GASP
PORE!
DIDN'T GO WELL, HUH? OKAY, I'LL COME CLEAN. THE *YAKUZA* HAVE TAKEN OVER THAT SUITE.
YOU OKAY?
YOU DON'T SAY!! SO WHY'D YOU SEND US OVER THERE?!
NO...
WITCH
JUST WANTED YOU TO GET A LOOK AT THE PLACE. YOU DO STILL WANT IT?
WHAT?!
Not amused.
YAKUZA HAVE TAKEN OVER, SO ALL YOU GOTTA DO IS TAKE IT BACK. YOU *ARE* A RECOVERY AGENCY, RIGHT?
THE LANDLORD WANTS HIS PLACE *RETURNED*. HEY MAN, I'M JUST TRYING TO GET YOU GUYS SOME WORK!
GEE. THANKS
WHADDYA THINK, BAN-CHAN?
...
HUH...
WE'RE THE BEST, *RIGHT*?
YEAH, BUT...
WE'LL DO IT!

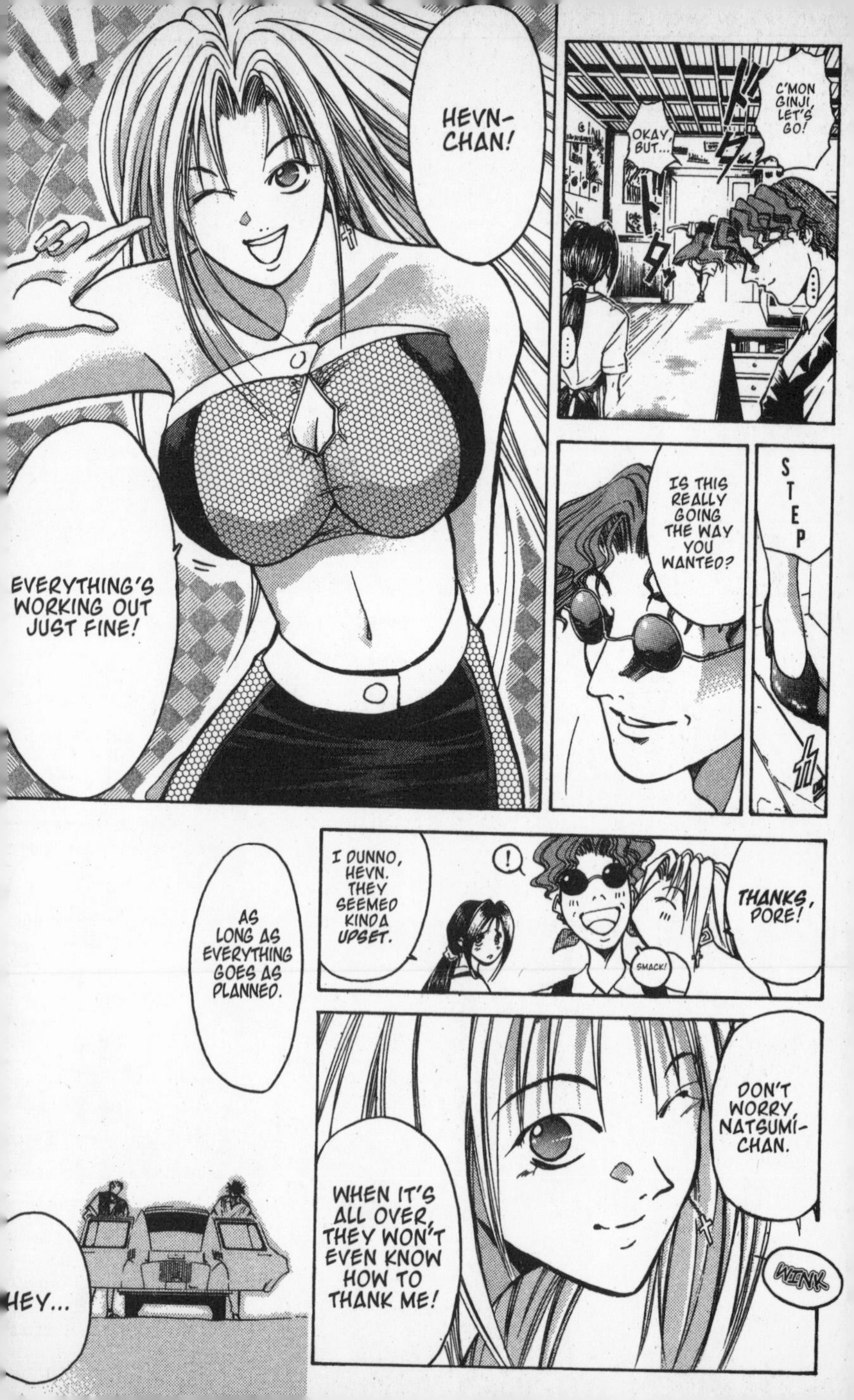

C'MON GINJI, LET'S GO!
OKAY, BUT...
STEP
IS THIS REALLY GOING THE WAY YOU WANTED?
HEVN-CHAN!
EVERYTHING'S WORKING OUT JUST FINE!
THANKS, PORE!
SMACK!
!
I DUNNO, HEVN. THEY SEEMED KINDA UPSET.
DON'T WORRY, NATSUMI-CHAN.
WHEN IT'S ALL OVER, THEY WON'T EVEN KNOW HOW TO THANK ME!
WINK
AS LONG AS EVERYTHING GOES AS PLANNED.
HEY...

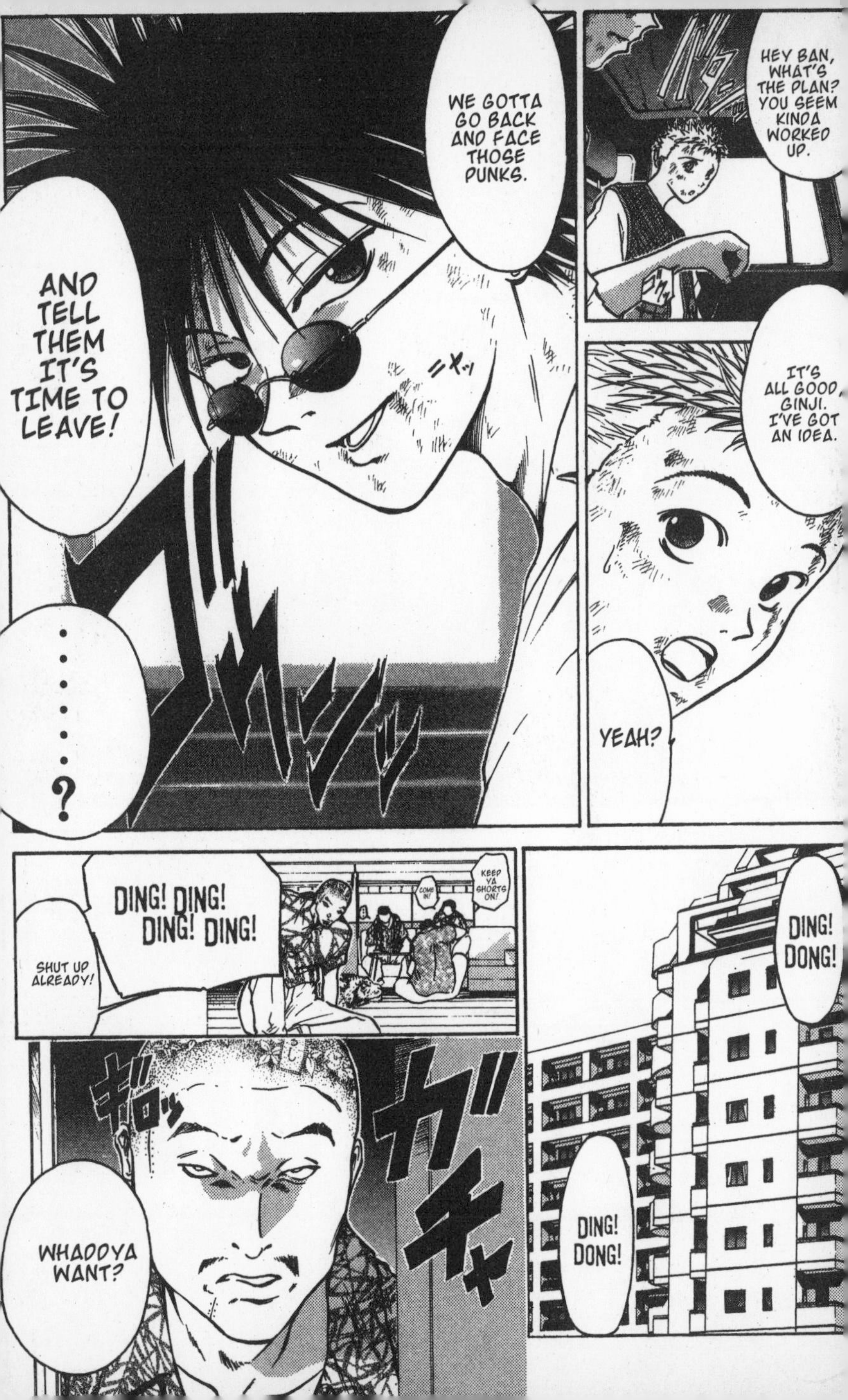
HEY BAN, WHAT'S THE PLAN? YOU SEEM KINDA WORKED UP.
IT'S ALL GOOD GINJI. I'VE GOT AN IDEA.
YEAH?
WE GOTTA GO BACK AND FACE THOSE PUNKS.
AND TELL THEM IT'S TIME TO LEAVE!
......?
DING! DONG!
DING! DONG!
DING! DING! DING! DING!
KEEP YA SHORTS ON!
COME IN!
SHUT UP ALREADY!
WHADDYA WANT?

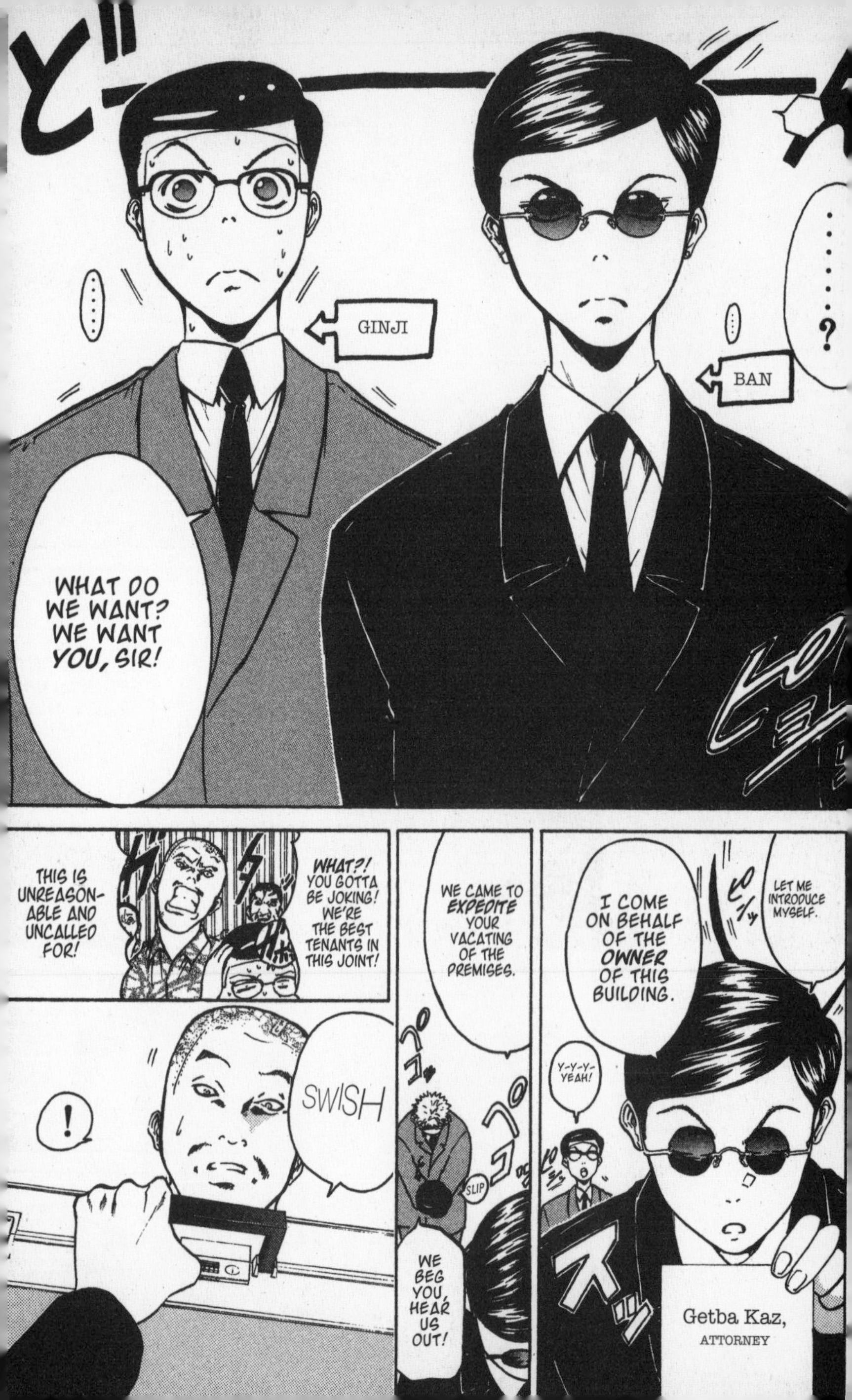

......?
...
BAN
...
GINJI
WHAT DO WE WANT? WE WANT YOU, SIR!
LET ME INTRODUCE MYSELF.
I COME ON BEHALF OF THE OWNER OF THIS BUILDING.
Y-Y-Y-YEAH!
Getba Kaz, ATTORNEY
WE CAME TO EXPEDITE YOUR VACATING OF THE PREMISES.
SLIP
WE BEG YOU, HEAR US OUT!
WHAT?! YOU GOTTA BE JOKING! WE'RE THE BEST TENANTS IN THIS JOINT!
THIS IS UNREASON-ABLE AND UNCALLED FOR!
SWISH
!

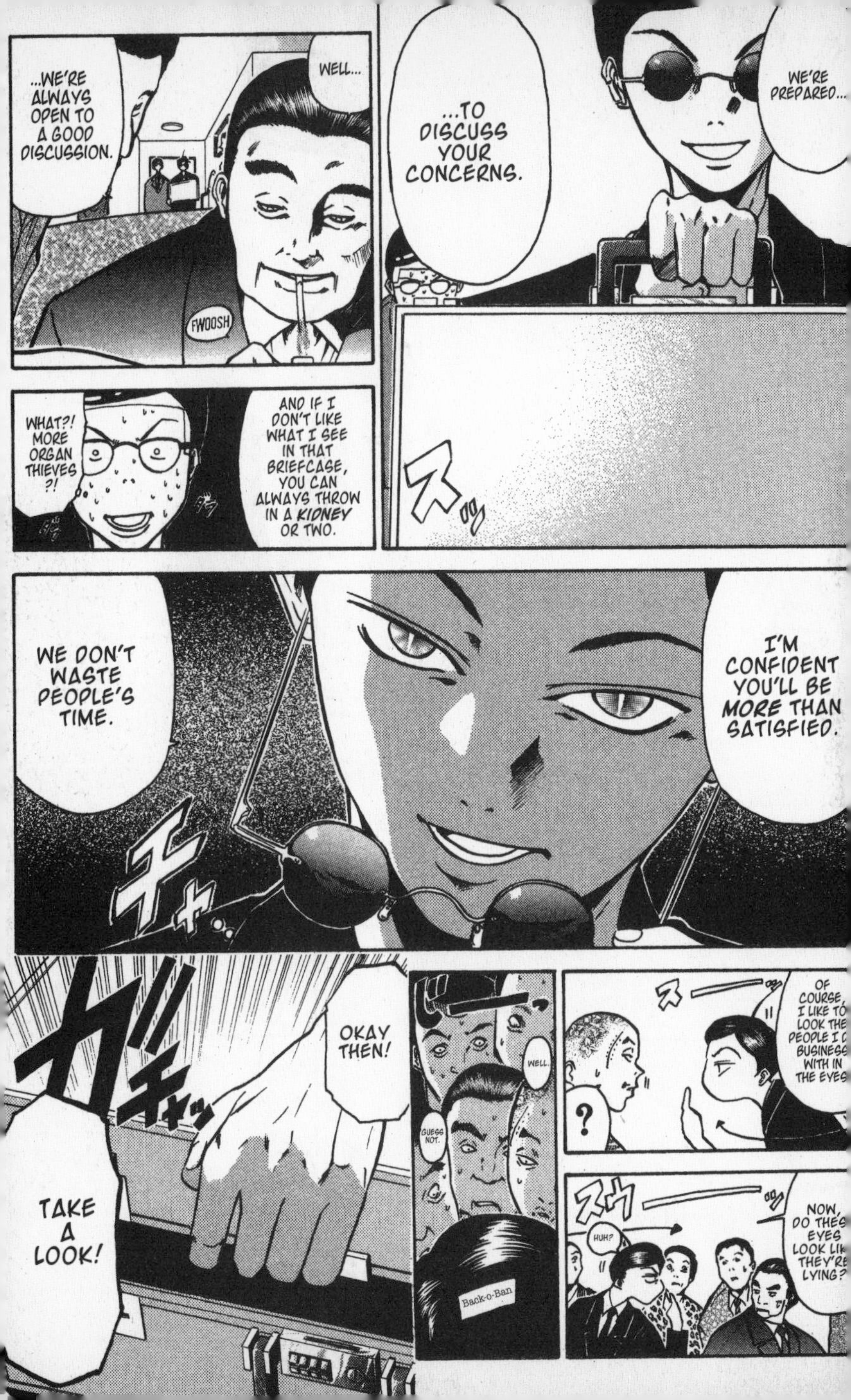

WE'RE PREPARED...
...TO DISCUSS YOUR CONCERNS.
WELL...
...WE'RE ALWAYS OPEN TO A GOOD DISCUSSION.
FWOOSH
AND IF I DON'T LIKE WHAT I SEE IN THAT BRIEFCASE, YOU CAN ALWAYS THROW IN A KIDNEY OR TWO.
WHAT?! MORE ORGAN THIEVES?!
I'M CONFIDENT YOU'LL BE MORE THAN SATISFIED.
WE DON'T WASTE PEOPLE'S TIME.
OF COURSE, I LIKE TO LOOK THE PEOPLE I D BUSINESS WITH IN THE EYES
?
NOW, DO THES EYES LOOK LIK THEY'RE LYING?
HUH?
WELL.
GUESS NOT.
Back-o-Ban
OKAY THEN!
TAKE A LOOK!

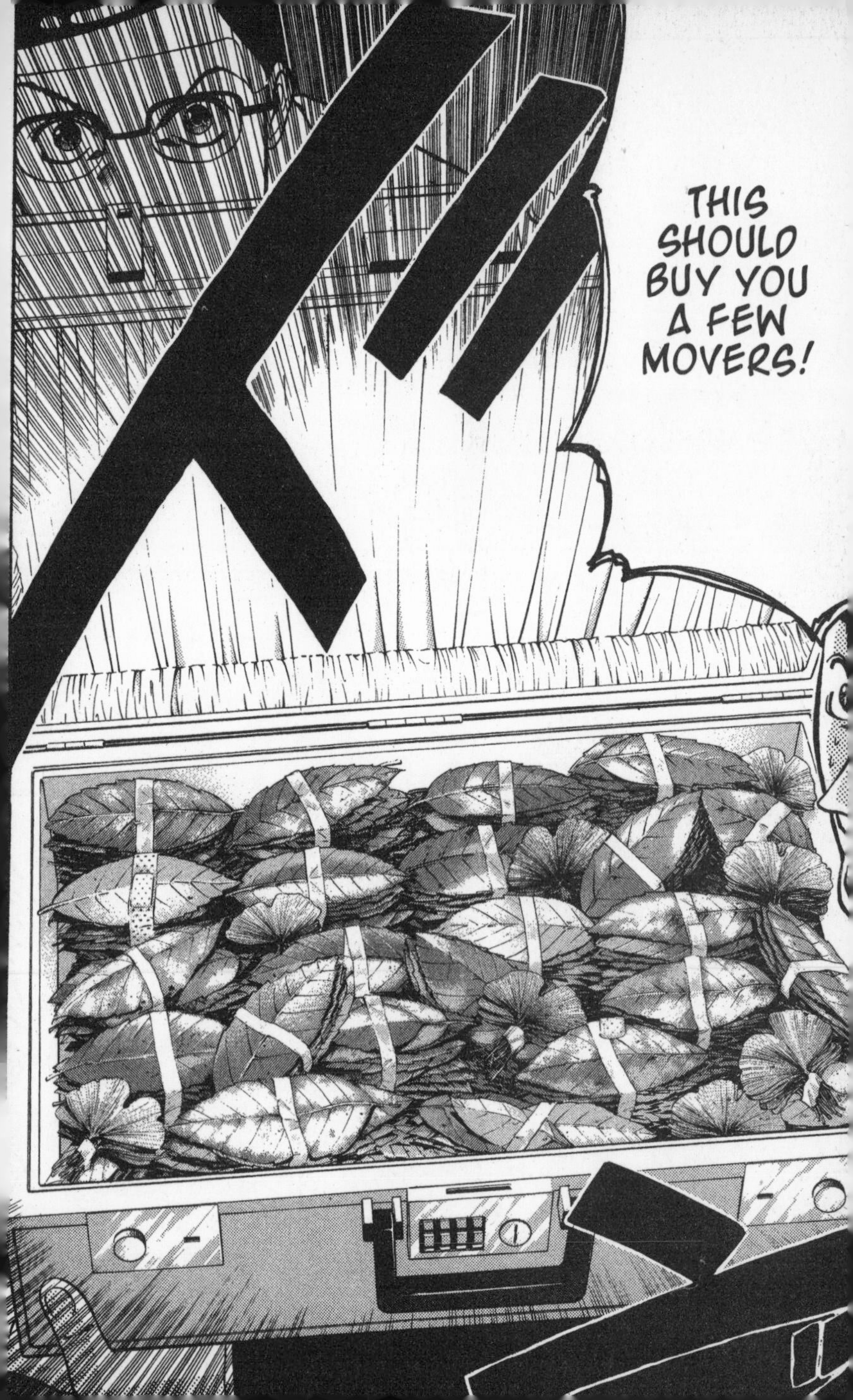
THIS SHOULD BUY YOU A FEW MOVERS!

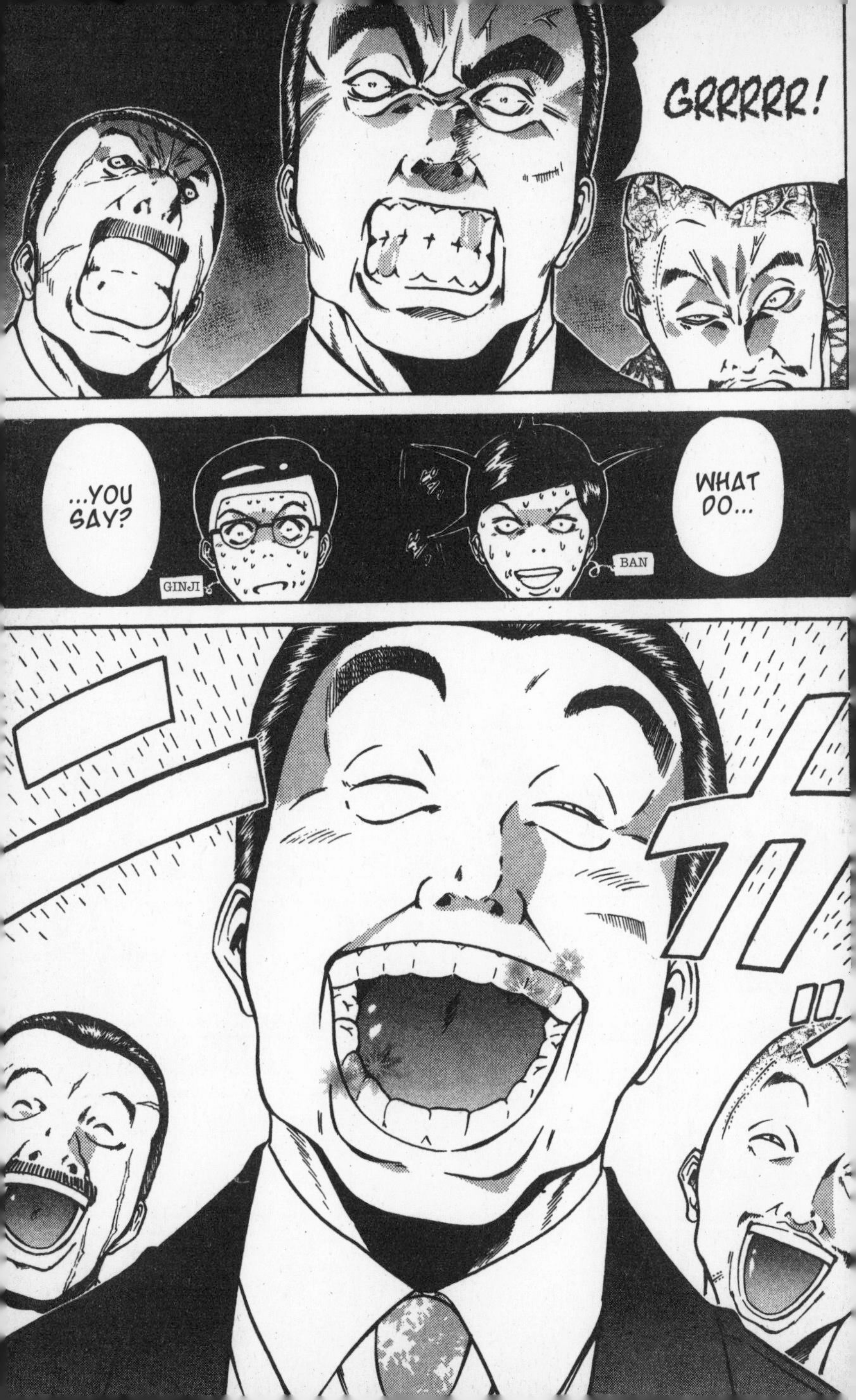
GRRRRR!
WHAT DO...
BAN
GINJI
...YOU SAY?

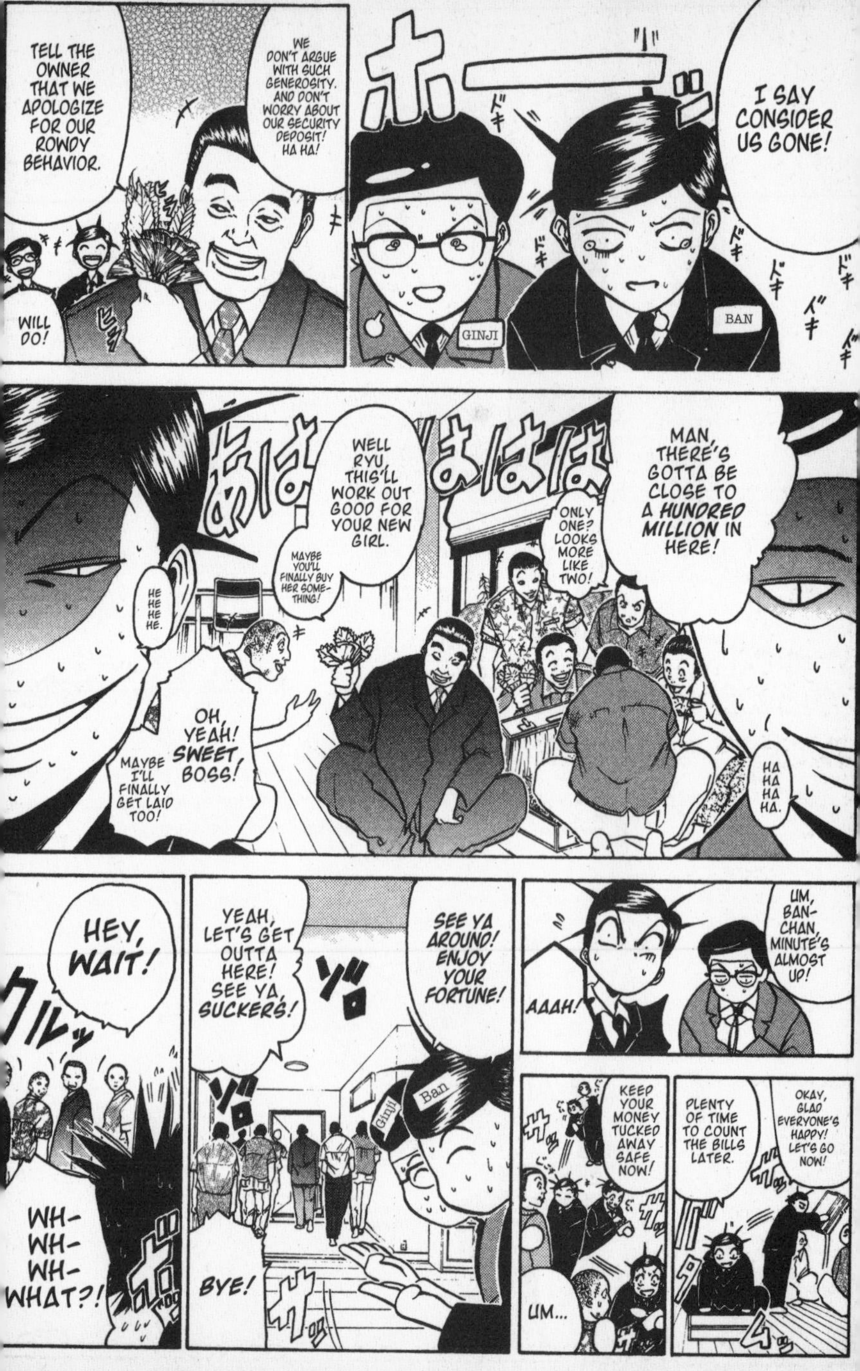
I SAY CONSIDER US GONE!
BAN
GINJI
WE DON'T ARGUE WITH SUCH GENEROSITY. AND DON'T WORRY ABOUT OUR SECURITY DEPOSIT! HA HA!
TELL THE OWNER THAT WE APOLOGIZE FOR OUR ROWDY BEHAVIOR.
WILL DO!
MAN, THERE'S GOTTA BE CLOSE TO A HUNDRED MILLION IN HERE!
ONLY ONE? LOOKS MORE LIKE TWO!
WELL RYU, THIS'LL WORK OUT GOOD FOR YOUR NEW GIRL.
MAYBE YOU'LL FINALLY BUY HER SOMETHING!
HE HE HE HE.
OH, YEAH! SWEET, BOSS!
MAYBE I'LL FINALLY GET LAID TOO!
HA HA HA HA.
UM, BAN-CHAN, MINUTE'S ALMOST UP!
AAAH!
OKAY, GLAD EVERYONE'S HAPPY! LET'S GO NOW!
PLENTY OF TIME TO COUNT THE BILLS LATER.
KEEP YOUR MONEY TUCKED AWAY SAFE NOW!
UM...
SEE YA AROUND! ENJOY YOUR FORTUNE!
YEAH, LET'S GET OUTTA HERE! SEE YA, SUCKERS!
Ban
Ginji
BYE!
HEY, WAIT!
WH-WH-WH-WHAT?!

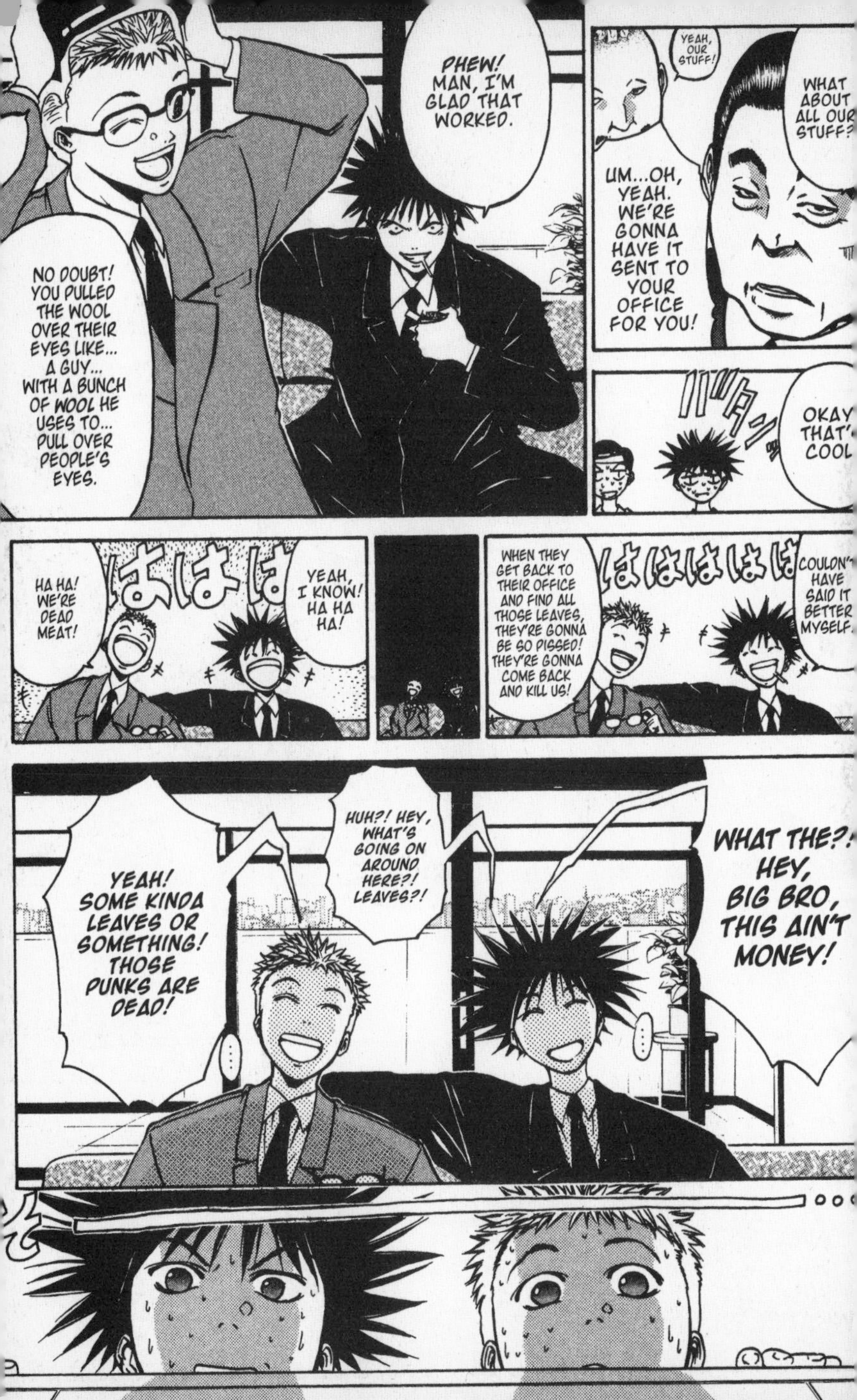
WHAT ABOUT ALL OUR STUFF?
YEAH, OUR STUFF!
UM...OH, YEAH. WE'RE GONNA HAVE IT SENT TO YOUR OFFICE FOR YOU!
OKAY THAT'S COOL
PHEW! MAN, I'M GLAD THAT WORKED.
NO DOUBT! YOU PULLED THE WOOL OVER THEIR EYES LIKE... A GUY... WITH A BUNCH OF WOOL HE USES TO... PULL OVER PEOPLE'S EYES.
はははは
COULDN'T HAVE SAID IT BETTER MYSELF.
WHEN THEY GET BACK TO THEIR OFFICE AND FIND ALL THOSE LEAVES, THEY'RE GONNA BE SO PISSED! THEY'RE GONNA COME BACK AND KILL US!
YEAH, I KNOW! HA HA HA!
ははは
HA HA! WE'RE DEAD MEAT!
WHAT THE?! HEY, BIG BRO, THIS AIN'T MONEY!
HUH?! HEY, WHAT'S GOING ON AROUND HERE?! LEAVES?!
YEAH! SOME KINDA LEAVES OR SOMETHING! THOSE PUNKS ARE DEAD!
...
...

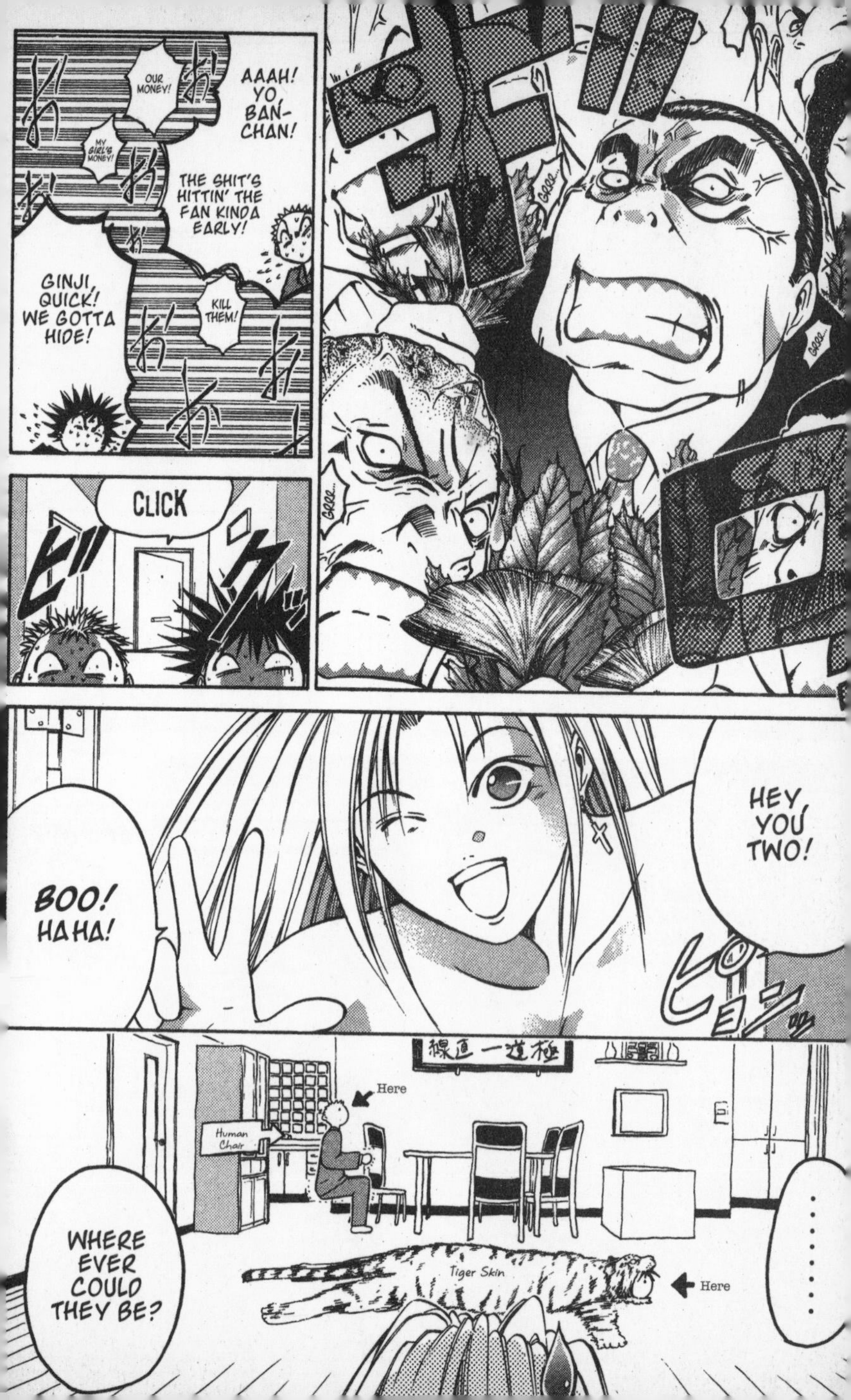
GRRR...
GRRR...
GRRR...
AAAH! YO BAN-CHAN!
THE SHIT'S HITTIN' THE FAN KINDA EARLY!
OUR MONEY!
MY GIRL'S MONEY!
KILL THEM!
GINJI, QUICK! WE GOTTA HIDE!
CLICK
HEY YOU TWO!
BOO! HAHA!
.....
極道一直線
Here
Human Chair
Tiger Skin
Here
WHERE EVER COULD THEY BE?

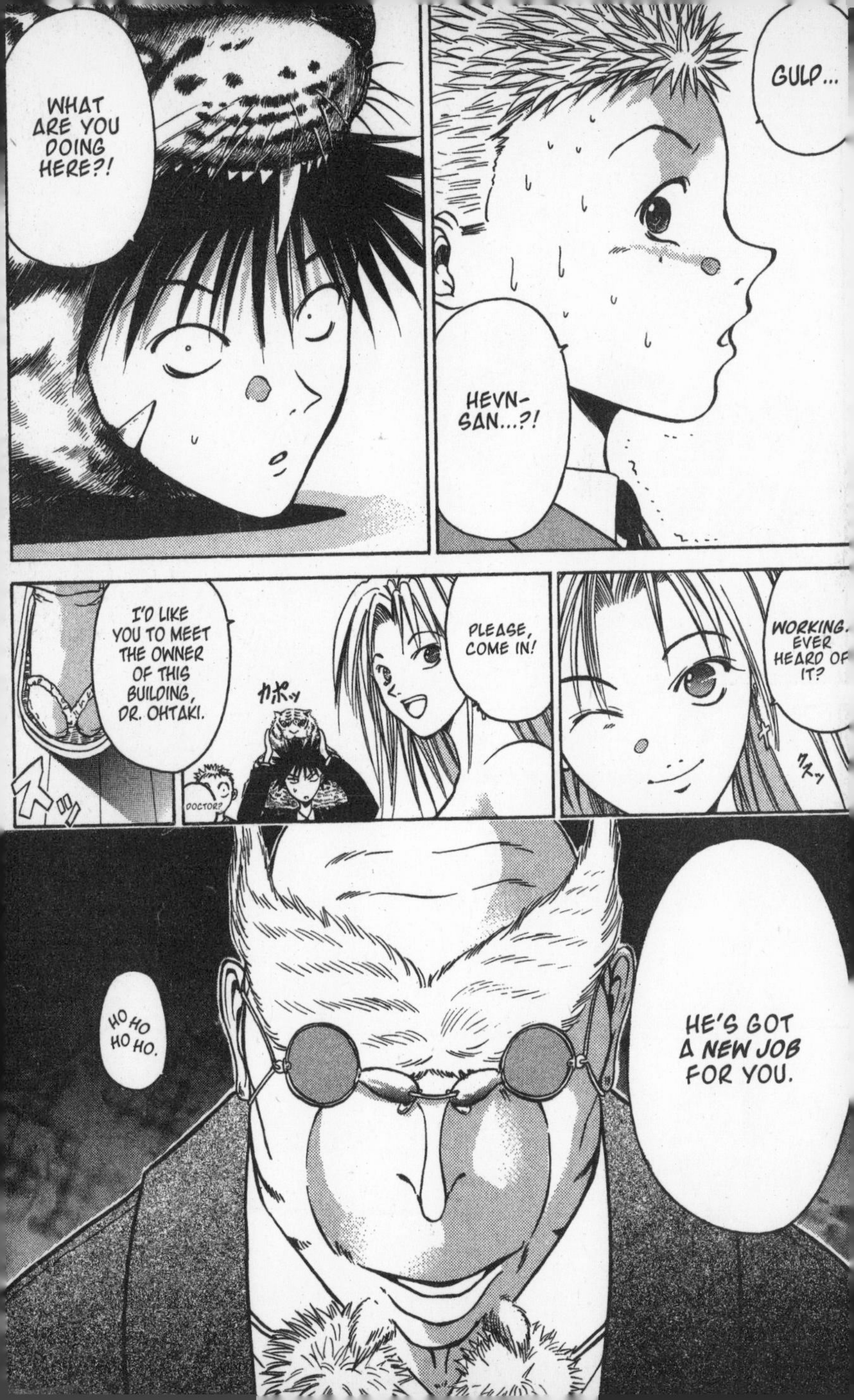
GULP...
HEVN-SAN...?!
WHAT ARE YOU DOING HERE?!
WORKING. EVER HEARD OF IT?
PLEASE, COME IN!
I'D LIKE YOU TO MEET THE OWNER OF THIS BUILDING, DR. OHTAKI.
DOCTOR?
HE'S GOT A NEW JOB FOR YOU.
HO HO HO HO.

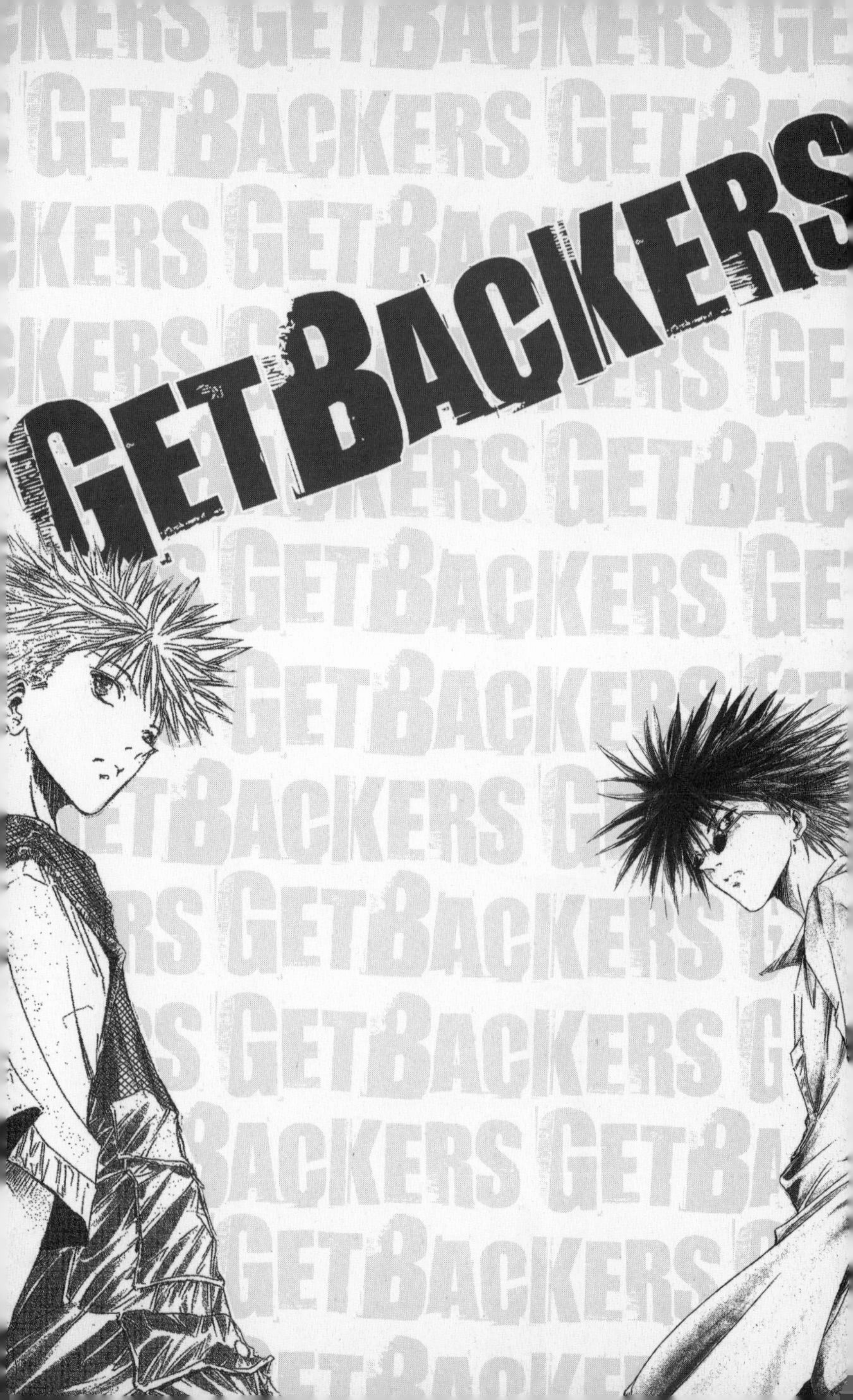
GETBACKERS

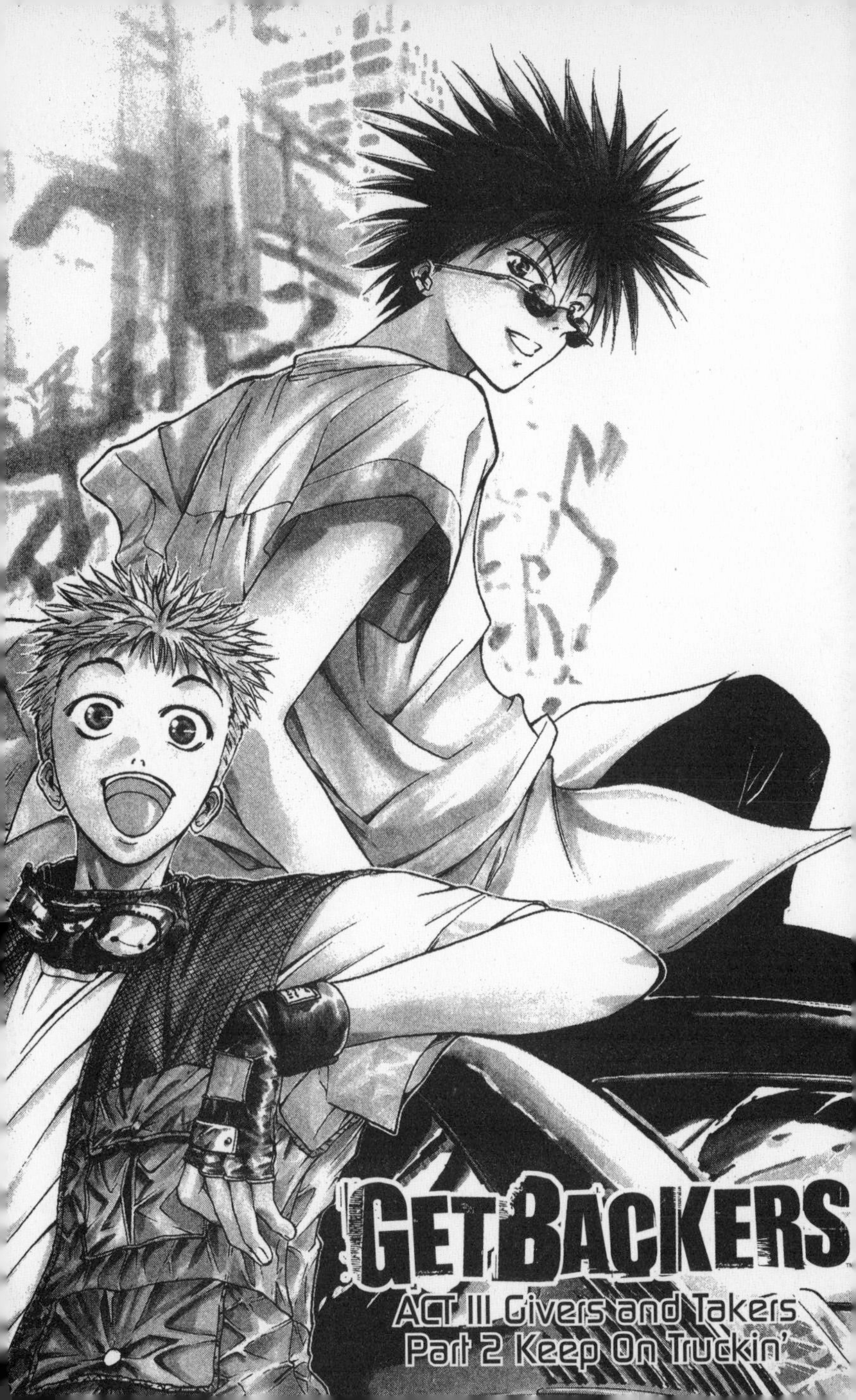
GET BACKERS
ACT III Givers and Takers
Part 2 Keep On Truckin'

Wan Pore found a new place for the GetBackers to live.
Great place, but unfortunately, it was overrun with Yakuza.

Ban used his Evil Eye to get them out, but the Yakuza soon realized they'd been tricked. And just as everything was going wrong, who should appear...?

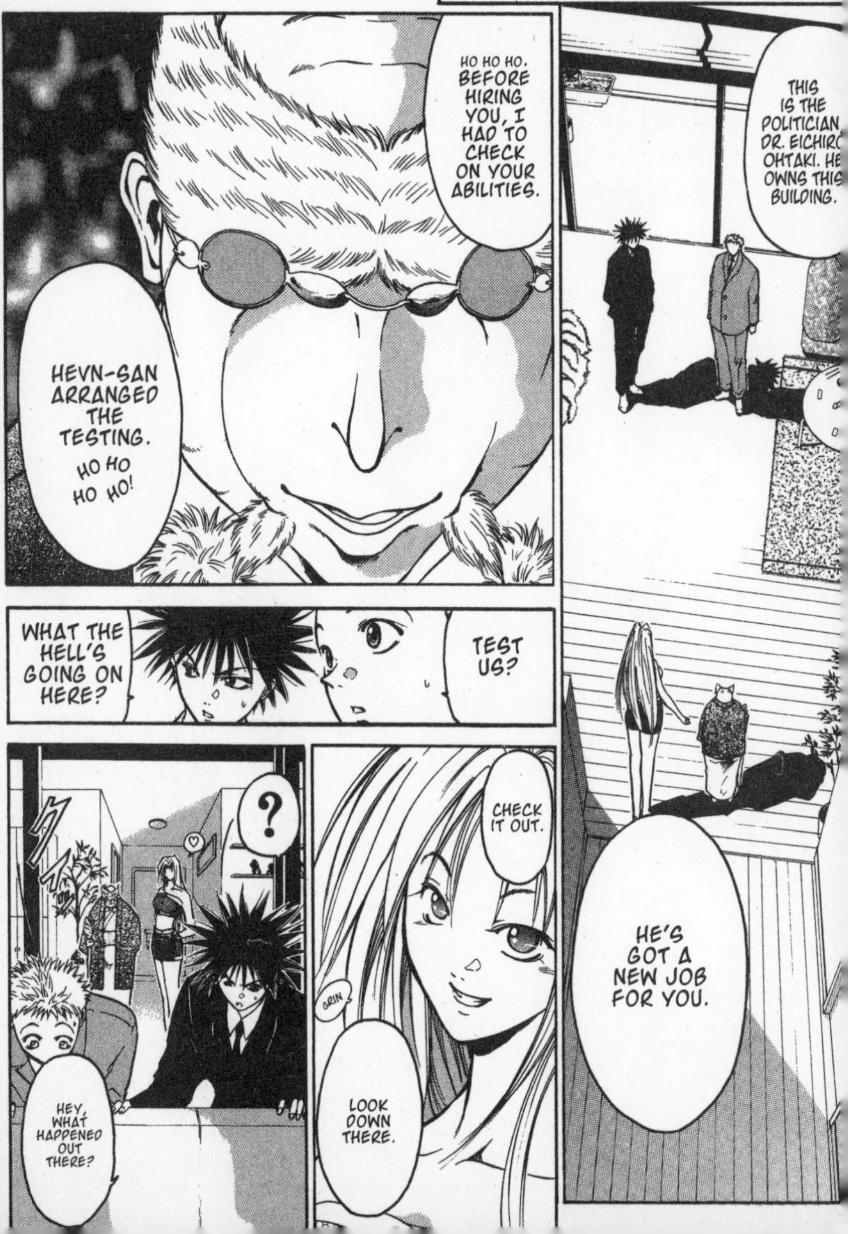

THIS IS THE POLITICIAN, DR. EICHIRO OHTAKI. HE OWNS THIS BUILDING.
HE'S GOT A NEW JOB FOR YOU.
HO HO HO. BEFORE HIRING YOU, I HAD TO CHECK ON YOUR ABILITIES.
HEVN-SAN ARRANGED THE TESTING.
HO HO HO HO!
TEST US?
WHAT THE HELL'S GOING ON HERE?
CHECK IT OUT.
GRIN
LOOK DOWN THERE.
?
HEY, WHAT HAPPENED OUT THERE?

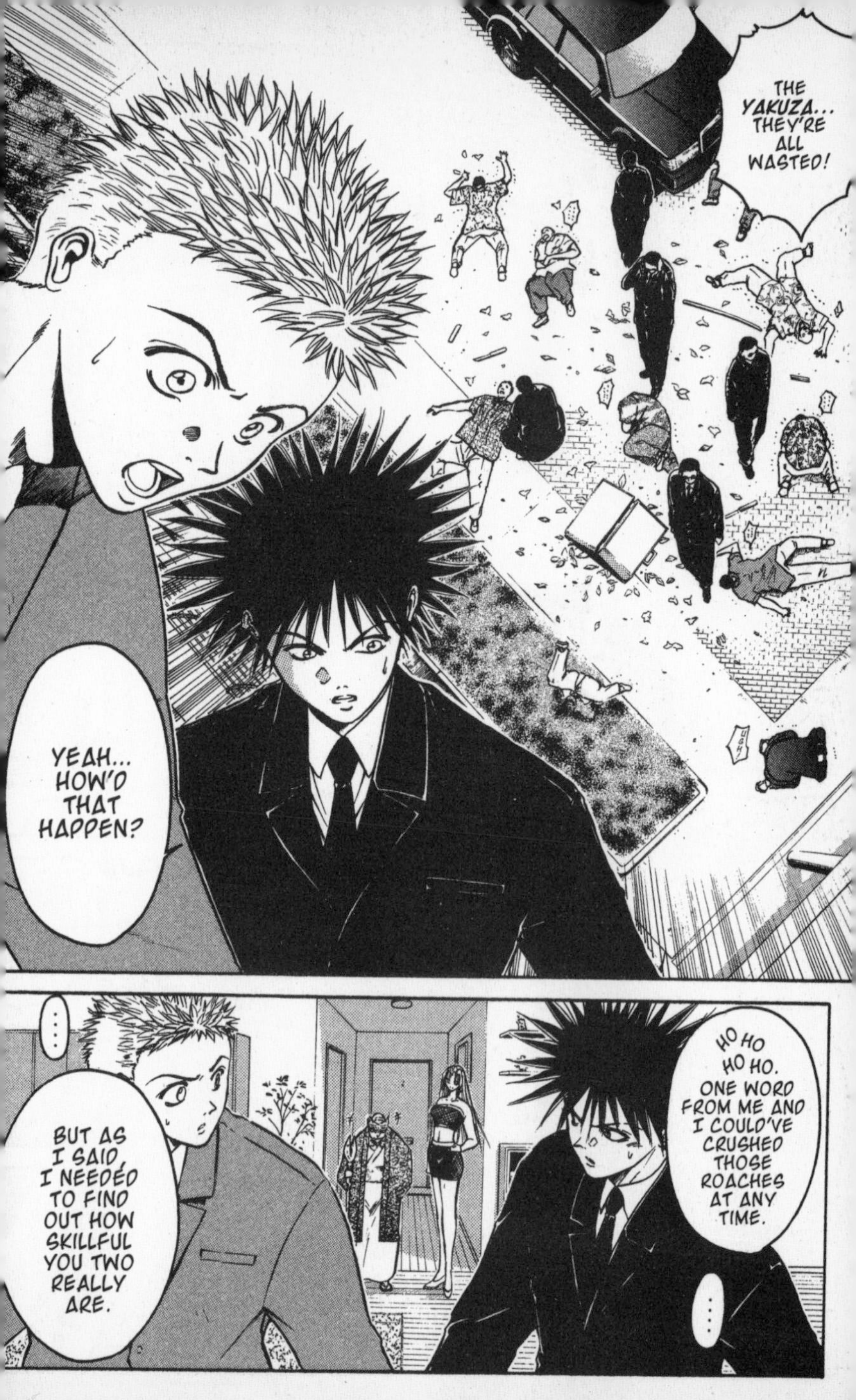
THE YAKUZA... THEY'RE ALL WASTED!
YEAH... HOW'D THAT HAPPEN?
HO HO HO HO. ONE WORD FROM ME AND I COULD'VE CRUSHED THOSE ROACHES AT ANY TIME.
....
....
BUT AS I SAID, I NEEDED TO FIND OUT HOW SKILLFUL YOU TWO REALLY ARE.

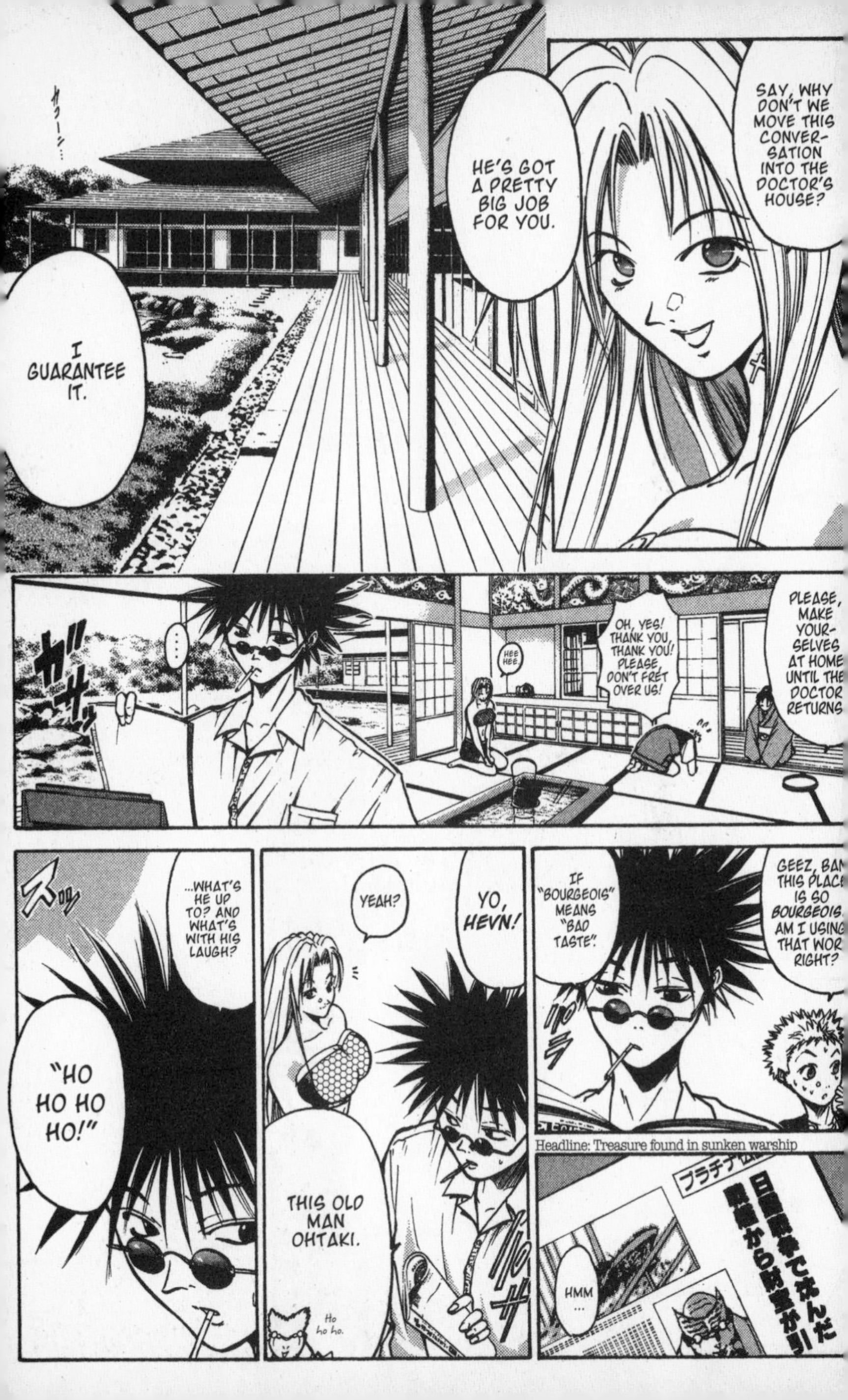
SAY, WHY DON'T WE MOVE THIS CONVER-SATION INTO THE DOCTOR'S HOUSE?
HE'S GOT A PRETTY BIG JOB FOR YOU.
I GUARANTEE IT.
PLEASE, MAKE YOUR-SELVES AT HOME UNTIL THE DOCTOR RETURNS
OH, YES! THANK YOU THANK YOU! PLEASE, DON'T FRET OVER US!
HEE HEE.
....
ガサッ
GEEZ, BAN THIS PLACE IS SO BOURGEOIS AM I USING THAT WOR RIGHT?
IF "BOURGEOIS" MEANS "BAD TASTE".
Headline: Treasure found in sunken warship
日露戦争で沈んだ
戦艦から財宝が引
HMM ...
YO, HEVN!
YEAH?
THIS OLD MAN OHTAKI.
Ho ho ho.
...WHAT'S HE UP TO? AND WHAT'S WITH HIS LAUGH?
"HO HO HO HO!"
ス

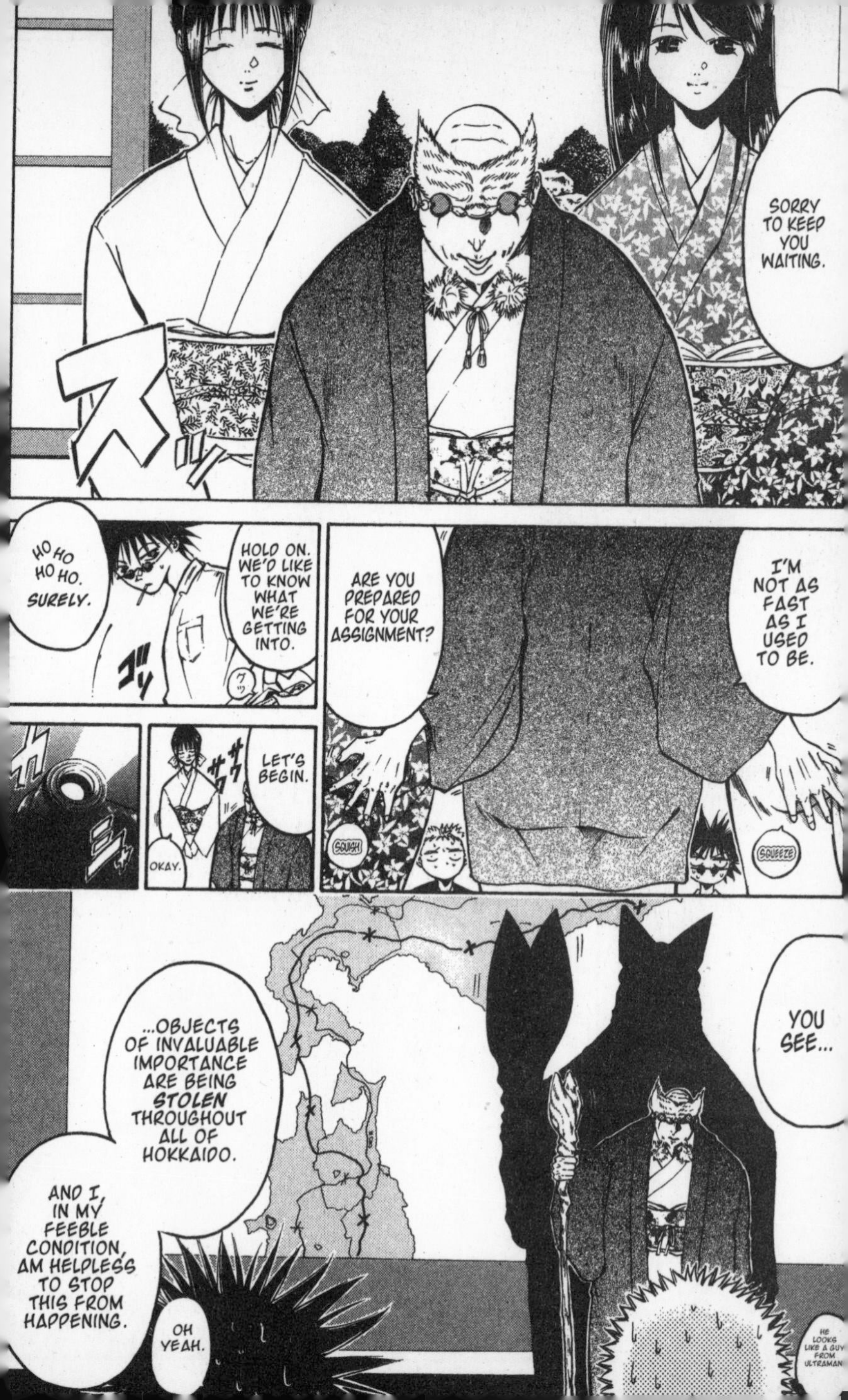
SORRY TO KEEP YOU WAITING.
I'M NOT AS FAST AS I USED TO BE.
ARE YOU PREPARED FOR YOUR ASSIGNMENT?
SQUEEZE
SOUGH
HOLD ON. WE'D LIKE TO KNOW WHAT WE'RE GETTING INTO.
HO HO HO HO. SURELY.
LET'S BEGIN.
OKAY.
YOU SEE...
...OBJECTS OF INVALUABLE IMPORTANCE ARE BEING STOLEN THROUGHOUT ALL OF HOKKAIDO.
AND I, IN MY FEEBLE CONDITION, AM HELPLESS TO STOP THIS FROM HAPPENING.
OH YEAH.
HE LOOKS LIKE A GUY FROM ULTRAMAN

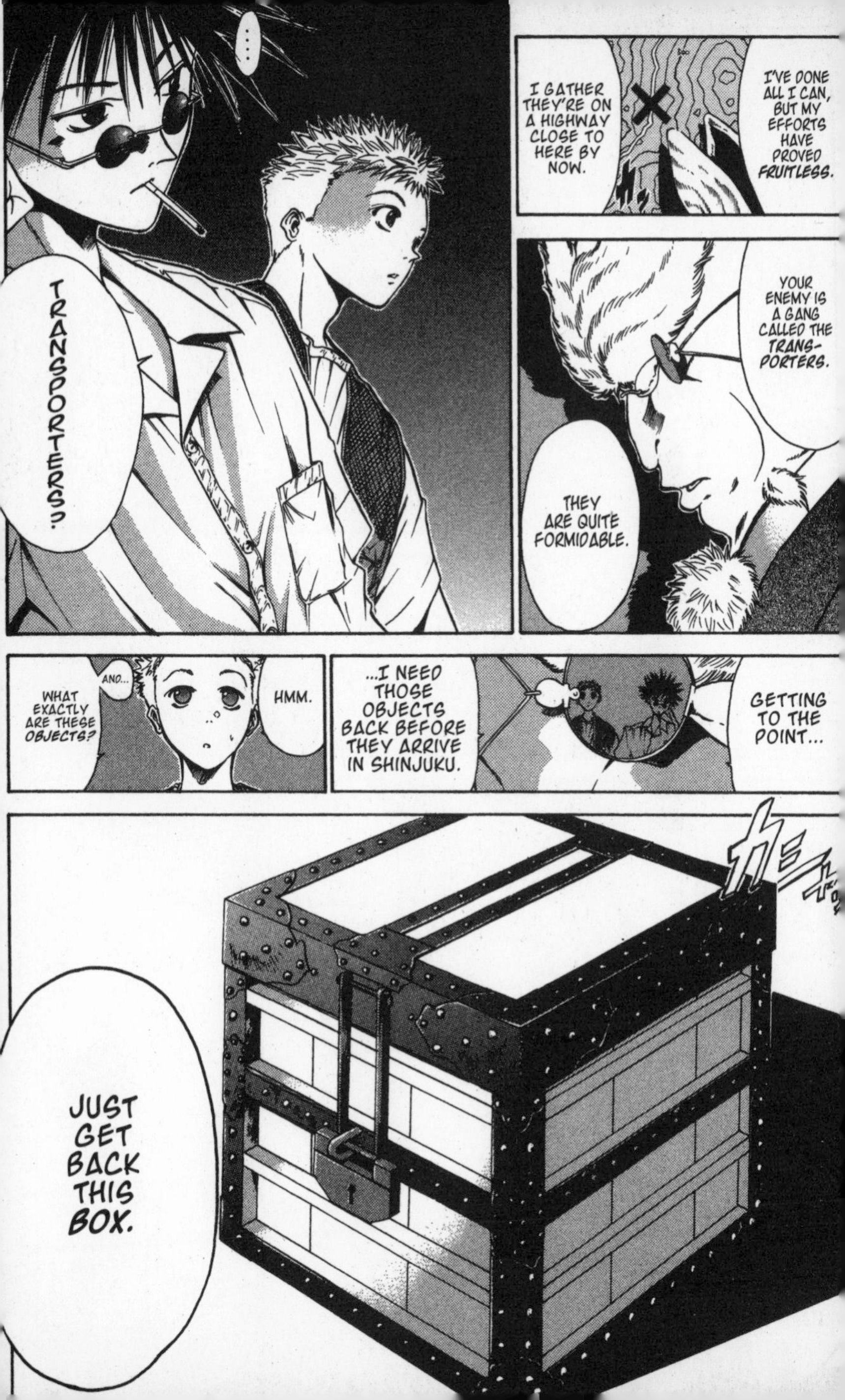
I'VE DONE ALL I CAN, BUT MY EFFORTS HAVE PROVED FRUITLESS.
I GATHER THEY'RE ON A HIGHWAY CLOSE TO HERE BY NOW.
YOUR ENEMY IS A GANG CALLED THE TRANSPORTERS.
THEY ARE QUITE FORMIDABLE.
...
TRANSPORTERS?
GETTING TO THE POINT...
...I NEED THOSE OBJECTS BACK BEFORE THEY ARRIVE IN SHINJUKU.
HMM.
AND...
WHAT EXACTLY ARE THESE OBJECTS?
JUST GET BACK THIS BOX.

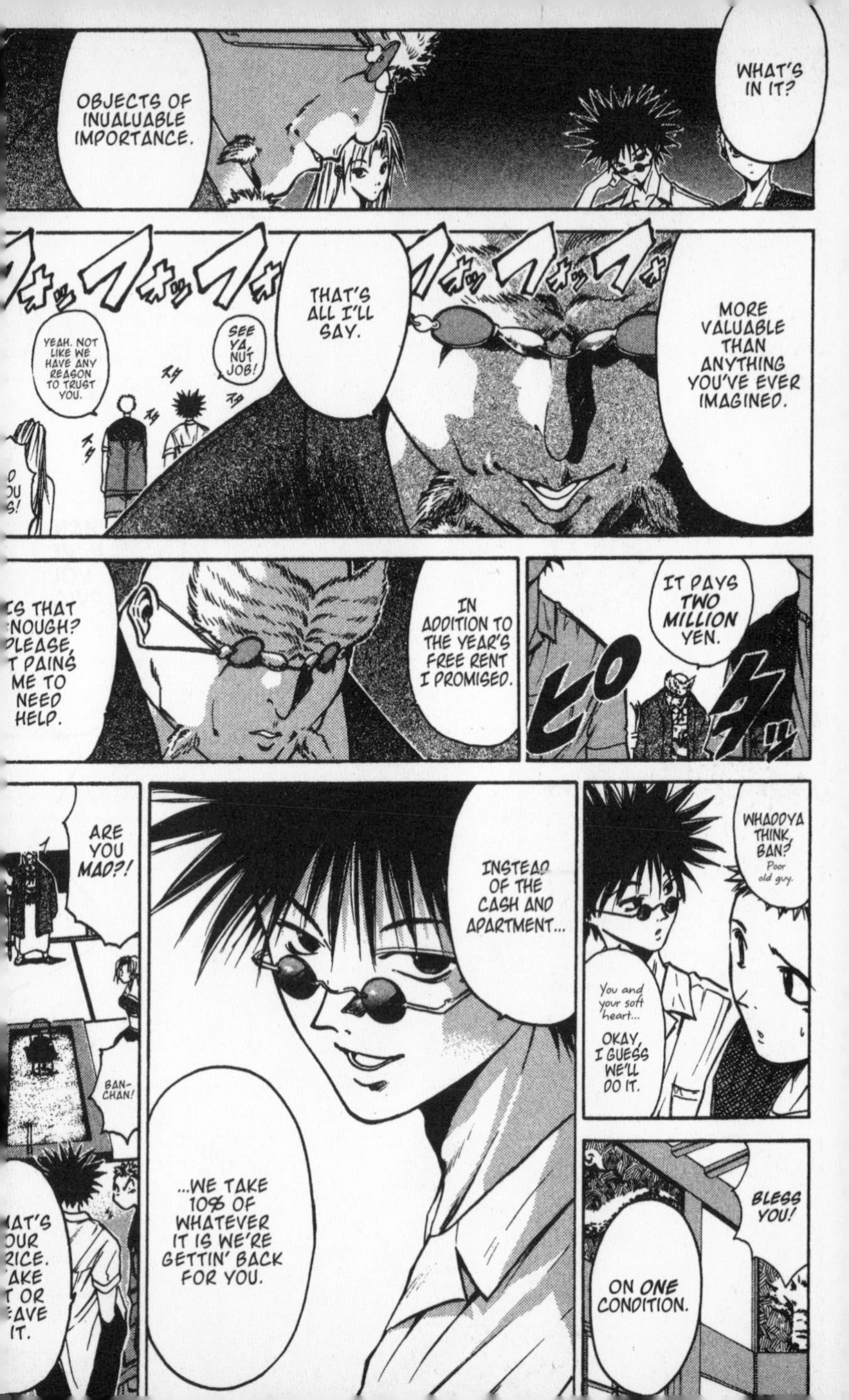
WHAT'S IN IT?
OBJECTS OF INUALUABLE IMPORTANCE.
MORE VALUABLE THAN ANYTHING YOU'VE EVER IMAGINED.
THAT'S ALL I'LL SAY.
SEE YA, NUT JOB!
YEAH. NOT LIKE WE HAVE ANY REASON TO TRUST YOU.
IT PAYS TWO MILLION YEN.
IN ADDITION TO THE YEAR'S FREE RENT I PROMISED.
S THAT ENOUGH? PLEASE, T PAINS ME TO NEED HELP.
WHADDOYA THINK, BAN?
Poor old guy.
You and your soft heart...
OKAY, I GUESS WE'LL DO IT.
BLESS YOU!
ON ONE CONDITION.
INSTEAD OF THE CASH AND APARTMENT...
...WE TAKE 10% OF WHATEVER IT IS WE'RE GETTIN' BACK FOR YOU.
ARE YOU MAD?!
BAN-CHAN!
AT'S OUR RICE. AKE T OR EAVE IT.

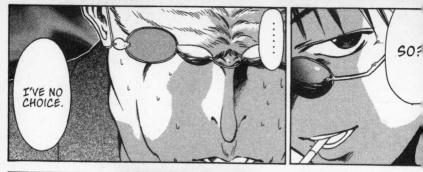

I'VE NO CHOICE.

SO?

THEN WE'RE AT YOUR SERVICE!

HEY, BAN-CHAN...

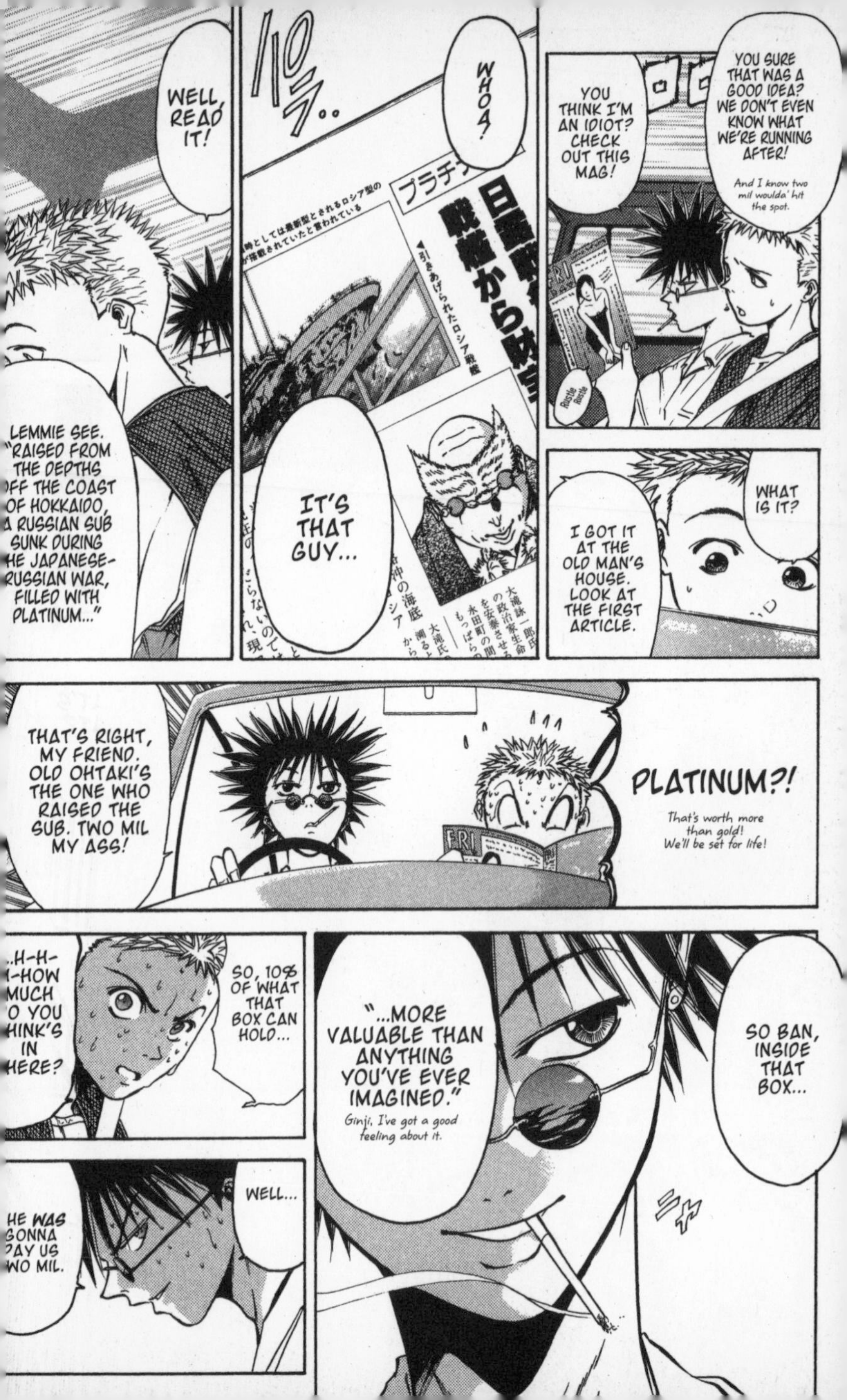

YOU SURE THAT WAS A GOOD IDEA? WE DON'T EVEN KNOW WHAT WE'RE RUNNING AFTER!
And I know two mil woulda' hit the spot.
YOU THINK I'M AN IDIOT? CHECK OUT THIS MAG!
Rustle Rustle
WHAT IS IT?
I GOT IT AT THE OLD MAN'S HOUSE. LOOK AT THE FIRST ARTICLE.
WHOA!
IT'S THAT GUY...
戦艦から財宝
引きあげられたロシア戦艦
WELL, READ IT!
LEMMIE SEE. "RAISED FROM THE DEPTHS OFF THE COAST OF HOKKAIDO, A RUSSIAN SUB SUNK DURING HE JAPANESE-RUSSIAN WAR, FILLED WITH PLATINUM..."
PLATINUM?!
That's worth more than gold! We'll be set for life!
THAT'S RIGHT, MY FRIEND. OLD OHTAKI'S THE ONE WHO RAISED THE SUB. TWO MIL MY ASS!
SO BAN, INSIDE THAT BOX...
"...MORE VALUABLE THAN ANYTHING YOU'VE EVER IMAGINED."
Ginji, I've got a good feeling about it.
SO, 10% OF WHAT THAT BOX CAN HOLD...
..H-H-H-HOW MUCH O YOU HINK'S IN HERE?
WELL...
HE WAS GONNA PAY US WO MIL.

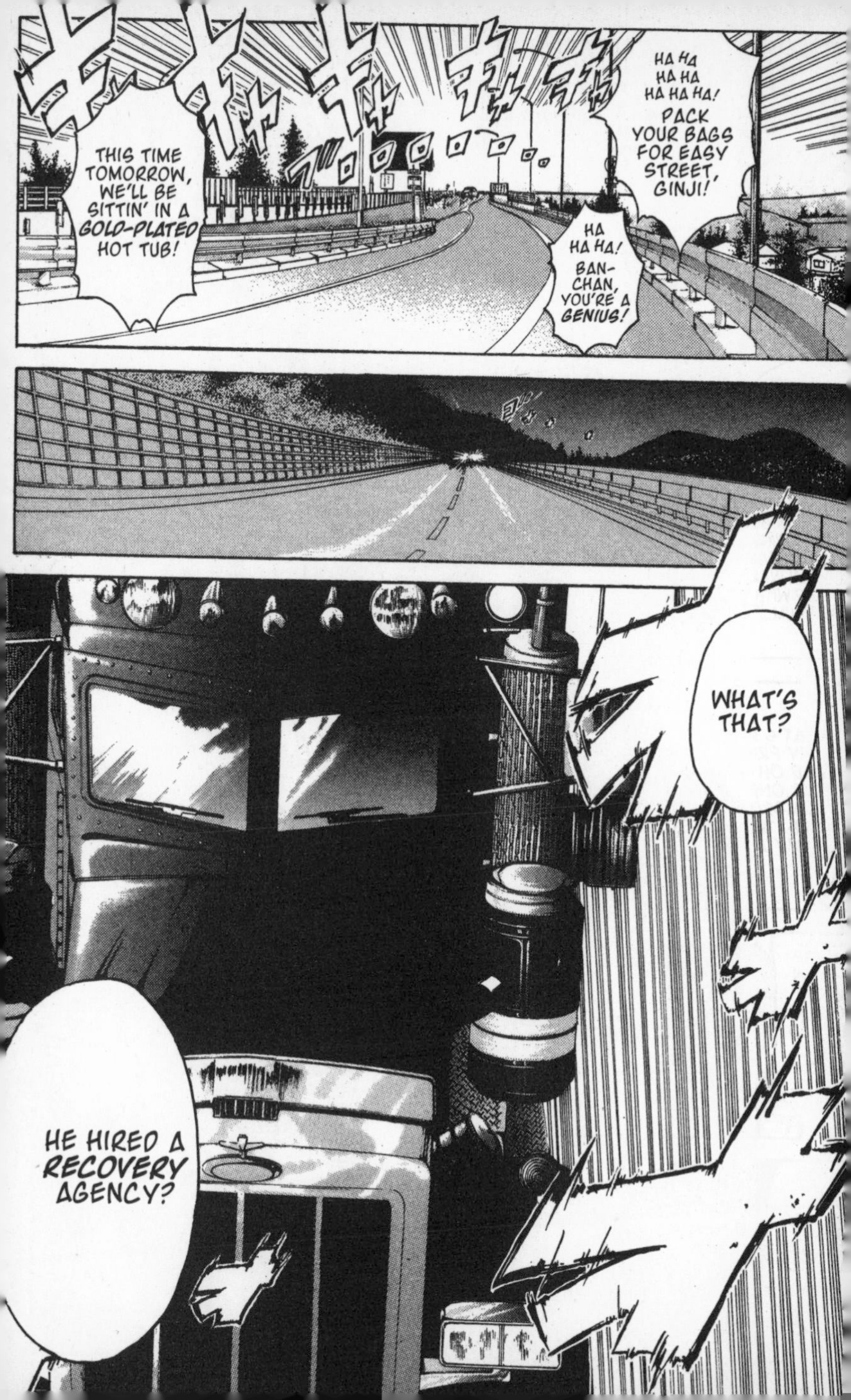
HA HA HA HA HA HA HA! PACK YOUR BAGS FOR EASY STREET, GINJI!
HA HA HA! BAN-CHAN, YOU'RE A *GENIUS!*
THIS TIME TOMORROW, WE'LL BE SITTIN' IN A *GOLD-PLATED* HOT TUB!
WHAT'S THAT?
HE HIRED A *RECOVERY* AGENCY?

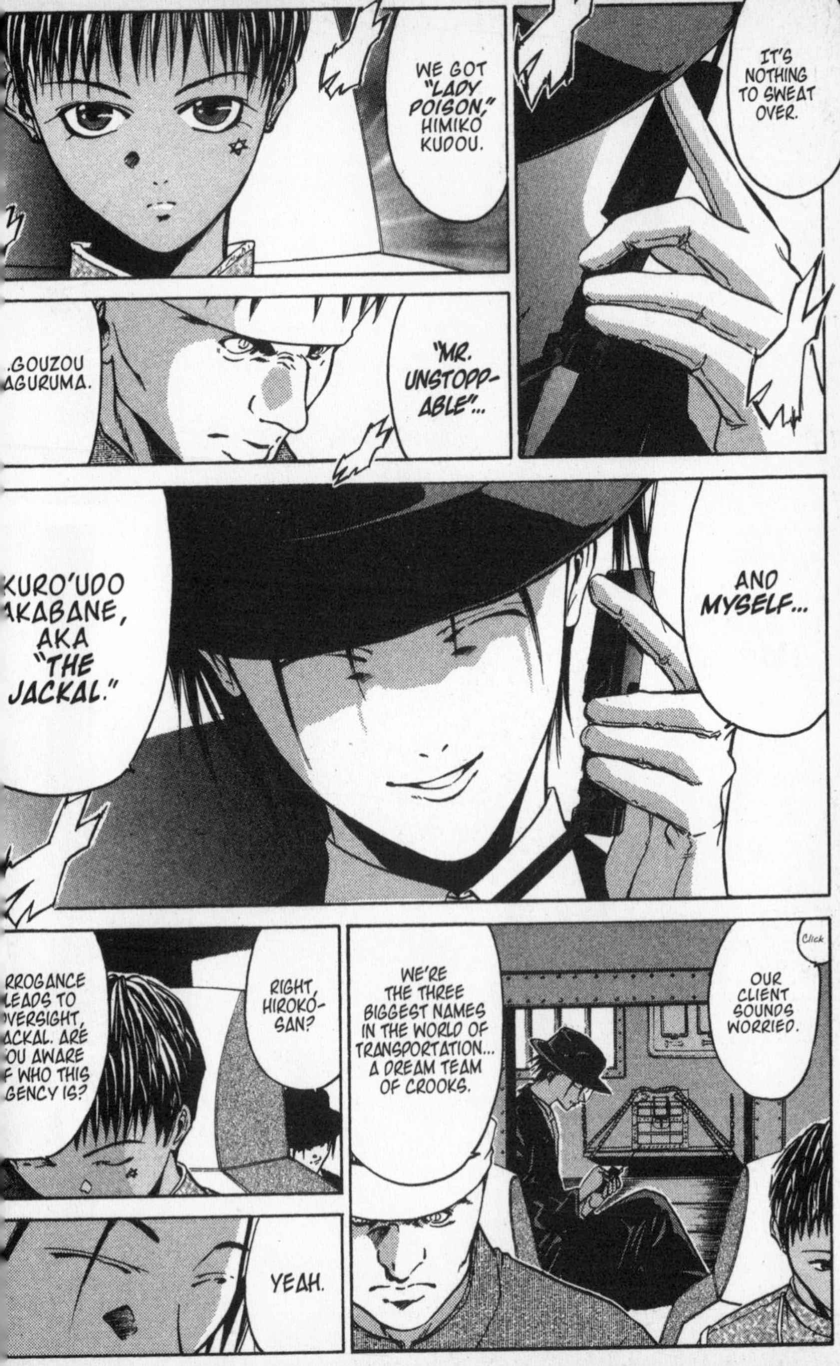
IT'S NOTHING TO SWEAT OVER.
WE GOT "LADY POISON," HIMIKO KUDOU.
"MR. UNSTOPP-ABLE"...
.GOUZOU AGURUMA.
AND MYSELF...
KURO'UDO AKABANE, AKA "THE JACKAL."
Click
OUR CLIENT SOUNDS WORRIED.
WE'RE THE THREE BIGGEST NAMES IN THE WORLD OF TRANSPORTATION... A DREAM TEAM OF CROOKS.
RIGHT, HIROKO-SAN?
RROGANCE LEADS TO VERSIGHT, ACKAL. ARE OU AWARE F WHO THIS GENCY IS?
YEAH.

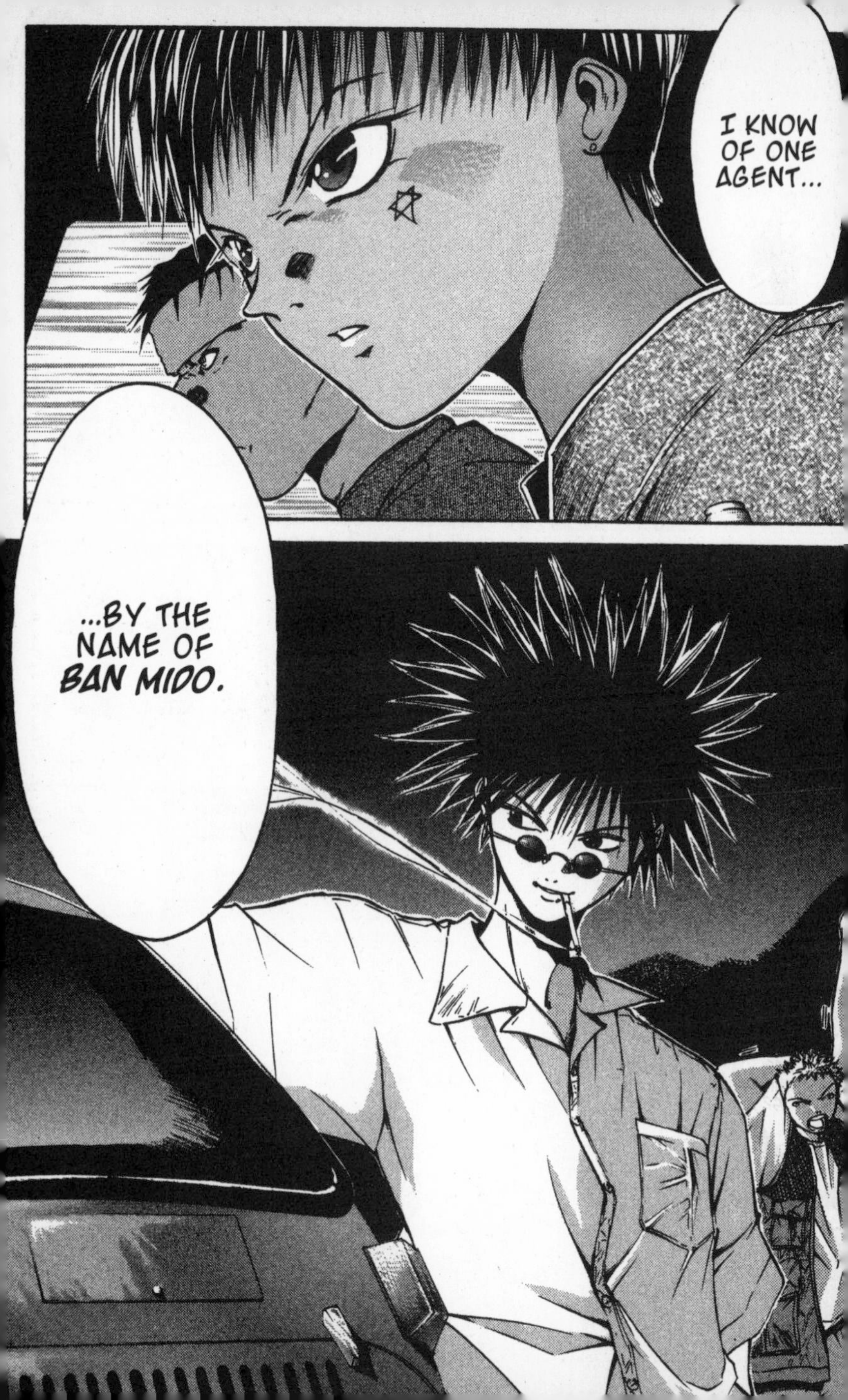
I KNOW OF ONE AGENT...
...BY THE NAME OF BAN MIDO.

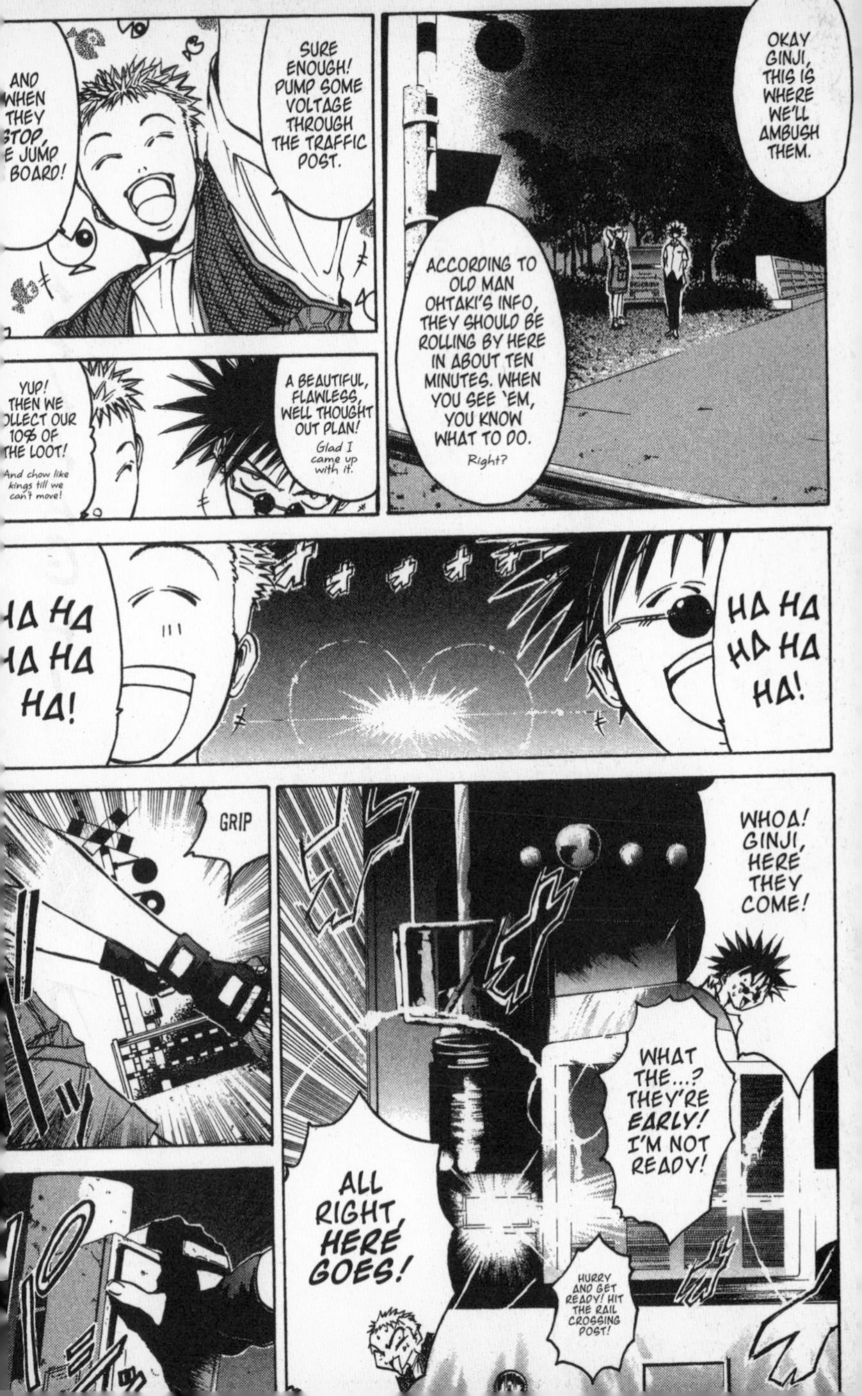
OKAY GINJI, THIS IS WHERE WE'LL AMBUSH THEM.
ACCORDING TO OLD MAN OHTAKI'S INFO, THEY SHOULD BE ROLLING BY HERE IN ABOUT TEN MINUTES. WHEN YOU SEE 'EM, YOU KNOW WHAT TO DO.
Right?
SURE ENOUGH! PUMP SOME VOLTAGE THROUGH THE TRAFFIC POST.
AND WHEN THEY STOP, E JUMP BOARD!
A BEAUTIFUL, FLAWLESS, WELL THOUGHT OUT PLAN!
Glad I came up with it.
YUP! THEN WE OLLECT OUR 10% OF THE LOOT!
And chow like kings till we can't move!
HA HA HA HA HA!
HA HA HA HA HA!
WHOA! GINJI, HERE THEY COME!
WHAT THE...? THEY'RE *EARLY!* I'M NOT READY!
HURRY AND GET READY! HIT THE RAIL CROSSING POST!
ALL RIGHT *HERE* GOES!
GRIP

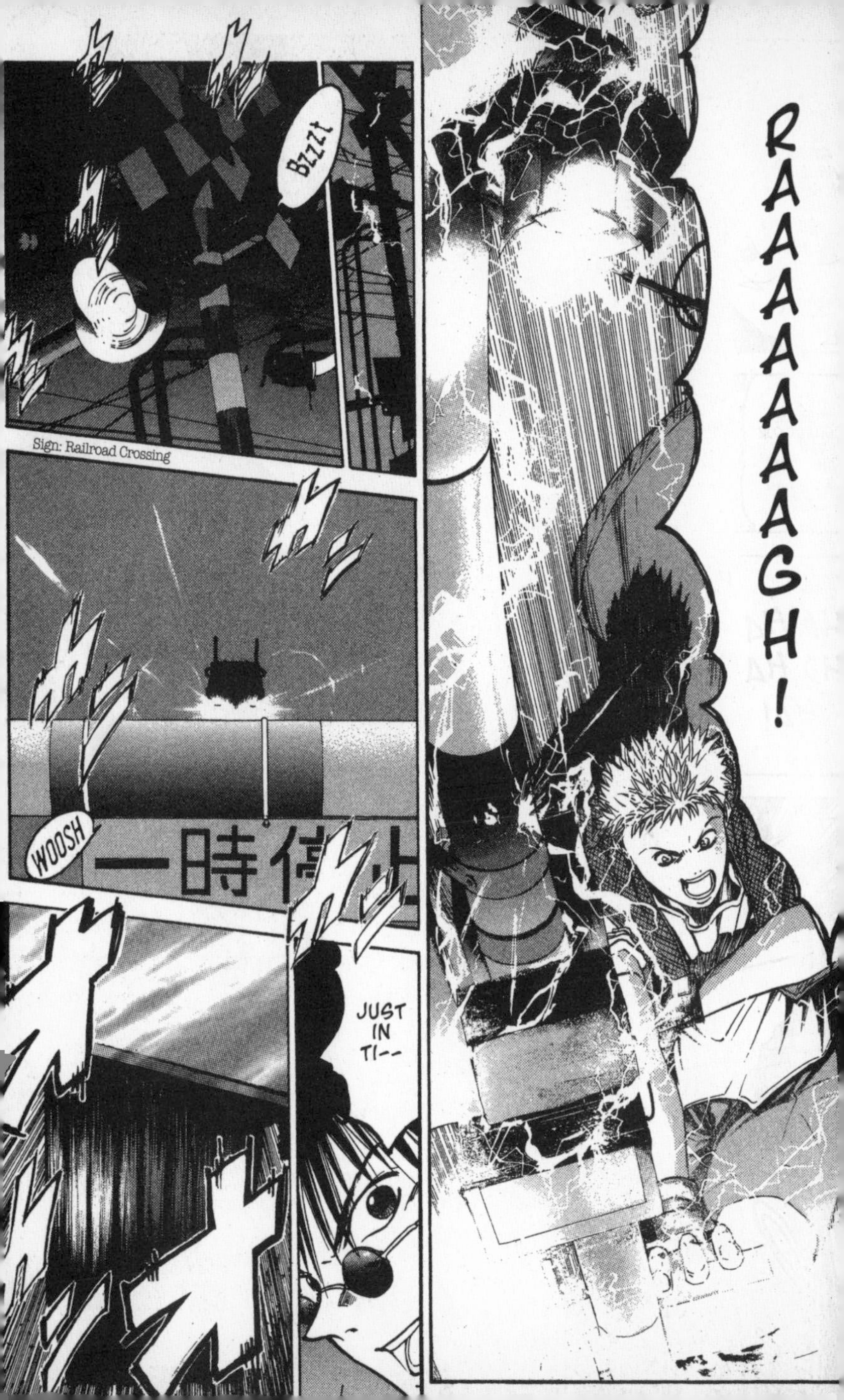
RAAAAAAAAGH!
Bzzzt
WOOSH
一時停
JUST IN TI--
Sign: Railroad Crossing

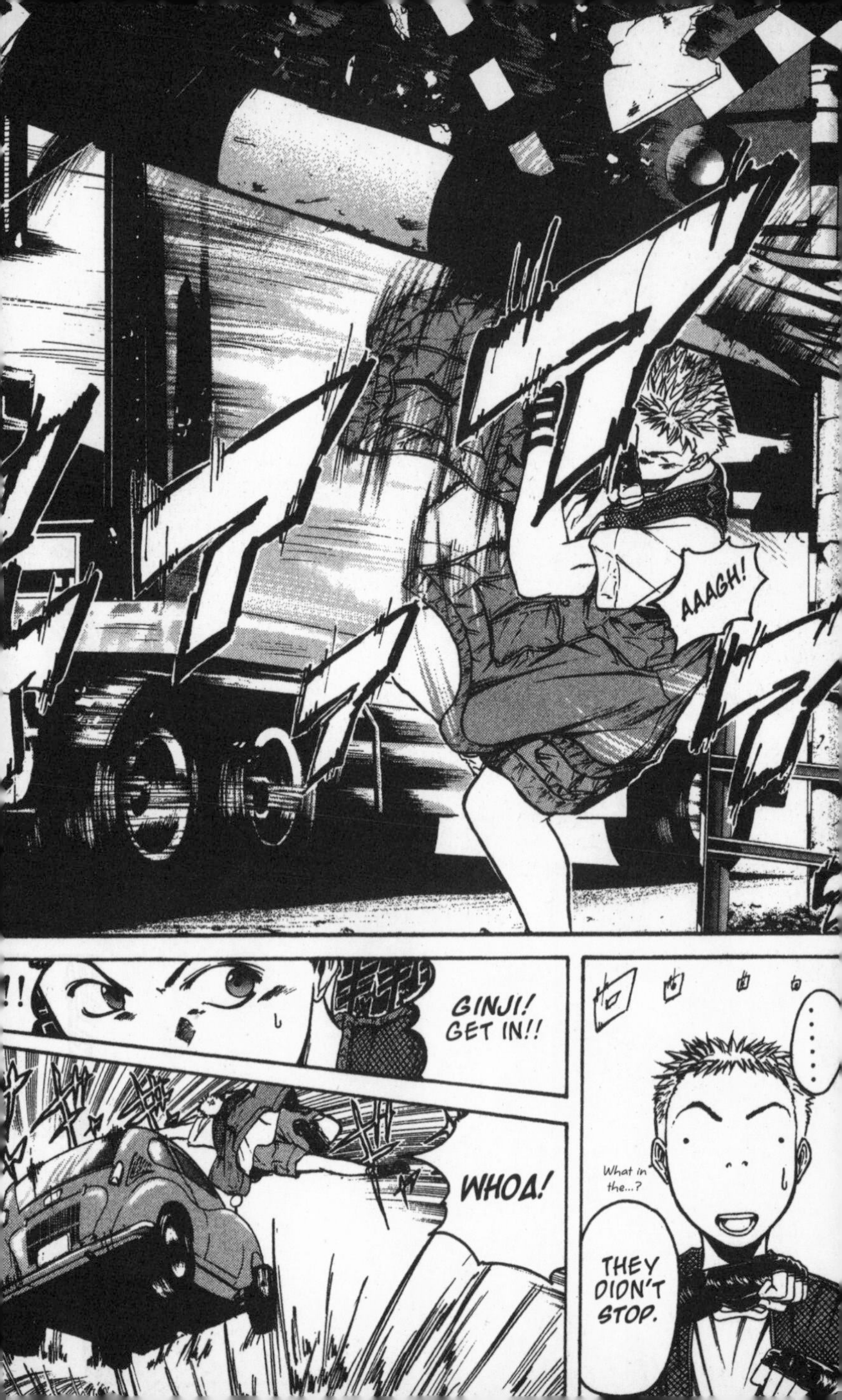
AAAGH!
......
What in the...?
THEY DIDN'T STOP.
!!
GINJI! GET IN!!
WHOA!

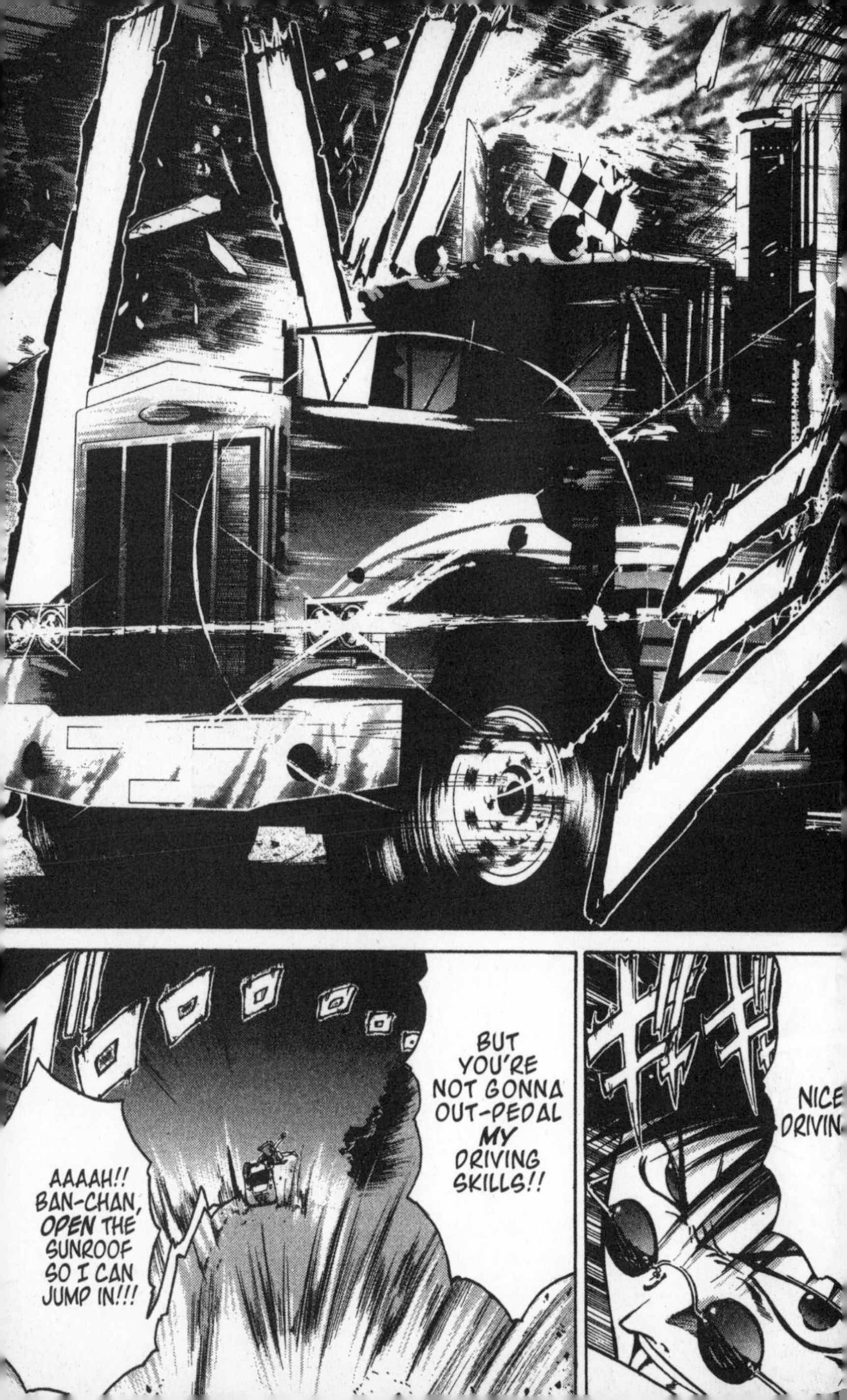
NICE DRIVIN
BUT YOU'RE NOT GONNA OUT-PEDAL MY DRIVING SKILLS!!
AAAAH!! BAN-CHAN, OPEN THE SUNROOF SO I CAN JUMP IN!!!

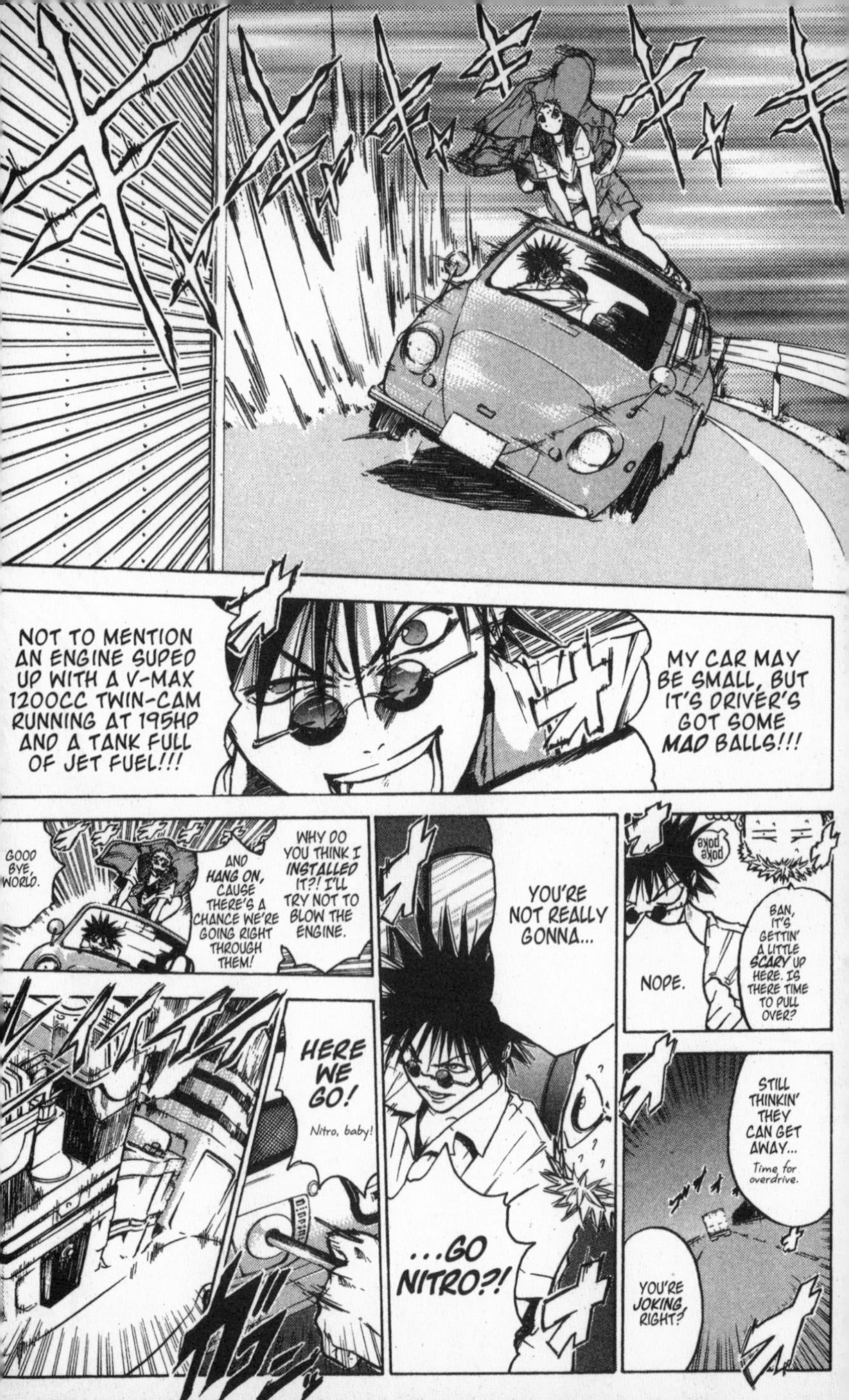

MY CAR MAY BE SMALL, BUT IT'S DRIVER'S GOT SOME MAD BALLS!!!
NOT TO MENTION AN ENGINE SUPED UP WITH A V-MAX 1200CC TWIN-CAM RUNNING AT 195HP AND A TANK FULL OF JET FUEL!!!
poke poke
BAN, IT'S GETTIN' A LITTLE SCARY UP HERE. IS THERE TIME TO PULL OVER?
NOPE.
STILL THINKIN' THEY CAN GET AWAY...
Time for overdrive.
YOU'RE JOKING, RIGHT?
YOU'RE NOT REALLY GONNA...
...GO NITRO?!
WHY DO YOU THINK I INSTALLED IT?! I'LL TRY NOT TO BLOW THE ENGINE.
AND HANG ON, CAUSE THERE'S A CHANCE WE'RE GOING RIGHT THROUGH THEM!
GOOD BYE, WORLD.
HERE WE GO!
Nitro, baby!

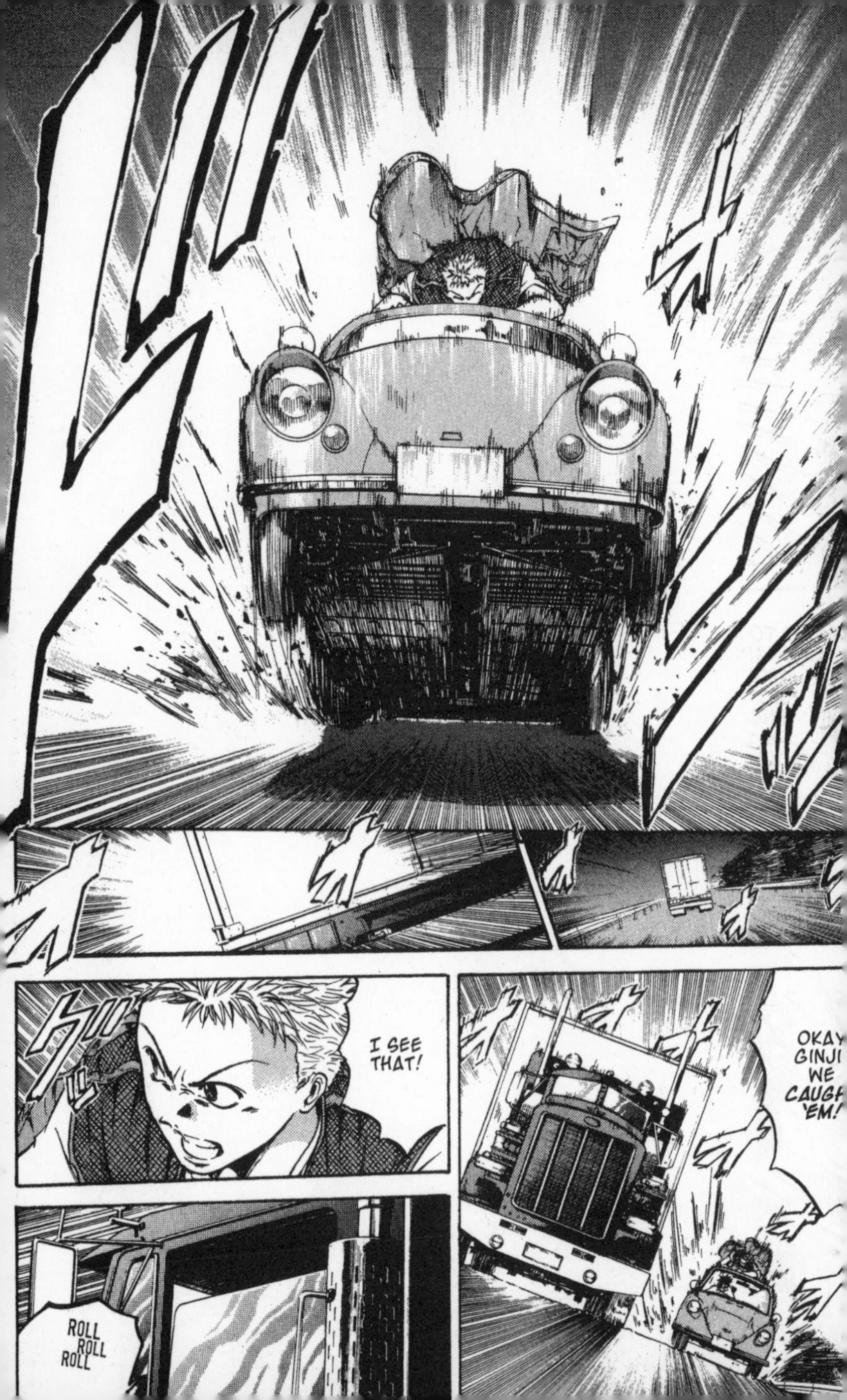
OKAY GINJI WE CAUGHT 'EM!
I SEE THAT!
ROLL ROLL ROLL

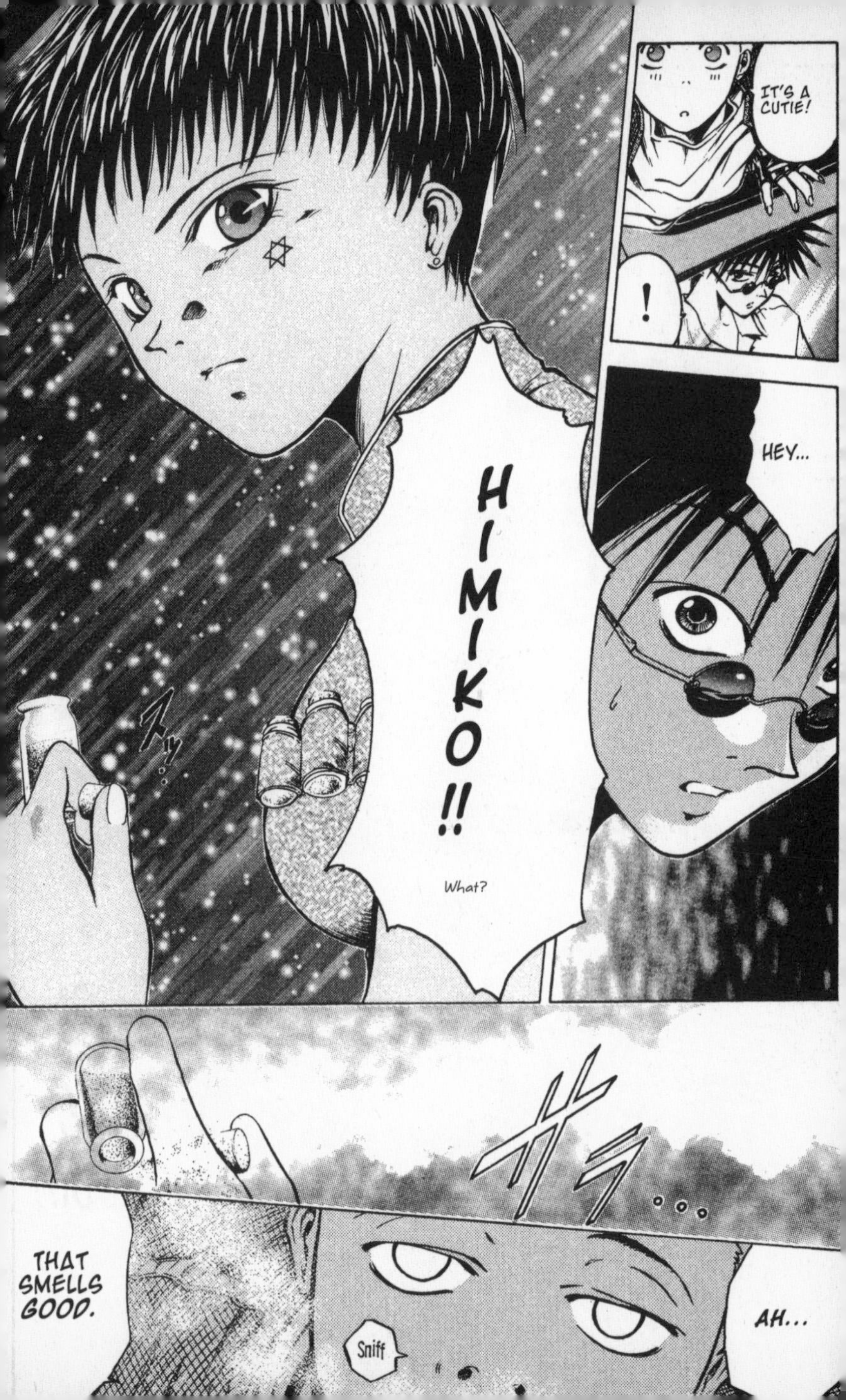
IT'S A CUTIE!
!
HEY...
HIMIKO!!
What?
AH...
Sniff
THAT SMELLS GOOD.

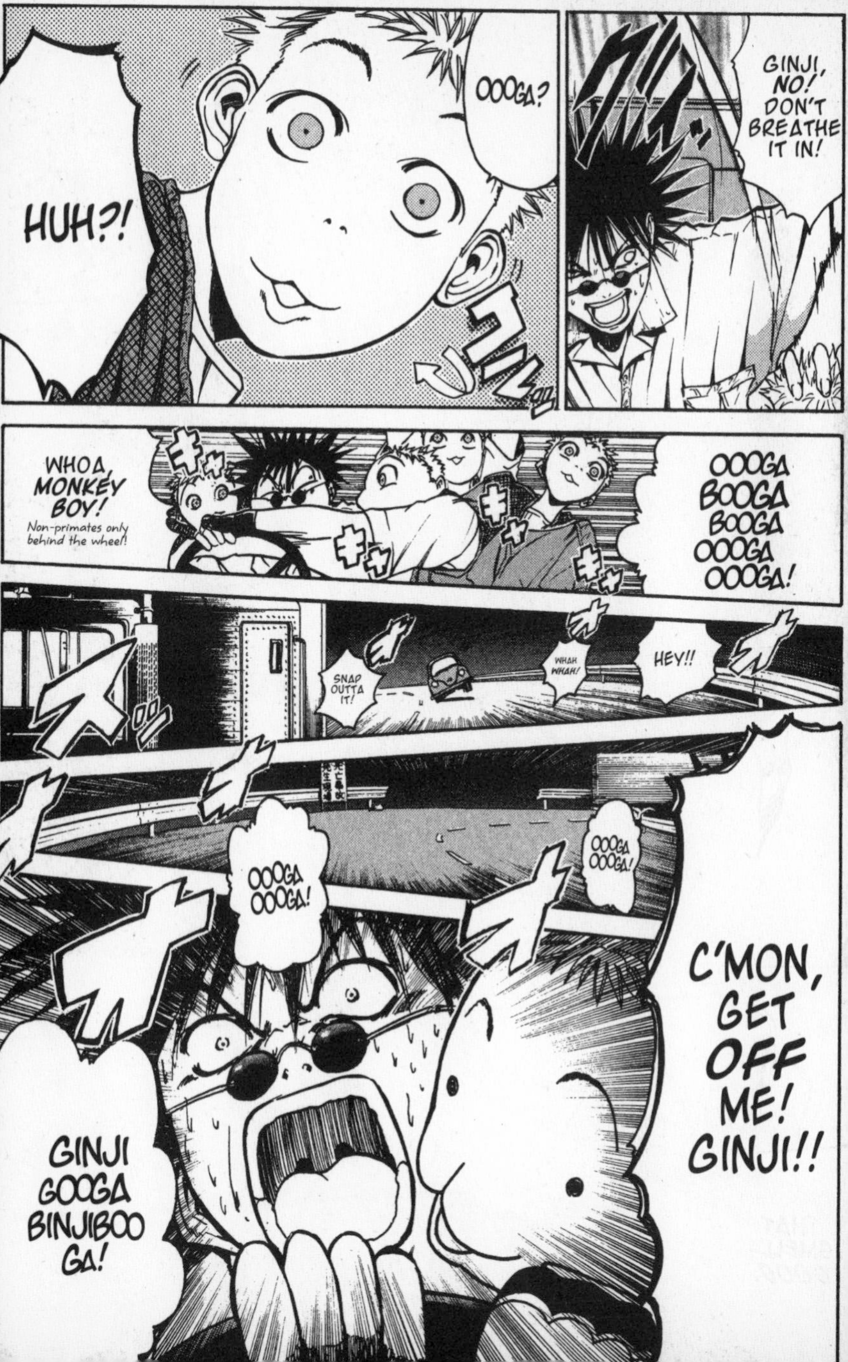
GINJI, NO! DON'T BREATHE IT IN!
OOOGA?
HUH?!
OOOGA BOOGA BOOGA OOOGA OOOGA!
WHOA, MONKEY BOY!
Non-primates only behind the wheel!
HEY!!
WHAH WHAH!
SNAP OUTTA IT!
C'MON, GET OFF ME! GINJI!!
OOOGA OOOGA!
OOOGA OOOGA!
GINJI GOOGA BINJIBOO GA!

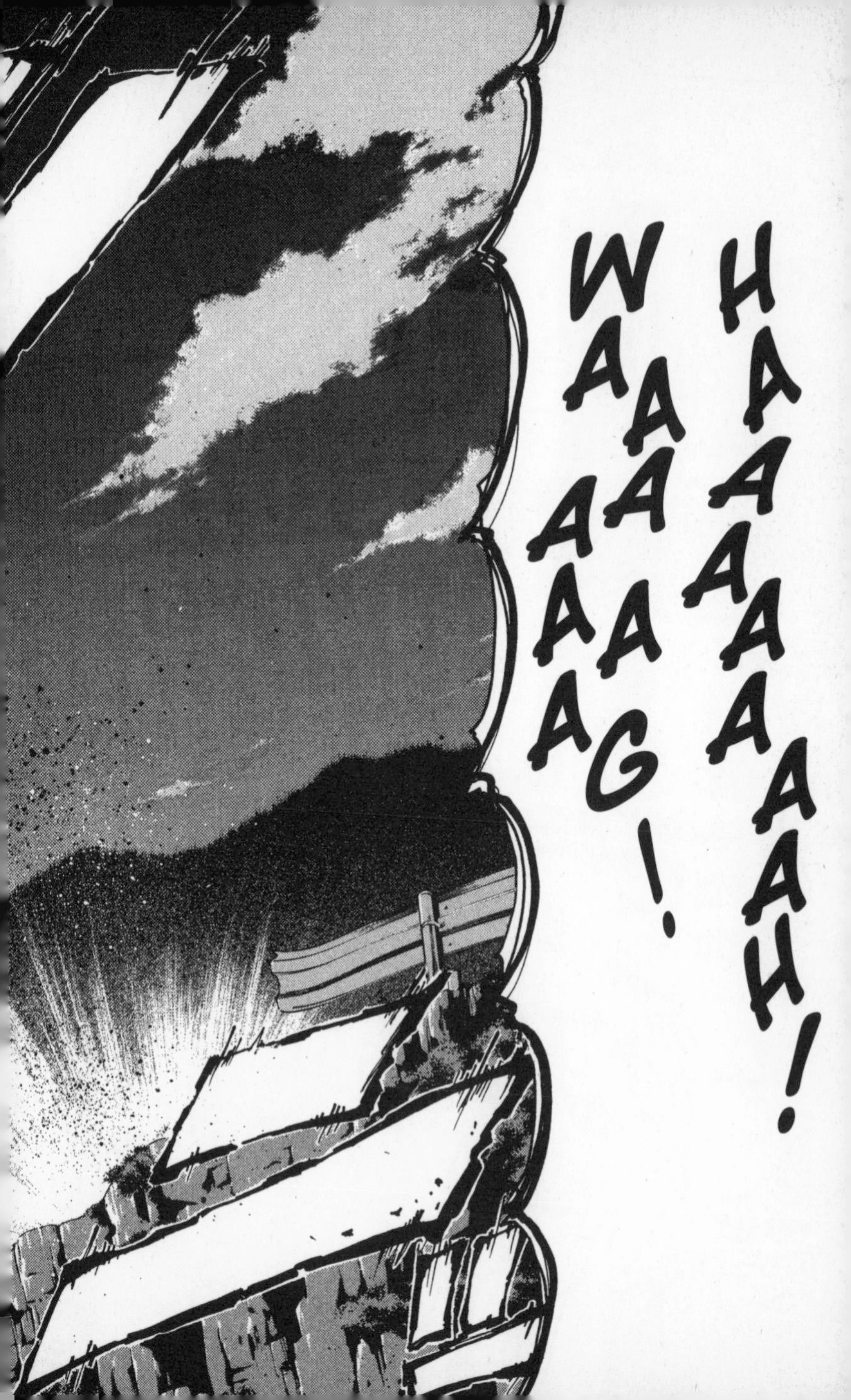
WAAAAAAAG!
HAAAAAAAH!

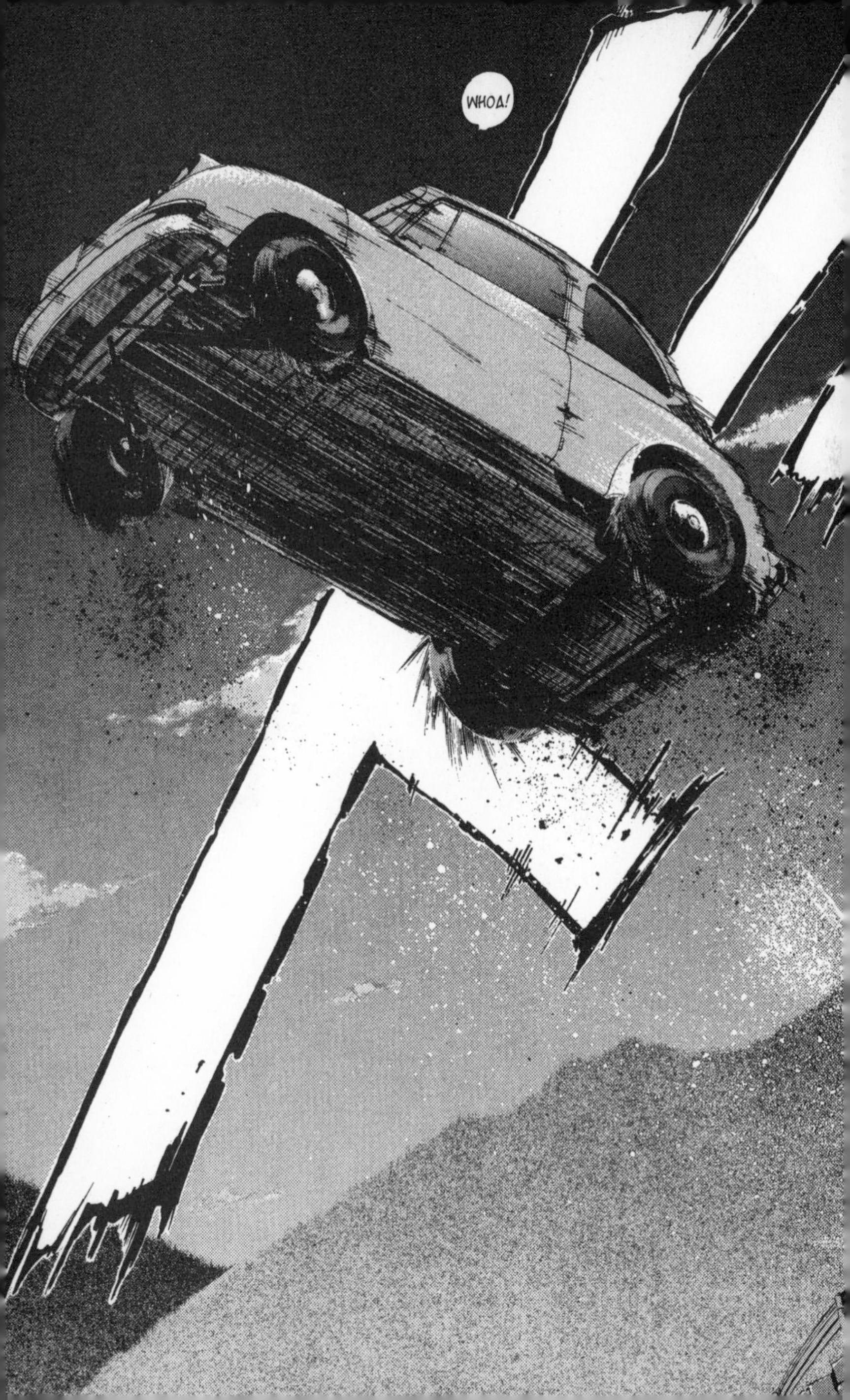
WHOA!

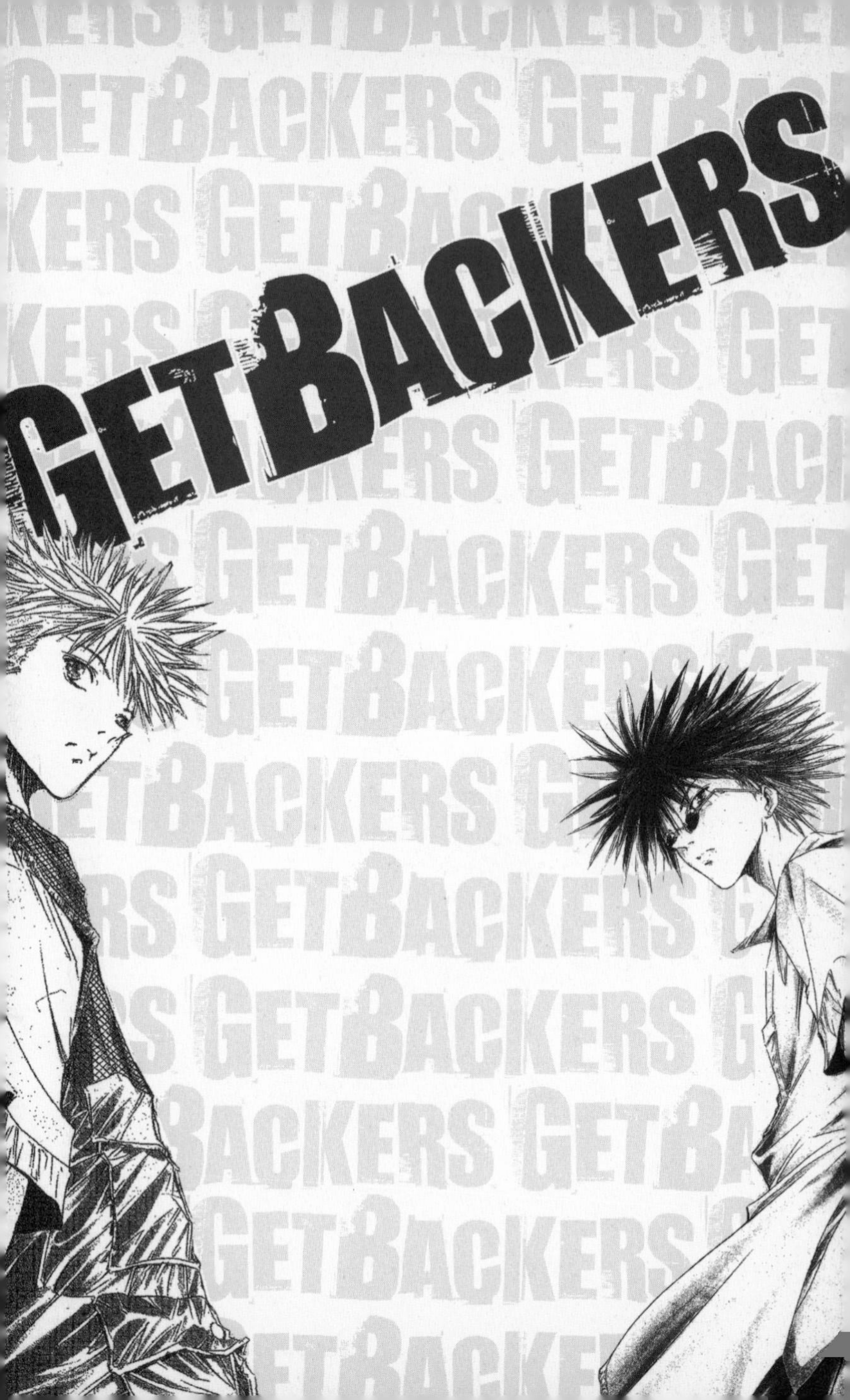
GETBACKERS

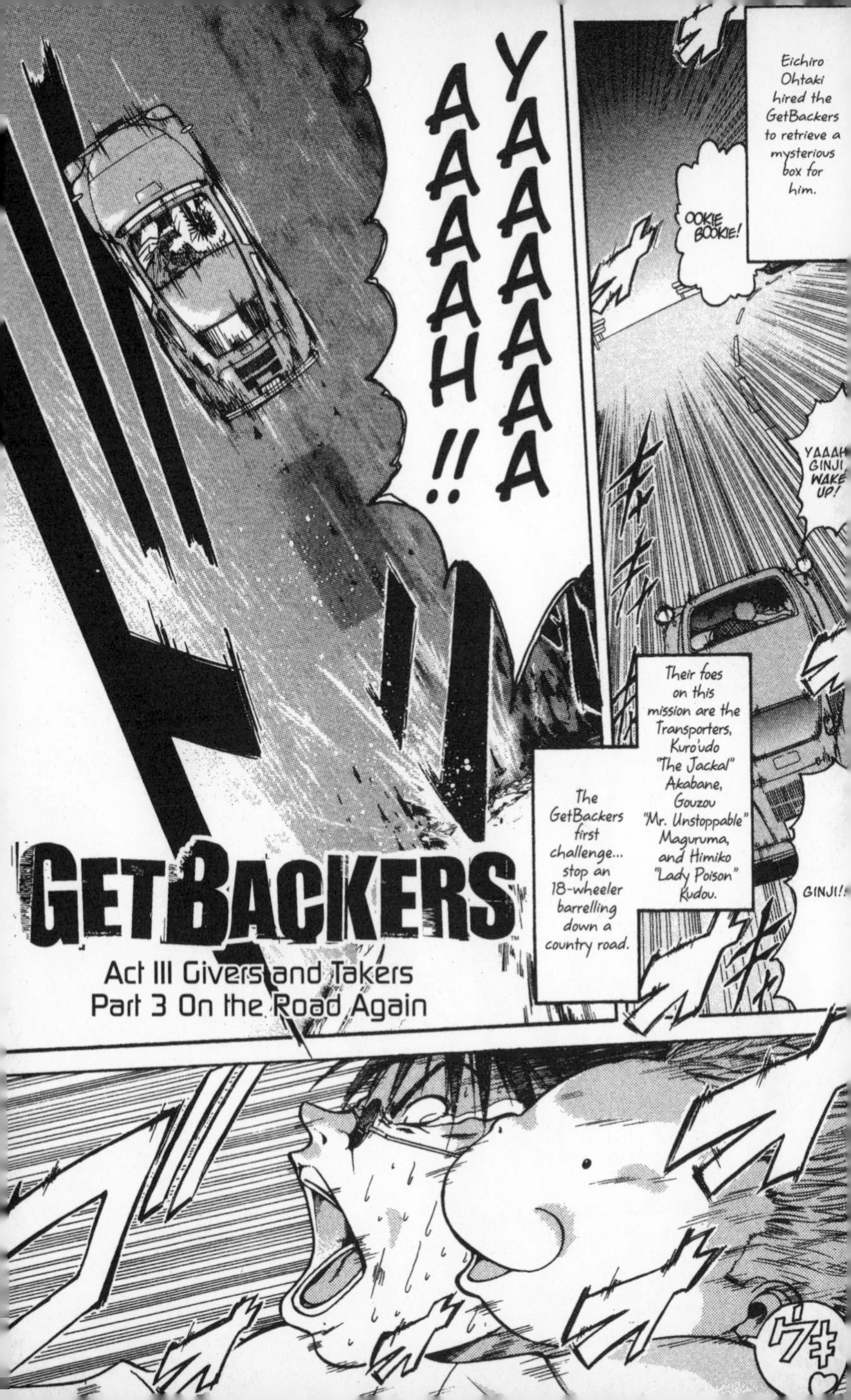
Eichiro Ohtaki hired the GetBackers to retrieve a mysterious box for him.
OOKIE BOOKIE!
YAAAH GINJI WAKE UP!
Their foes on this mission are the Transporters, Kuro'udo "The Jackal" Akabane, Gouzou "Mr. Unstoppable" Maguruma, and Himiko "Lady Poison" Kudou.
The GetBackers first challenge... stop an 18-wheeler barrelling down a country road.
GINJI!!
YAAAAAAA
AAAAAH!!
GETBACKERS™
Act III Givers and Takers
Part 3 On the Road Again
ウキ

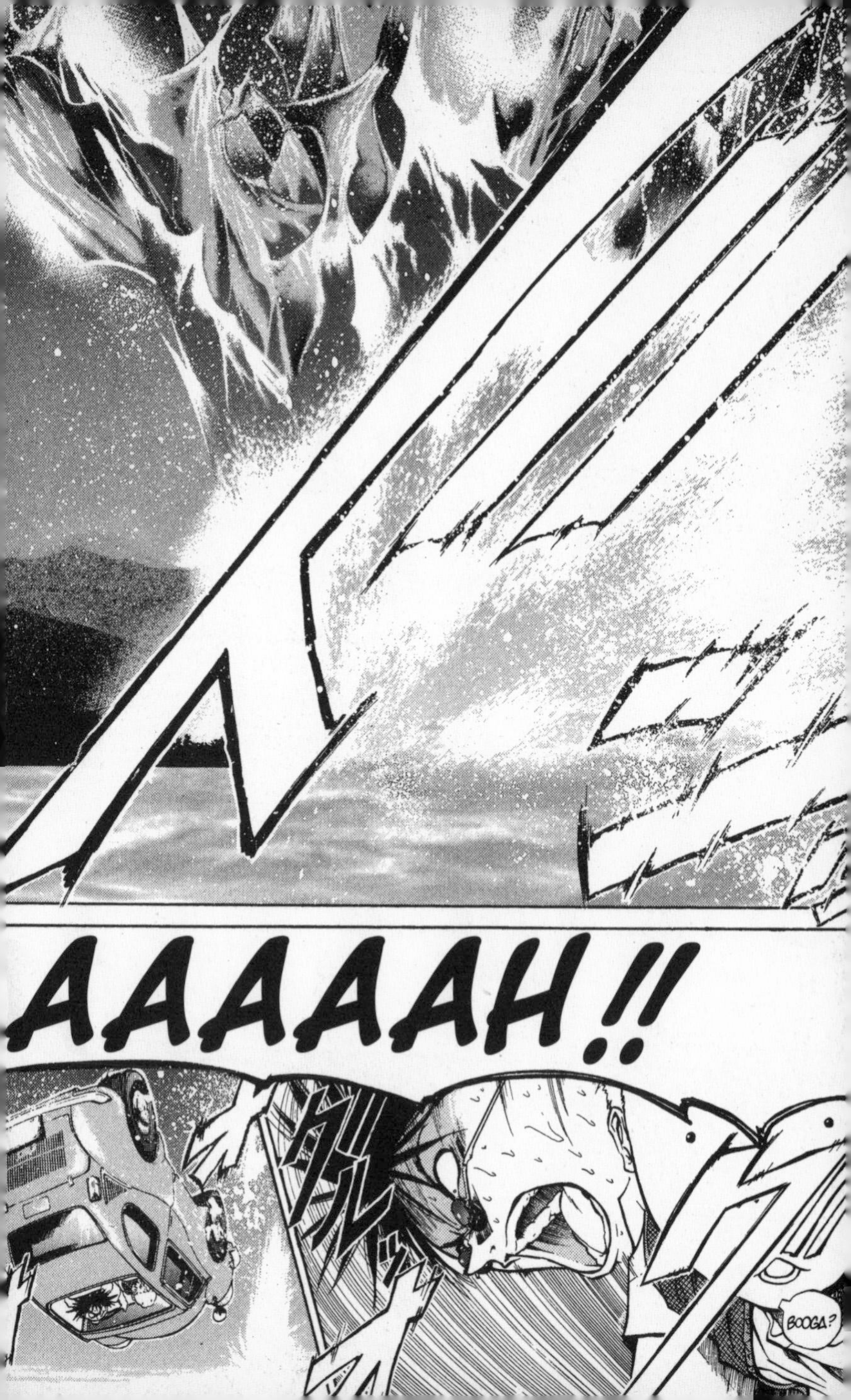
AAAAAH!!
BOOGA?

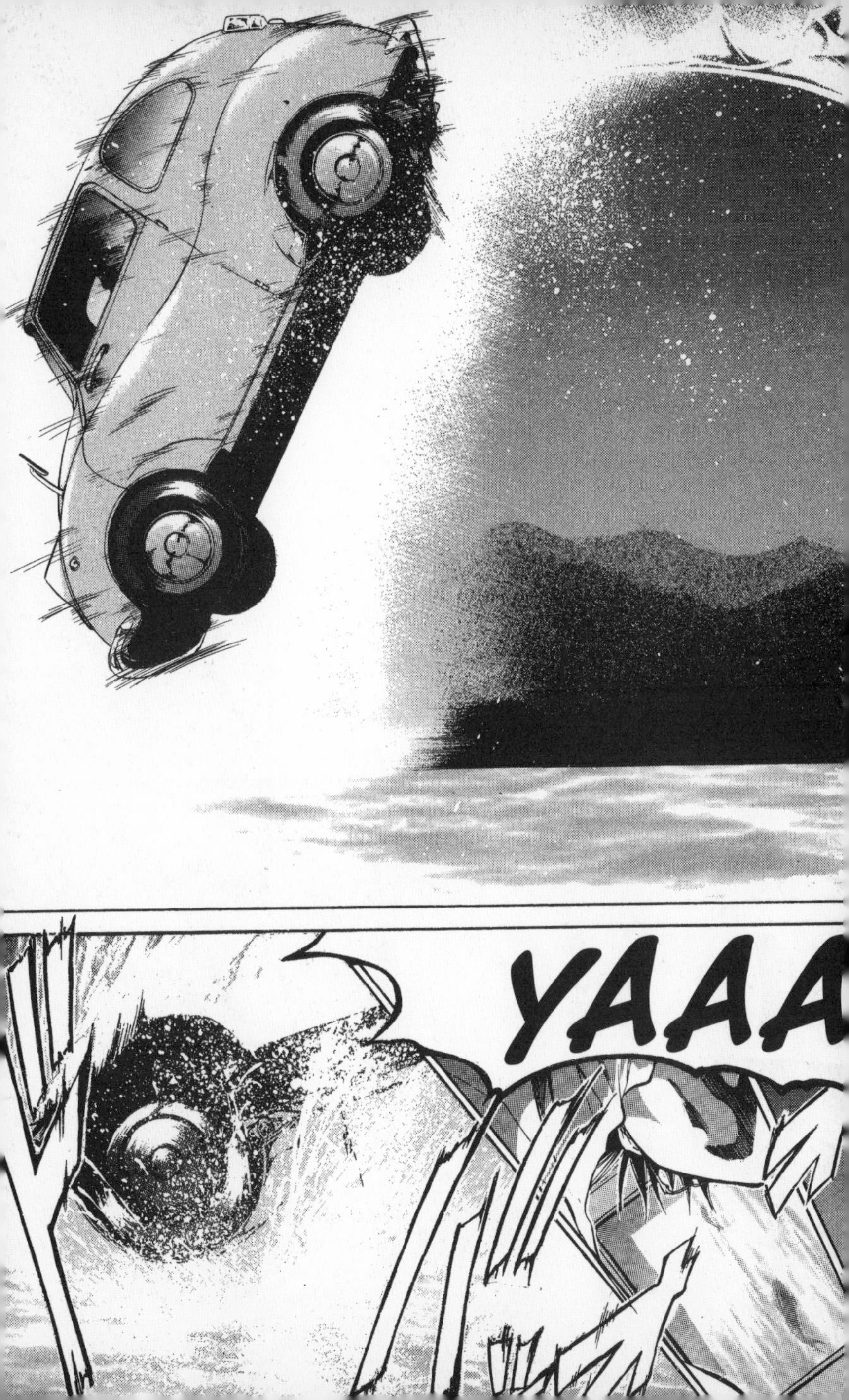
YAAA

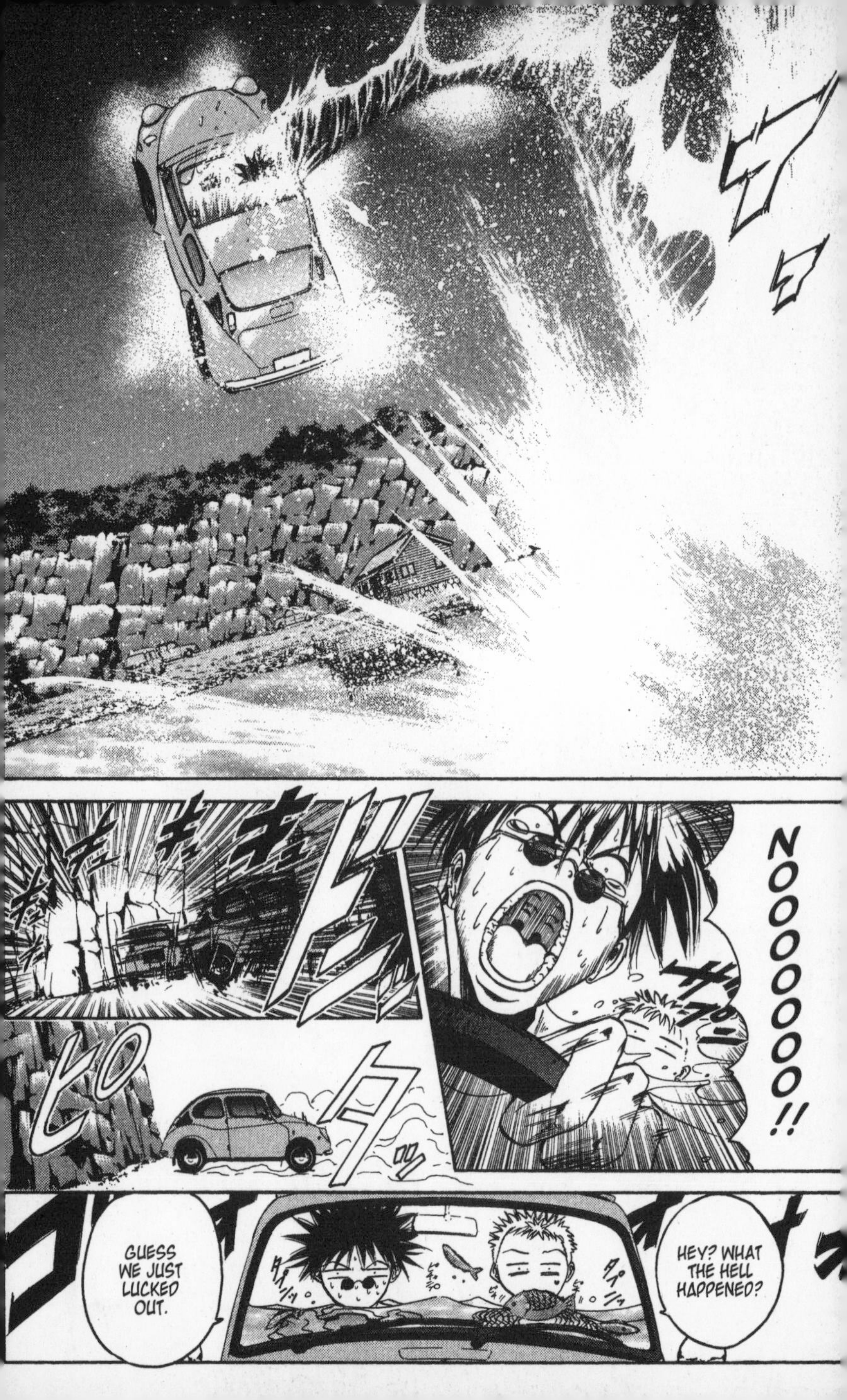
NOOOOOOOO!!
HEY? WHAT THE HELL HAPPENED?
GUESS WE JUST LUCKED OUT.

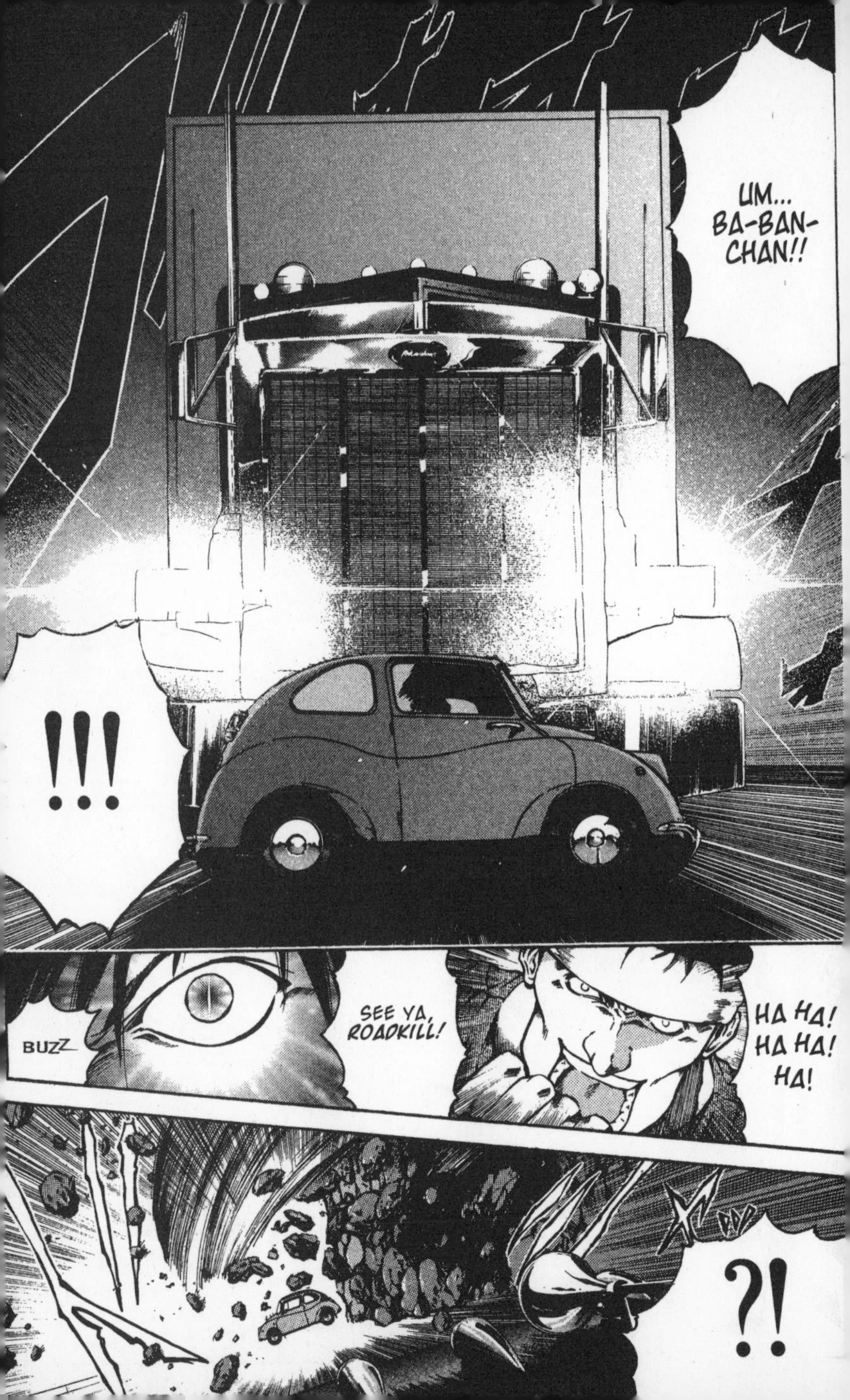
UM... BA-BAN-CHAN!!
!!!
HA HA! HA HA! HA!
SEE YA, ROADKILL!
BUZZ
?!

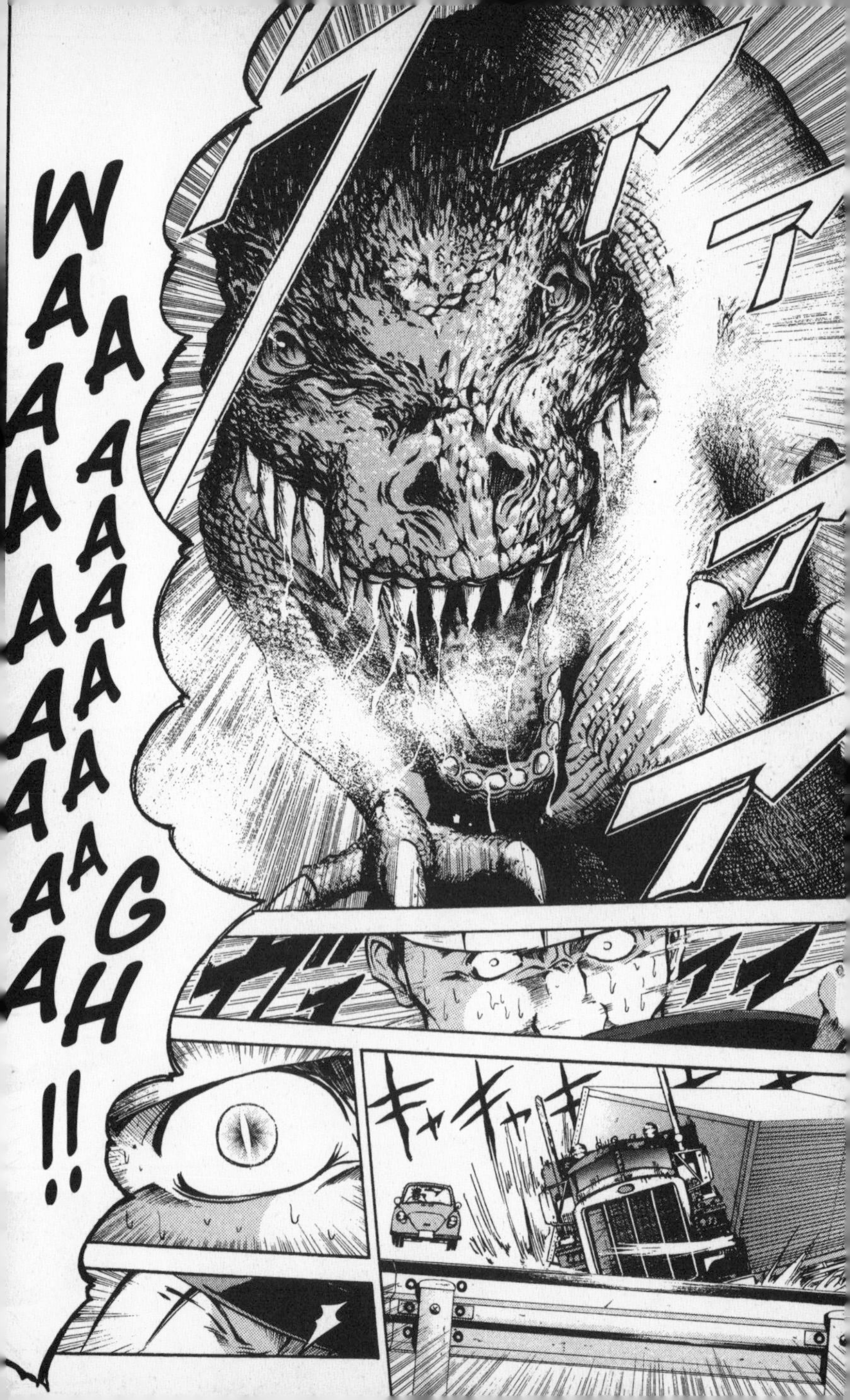
WAAAAAAAAAAAAAAAAAGH!!

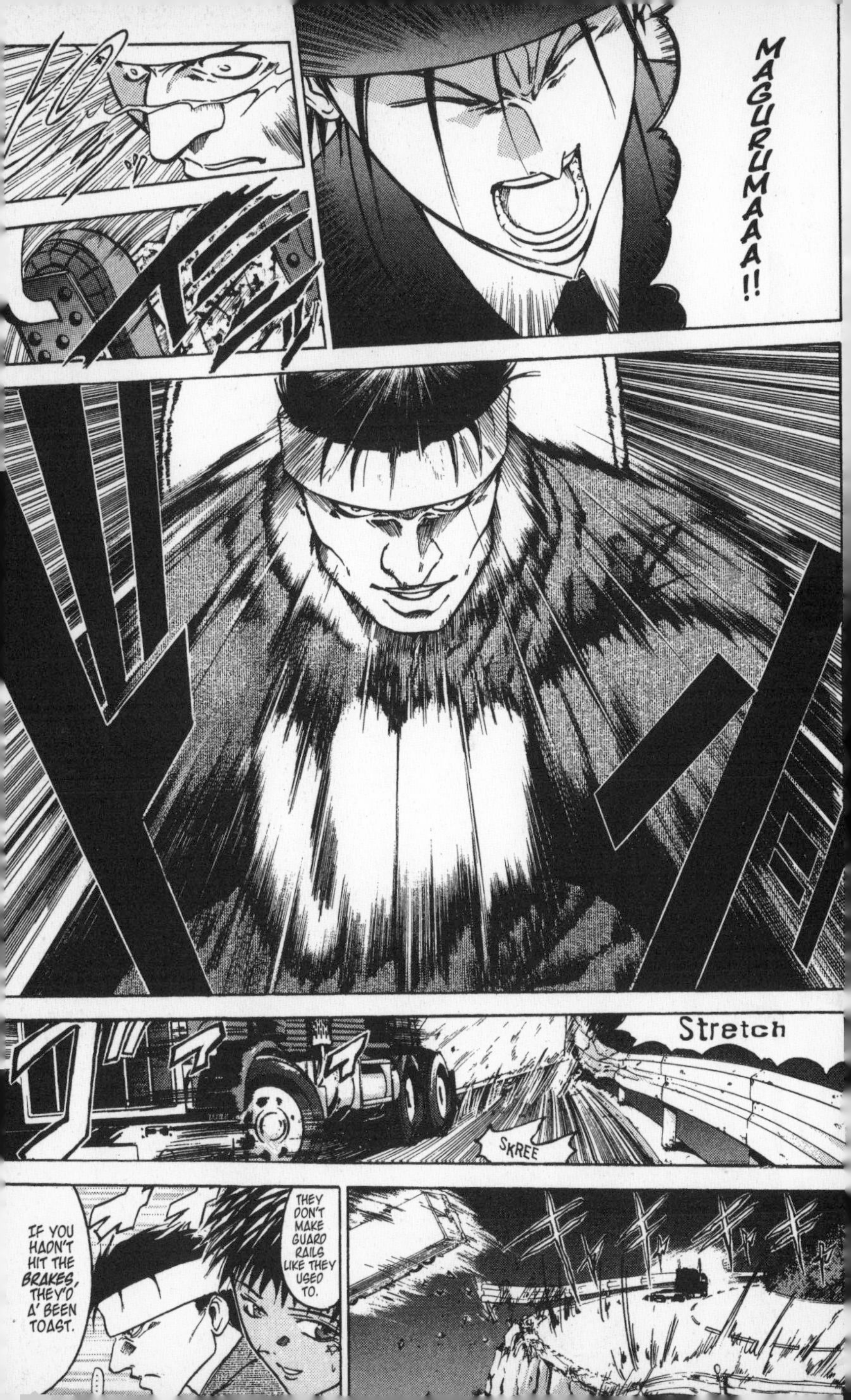

MAGURUMAAA!!
Stretch
SKREE
THEY DON'T MAKE GUARD RAILS LIKE THEY USED TO.
IF YOU HADN'T HIT THE BRAKES, THEY'D A' BEEN TOAST.

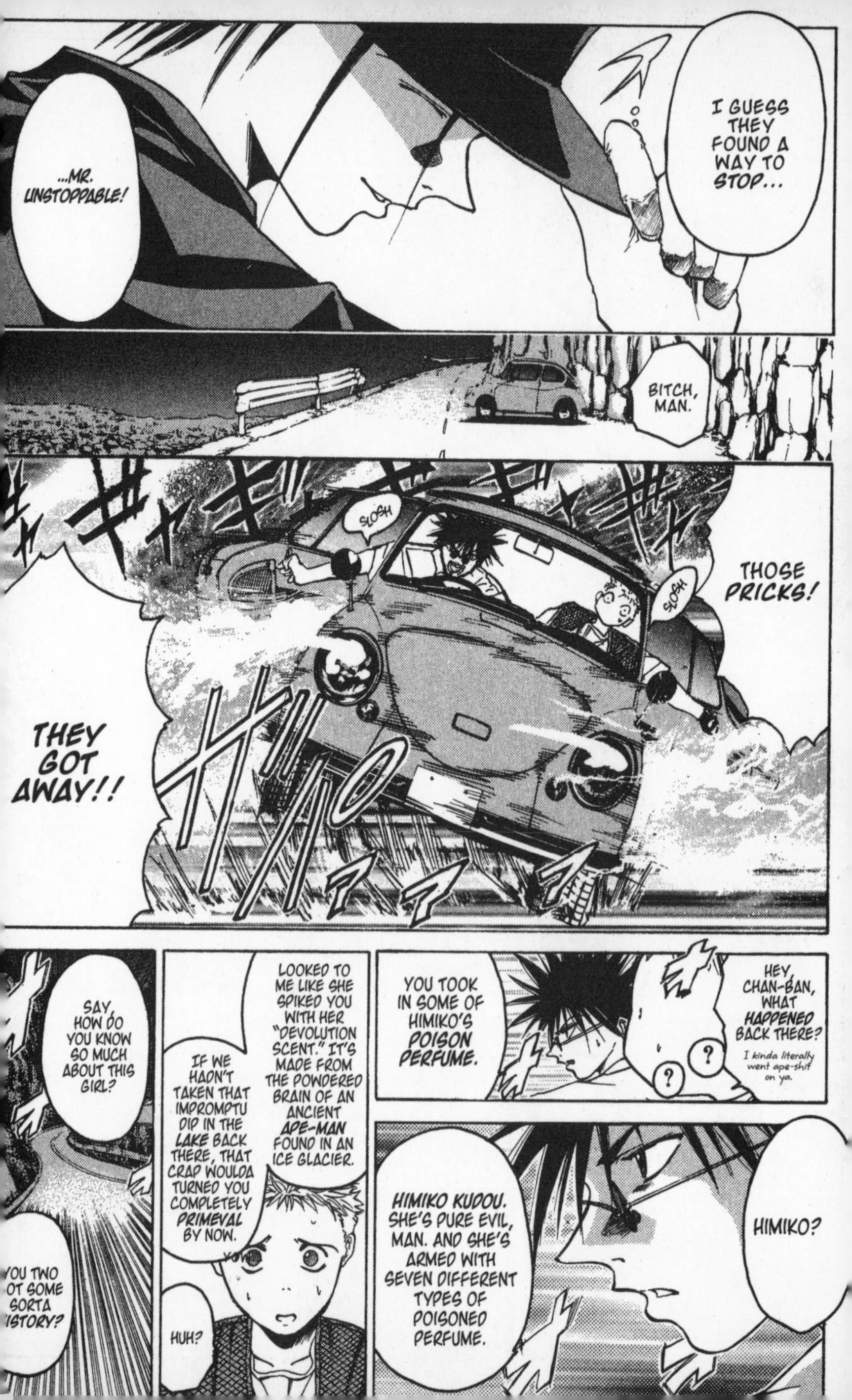

I GUESS THEY FOUND A WAY TO STOP...
...MR. UNSTOPPABLE!
BITCH, MAN.
THOSE PRICKS!
SLOSH
SLOSH
THEY GOT AWAY!!
HEY, CHAN-BAN, WHAT HAPPENED BACK THERE?
I kinda literally went ape-shit on ya.
?
?
YOU TOOK IN SOME OF HIMIKO'S POISON PERFUME.
HIMIKO?
HIMIKO KUDOU. SHE'S PURE EVIL, MAN. AND SHE'S ARMED WITH SEVEN DIFFERENT TYPES OF POISONED PERFUME.
LOOKED TO ME LIKE SHE SPIKED YOU WITH HER "DEVOLUTION SCENT." IT'S MADE FROM THE POWDERED BRAIN OF AN ANCIENT APE-MAN FOUND IN AN ICE GLACIER.
IF WE HADN'T TAKEN THAT IMPROMPTU DIP IN THE LAKE BACK THERE, THAT CRAP WOULDA TURNED YOU COMPLETELY PRIMEVAL BY NOW.
HUH?
SAY, HOW DO YOU KNOW SO MUCH ABOUT THIS GIRL?
YOU TWO OT SOME SORTA ISTORY?

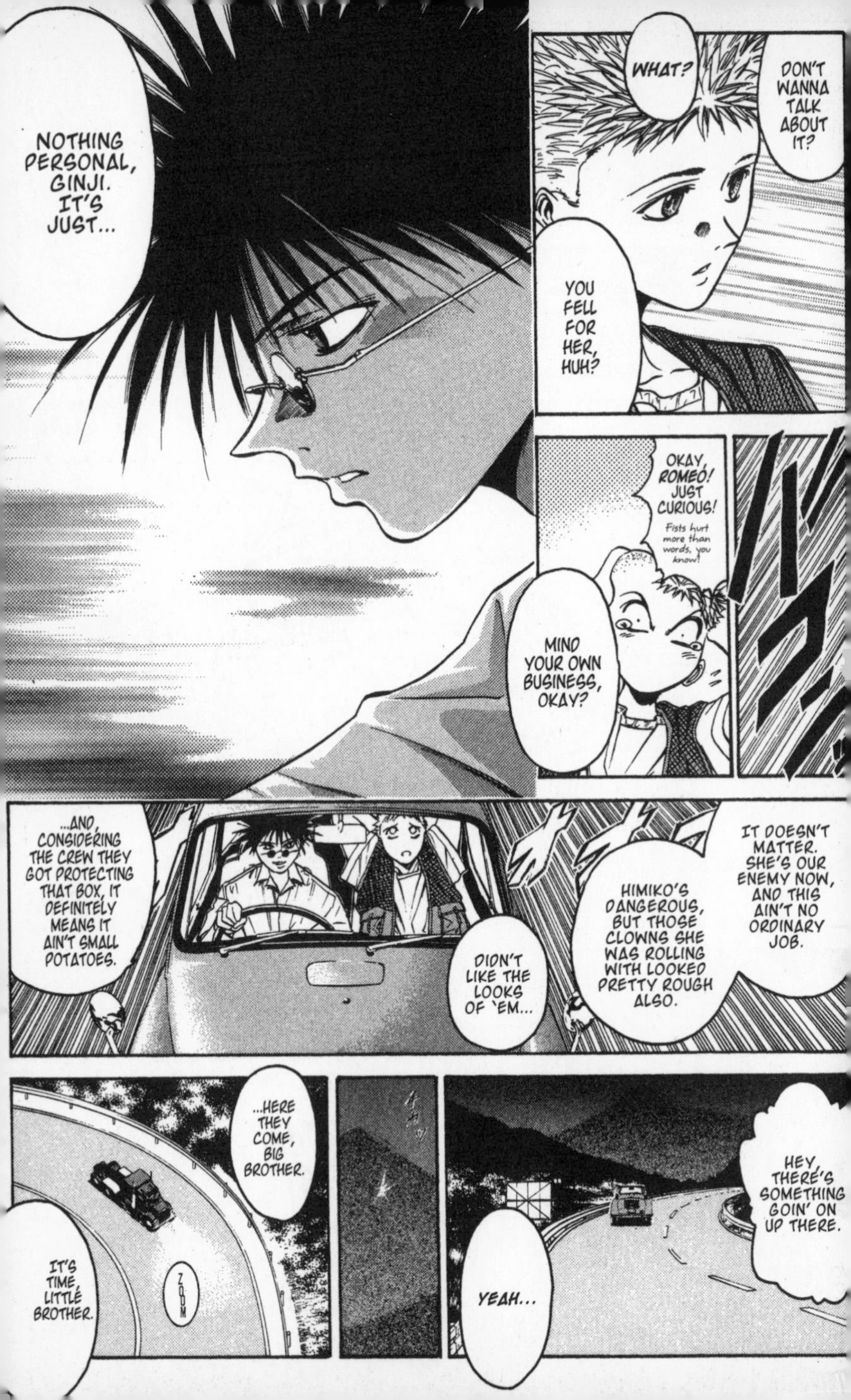
DON'T WANNA TALK ABOUT IT?
WHAT?
YOU FELL FOR HER, HUH?
OKAY, ROMEO! JUST CURIOUS!
Fists hurt more than words, you know!
MIND YOUR OWN BUSINESS, OKAY?
NOTHING PERSONAL, GINJI. IT'S JUST...
IT DOESN'T MATTER. SHE'S OUR ENEMY NOW, AND THIS AIN'T NO ORDINARY JOB.
HIMIKO'S DANGEROUS, BUT THOSE CLOWNS SHE WAS ROLLING WITH LOOKED PRETTY ROUGH ALSO.
DIDN'T LIKE THE LOOKS OF 'EM...
...AND, CONSIDERING THE CREW THEY GOT PROTECTING THAT BOX, IT DEFINITELY MEANS IT AIN'T SMALL POTATOES.
HEY, THERE'S SOMETHING GOIN' ON UP THERE.
YEAH...
...HERE THEY COME, BIG BROTHER.
IT'S TIME, LITTLE BROTHER.
ZOOM

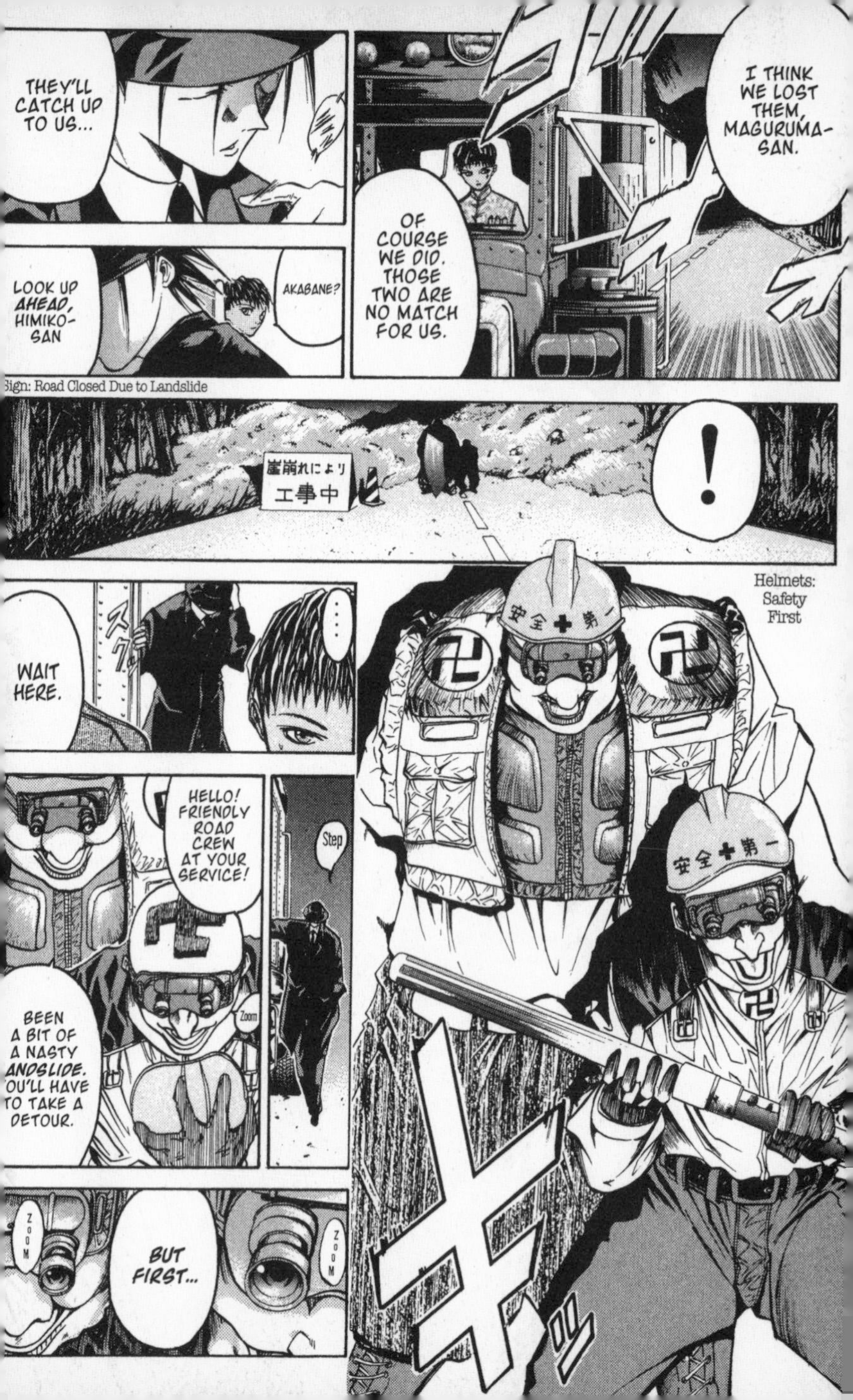
I THINK WE LOST THEM, MAGURUMA-SAN.
OF COURSE WE DID. THOSE TWO ARE NO MATCH FOR US.
THEY'LL CATCH UP TO US...
AKABANE?
LOOK UP AHEAD, HIMIKO-SAN
Sign: Road Closed Due to Landslide
!
崖崩れにより
工事中
Helmets: Safety First
安全✚第一
....
WAIT HERE.
Step
HELLO! FRIENDLY ROAD CREW AT YOUR SERVICE!
Zoom
BEEN A BIT OF A NASTY ANDSLIDE. OU'LL HAVE TO TAKE A DETOUR.
ZOOM
BUT FIRST...
ZOOM

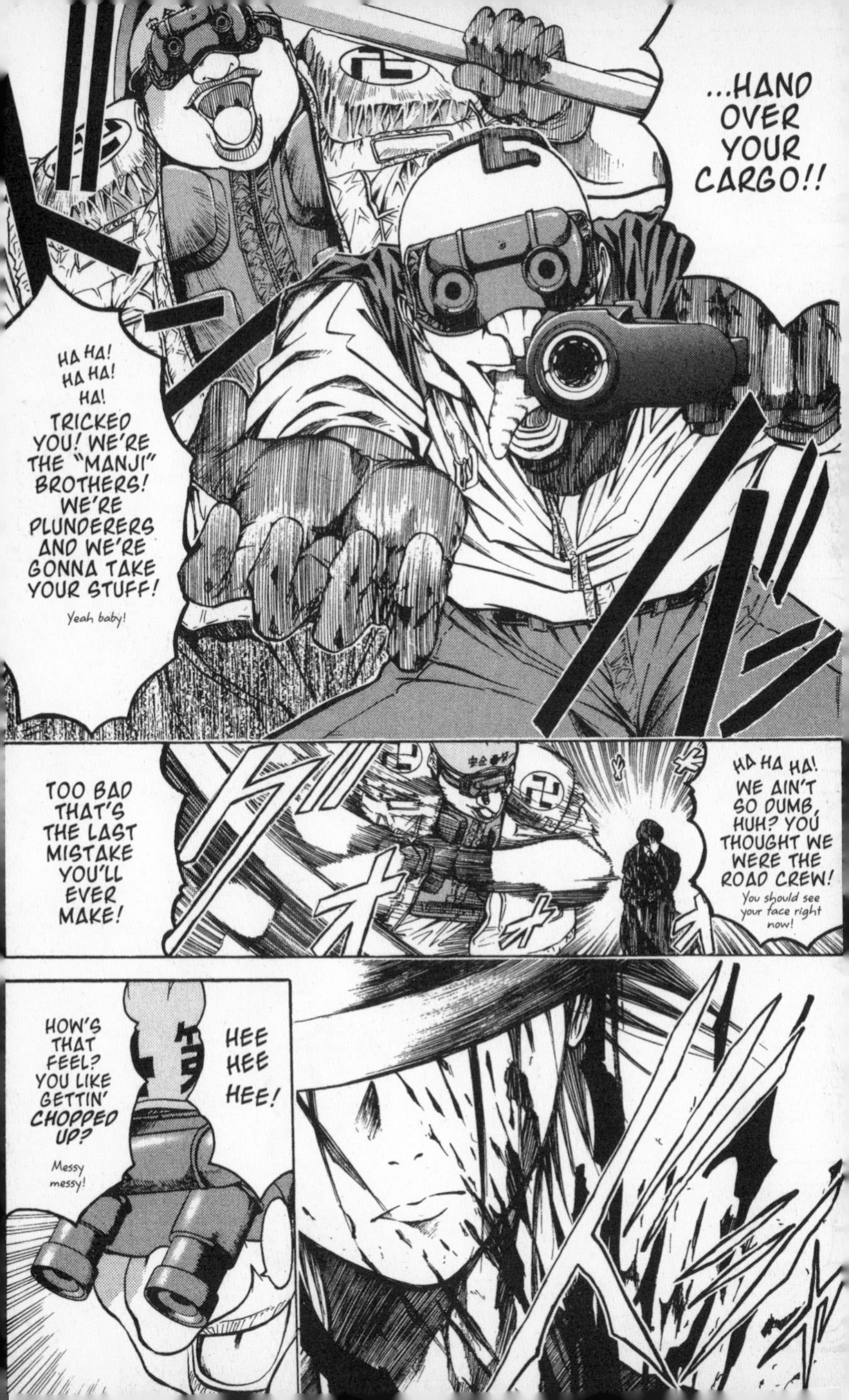
...HAND OVER YOUR CARGO!!
HA HA! HA HA! HA! TRICKED YOU! WE'RE THE "MANJI" BROTHERS! WE'RE PLUNDERERS AND WE'RE GONNA TAKE YOUR STUFF!
Yeah baby!
HA HA HA! WE AIN'T SO DUMB, HUH? YOU THOUGHT WE WERE THE ROAD CREW!
You should see your face right now!
TOO BAD THAT'S THE LAST MISTAKE YOU'LL EVER MAKE!
HEE HEE HEE!
HOW'S THAT FEEL? YOU LIKE GETTIN' CHOPPED UP?
Messy messy!

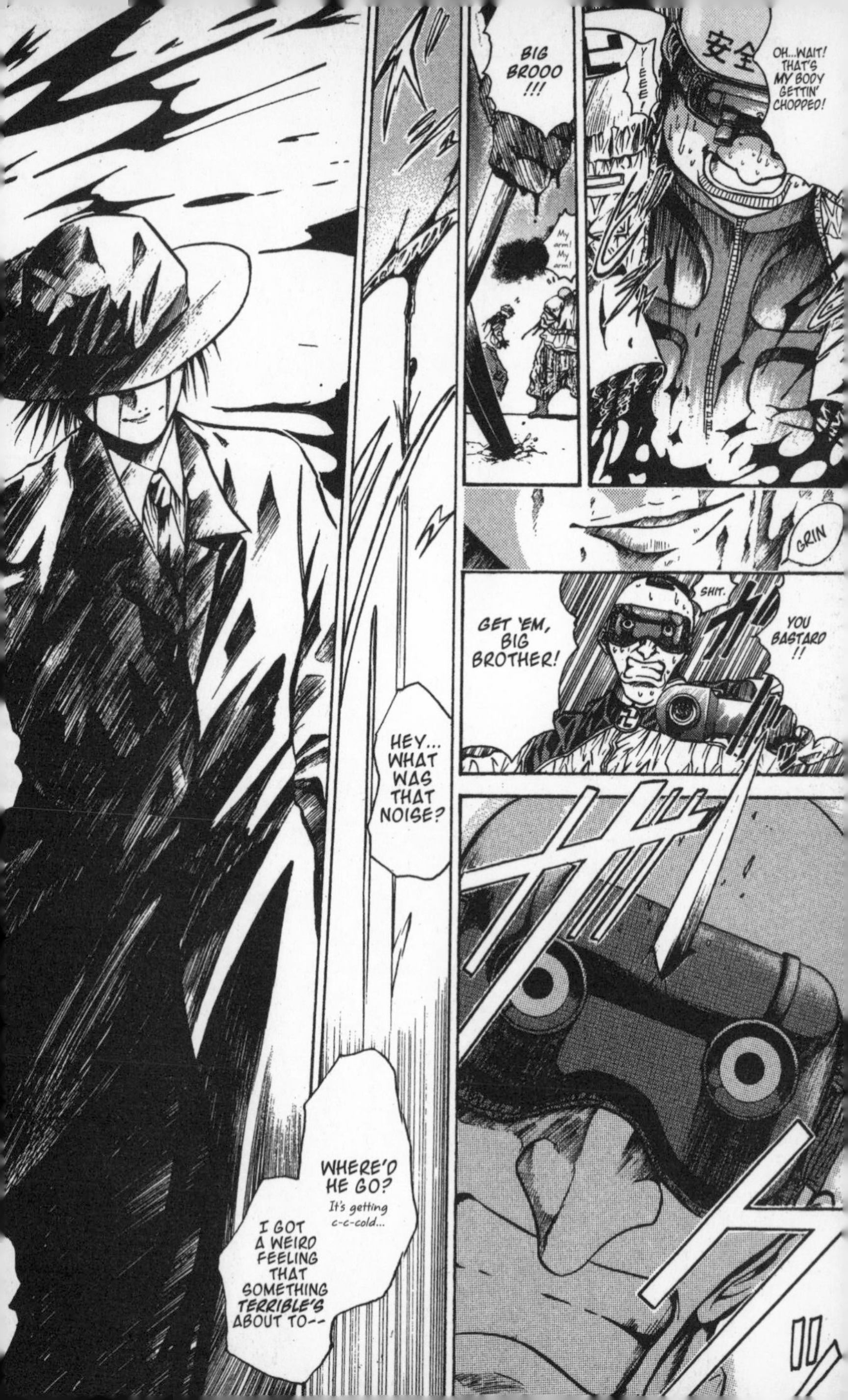
OH...WAIT! THAT'S MY BODY GETTIN' CHOPPED!
YIEEE!
BIG BROOO!!!
My arm! My arm!
GRIN
YOU BASTARD!!
SHIT.
GET 'EM, BIG BROTHER!
HEY... WHAT WAS THAT NOISE?
WHERE'D HE GO?
It's getting c-c-cold...
I GOT A WEIRD FEELING THAT SOMETHING TERRIBLE'S ABOUT TO--

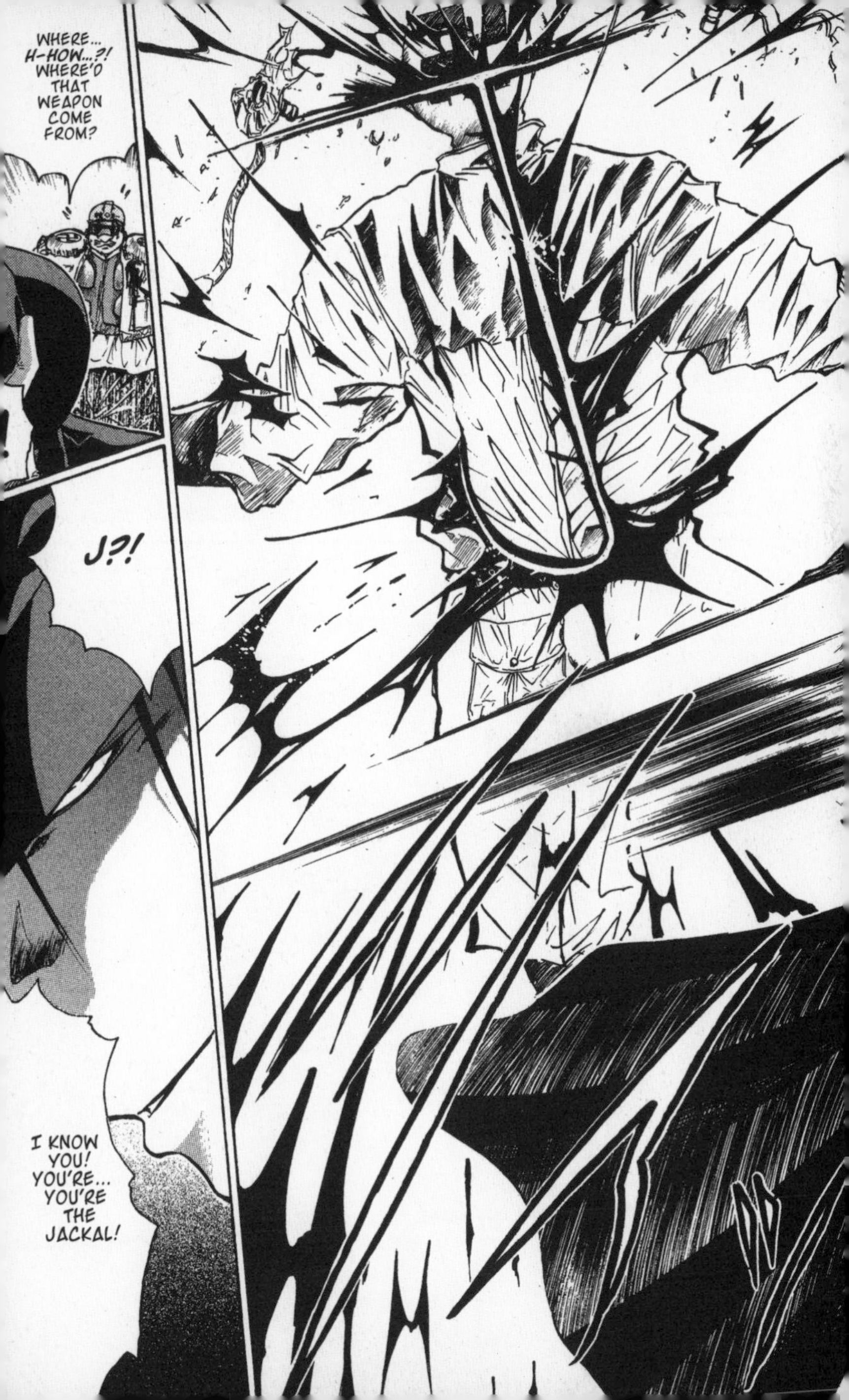
WHERE... H-HOW...?! WHERE'D THAT WEAPON COME FROM?
J?!
I KNOW YOU! YOU'RE... YOU'RE THE JACKAL!

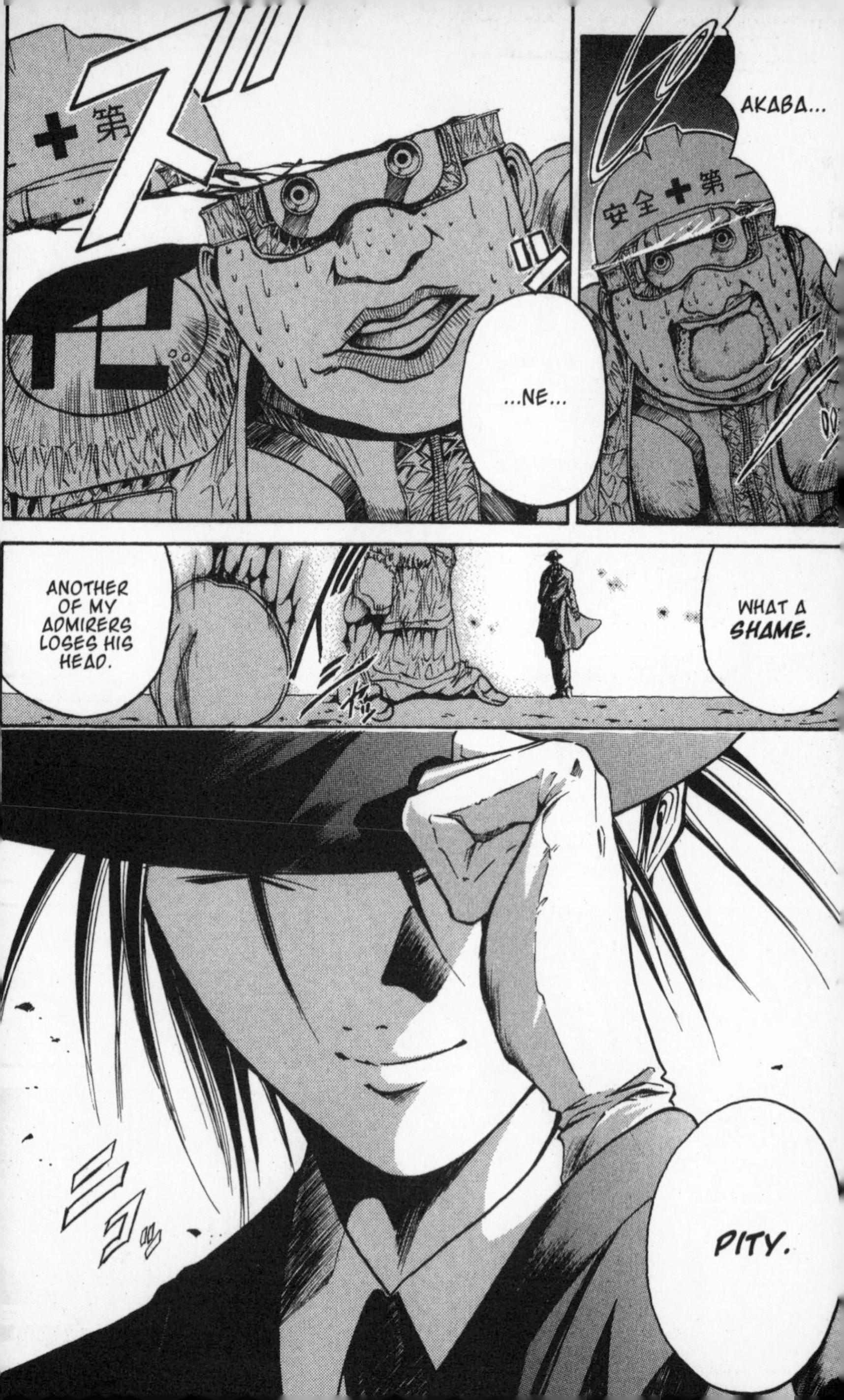
AKABA...
...NE...
WHAT A SHAME.
ANOTHER OF MY ADMIRERS LOSES HIS HEAD.
PITY.

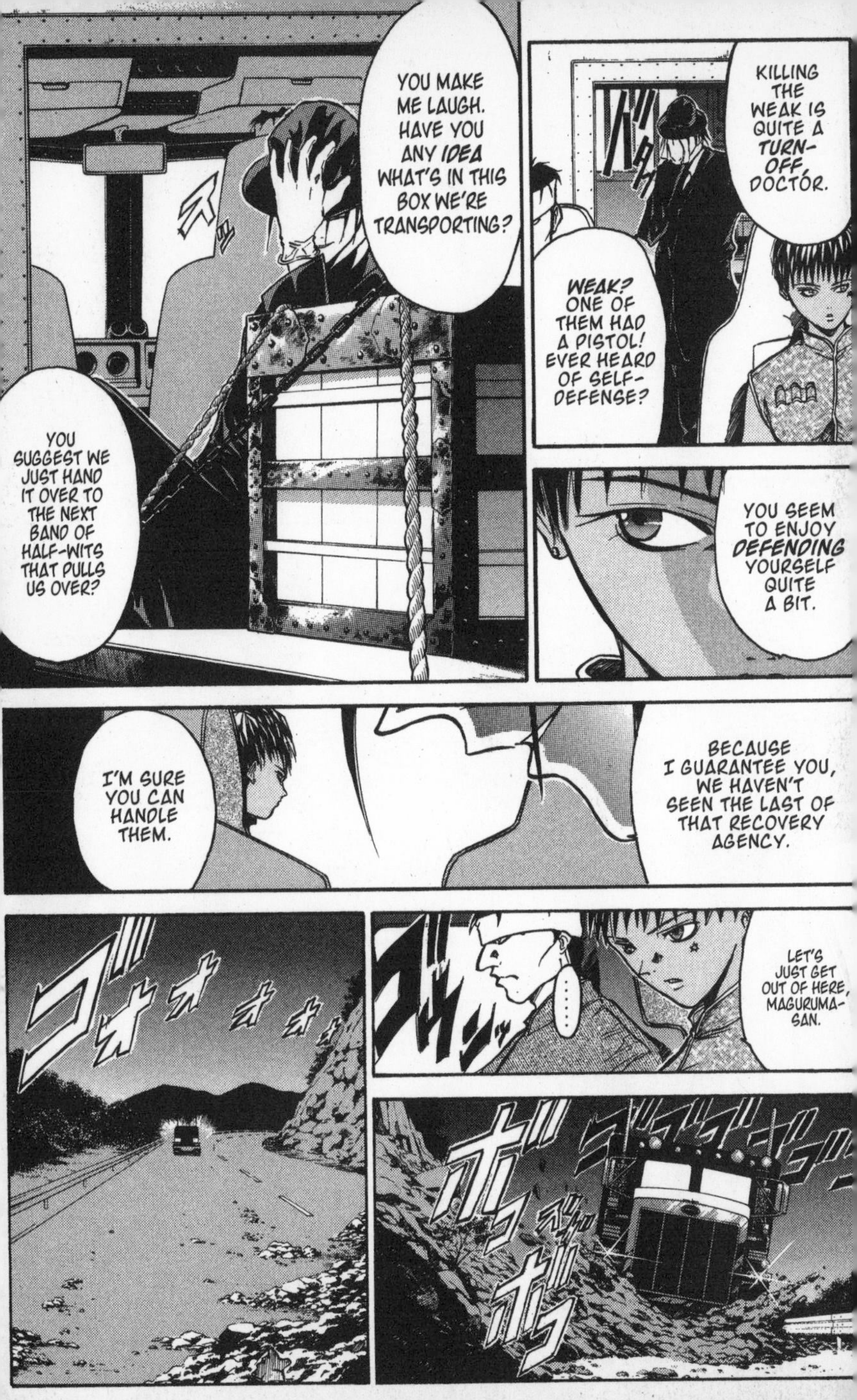
KILLING THE WEAK IS QUITE A *TURN-OFF*, DOCTOR.
WEAK? ONE OF THEM HAD A PISTOL! EVER HEARD OF SELF-DEFENSE?
YOU SEEM TO ENJOY *DEFENDING* YOURSELF QUITE A BIT.
YOU MAKE ME LAUGH. HAVE YOU ANY *IDEA* WHAT'S IN THIS BOX WE'RE TRANSPORTING?
YOU SUGGEST WE JUST HAND IT OVER TO THE NEXT BAND OF HALF-WITS THAT PULLS US OVER?
BECAUSE I GUARANTEE YOU, WE HAVEN'T SEEN THE LAST OF THAT RECOVERY AGENCY.
I'M SURE YOU CAN HANDLE THEM.
LET'S JUST GET OUT OF HERE, MAGURUMA-SAN.

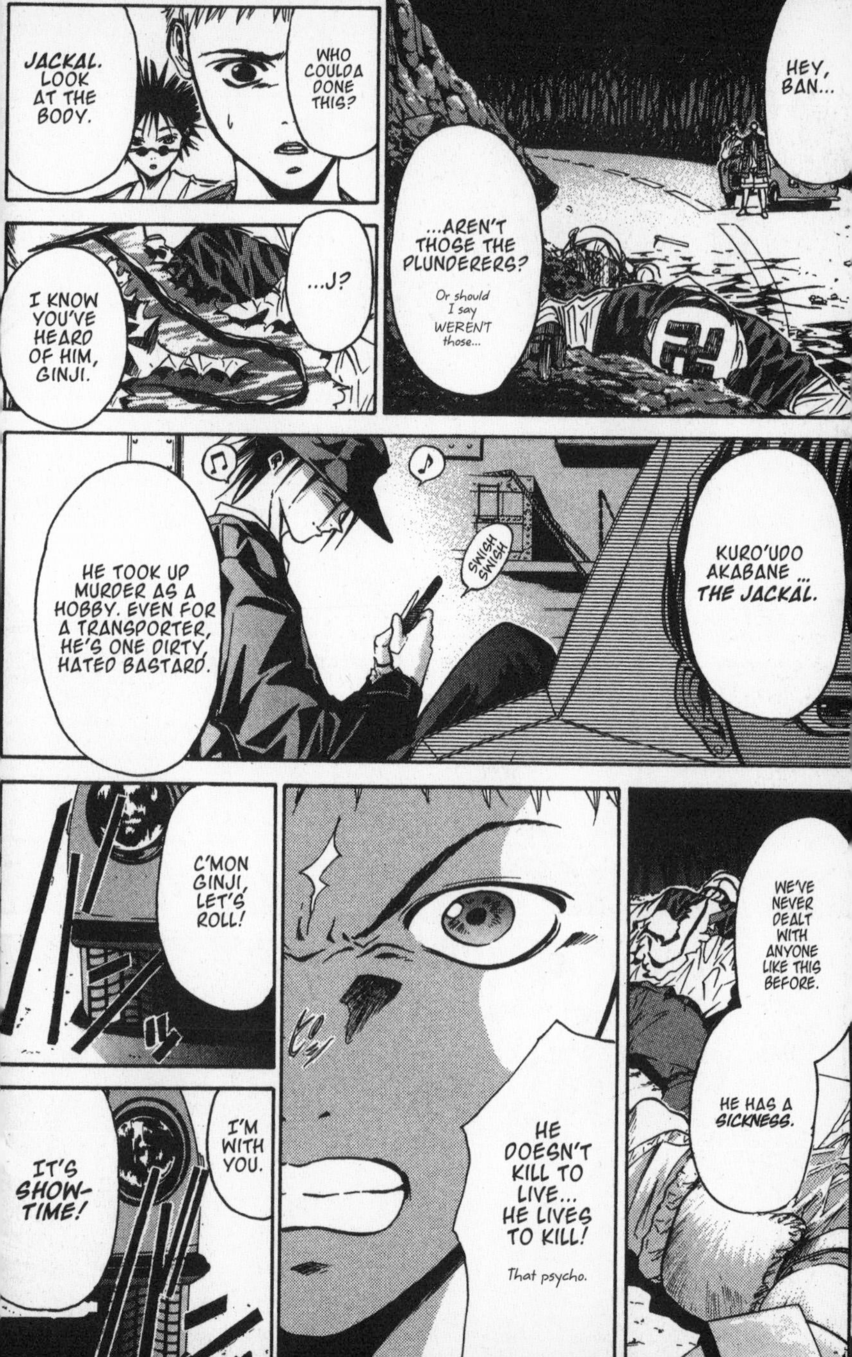
HEY, BAN...
...AREN'T THOSE THE PLUNDERERS?
Or should I say WEREN'T those...
WHO COULDA DONE THIS?
JACKAL. LOOK AT THE BODY.
...J?
I KNOW YOU'VE HEARD OF HIM, GINJI.
KURO'UDO AKABANE... THE JACKAL.
SWISH SWISH
HE TOOK UP MURDER AS A HOBBY. EVEN FOR A TRANSPORTER, HE'S ONE DIRTY, HATED BASTARD.
WE'VE NEVER DEALT WITH ANYONE LIKE THIS BEFORE.
HE HAS A SICKNESS.
HE DOESN'T KILL TO LIVE... HE LIVES TO KILL!
That psycho.
C'MON GINJI, LET'S ROLL!
I'M WITH YOU.
IT'S SHOW-TIME!

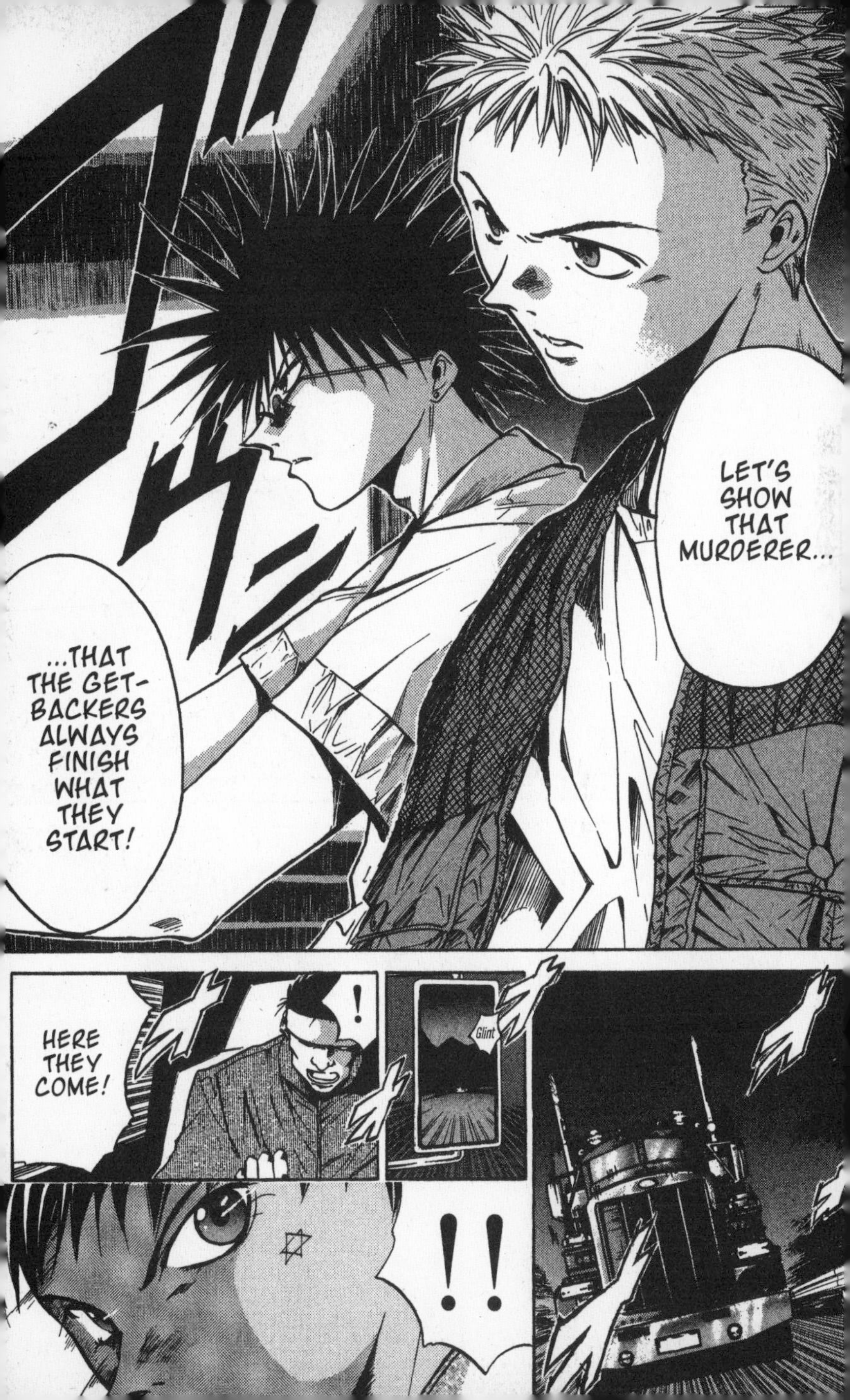
LET'S SHOW THAT MURDERER...
...THAT THE GET-BACKERS ALWAYS FINISH WHAT THEY START!
Glint
!
HERE THEY COME!
!!

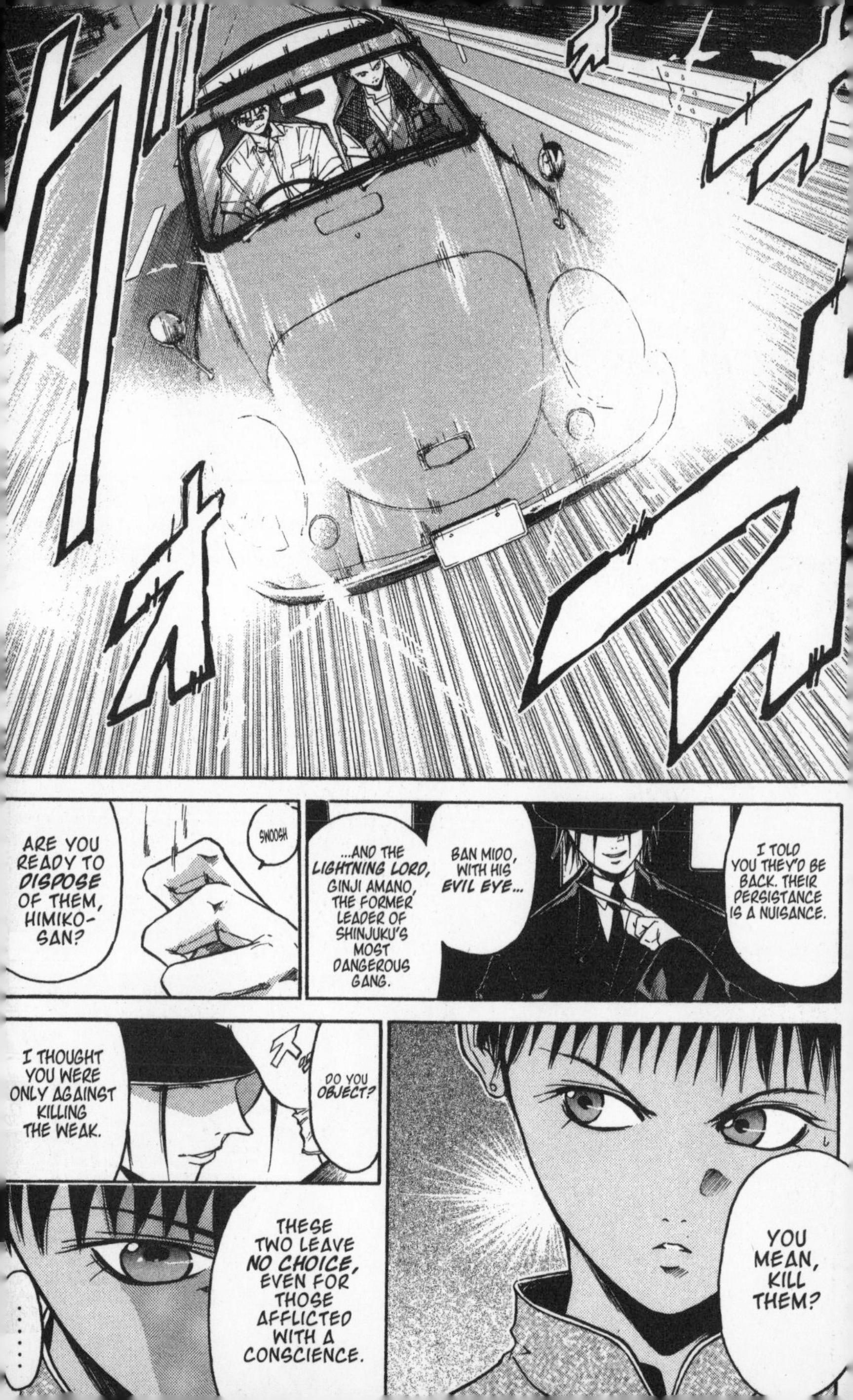
I TOLD YOU THEY'D BE BACK. THEIR PERSISTANCE IS A NUISANCE.
BAN MIDO, WITH HIS *EVIL EYE*...
...AND THE *LIGHTNING LORD*, GINJI AMANO, THE FORMER LEADER OF SHINJUKU'S MOST DANGEROUS GANG.
SWOOSH
ARE YOU READY TO *DISPOSE* OF THEM, HIMIKO-SAN?
YOU MEAN, KILL THEM?
DO YOU *OBJECT?*
I THOUGHT YOU WERE ONLY AGAINST KILLING THE WEAK.
THESE TWO LEAVE **NO CHOICE**, EVEN FOR THOSE AFFLICTED WITH A CONSCIENCE.

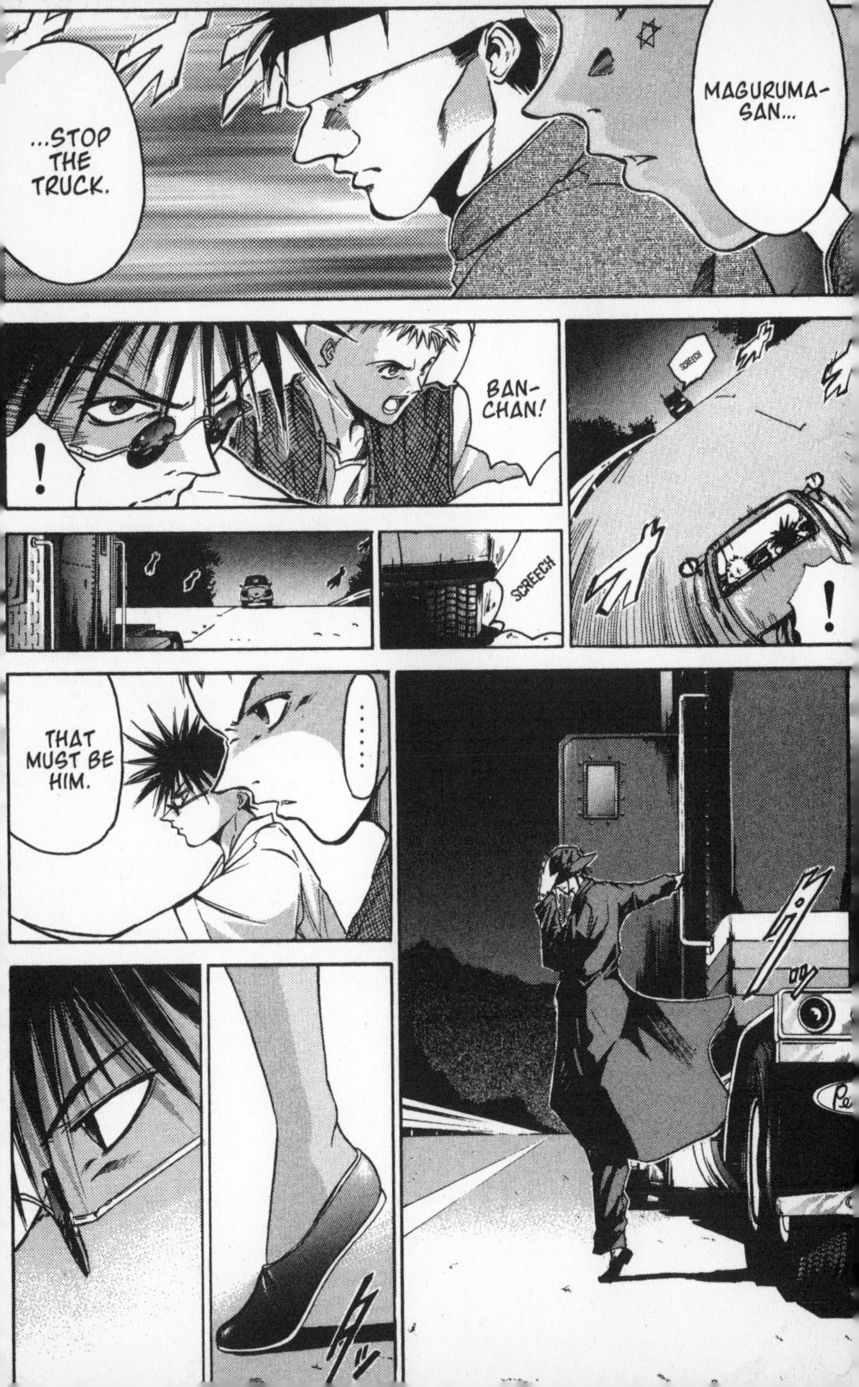
MAGURUMA-SAN...
...STOP THE TRUCK.
SCREECH
!
BAN-CHAN!
!
SCREECH
......
THAT MUST BE HIM.

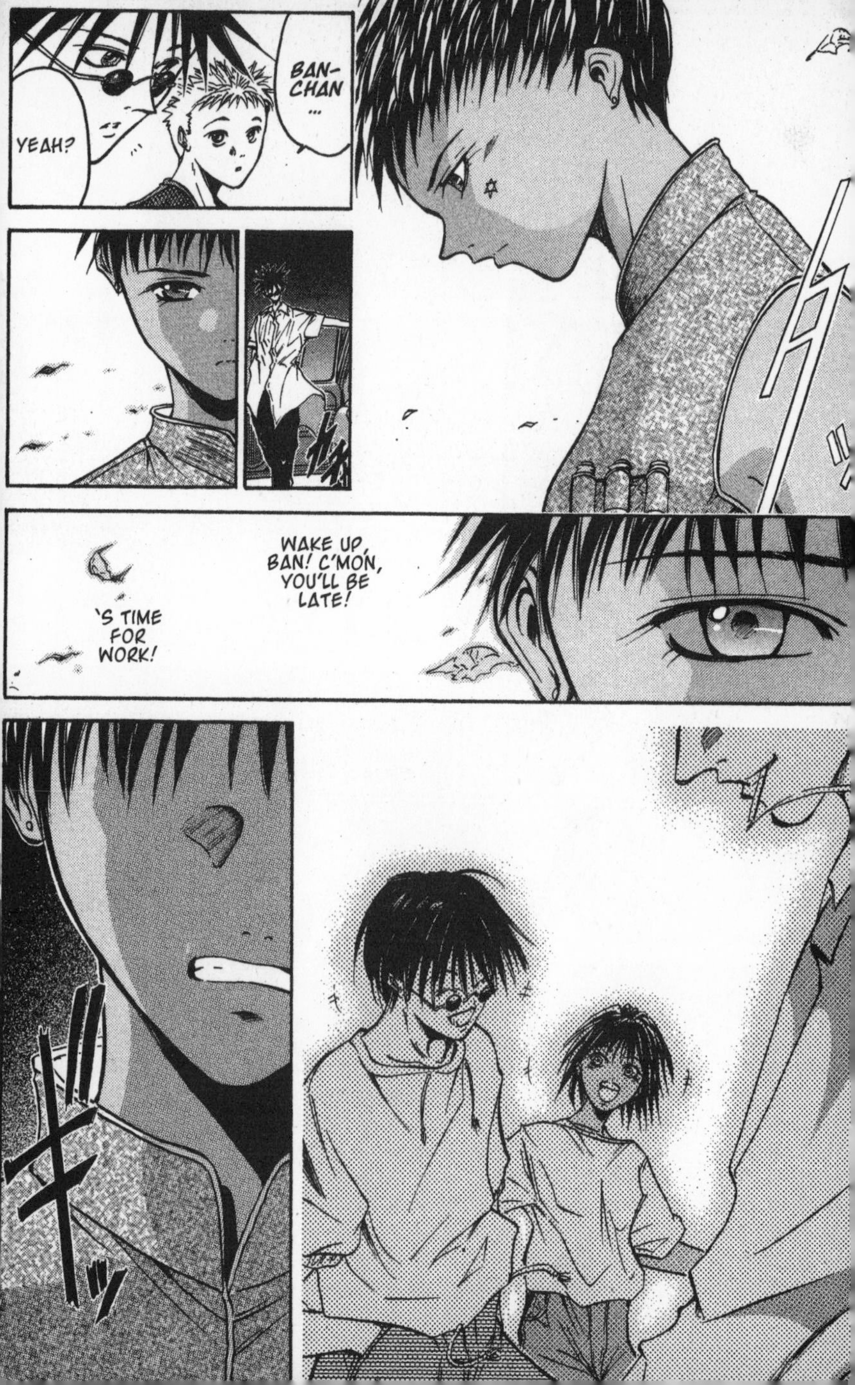

BAN-CHAN ...
YEAH?
WAKE UP, BAN! C'MON, YOU'LL BE LATE!
'S TIME FOR WORK!

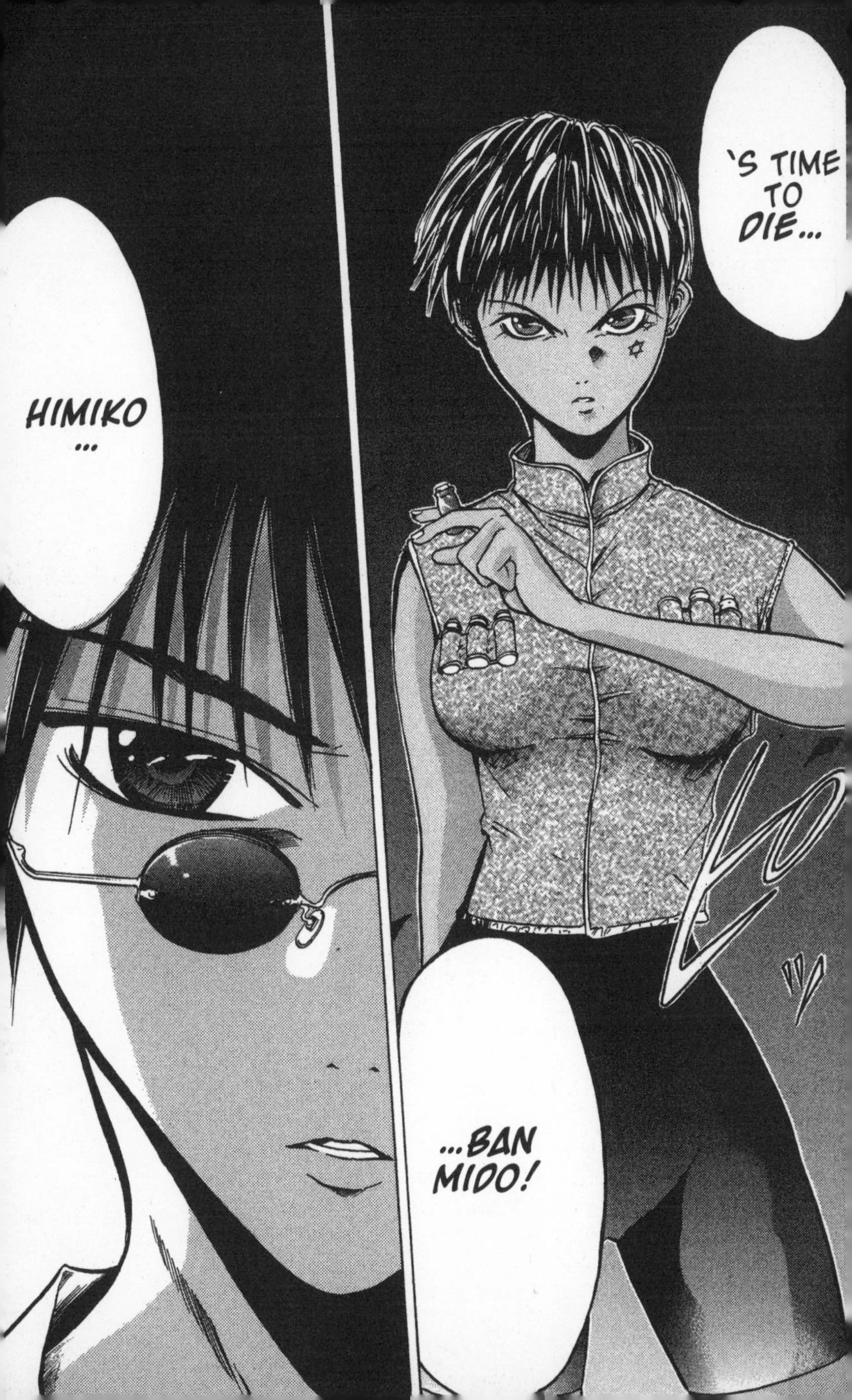
`S TIME TO DIE...
...BAN MIDO!
HIMIKO ...

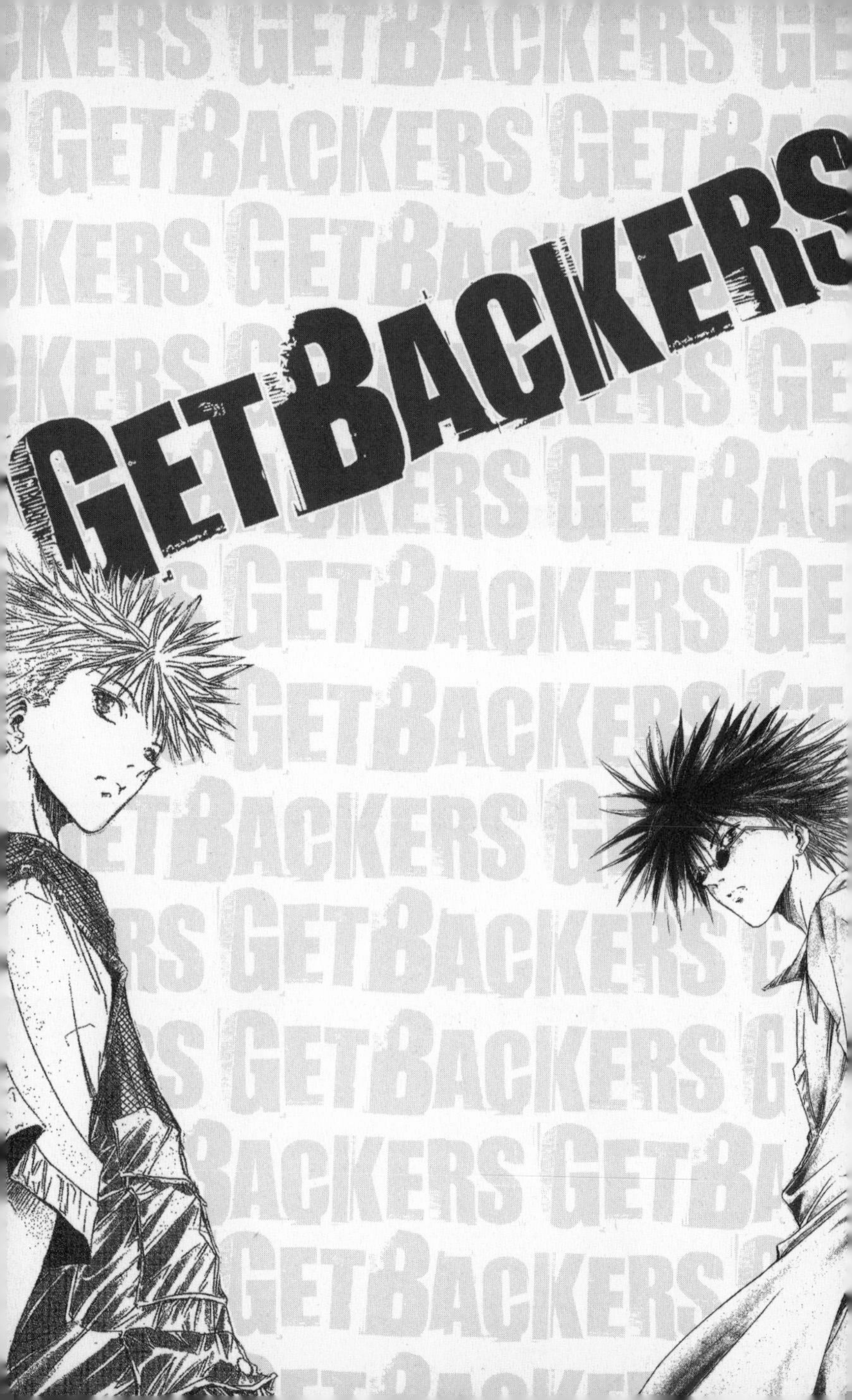
GETBACKERS

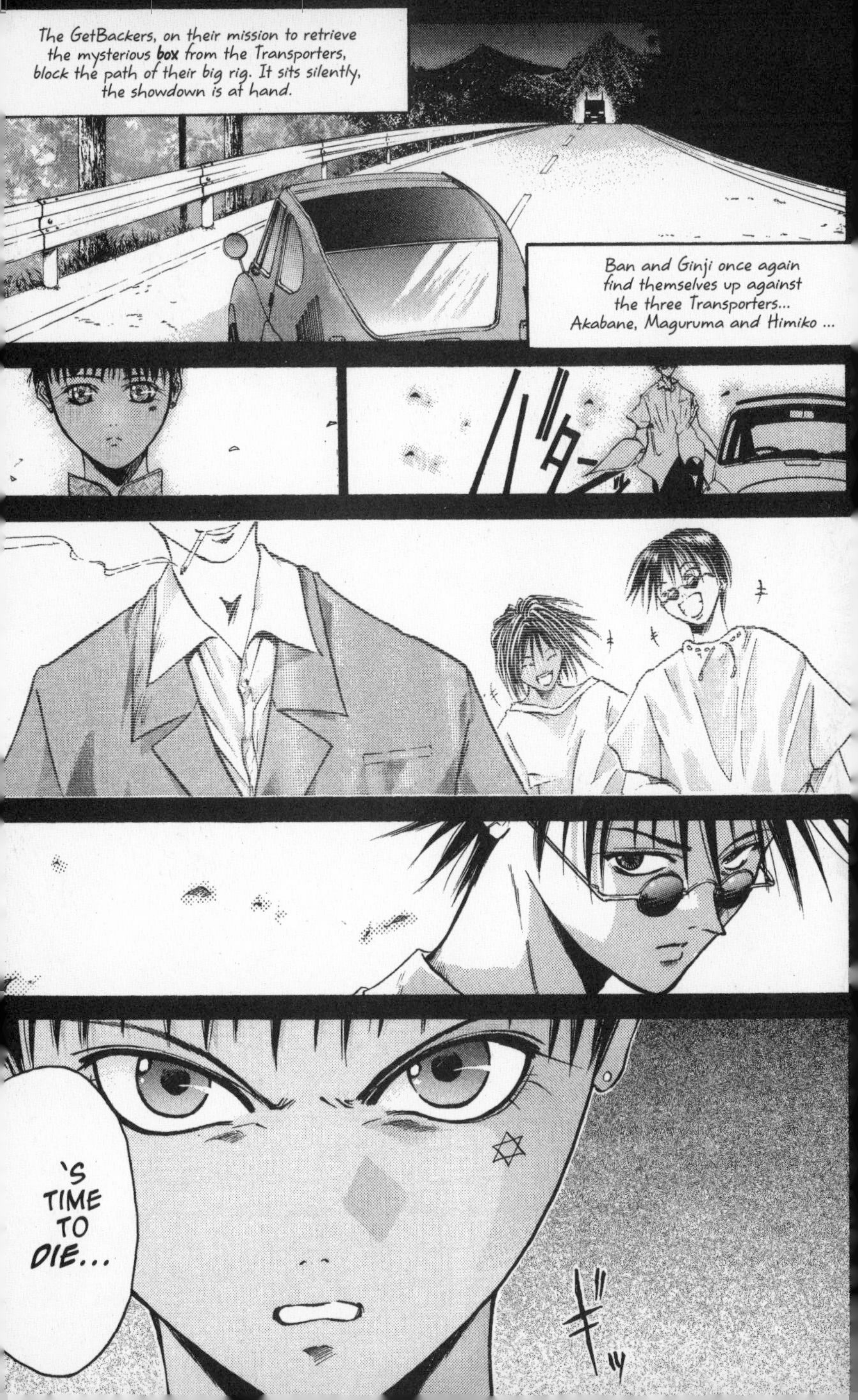
The GetBackers, on their mission to retrieve the mysterious box from the Transporters, block the path of their big rig. It sits silently, the showdown is at hand.
Ban and Ginji once again find themselves up against the three Transporters... Akabane, Maguruma and Himiko ...
'S TIME TO DIE...

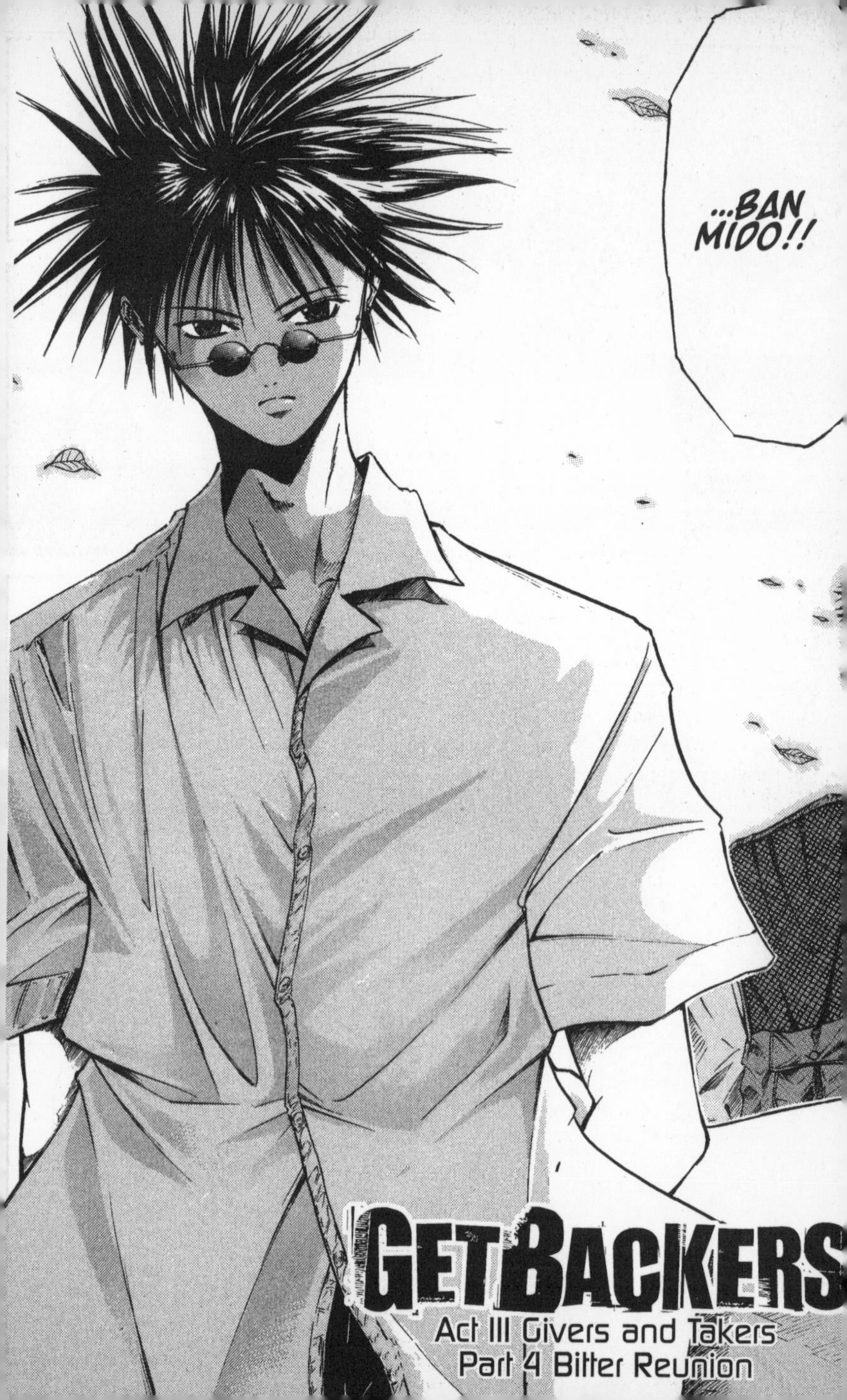
...BAN MIDO!!
GETBACKERS
Act III Givers and Takers
Part 4 Bitter Reunion

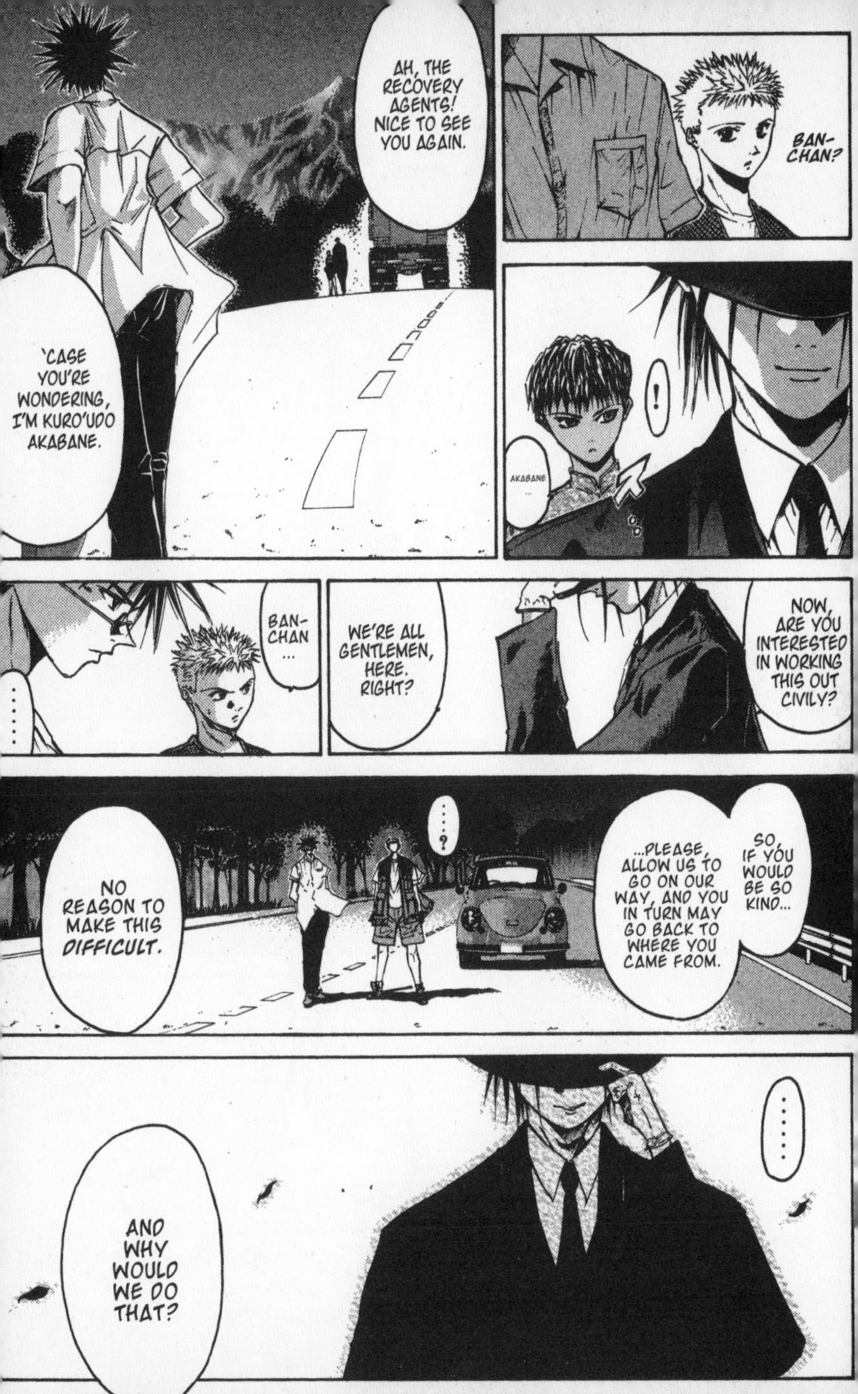
BAN-CHAN?
!
AKABANE ...
AH, THE RECOVERY AGENTS! NICE TO SEE YOU AGAIN.
'CASE YOU'RE WONDERING, I'M KURO'UDO AKABANE.
NOW, ARE YOU INTERESTED IN WORKING THIS OUT CIVILY?
WE'RE ALL GENTLEMEN, HERE. RIGHT?
BAN-CHAN ...
......
SO, IF YOU WOULD BE SO KIND...
...PLEASE, ALLOW US TO GO ON OUR WAY, AND YOU IN TURN MAY GO BACK TO WHERE YOU CAME FROM.
...?
NO REASON TO MAKE THIS *DIFFICULT*.
......
AND WHY WOULD WE DO THAT?

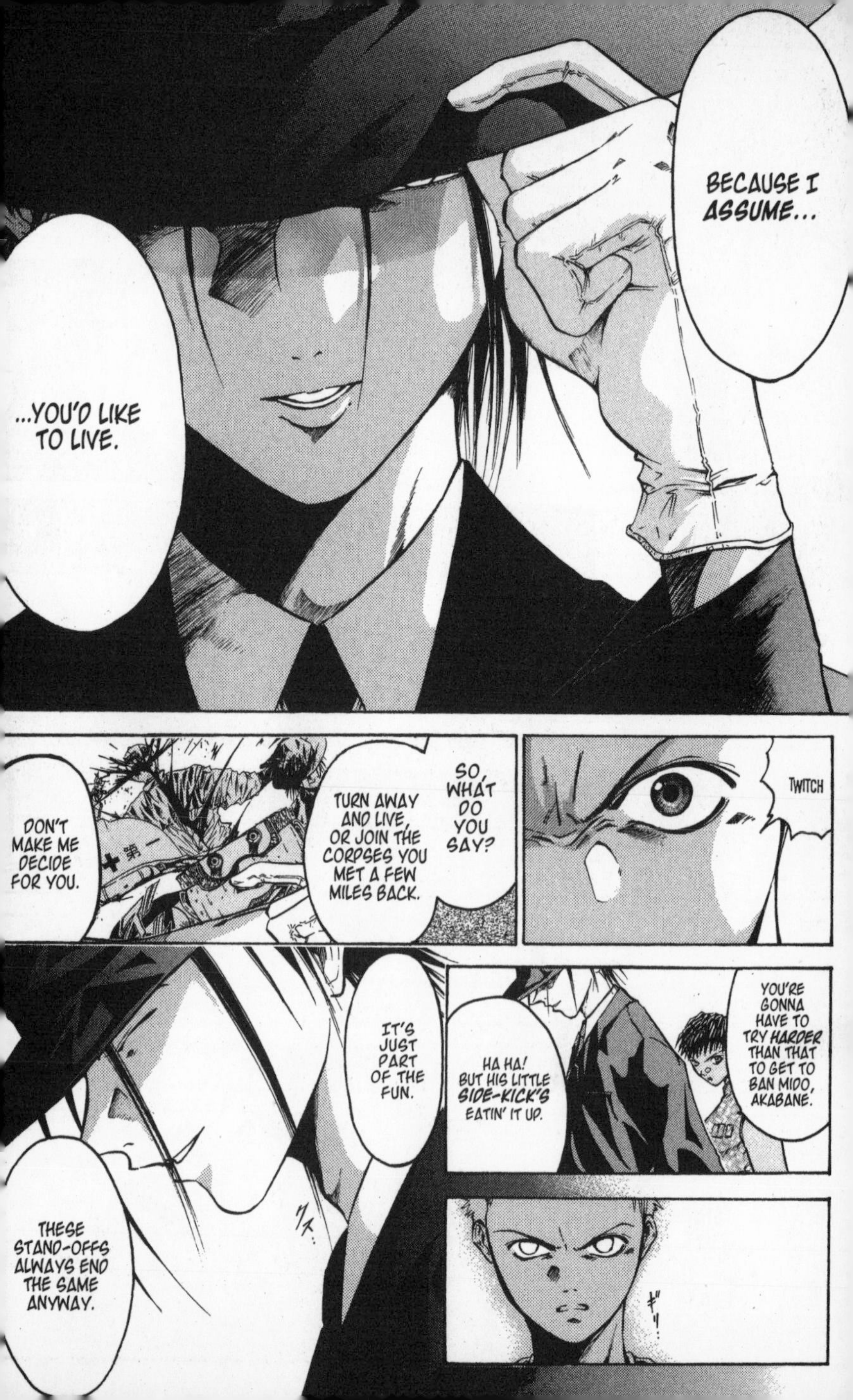
BECAUSE I ASSUME...
...YOU'D LIKE TO LIVE.
TWITCH
SO, WHAT DO YOU SAY?
TURN AWAY AND LIVE, OR JOIN THE CORPSES YOU MET A FEW MILES BACK.
DON'T MAKE ME DECIDE FOR YOU.
YOU'RE GONNA HAVE TO TRY HARDER THAN THAT TO GET TO BAN MIDO, AKABANE.
HA HA! BUT HIS LITTLE SIDE-KICK'S EATIN' IT UP.
IT'S JUST PART OF THE FUN.
THESE STAND-OFFS ALWAYS END THE SAME ANYWAY.

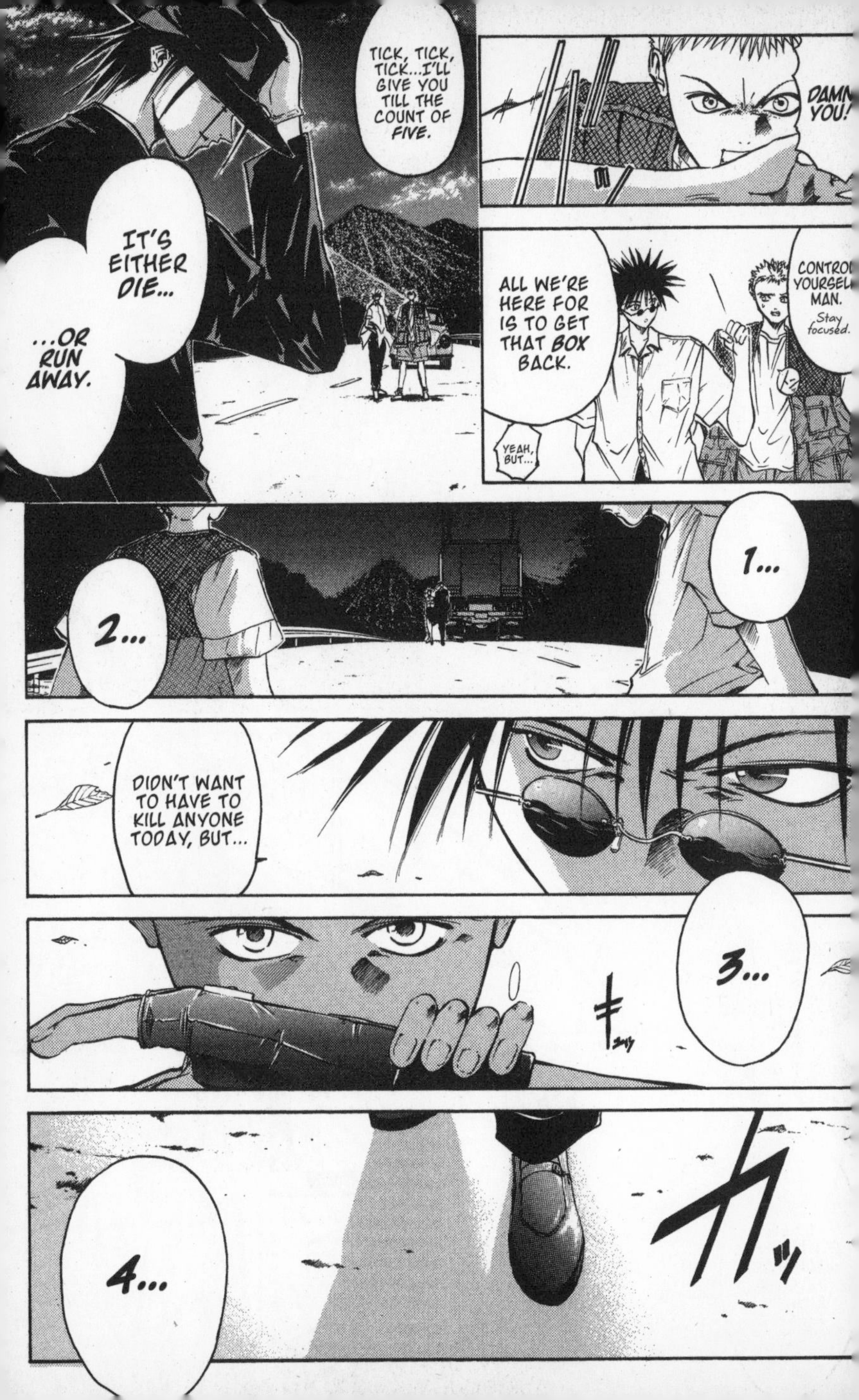
DAMN YOU!
CONTROL YOURSEL MAN. Stay focused.
ALL WE'RE HERE FOR IS TO GET THAT BOX BACK.
YEAH, BUT...
TICK, TICK, TICK...I'LL GIVE YOU TILL THE COUNT OF FIVE.
IT'S EITHER DIE...
...OR RUN AWAY.
1...
2...
DIDN'T WANT TO HAVE TO KILL ANYONE TODAY, BUT...
3...
4...

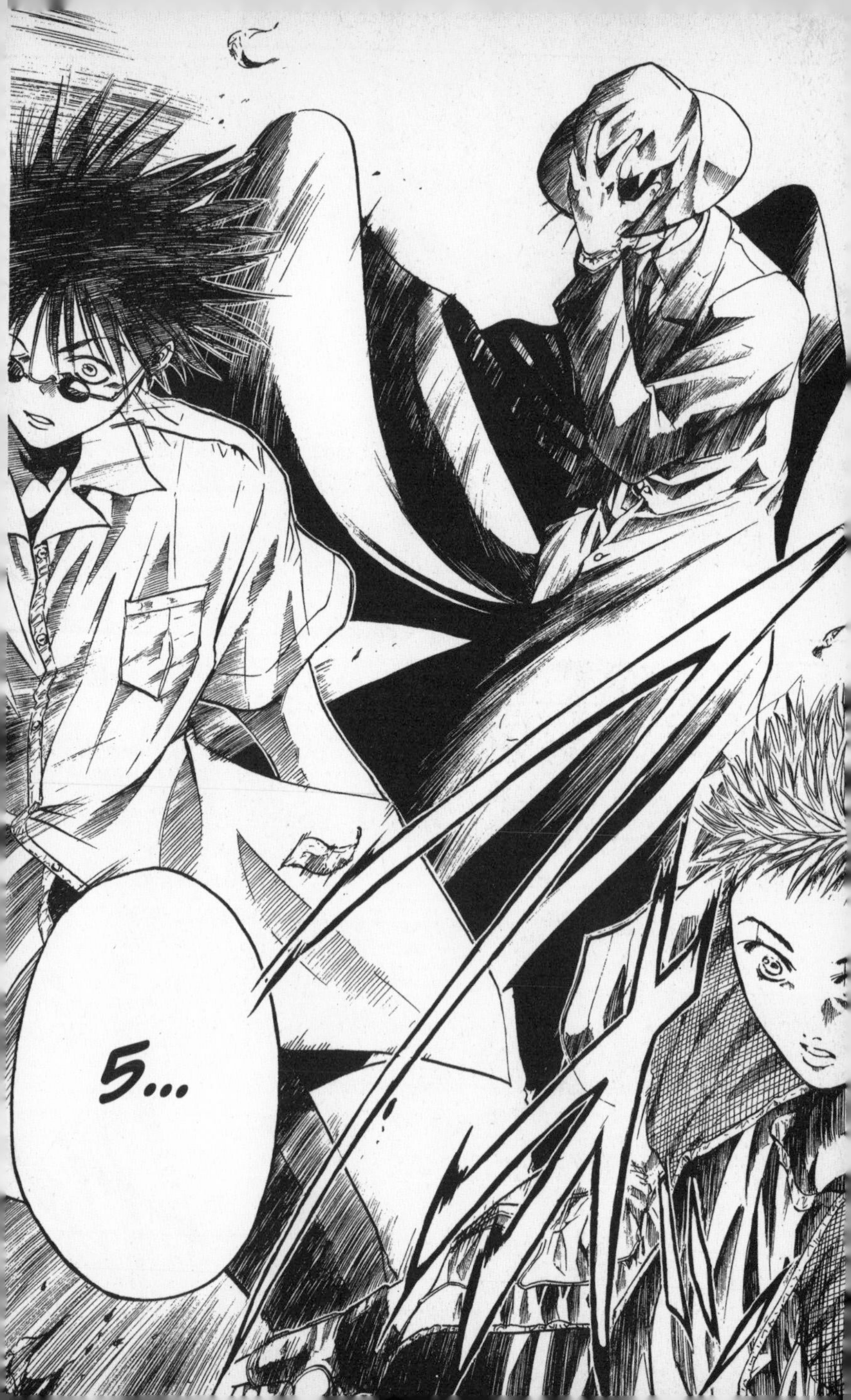
5...

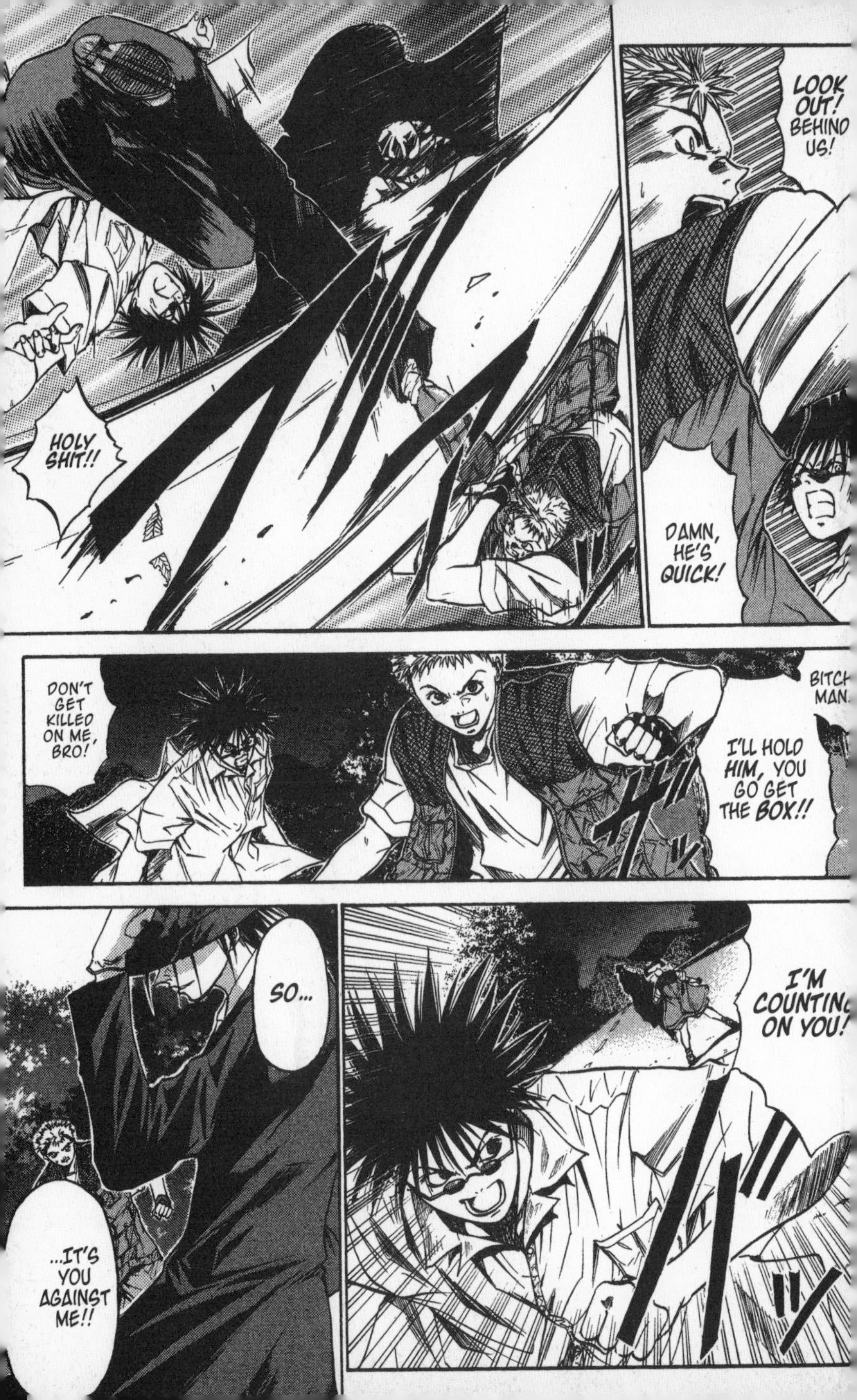
LOOK OUT! BEHIND US!
DAMN, HE'S QUICK!
HOLY SHIT!!
BITCH MAN
I'LL HOLD HIM, YOU GO GET THE BOX!!
DON'T GET KILLED ON ME, BRO!
I'M COUNTING ON YOU!
SO...
...IT'S YOU AGAINST ME!!

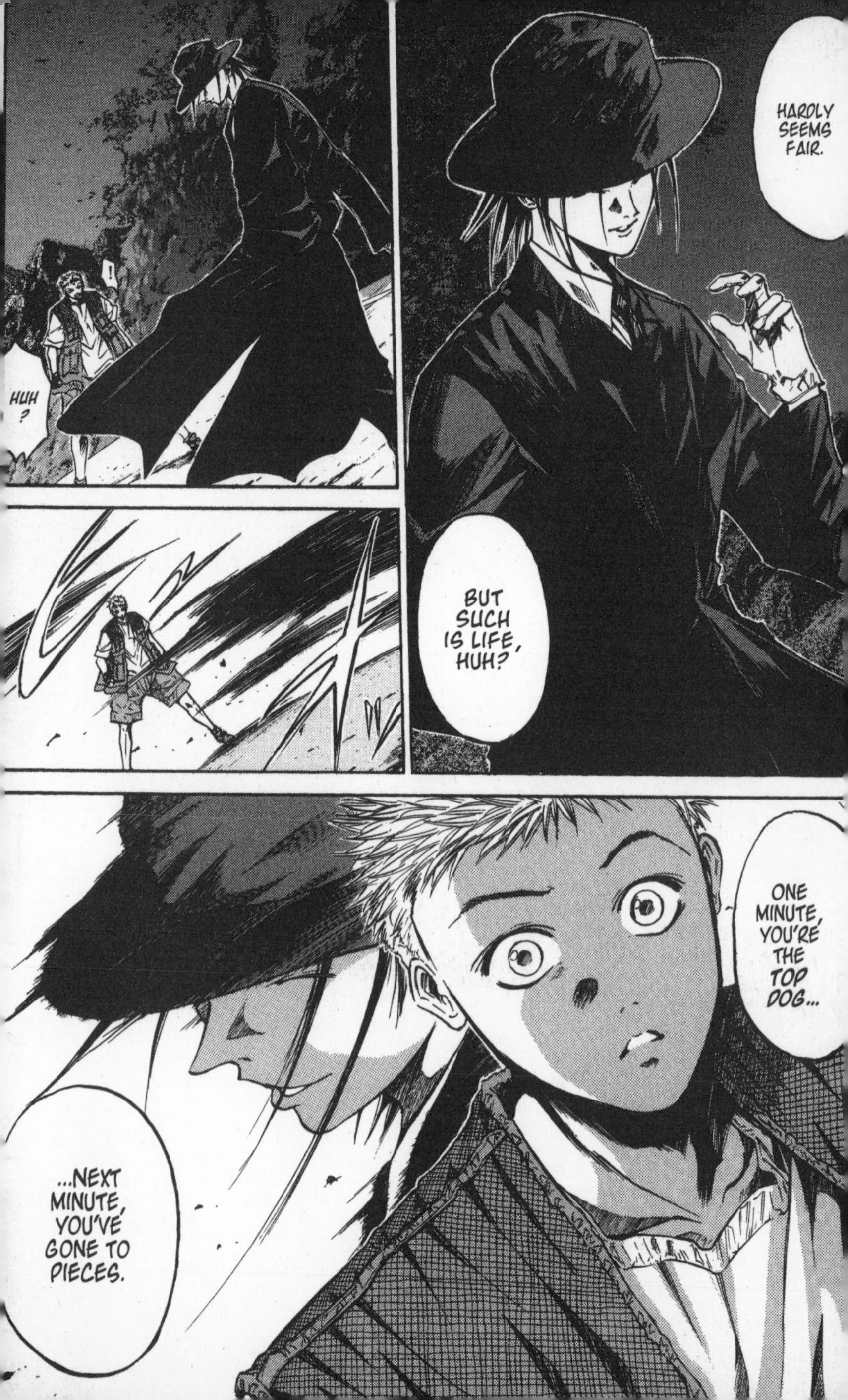
HARDLY SEEMS FAIR.
BUT SUCH IS LIFE, HUH?
!
HUH?
ONE MINUTE, YOU'RE THE TOP DOG...
...NEXT MINUTE, YOU'VE GONE TO PIECES.

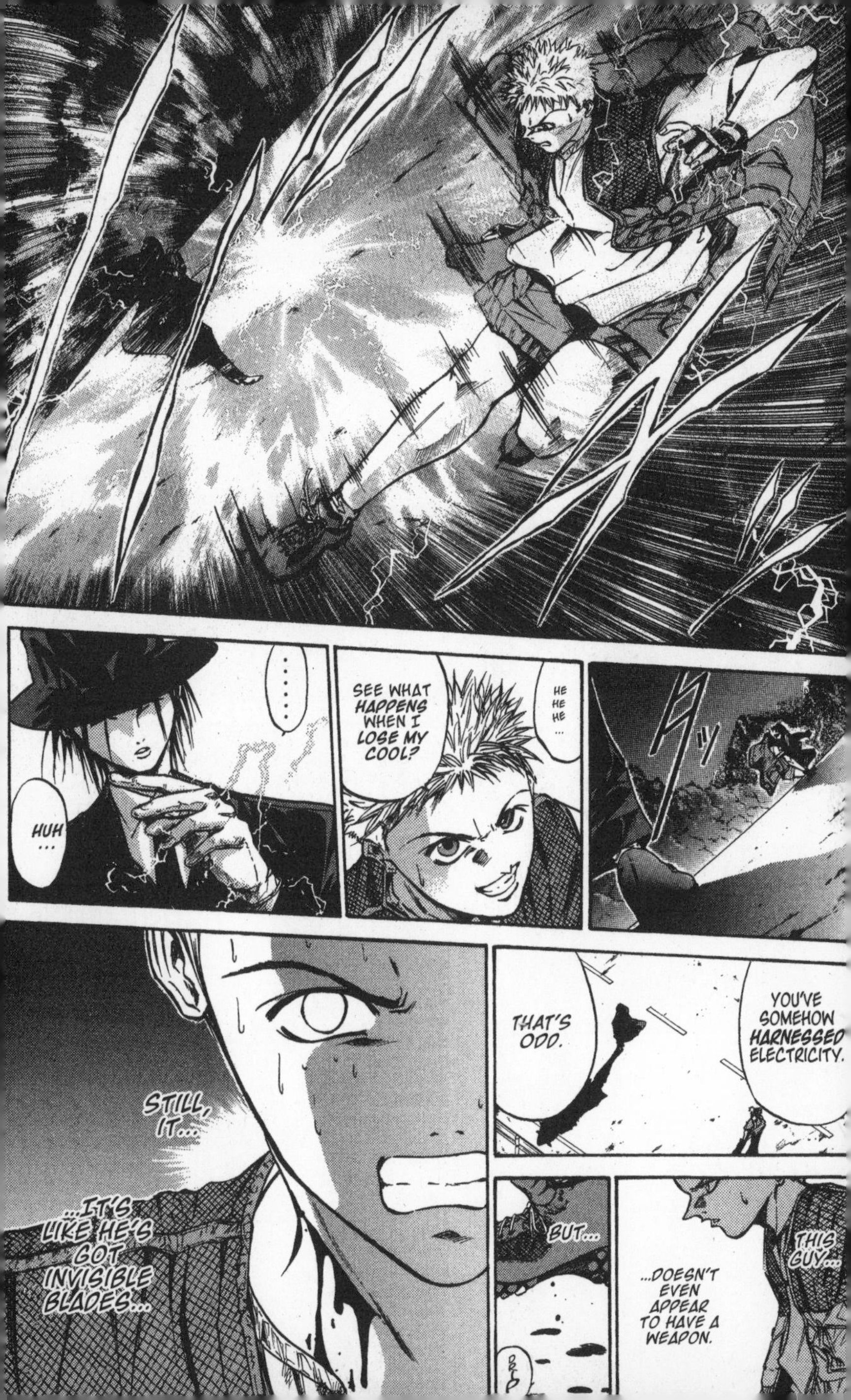
HE HE HE...
SEE WHAT HAPPENS WHEN I LOSE MY COOL?
......
HUH...
YOU'VE SOMEHOW HARNESSED ELECTRICITY.
THAT'S ODD.
THIS GUY...
...DOESN'T EVEN APPEAR TO HAVE A WEAPON.
BUT...
DRIP
STILL, IT...
...IT'S LIKE HE'S GOT INVISIBLE BLADES...

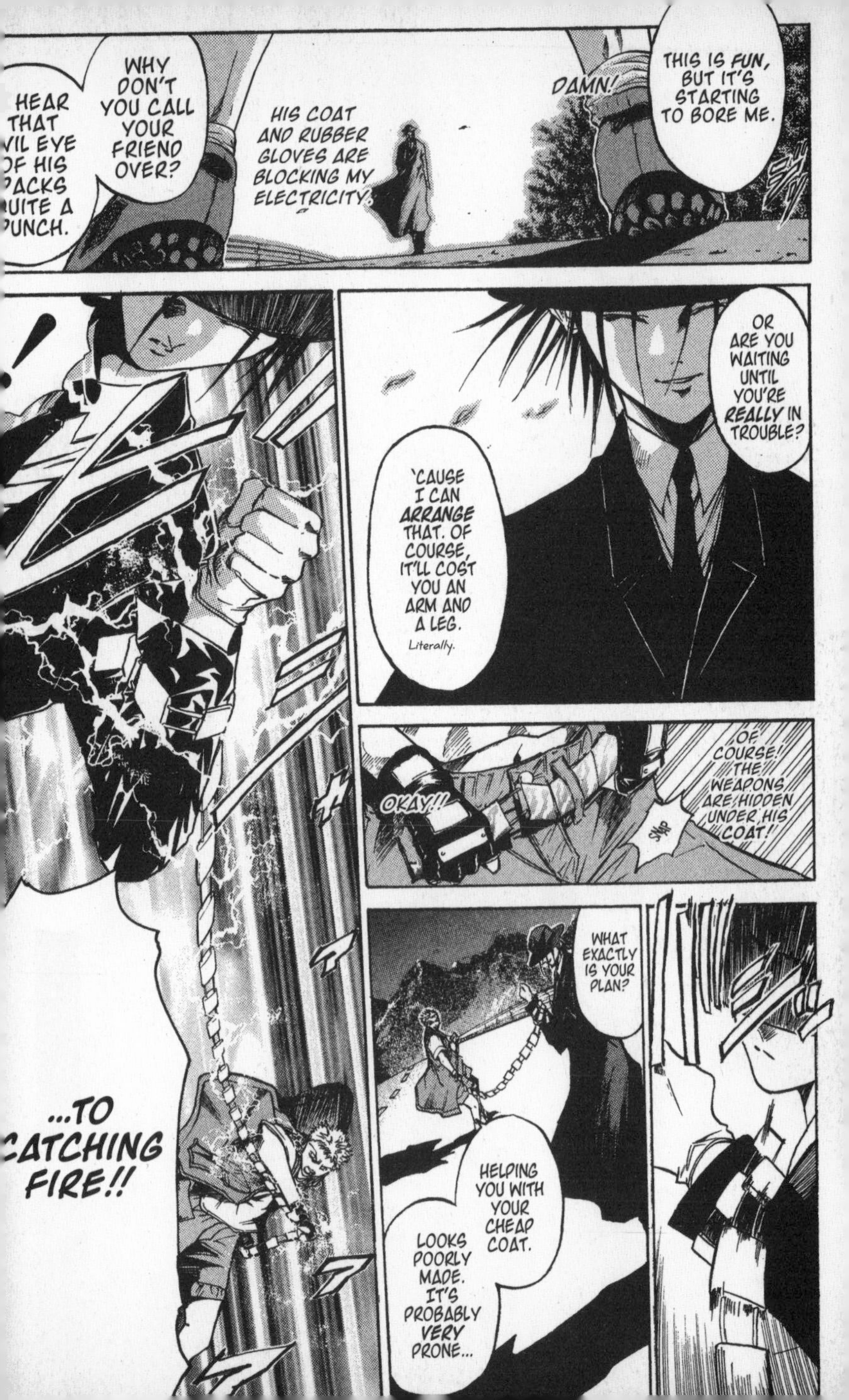
THIS IS FUN, BUT IT'S STARTING TO BORE ME.
DAMN!
HIS COAT AND RUBBER GLOVES ARE BLOCKING MY ELECTRICITY.
WHY DON'T YOU CALL YOUR FRIEND OVER?
HEAR THAT VIL EYE OF HIS ACKS UITE A UNCH.
OR ARE YOU WAITING UNTIL YOU'RE REALLY IN TROUBLE?
'CAUSE I CAN ARRANGE THAT. OF COURSE, IT'LL COST YOU AN ARM AND A LEG.
Literally.
OF COURSE! THE WEAPONS ARE HIDDEN UNDER HIS COAT!
SNAP
OKAY!!
WHAT EXACTLY IS YOUR PLAN?
HELPING YOU WITH YOUR CHEAP COAT.
LOOKS POORLY MADE. IT'S PROBABLY VERY PRONE...
!
...TO ATCHING FIRE!!

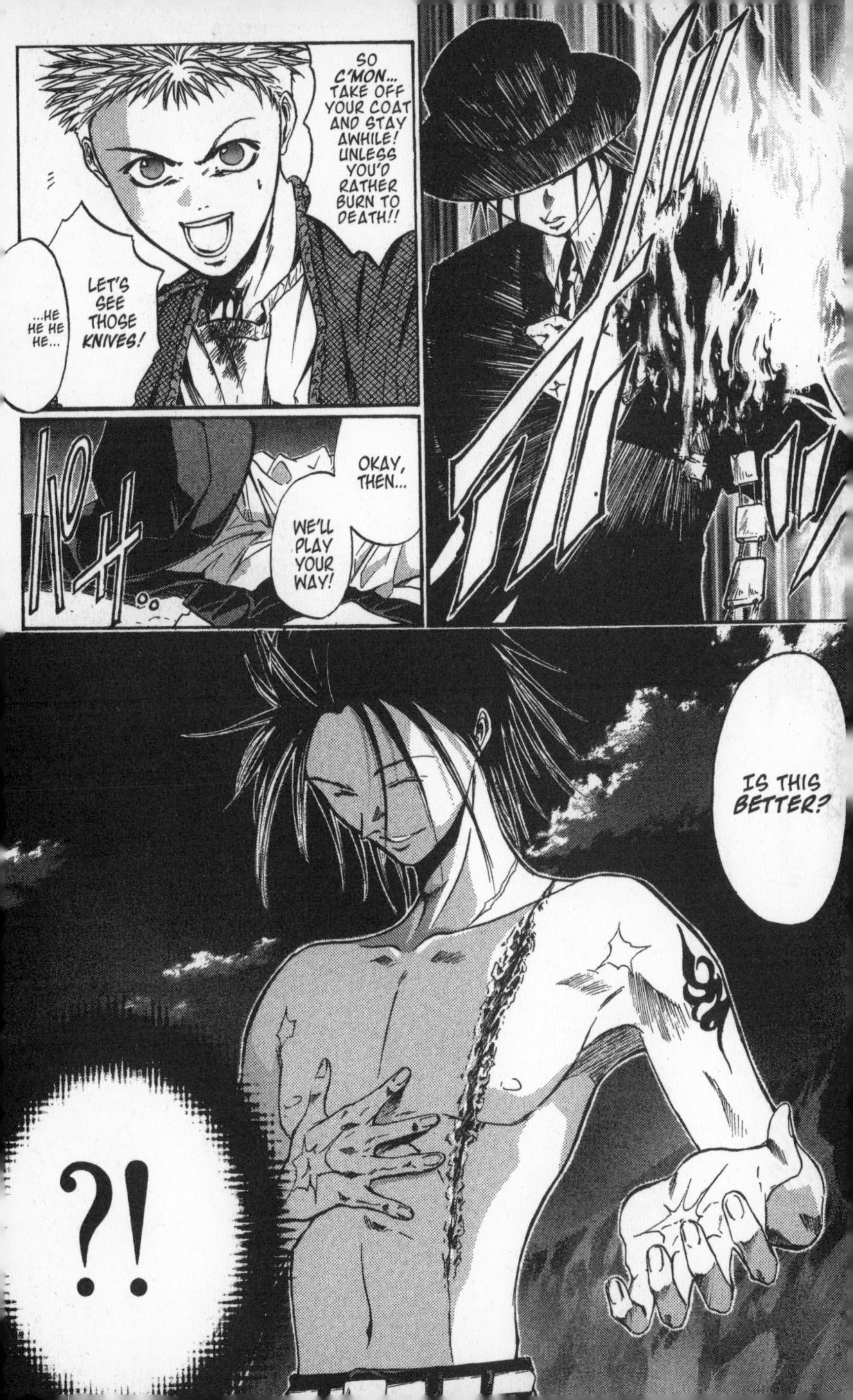
SO C'MON... TAKE OFF YOUR COAT AND STAY AWHILE! UNLESS YOU'D RATHER BURN TO DEATH!!
LET'S SEE THOSE KNIVES!
...HE HE HE HE...
OKAY, THEN...
WE'LL PLAY YOUR WAY!
IS THIS BETTER?
?!

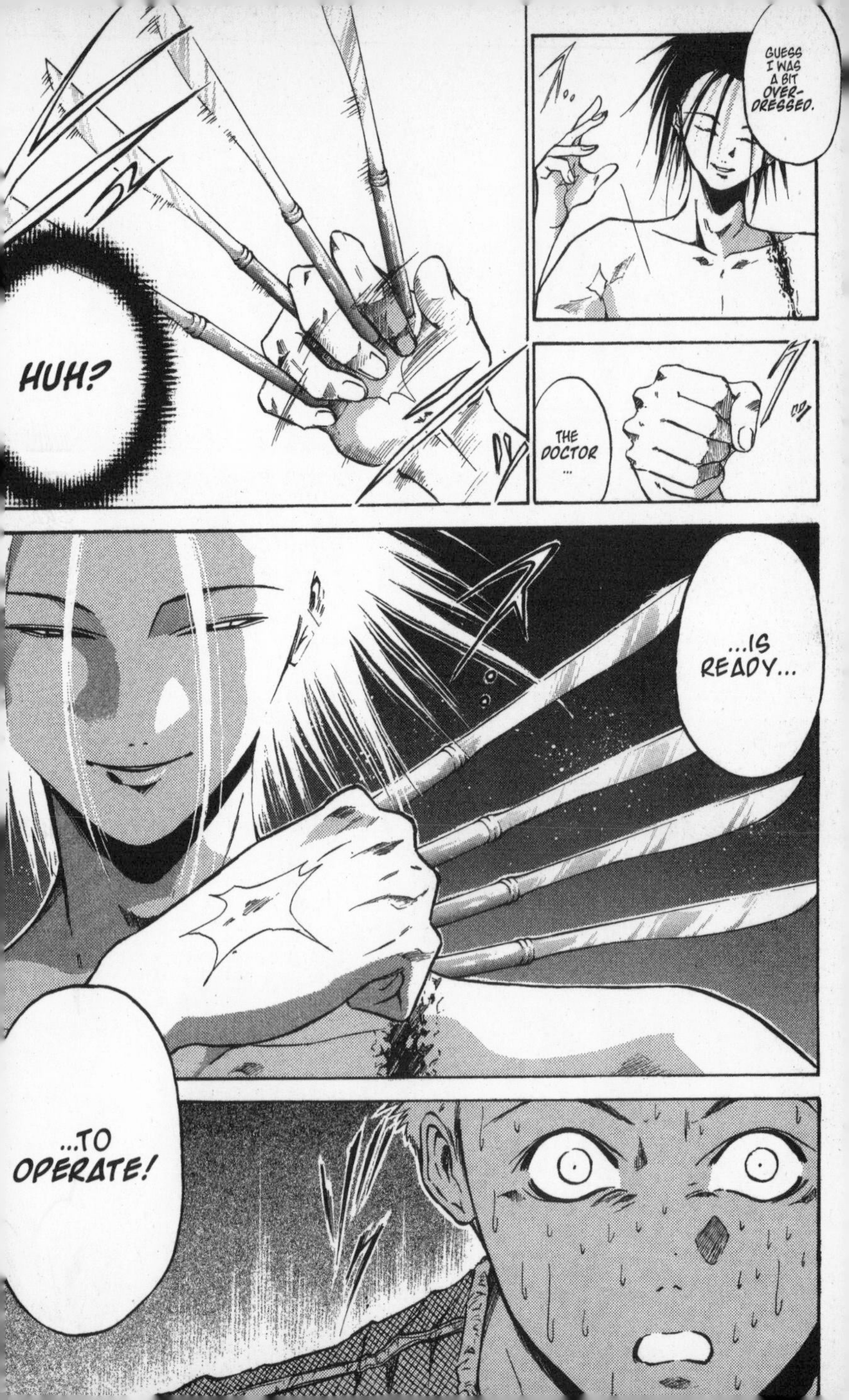
GUESS I WAS A BIT OVER-DRESSED.
THE DOCTOR ...
HUH?
...IS READY...
...TO OPERATE!

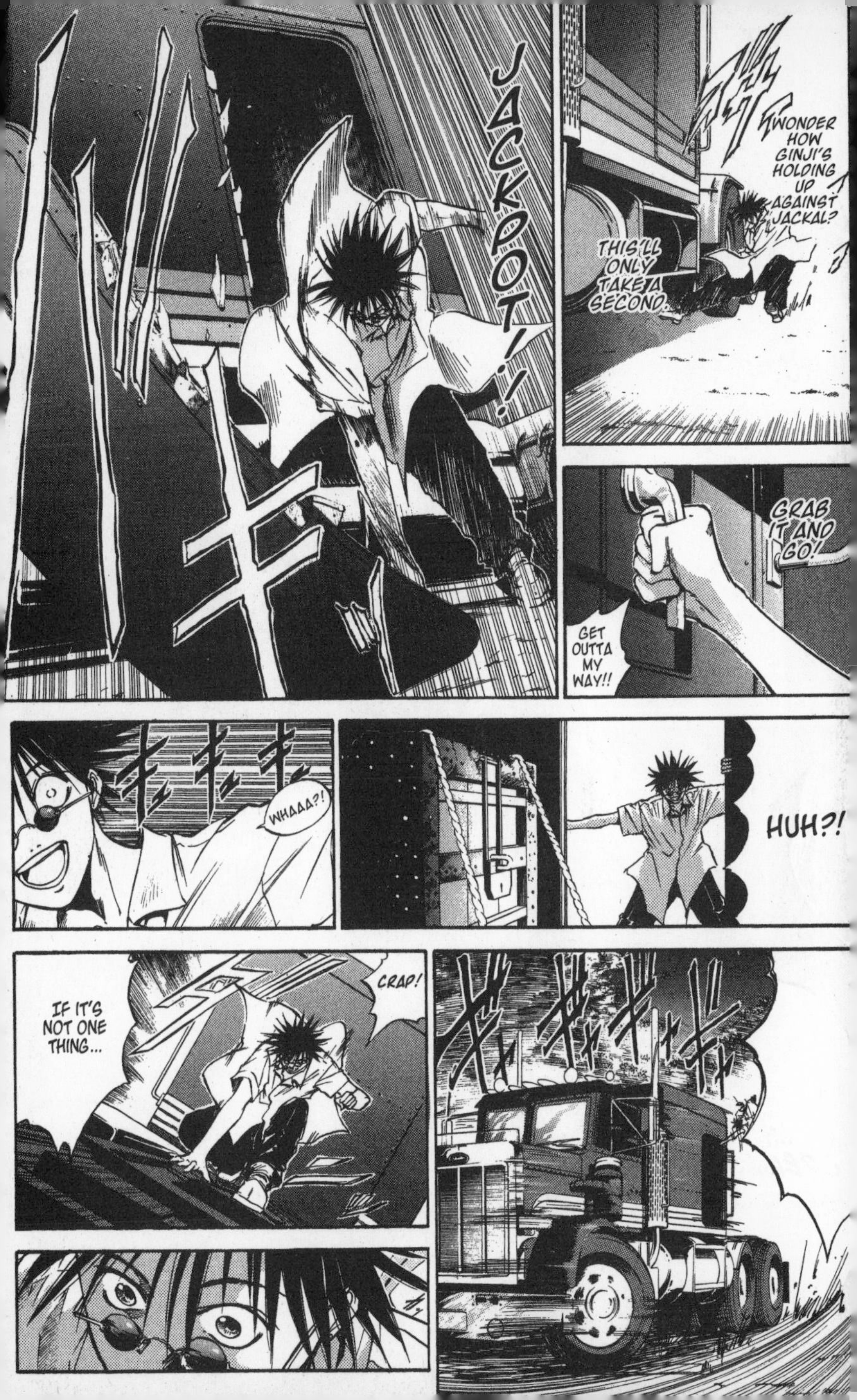
I WONDER HOW GINJI'S HOLDING UP AGAINST JACKAL?
THIS'LL ONLY TAKE A SECOND.
GRAB IT AND GO!
GET OUTTA MY WAY!!
JACKPOT!!
HUH?!
WHAAA?!
CRAP!
IF IT'S NOT ONE THING...

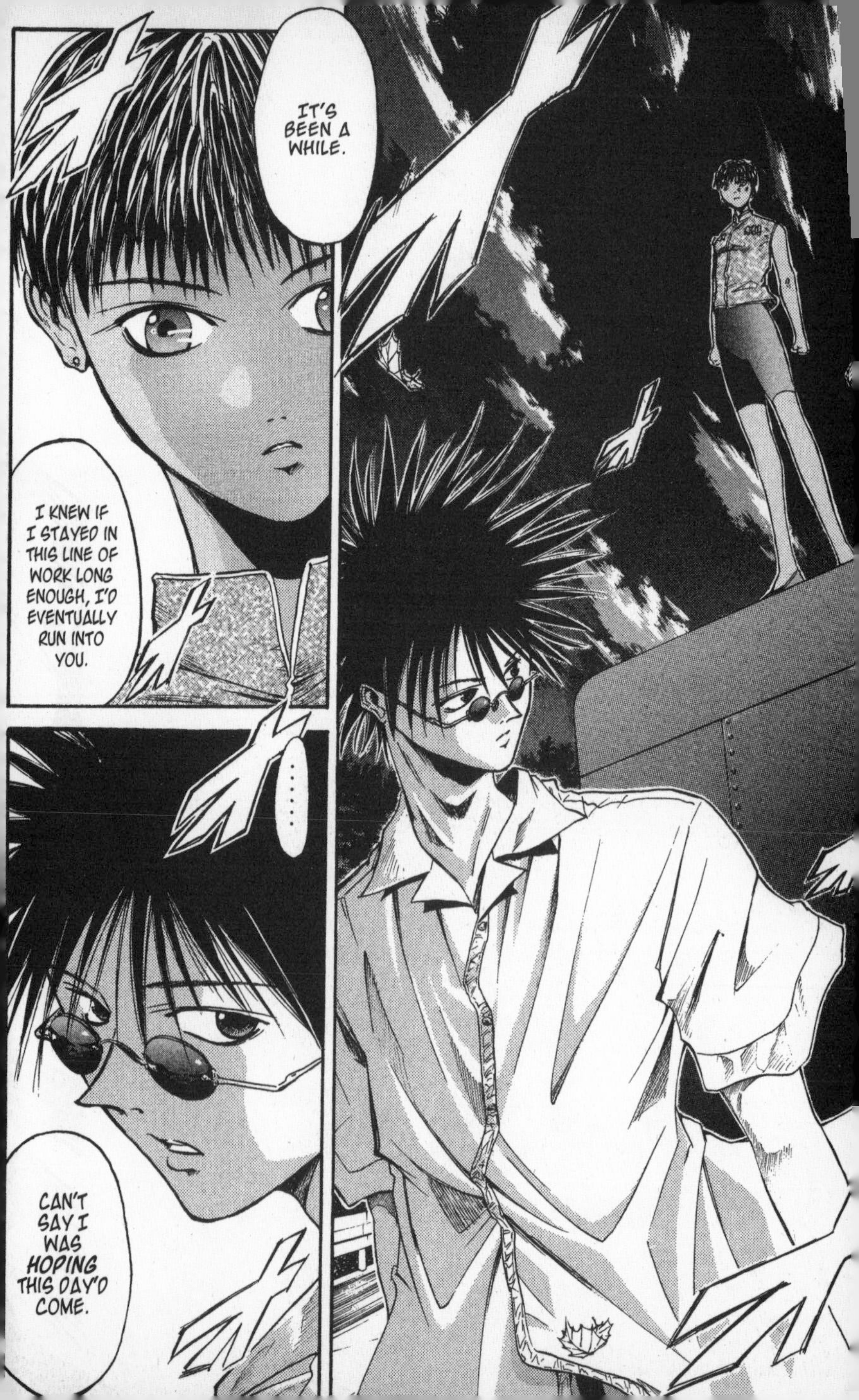
IT'S BEEN A WHILE.
I KNEW IF I STAYED IN THIS LINE OF WORK LONG ENOUGH, I'D EVENTUALLY RUN INTO YOU.
......
CAN'T SAY I WAS *HOPING* THIS DAY'D COME.

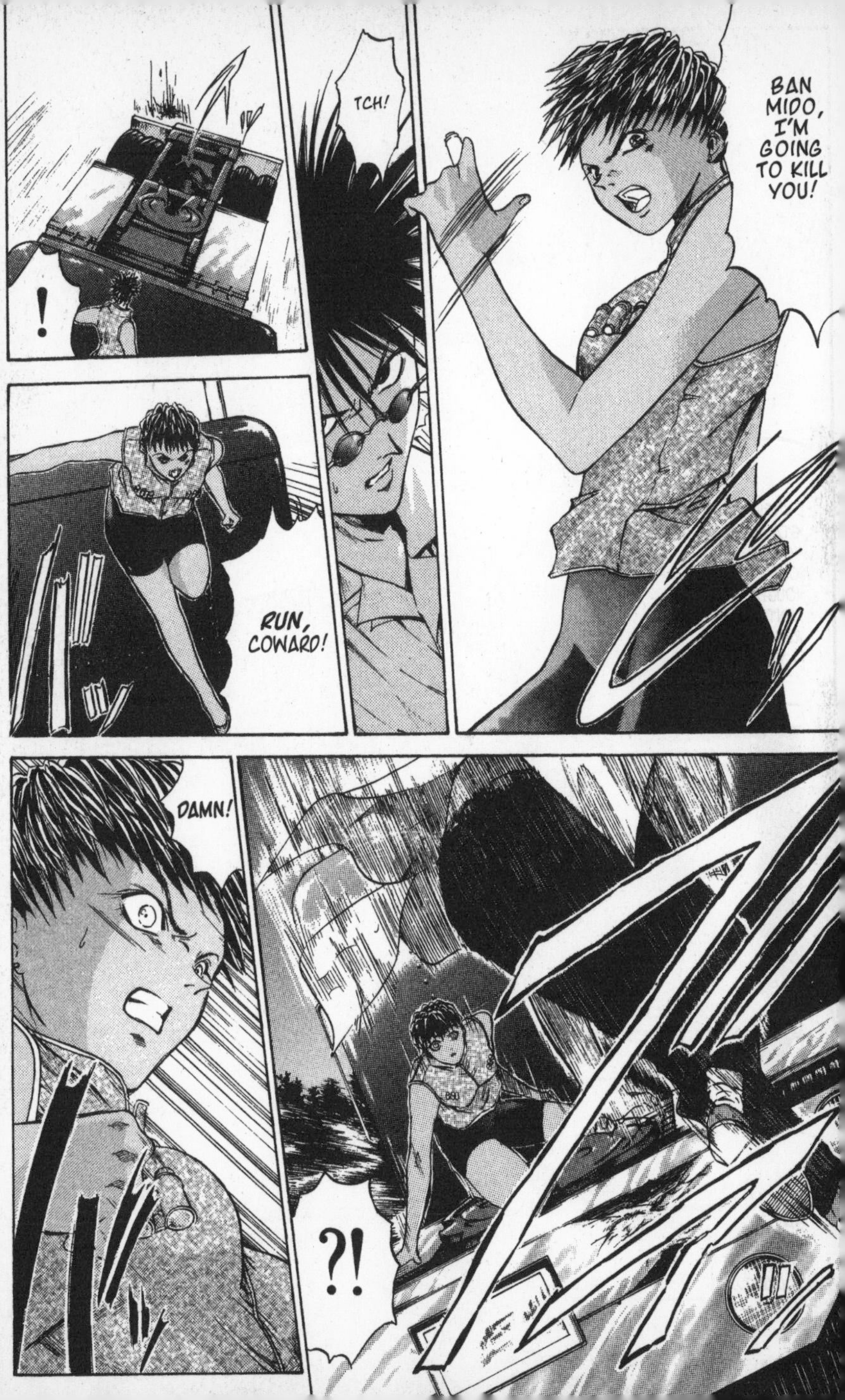
BAN MIDO, I'M GOING TO KILL YOU!
TCH!
!
RUN, COWARD!
DAMN!
?!

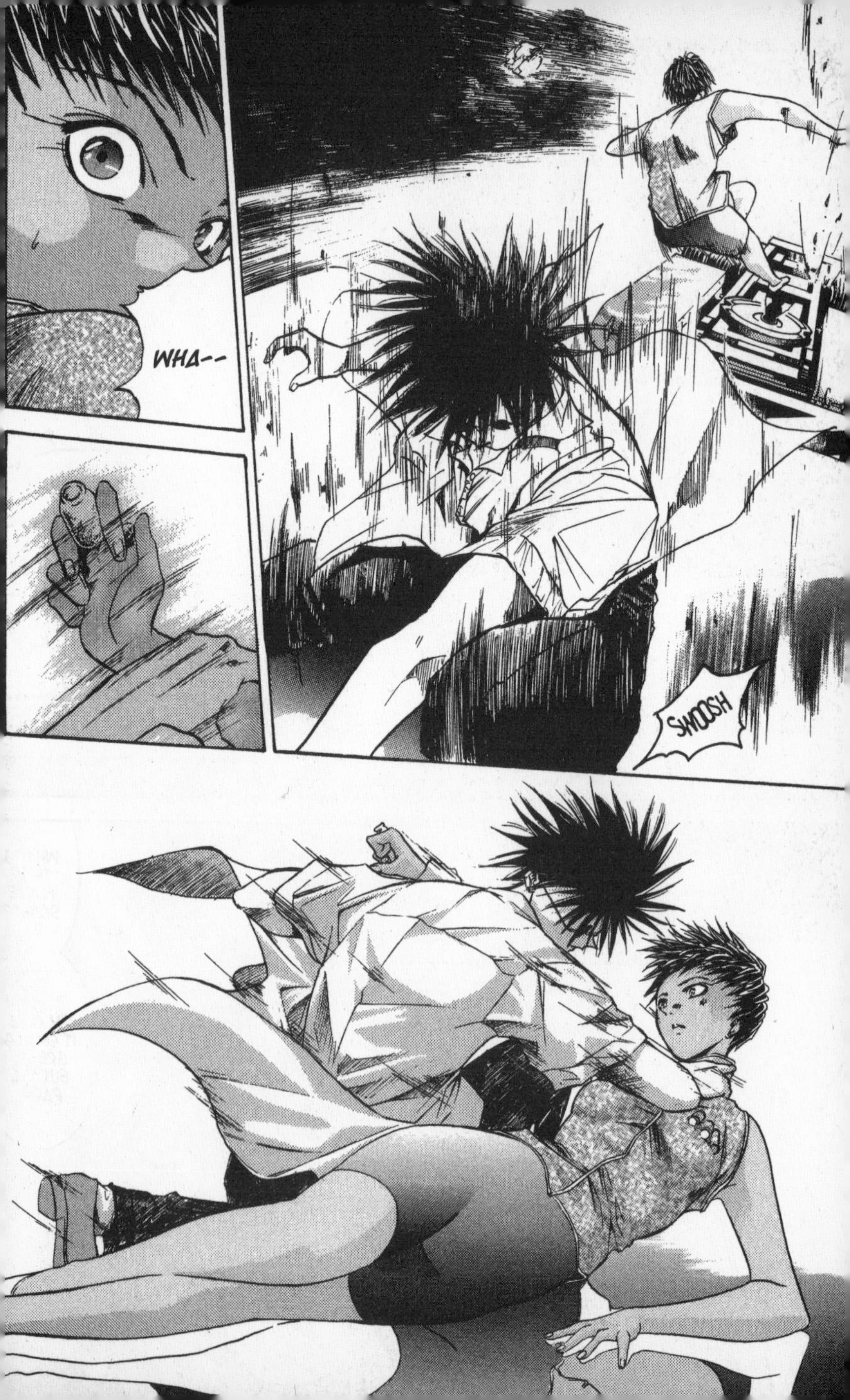
SHOOSH
WHA--

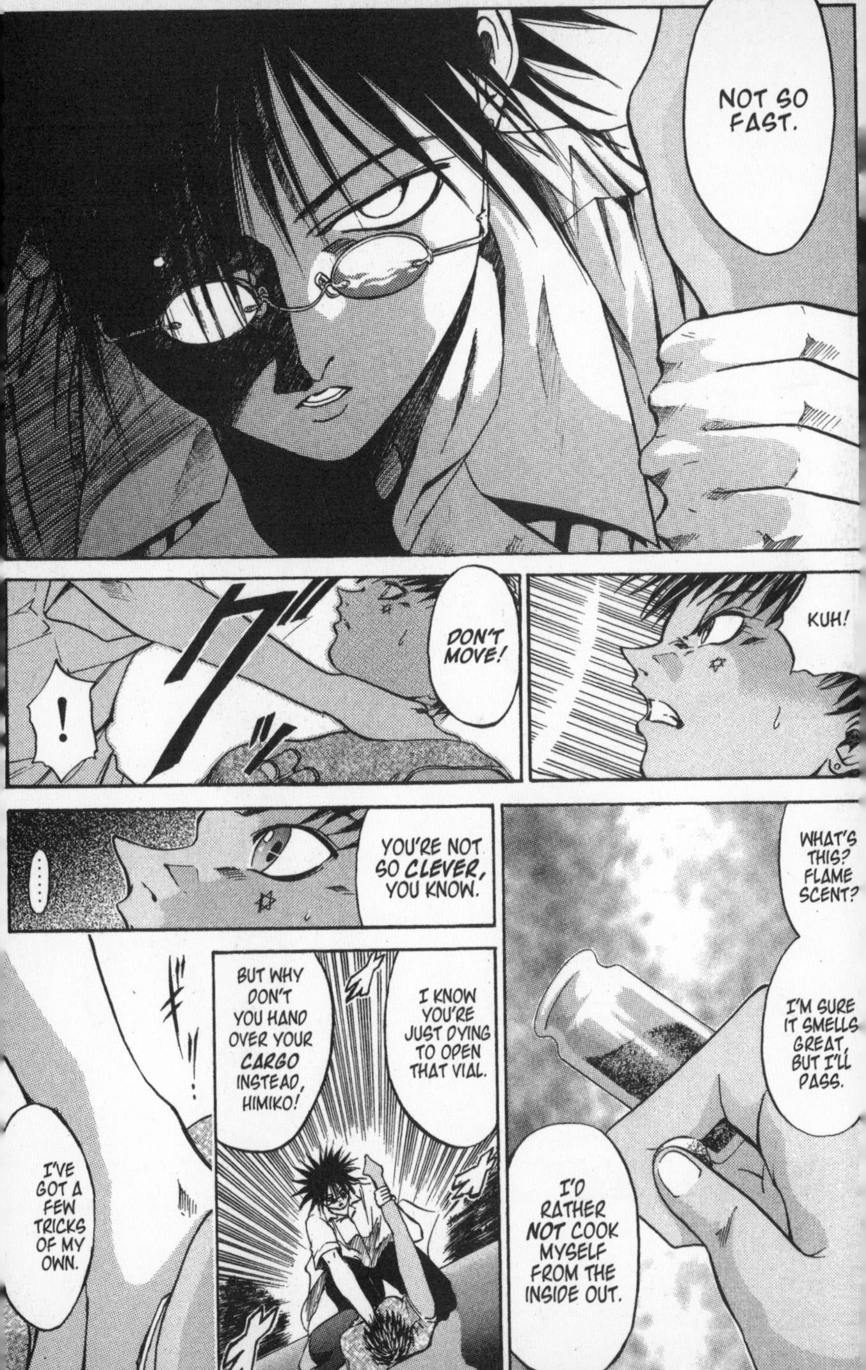
NOT SO FAST.
KUH!
DON'T MOVE!
!
WHAT'S THIS? FLAME SCENT?
I'M SURE IT SMELLS GREAT, BUT I'LL PASS.
I'D RATHER NOT COOK MYSELF FROM THE INSIDE OUT.
YOU'RE NOT SO CLEVER, YOU KNOW.
......
I KNOW YOU'RE JUST DYING TO OPEN THAT VIAL.
BUT WHY DON'T YOU HAND OVER YOUR CARGO INSTEAD, HIMIKO!
I'VE GOT A FEW TRICKS OF MY OWN.

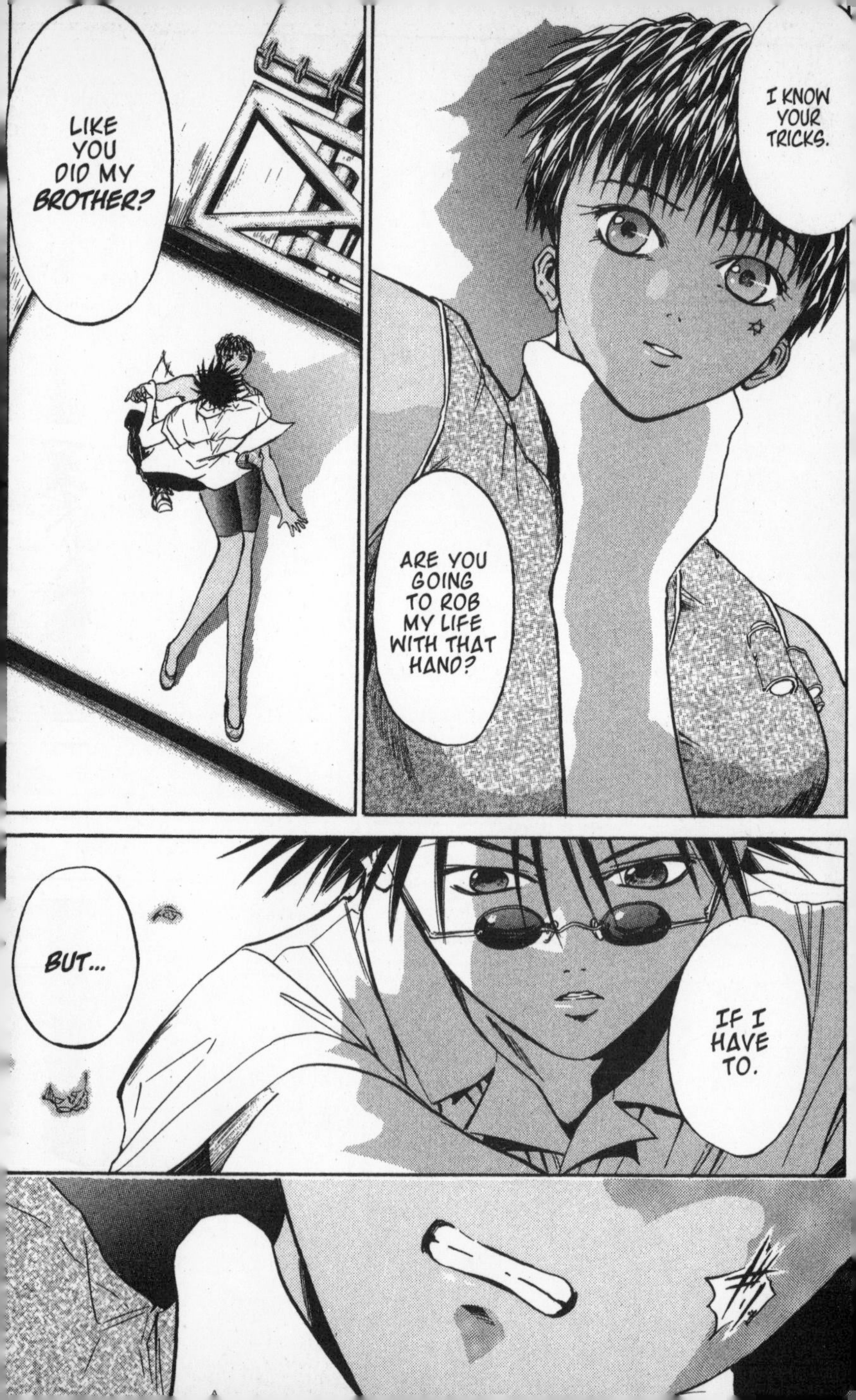
I KNOW YOUR TRICKS.
ARE YOU GOING TO ROB MY LIFE WITH THAT HAND?
LIKE YOU DID MY BROTHER?
IF I HAVE TO.
BUT...

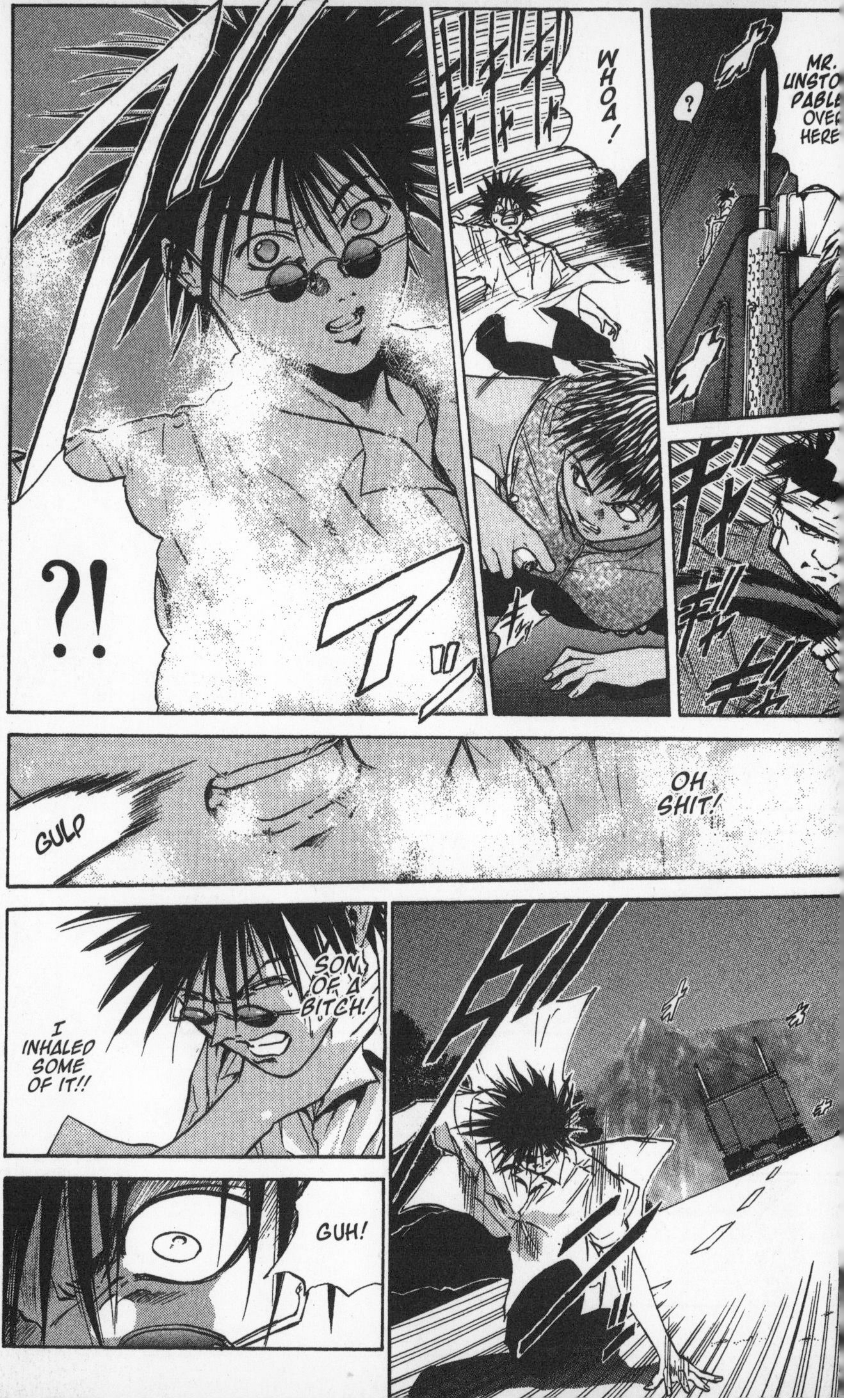
MR. UNSTO PABLE OVER HERE
?
WHOA!
?!
OH SHIT!
GULP
SON OF A BITCH!
I INHALED SOME OF IT!!
GUH!

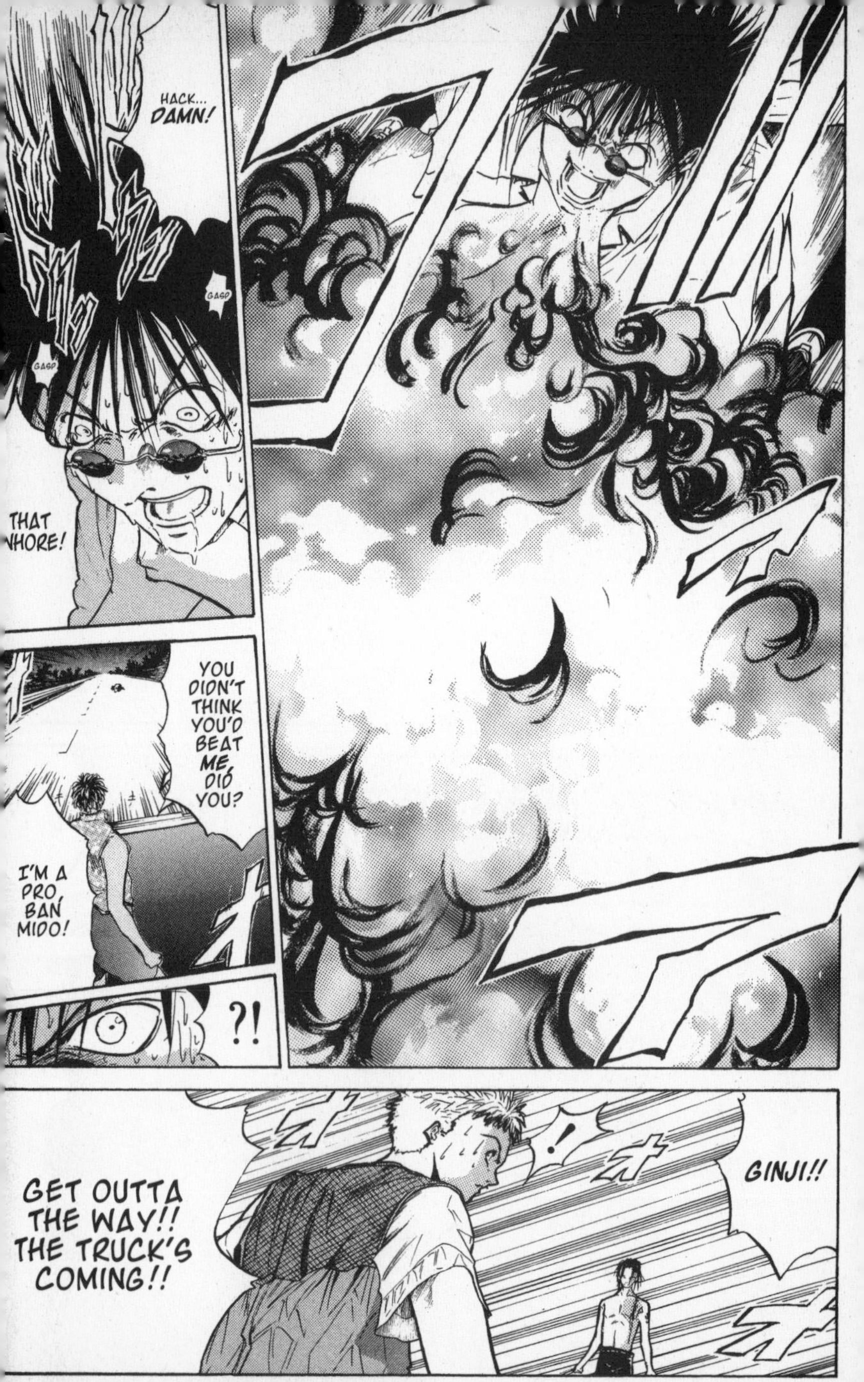
HACK... DAMN!
GASP
GASP
THAT WHORE!
YOU DIDN'T THINK YOU'D BEAT ME, DID YOU?
I'M A PRO, BAN MIDO!
?!
GINJI!!
GET OUTTA THE WAY!! THE TRUCK'S COMING!!

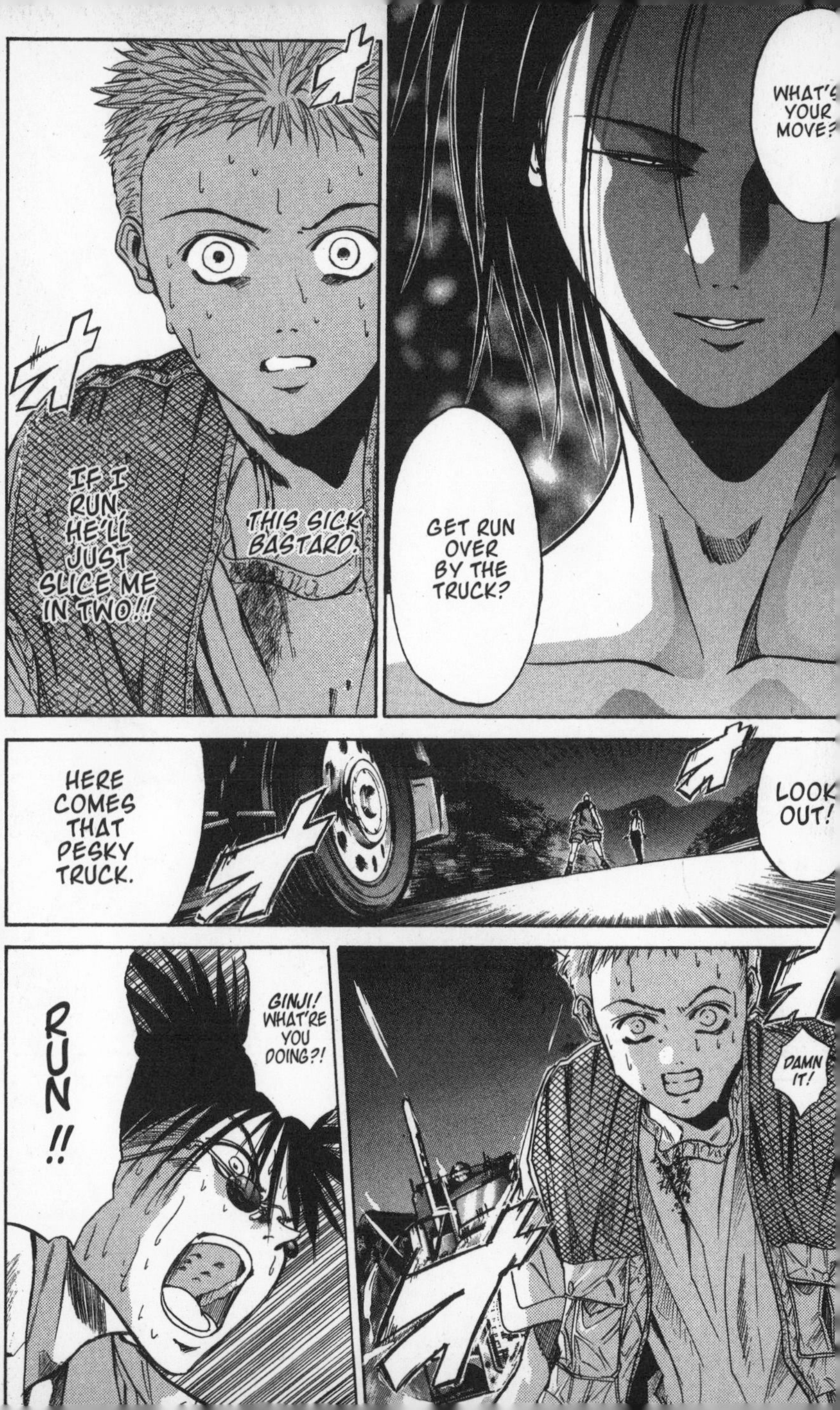
WHAT'S YOUR MOVE?
GET RUN OVER BY THE TRUCK?
THIS SICK BASTARD.
IF I RUN HE'LL JUST SLICE ME IN TWO!!
LOOK OUT!
HERE COMES THAT PESKY TRUCK.
DAMN IT!
GINJI! WHAT'RE YOU DOING?!
RUN!!

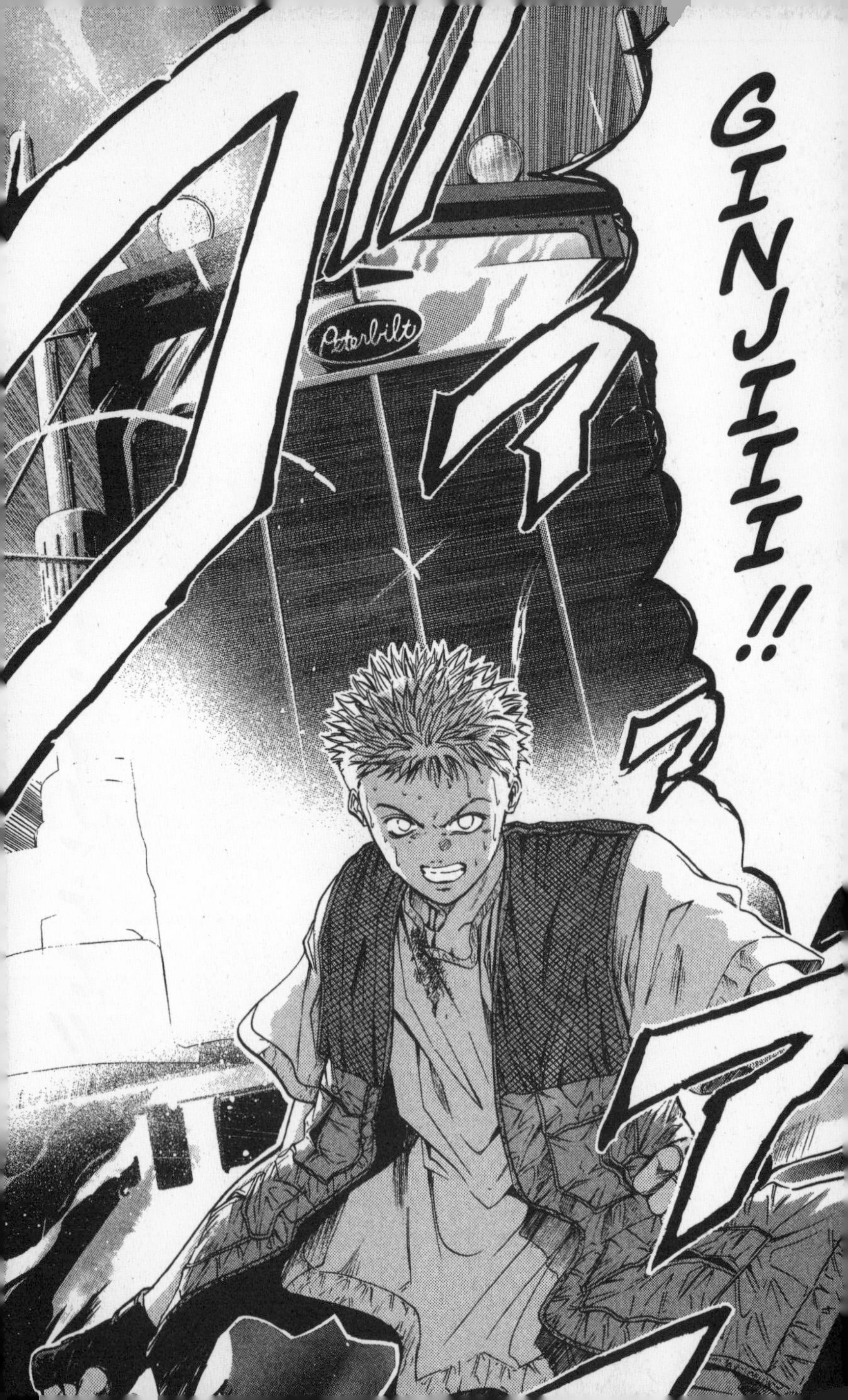
GINJIIII!!
Peterbilt

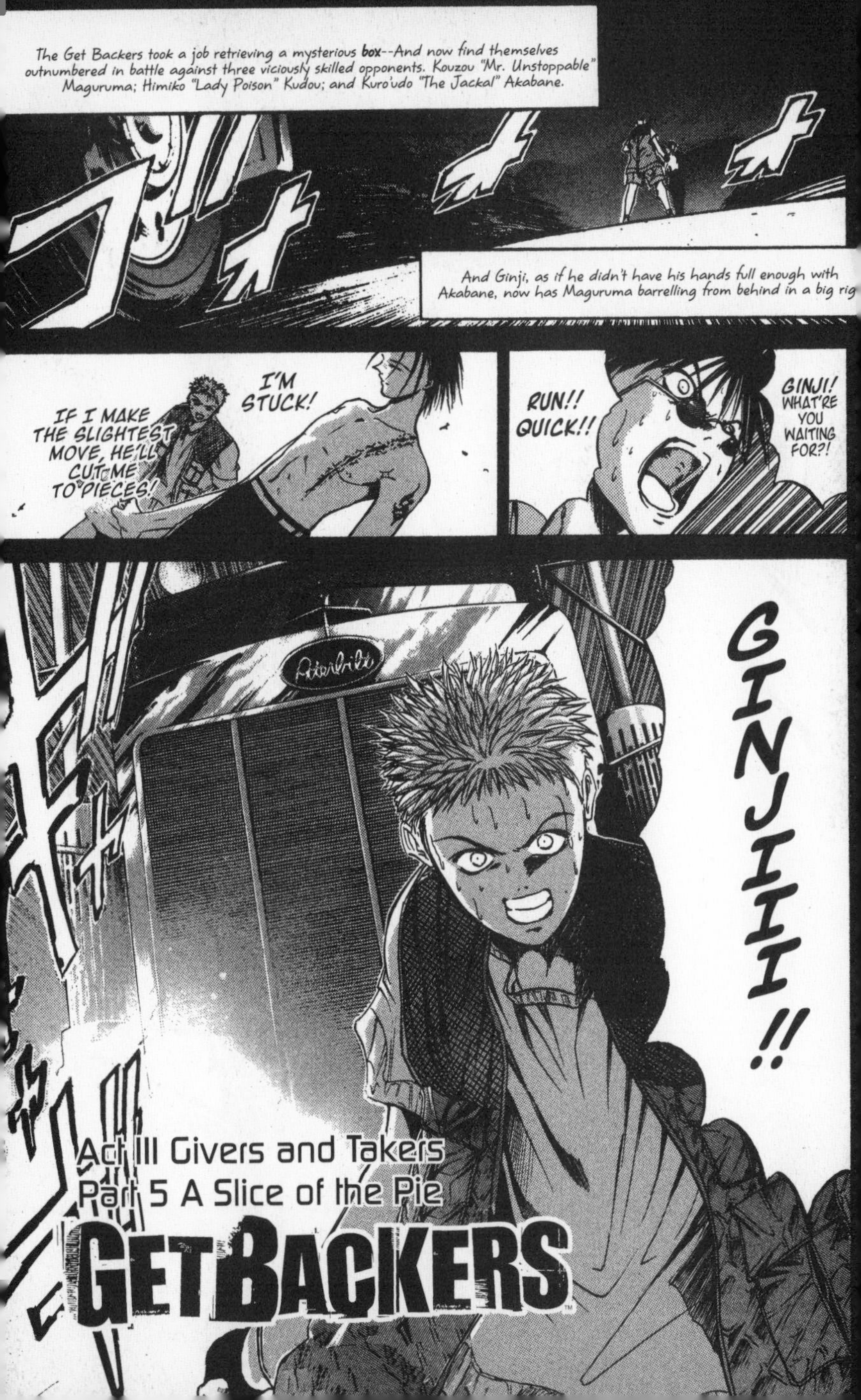
The Get Backers took a job retrieving a mysterious **box**--And now find themselves outnumbered in battle against three viciously skilled opponents. Kouzou "Mr. Unstoppable" Maguruma; Himiko "Lady Poison" Kudou; and Kuro'udo "The Jackal" Akabane.
And Ginji, as if he didn't have his hands full enough with Akabane, now has Maguruma barrelling from behind in a big rig
GINJI! WHAT'RE YOU WAITING FOR?!
RUN!! QUICK!!
I'M STUCK!
IF I MAKE THE SLIGHTEST MOVE, HE'LL CUT ME TO PIECES!
GINJIII!!
Act III Givers and Takers
Part 5 A Slice of the Pie
GETBACKERS

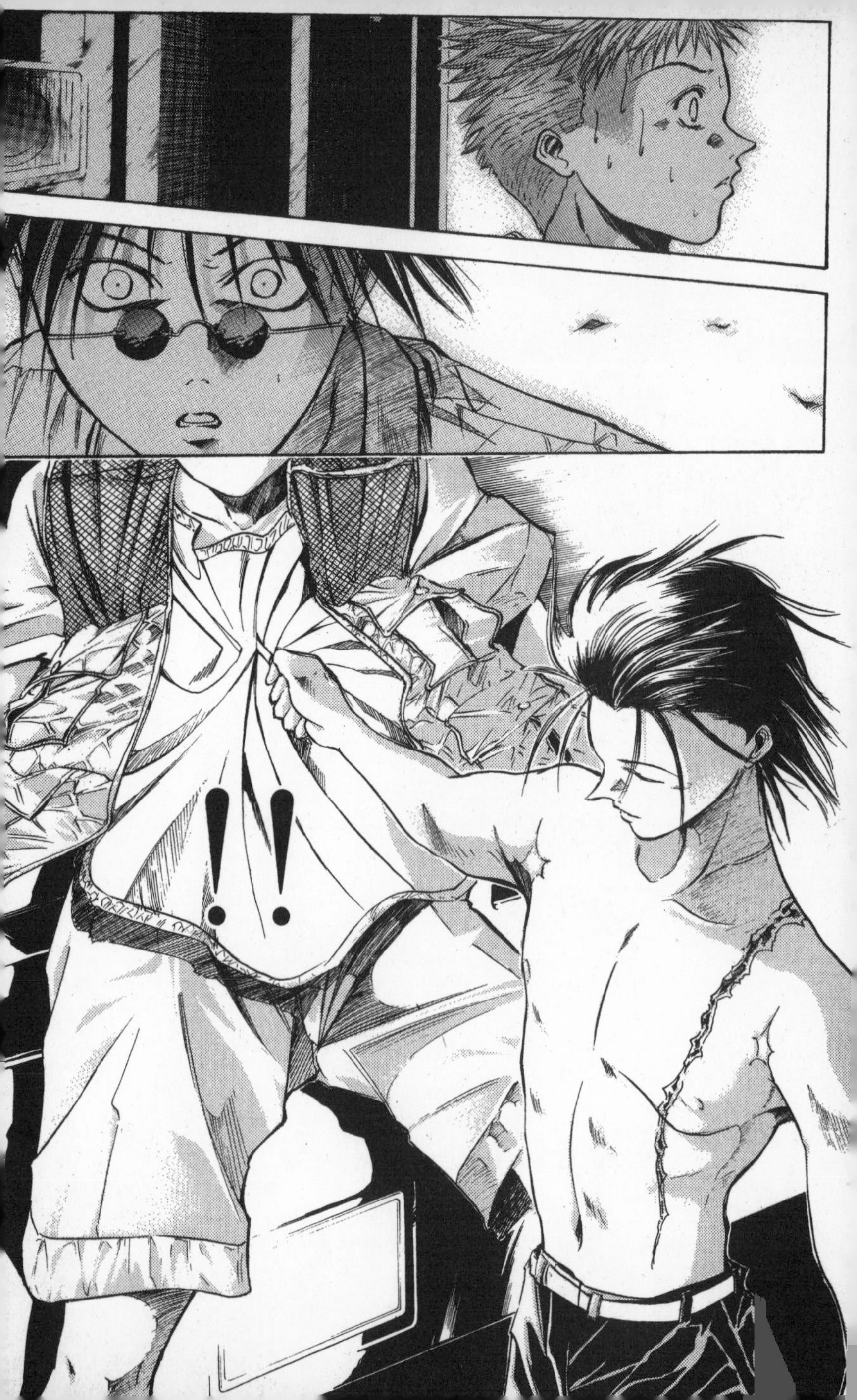
!!

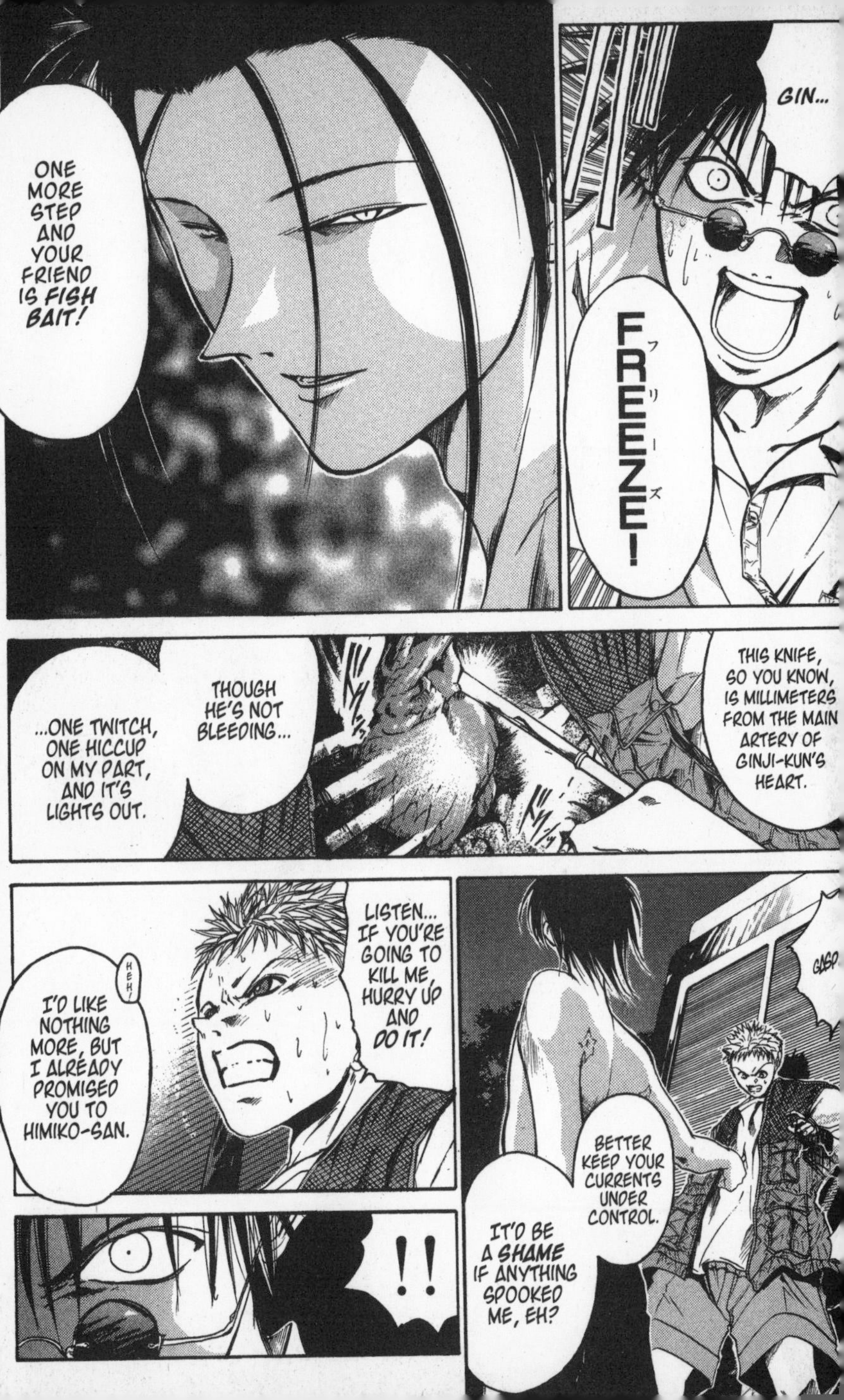

GIN...
FREEZE!
フリーズ
ONE MORE STEP AND YOUR FRIEND IS FISH BAIT!
THIS KNIFE, SO YOU KNOW, IS MILLIMETERS FROM THE MAIN ARTERY OF GINJI-KUN'S HEART.
THOUGH HE'S NOT BLEEDING...
...ONE TWITCH, ONE HICCUP ON MY PART, AND IT'S LIGHTS OUT.
GASP
BETTER KEEP YOUR CURRENTS UNDER CONTROL.
IT'D BE A SHAME IF ANYTHING SPOOKED ME, EH?
LISTEN... IF YOU'RE GOING TO KILL ME, HURRY UP AND DO IT!
HEH!
I'D LIKE NOTHING MORE, BUT I ALREADY PROMISED YOU TO HIMIKO-SAN.
!!

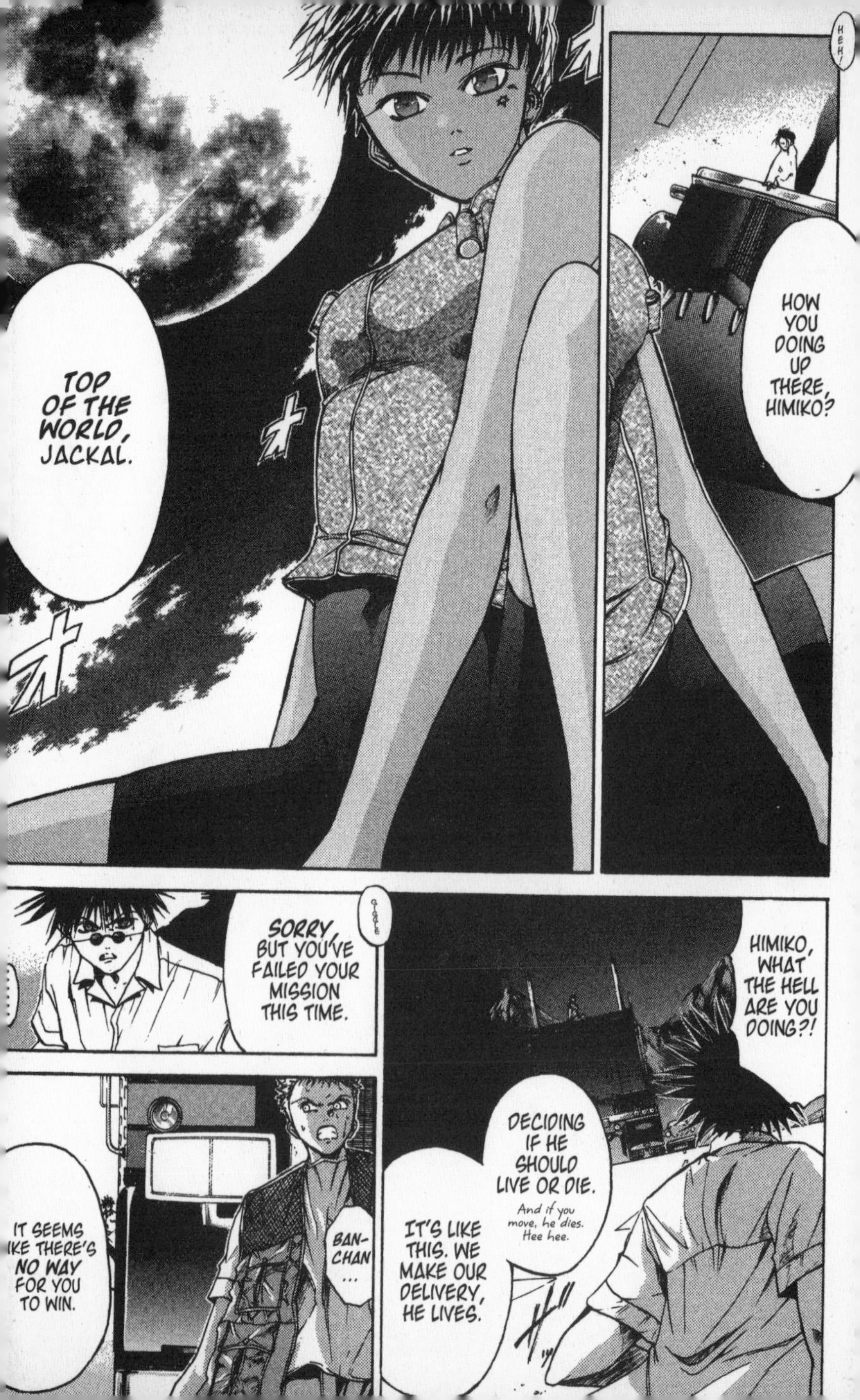
HEH!
HOW YOU DOING UP THERE, HIMIKO?
TOP OF THE WORLD, JACKAL.
HIMIKO, WHAT THE HELL ARE YOU DOING?!
GIGGLE
SORRY, BUT YOU'VE FAILED YOUR MISSION THIS TIME.
......
DECIDING IF HE SHOULD LIVE OR DIE.
And if you move, he dies. Hee hee.
IT'S LIKE THIS. WE MAKE OUR DELIVERY, HE LIVES.
BAN-CHAN...
IT SEEMS IKE THERE'S NO WAY FOR YOU TO WIN.

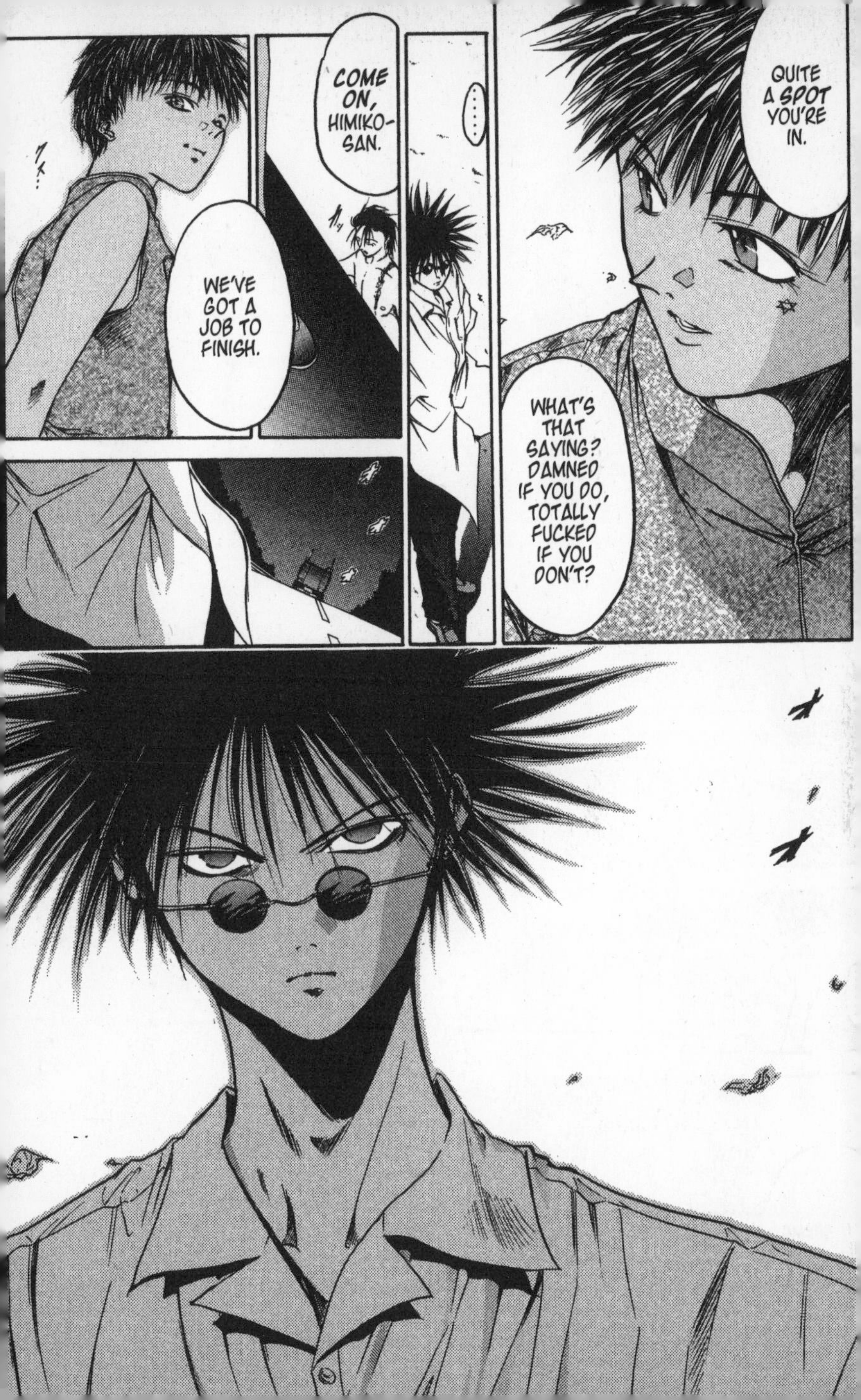

QUITE A SPOT YOU'RE IN.
WHAT'S THAT SAYING? DAMNED IF YOU DO, TOTALLY FUCKED IF YOU DON'T?
......
COME ON, HIMIKO-SAN.
WE'VE GOT A JOB TO FINISH.

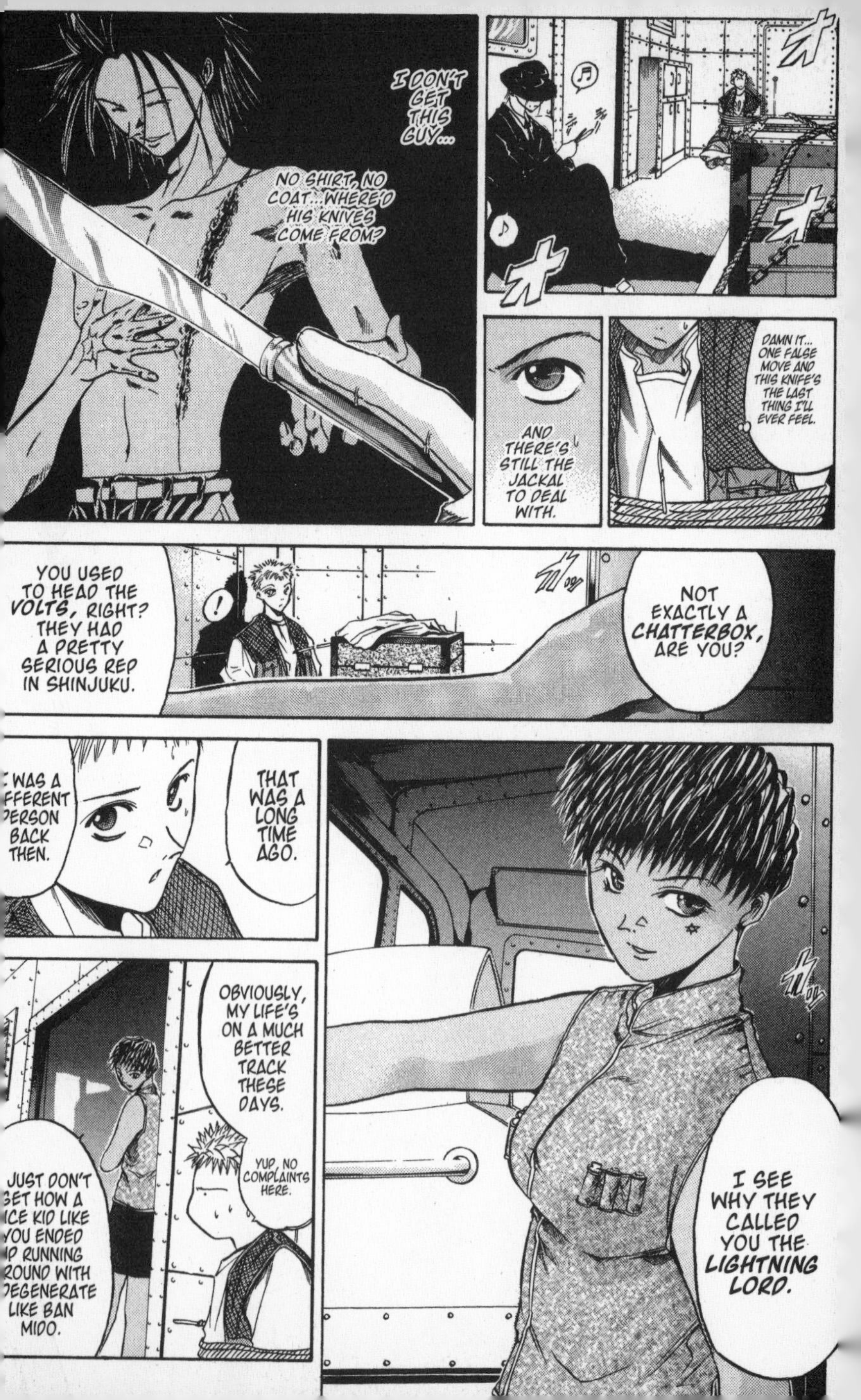

DAMN IT... ONE FALSE MOVE AND THIS KNIFE'S THE LAST THING I'LL EVER FEEL.
AND THERE'S STILL THE JACKAL TO DEAL WITH.
I DON'T GET THIS GUY...
NO SHIRT, NO COAT... WHERE'D HIS KNIVES COME FROM?
NOT EXACTLY A CHATTERBOX, ARE YOU?
YOU USED TO HEAD THE VOLTS, RIGHT? THEY HAD A PRETTY SERIOUS REP IN SHINJUKU.
I SEE WHY THEY CALLED YOU THE LIGHTNING LORD.
THAT WAS A LONG TIME AGO.
WAS A FFERENT ERSON BACK THEN.
OBVIOUSLY, MY LIFE'S ON A MUCH BETTER TRACK THESE DAYS.
YUP, NO COMPLAINTS HERE.
JUST DON'T GET HOW A ICE KID LIKE YOU ENDED IP RUNNING ROUND WITH DEGENERATE LIKE BAN MIDO.

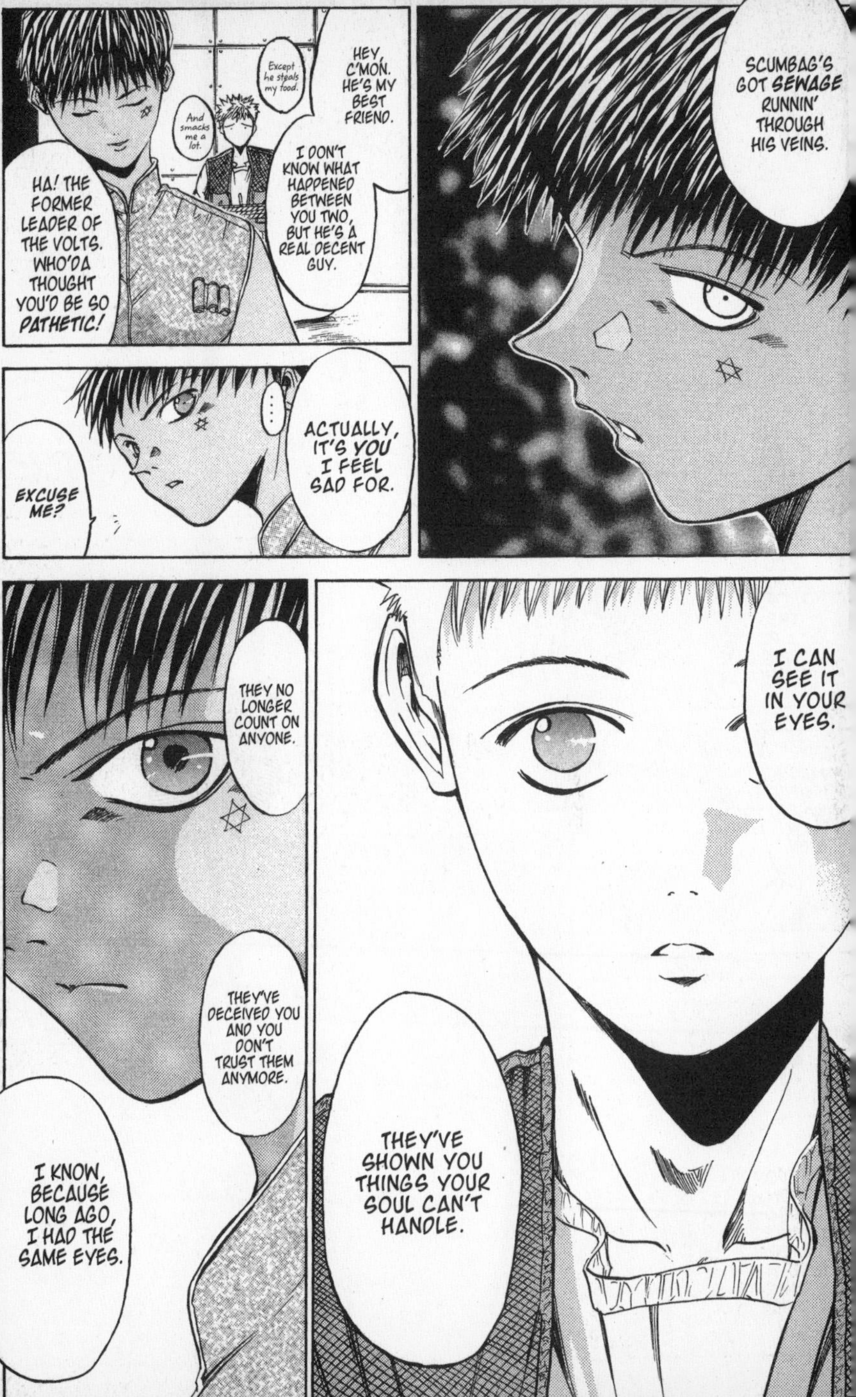
SCUMBAG'S GOT SEWAGE RUNNIN' THROUGH HIS VEINS.
HEY, C'MON. HE'S MY BEST FRIEND.
Except he steals my food.
I DON'T KNOW WHAT HAPPENED BETWEEN YOU TWO, BUT HE'S A REAL DECENT GUY.
And smacks me a lot.
HA! THE FORMER LEADER OF THE VOLTS. WHO'DA THOUGHT YOU'D BE SO PATHETIC!
...
ACTUALLY, IT'S YOU I FEEL SAD FOR.
EXCUSE ME?
I CAN SEE IT IN YOUR EYES.
THEY'VE SHOWN YOU THINGS YOUR SOUL CAN'T HANDLE.
THEY NO LONGER COUNT ON ANYONE.
THEY'VE DECEIVED YOU AND YOU DON'T TRUST THEM ANYMORE.
I KNOW, BECAUSE LONG AGO, I HAD THE SAME EYES.

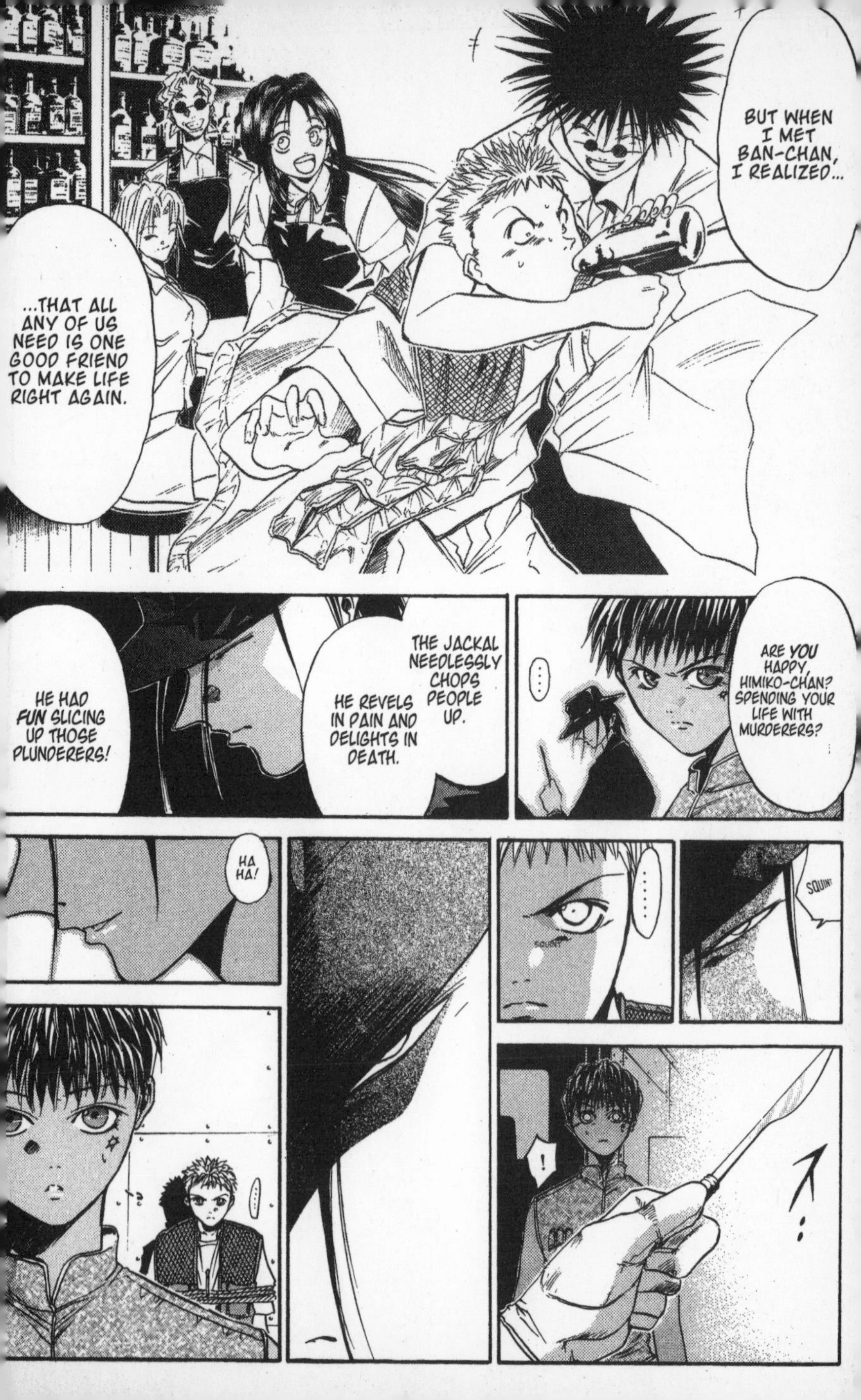
BUT WHEN I MET BAN-CHAN, I REALIZED...
...THAT ALL ANY OF US NEED IS ONE GOOD FRIEND TO MAKE LIFE RIGHT AGAIN.
ARE YOU HAPPY, HIMIKO-CHAN? SPENDING YOUR LIFE WITH MURDERERS?
...
THE JACKAL NEEDLESSLY CHOPS PEOPLE UP.
HE REVELS IN PAIN AND DELIGHTS IN DEATH.
HE HAD FUN SLICING UP THOSE PLUNDERERS!
SQUINT
......
SQUINT
HA HA!
!
?
...

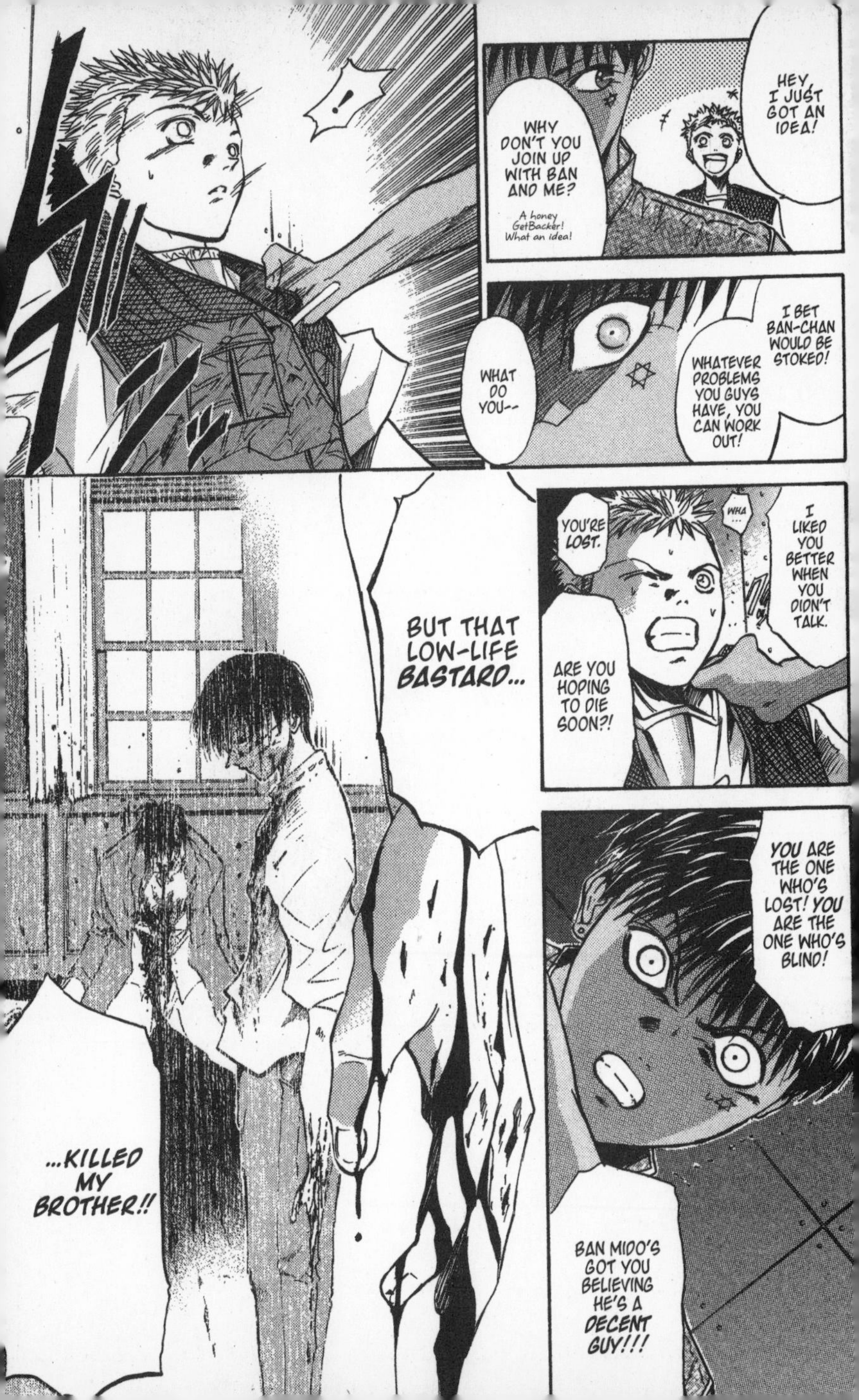

HEY, I JUST GOT AN IDEA!
WHY DON'T YOU JOIN UP WITH BAN AND ME?
A honey GetBacker! What an idea!
I BET BAN-CHAN WOULD BE STOKED!
WHATEVER PROBLEMS YOU GUYS HAVE, YOU CAN WORK OUT!
WHAT DO YOU--
!
I LIKED YOU BETTER WHEN YOU DIDN'T TALK.
WHA...
YOU'RE LOST.
ARE YOU HOPING TO DIE SOON?!
YOU ARE THE ONE WHO'S LOST! YOU ARE THE ONE WHO'S BLIND!
BAN MIDO'S GOT YOU BELIEVING HE'S A DECENT GUY!!!
BUT THAT LOW-LIFE BASTARD...
...KILLED MY BROTHER!!

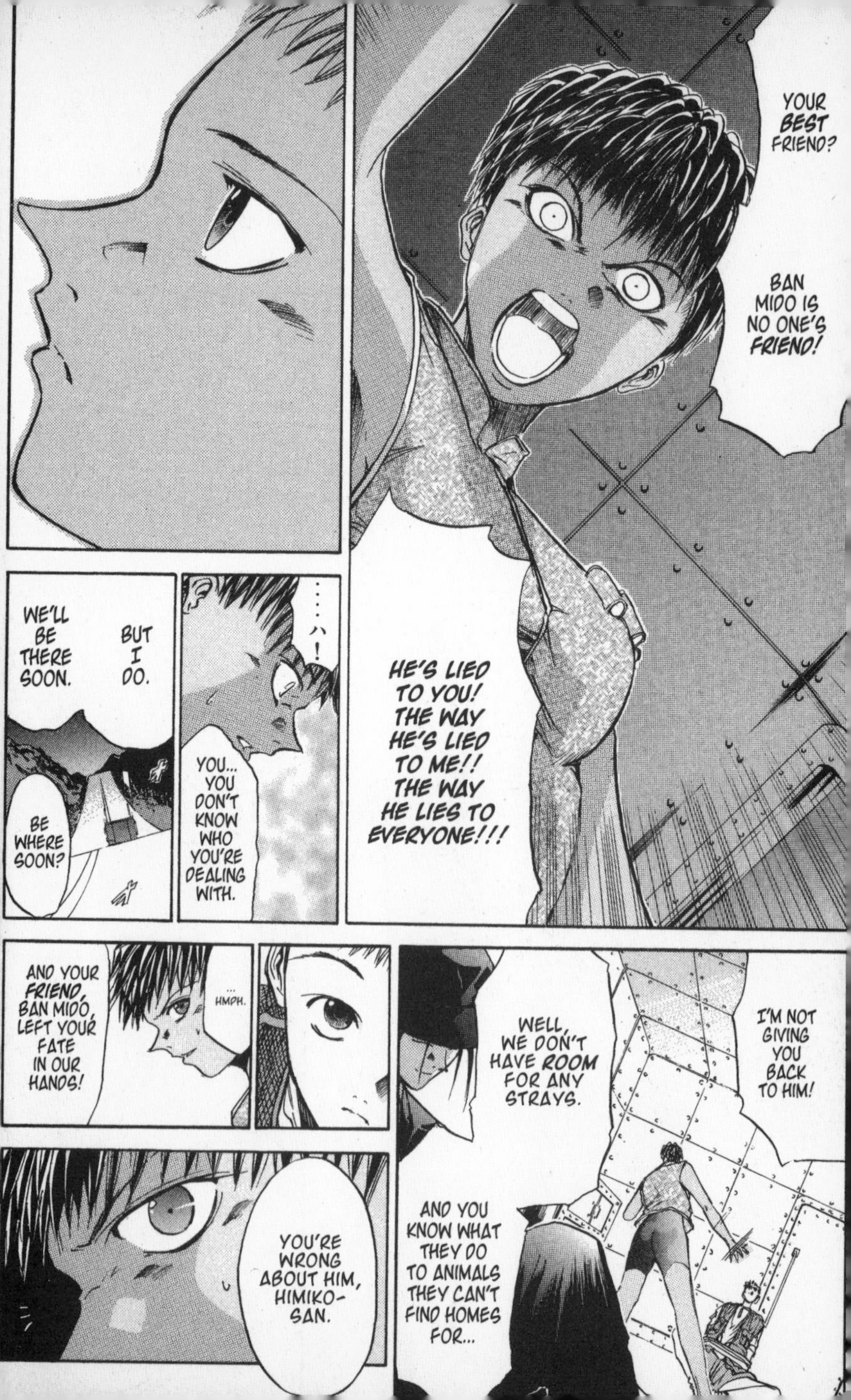
YOUR BEST FRIEND?
BAN MIDO IS NO ONE'S FRIEND!
HE'S LIED TO YOU! THE WAY HE'S LIED TO ME!! THE WAY HE LIES TO EVERYONE!!!
...ハ!
YOU... YOU DON'T KNOW WHO YOU'RE DEALING WITH.
BUT I DO.
WE'LL BE THERE SOON.
BE WHERE SOON?
I'M NOT GIVING YOU BACK TO HIM!
WELL, WE DON'T HAVE ROOM FOR ANY STRAYS.
AND YOU KNOW WHAT THEY DO TO ANIMALS THEY CAN'T FIND HOMES FOR...
...HMPH.
AND YOUR FRIEND, BAN MIDO, LEFT YOUR FATE IN OUR HANDS!
YOU'RE WRONG ABOUT HIM, HIMIKO-SAN.

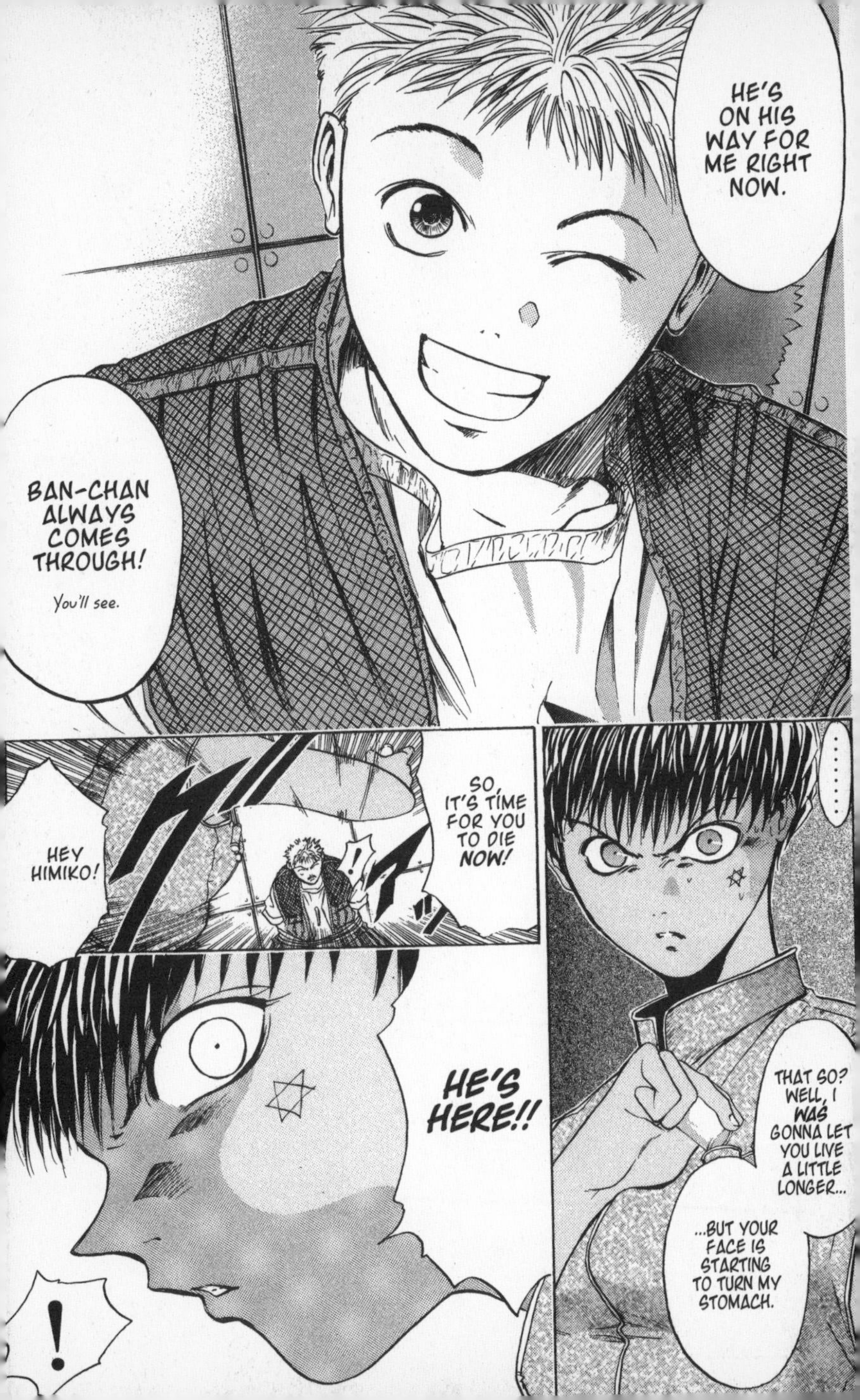
HE'S ON HIS WAY FOR ME RIGHT NOW.
BAN-CHAN ALWAYS COMES THROUGH!
You'll see.
......
THAT SO? WELL, I WAS GONNA LET YOU LIVE A LITTLE LONGER...
...BUT YOUR FACE IS STARTING TO TURN MY STOMACH.
SO, IT'S TIME FOR YOU TO DIE NOW!
HEY HIMIKO!
!
HE'S HERE!!
!

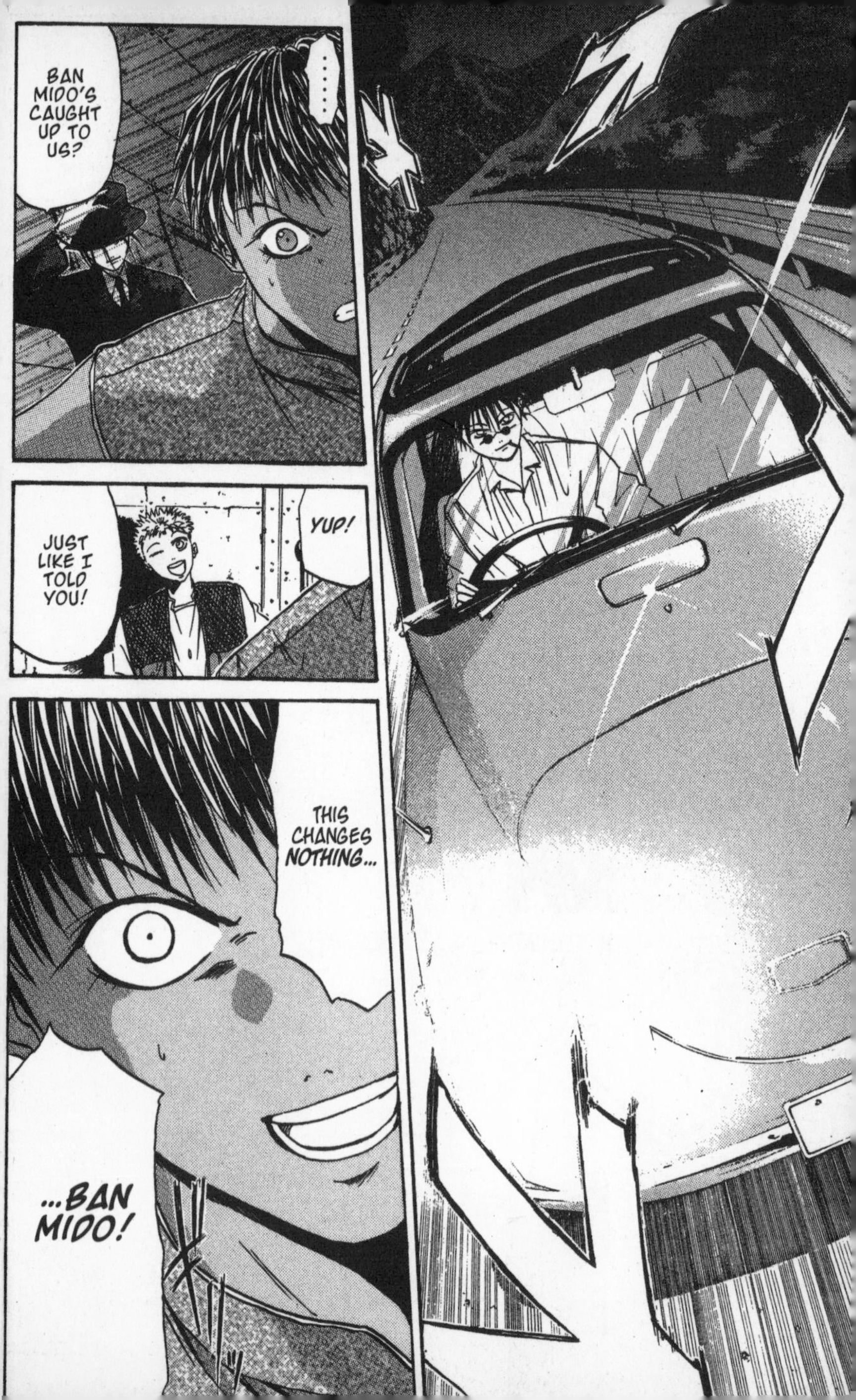
......
BAN MIDO'S CAUGHT UP TO US?
YUP!
JUST LIKE I TOLD YOU!
THIS CHANGES NOTHING...
...BAN MIDO!

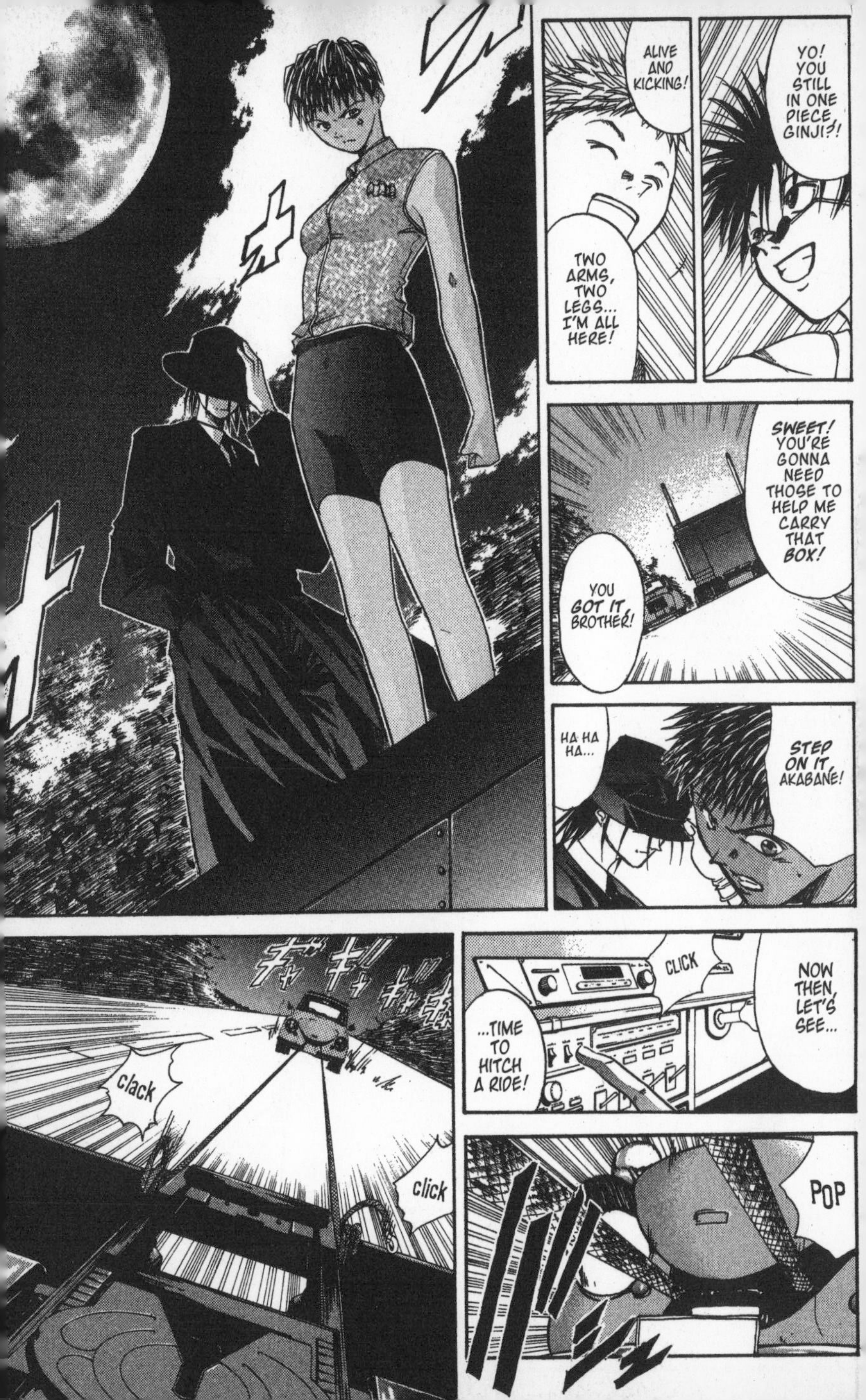
YO! YOU STILL IN ONE PIECE GINJI?!
ALIVE AND KICKING!
TWO ARMS, TWO LEGS... I'M ALL HERE!
SWEET! YOU'RE GONNA NEED THOSE TO HELP ME CARRY THAT BOX!
YOU GOT IT BROTHER!
STEP ON IT, AKABANE!
HA HA HA...
NOW THEN, LET'S SEE...
CLICK
...TIME TO HITCH A RIDE!
POP
clack
click

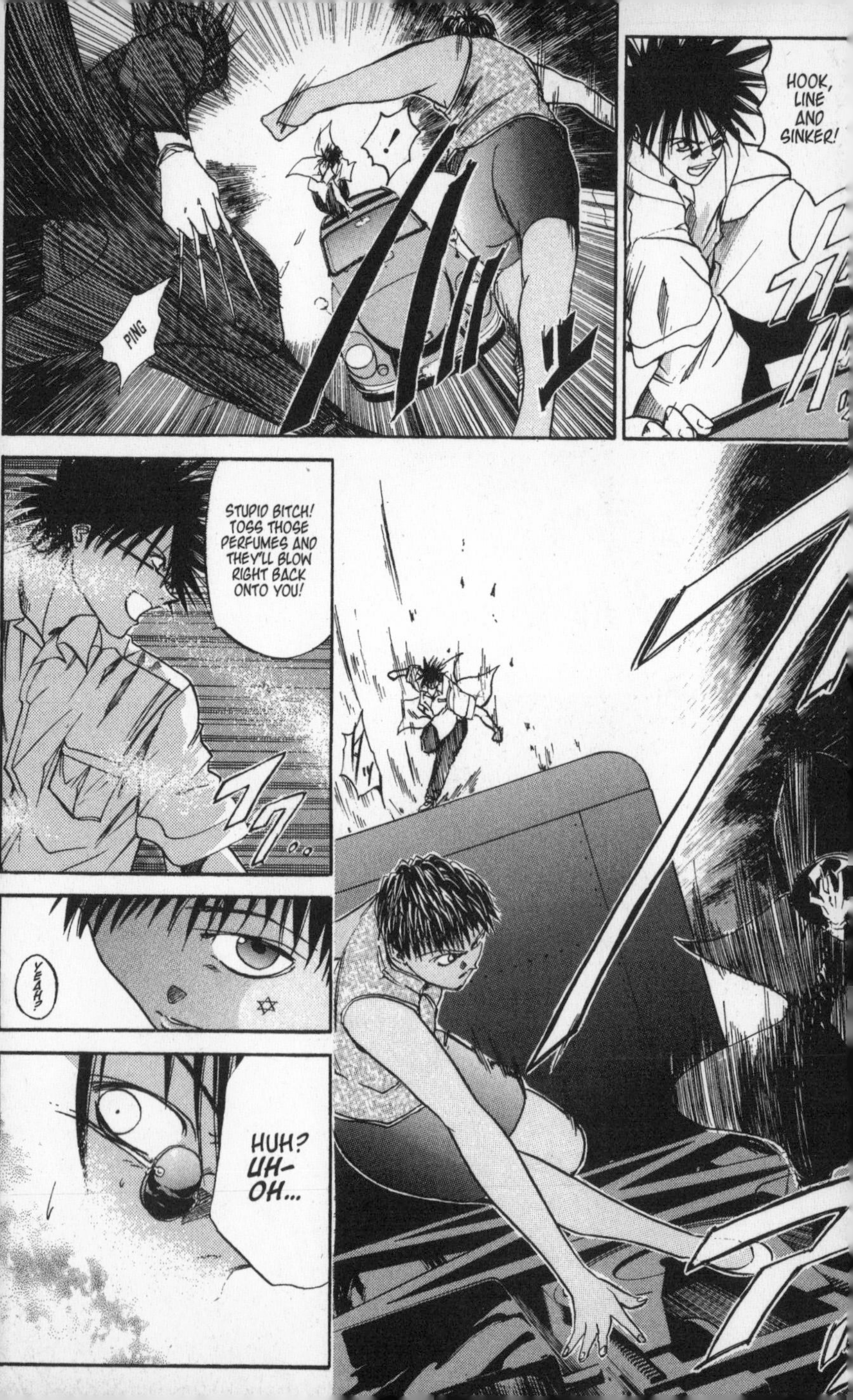
HOOK, LINE AND SINKER!
!
PING
STUPID BITCH! TOSS THOSE PERFUMES AND THEY'LL BLOW RIGHT BACK ONTO YOU!
YEAH?
HUH? UH-OH...

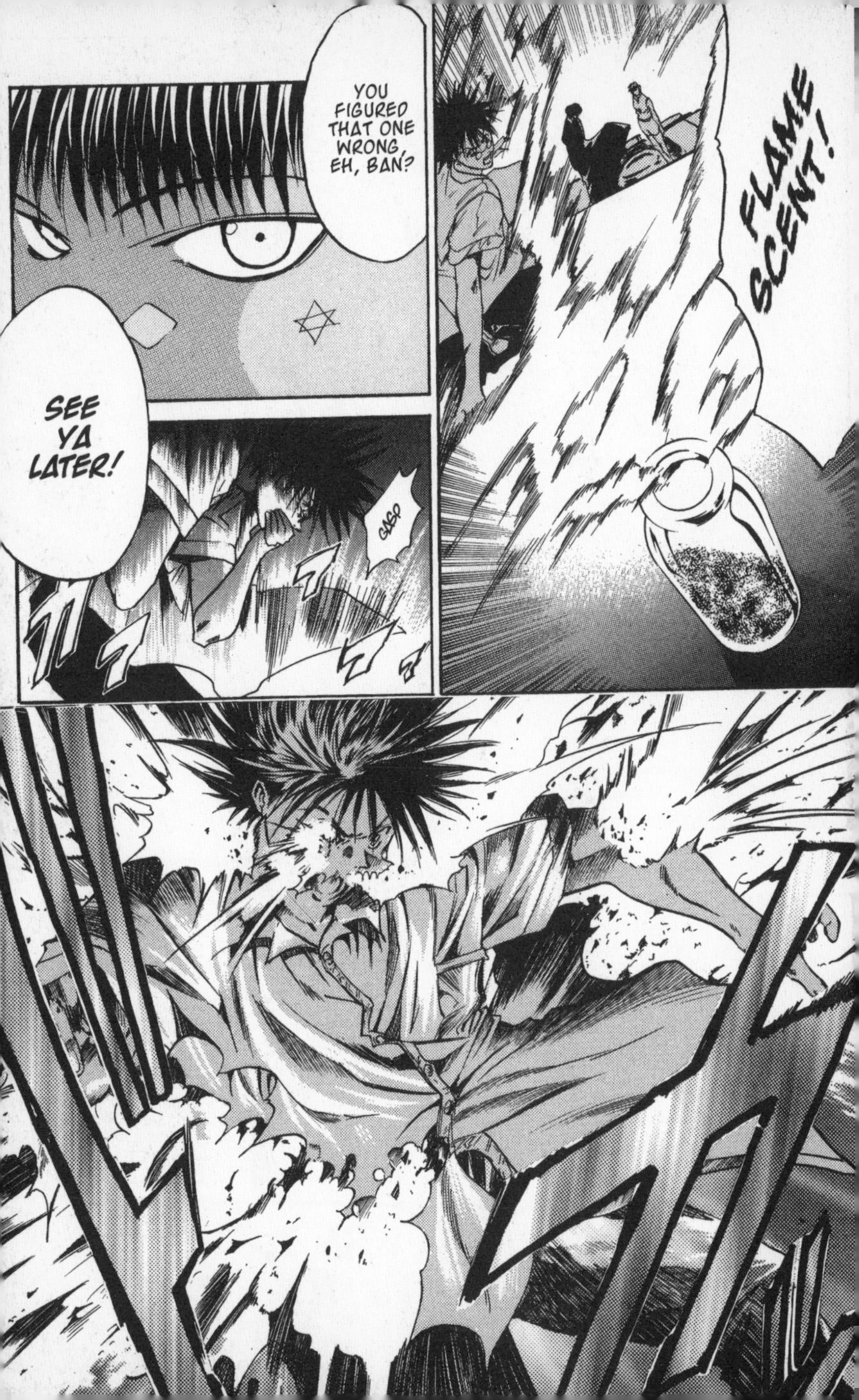
FLAME SCENT!
YOU FIGURED THAT ONE WRONG, EH, BAN?
SEE YA LATER!
GASP

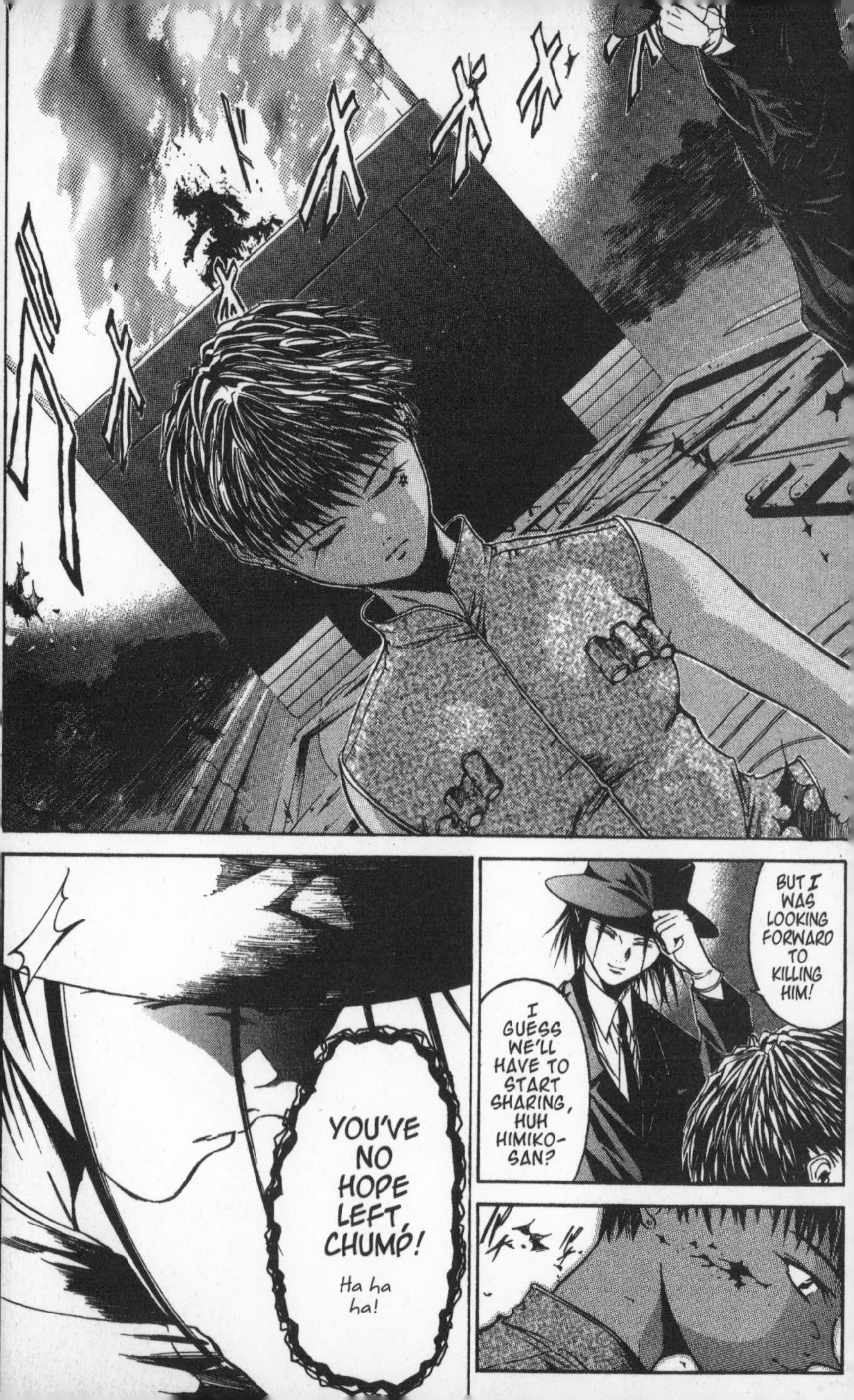
BUT I WAS LOOKING FORWARD TO KILLING HIM!
I GUESS WE'LL HAVE TO START SHARING, HUH HIMIKO-SAN?
YOU'VE NO HOPE LEFT, CHUMP!
Ha ha ha!

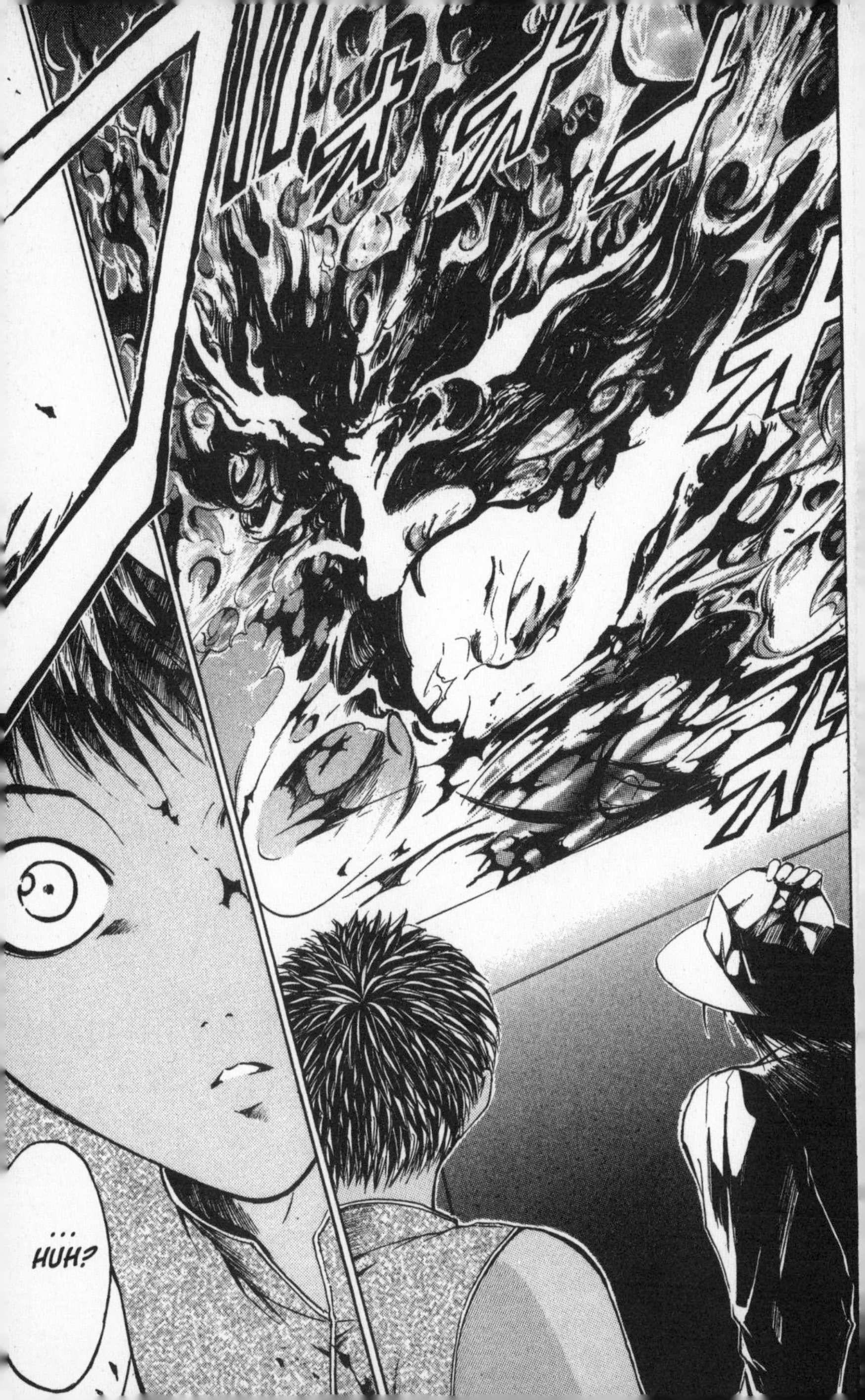
...HUH?

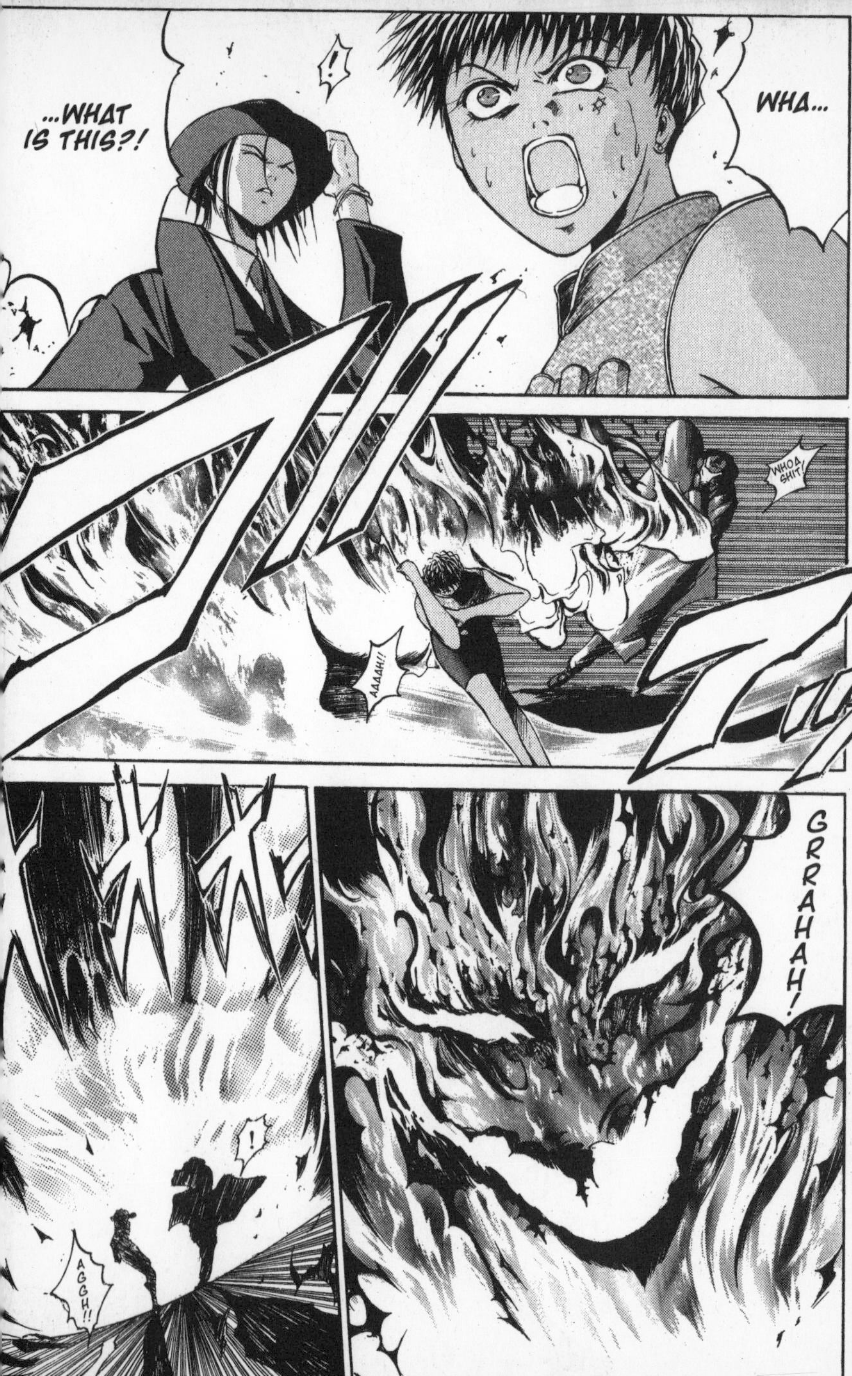
WHA...
!
...WHAT IS THIS?!
WHOA SHIT!
AAAAAH!!
GRRAHAH!
!
AGGGH!!

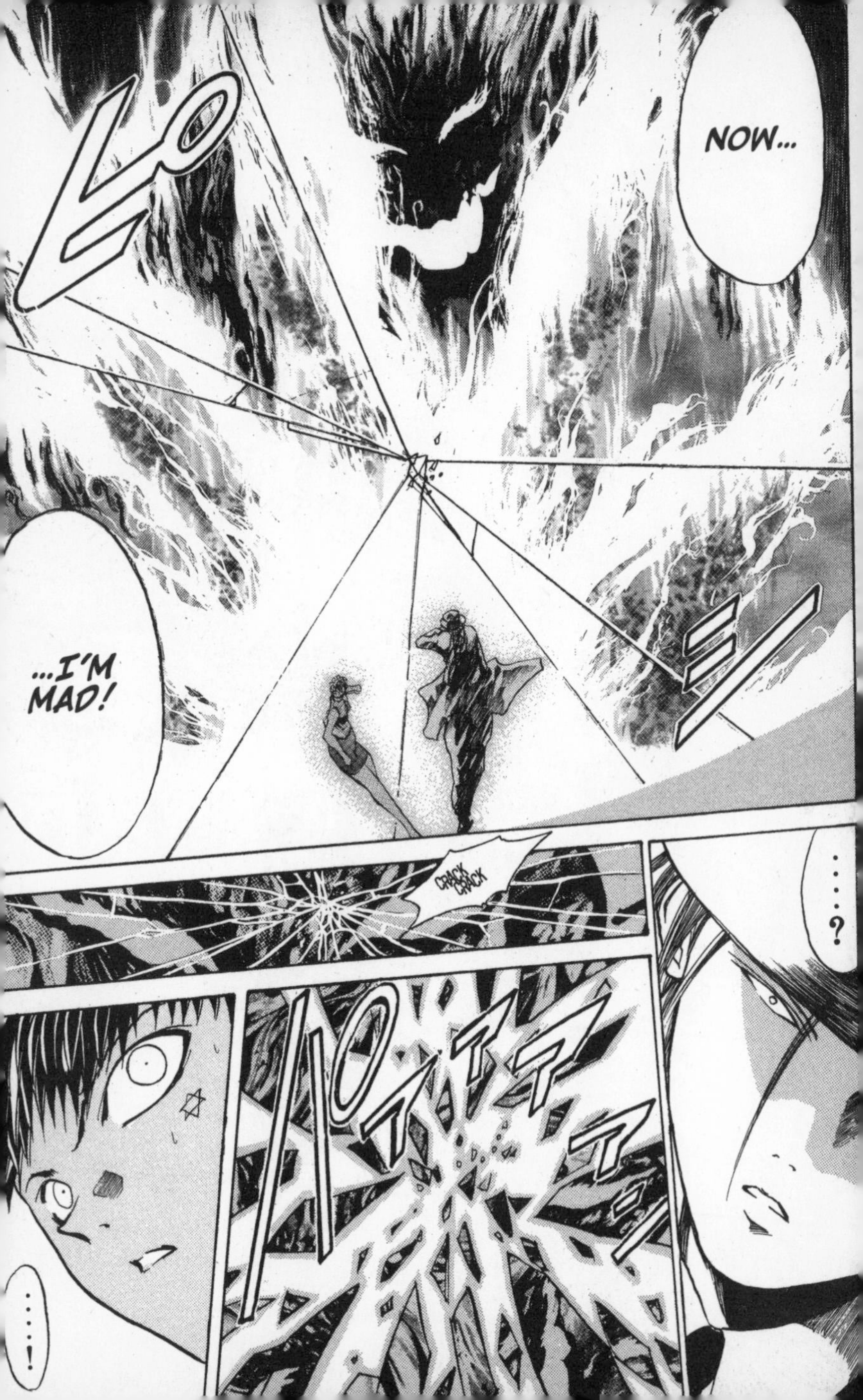
NOW...
...I'M MAD!
CRACK CRACK
....?
....!

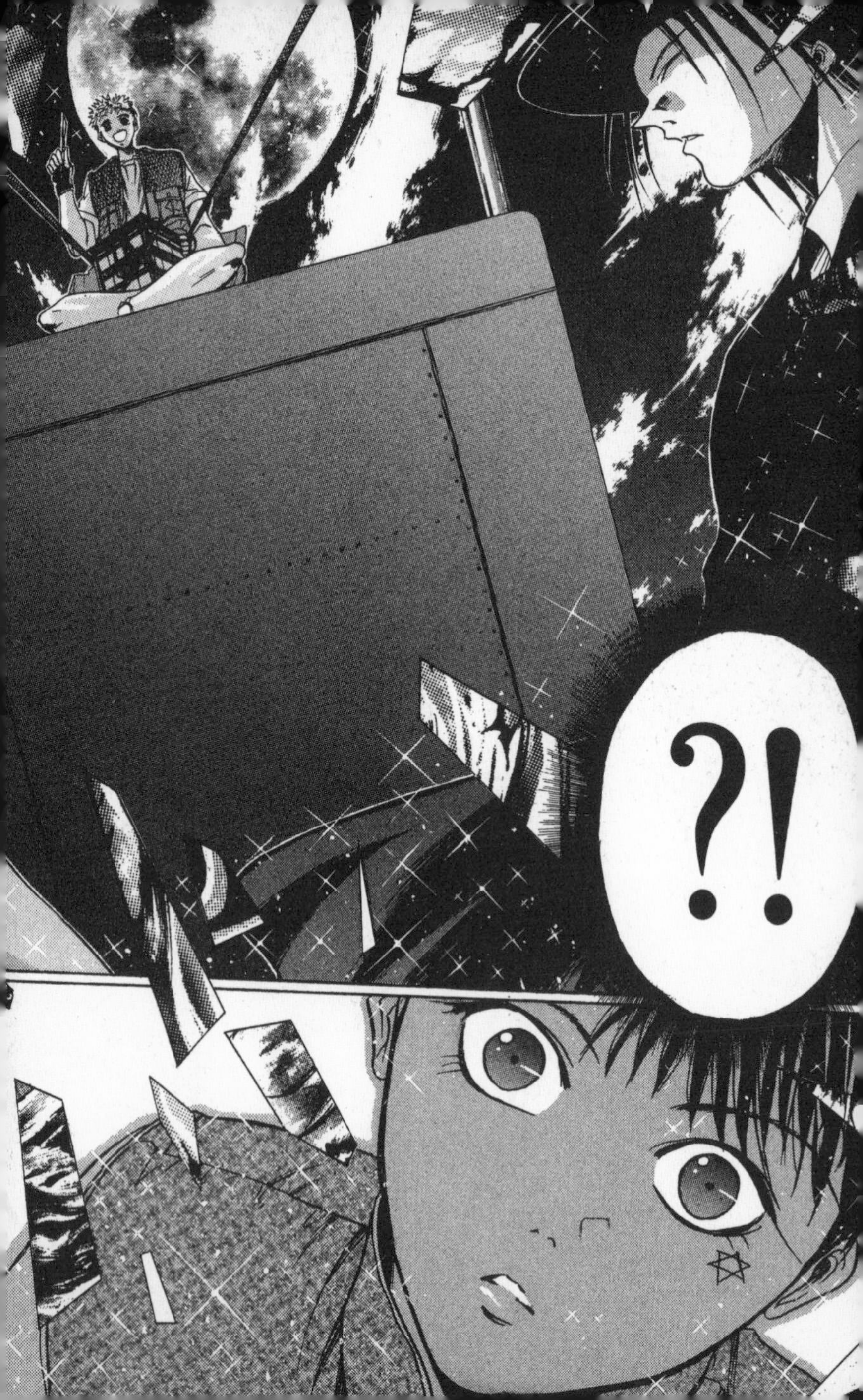
?!

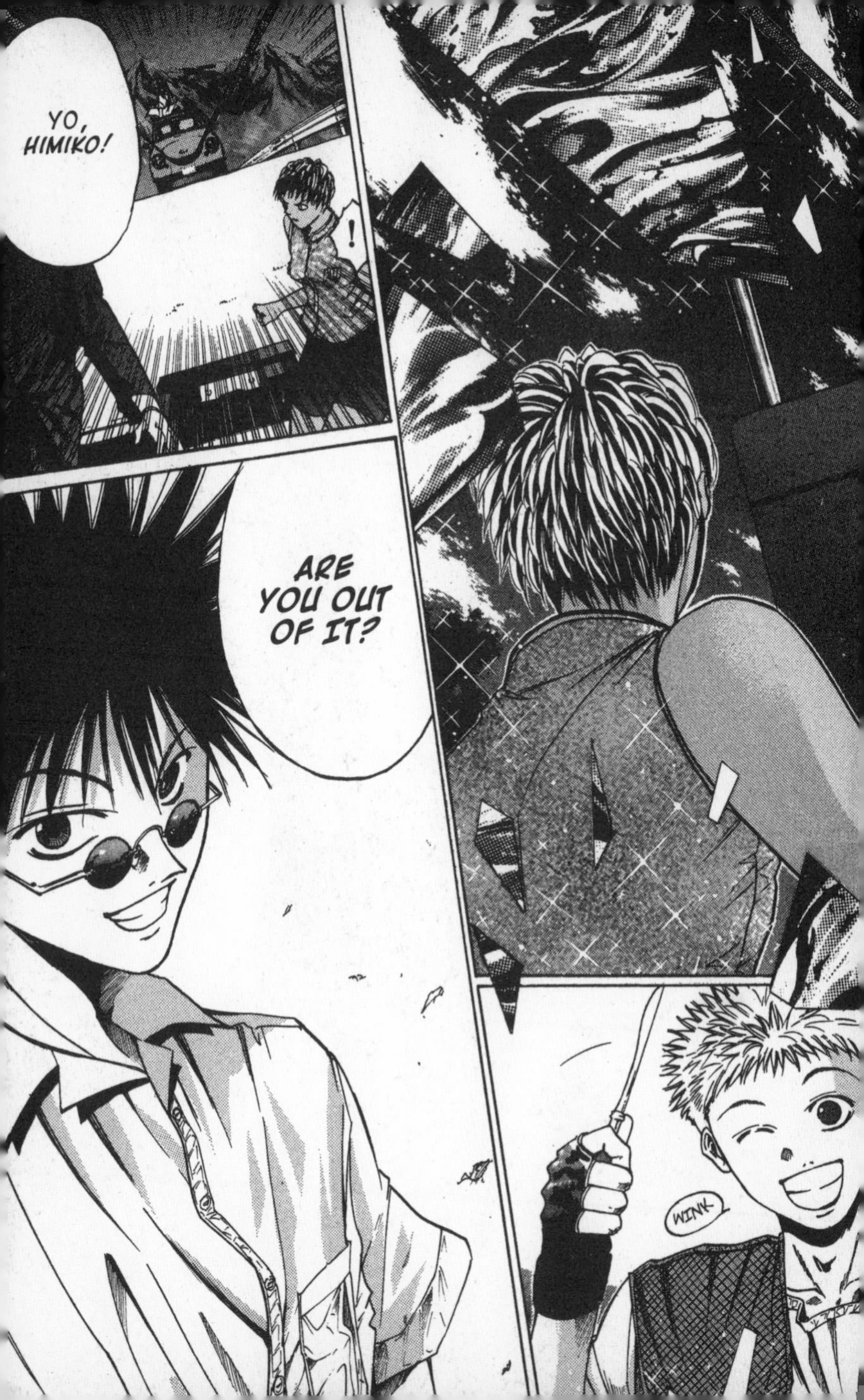
YO, HIMIKO!
!
WINK
ARE YOU OUT OF IT?

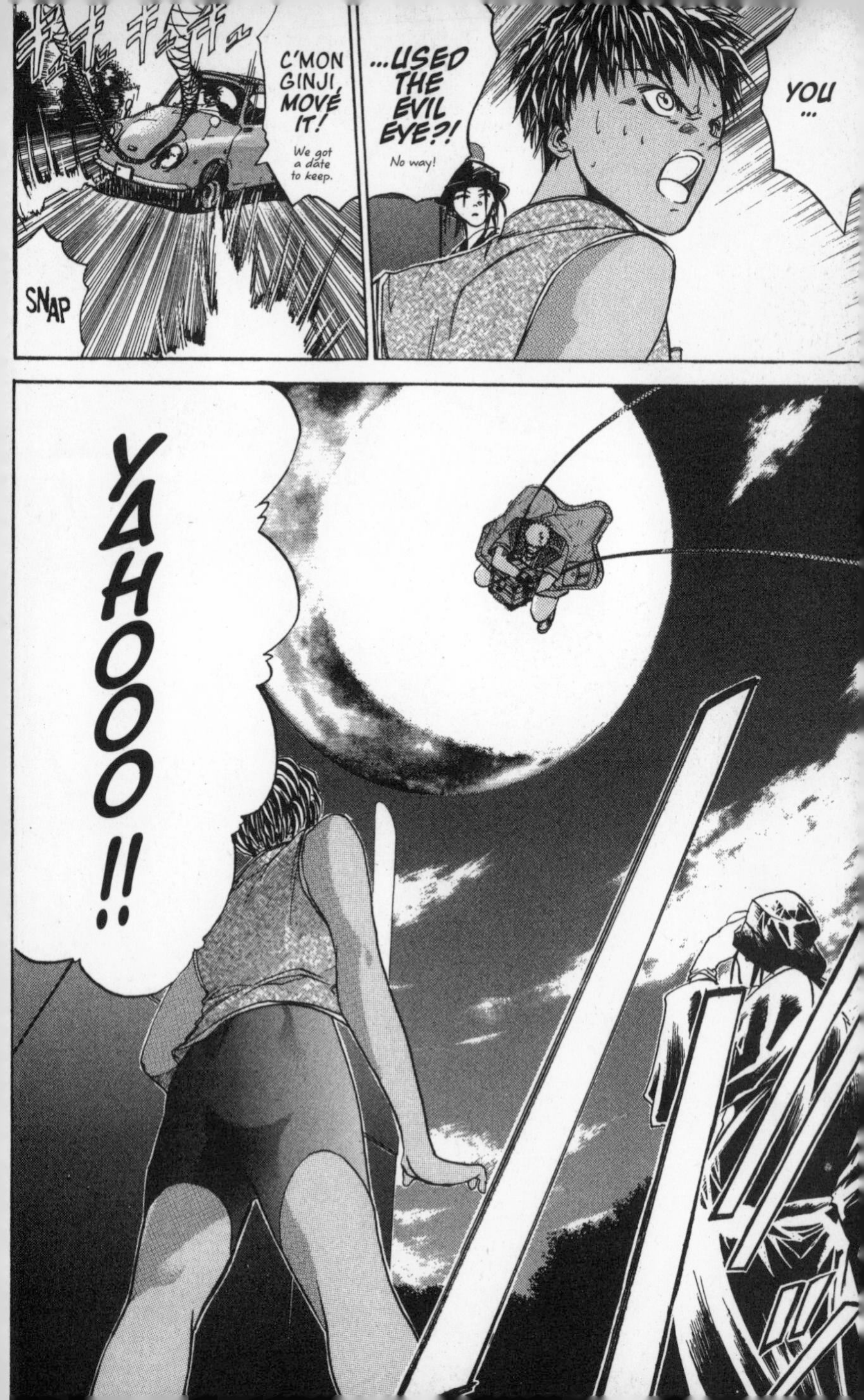
YOU ...
...USED THE EVIL EYE?!
No way!
C'MON GINJI, MOVE IT!
We got a date to keep.
SNAP
YAHOOOO!!

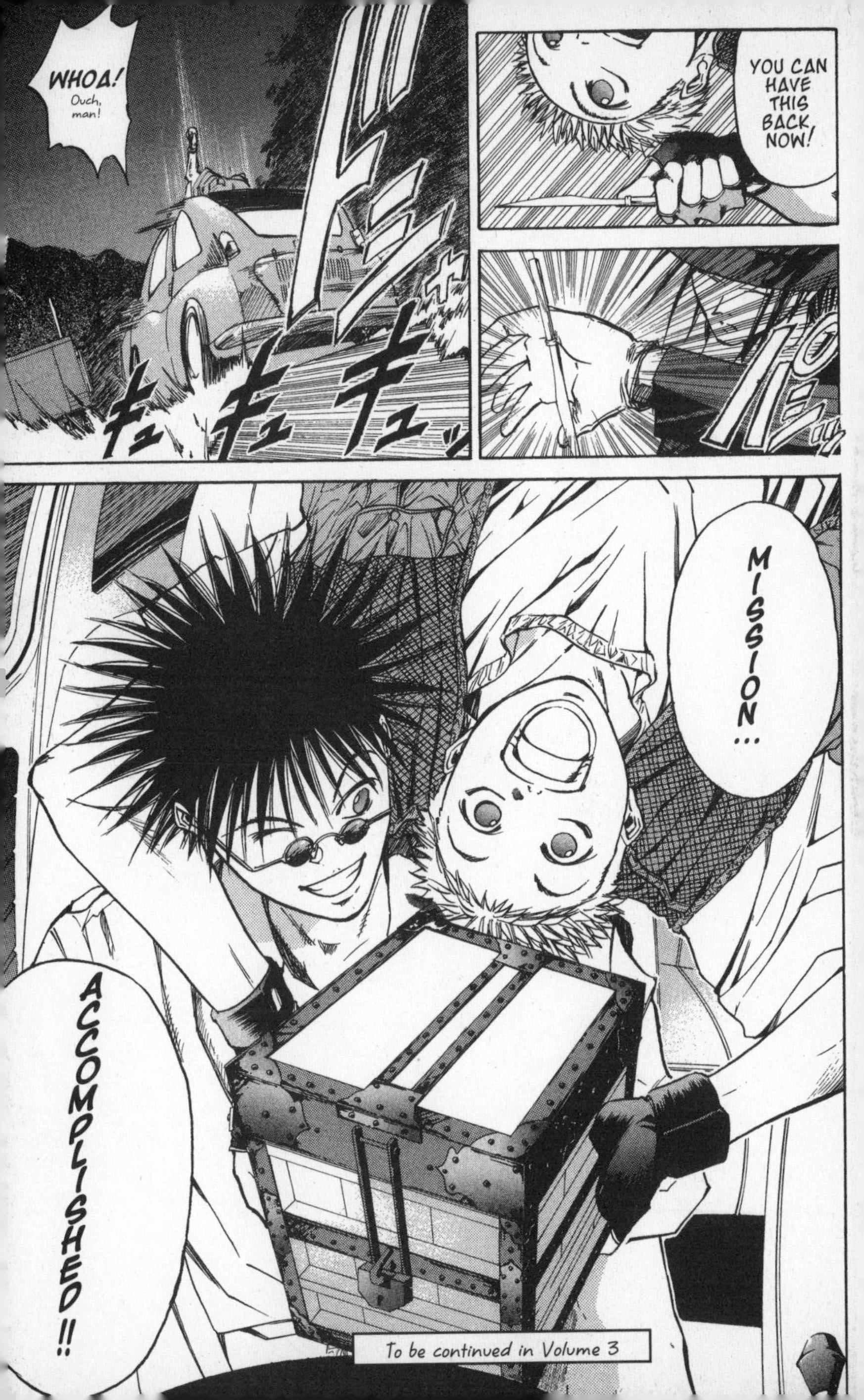
YOU CAN HAVE THIS BACK NOW!
WHOA! Ouch, man!
キュキュキュッ
MISSION...
ACCOMPLISHED!!
To be continued in Volume 3

スタッフ紹介 SUPPORT STAFF

伊川 良樹 YOSHIKI IKAWA

土屋 奈朋 NAHO TSUCHIYA

大久保 篤 ATSUSHI ŌKUBO

榎並 博昭 HIROAKI ENAMI

SPECIAL THANKS

近藤 太郎 TARO KONDO

藤狛 知弥 CHIHIRO FUJIKOMA

吉原 陽子 YOKO YOSHIHARA

辻 邦康 KUNIYASU TSUJI

EDITOR

SHIN KIBAYASHI

TOSHIMI HORIKAWA

KIICHIRŌ SUGAWARA

Thanks for all the fan letters! Every time I read their kind words, my spirits are raised! I'm really sorry I don't have time to respond to them all!! Well, I feel like drawing now, so catch you later! ^ ^ I really am sorry...
--Randy Ayamine

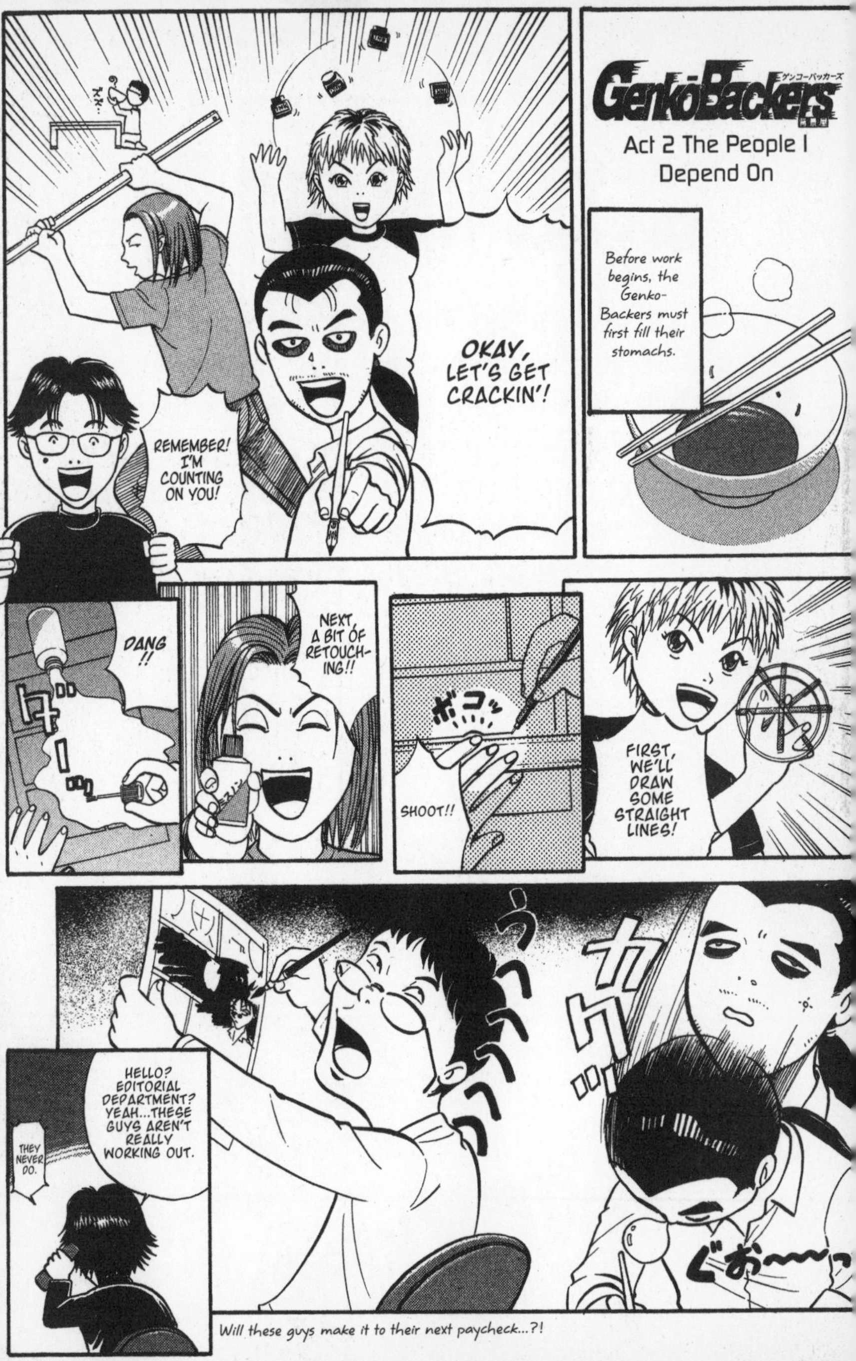
GenkōBackers
ゲンコーバッカーズ
Act 2 The People I Depend On
Before work begins, the Genko-Backers must first fill their stomachs.
OKAY, LET'S GET CRACKIN'!
REMEMBER! I'M COUNTING ON YOU!
FIRST, WE'LL DRAW SOME STRAIGHT LINES!
SHOOT!!
NEXT, A BIT OF RETOUCHING!!
DANG!!
HELLO? EDITORIAL DEPARTMENT? YEAH...THESE GUYS AREN'T REALLY WORKING OUT.
THEY NEVER DO.

Will these guys make it to their next paycheck...?!

In the next electrifying volume of

GETBACKERS™

The battle with the Transporters rages on... and the GetBackers are running out of aces. Ban has already used his Evil Eye, and Ginji has already spent quite a bit of charge. How are they going to retrieve the mysterious box and still get away with their asses intact? If they do, a young girl with a gift for music may be in their future.

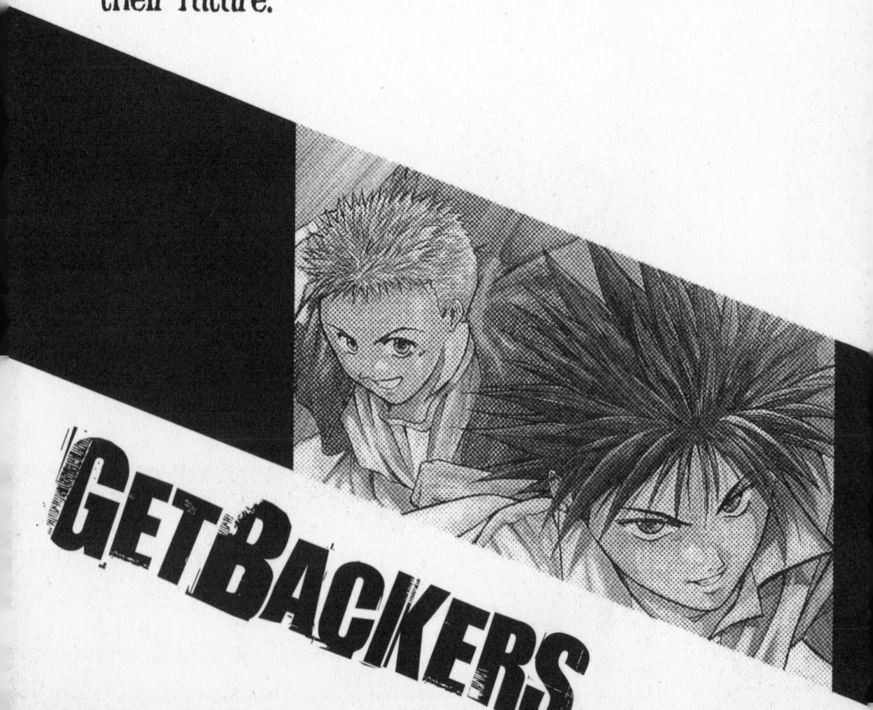
GETBACKERS™

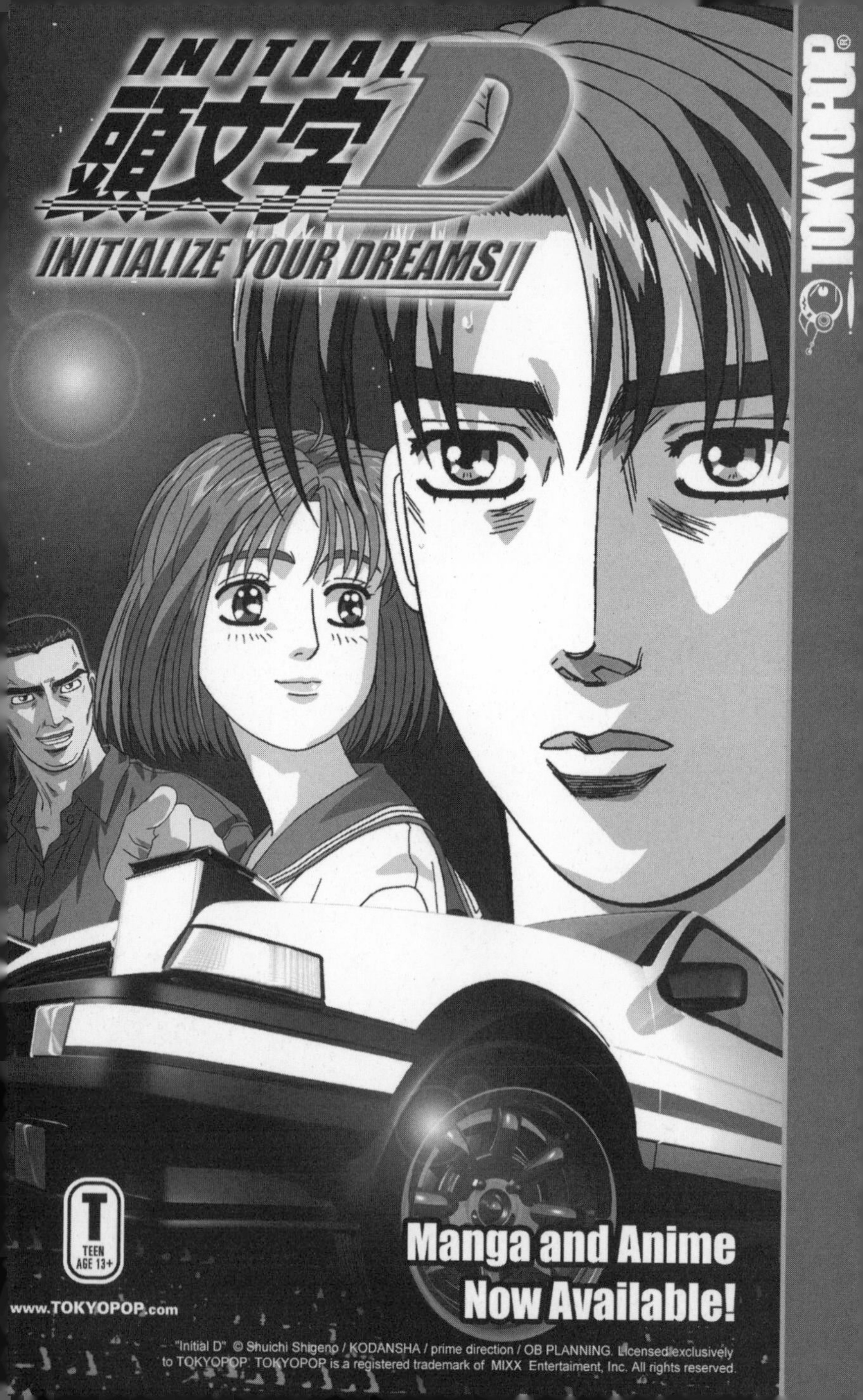
INITIAL
頭文字D
INITIALIZE YOUR DREAMS
TOKYOPOP
T
TEEN
AGE 13+
Manga and Anime
Now Available!
www.TOKYOPOP.com
"Initial D" © Shuichi Shigeno / KODANSHA / prime direction / OB PLANNING. Licensed exclusively to TOKYOPOP. TOKYOPOP is a registered trademark of MIXX Entertaiment, Inc. All rights reserved.

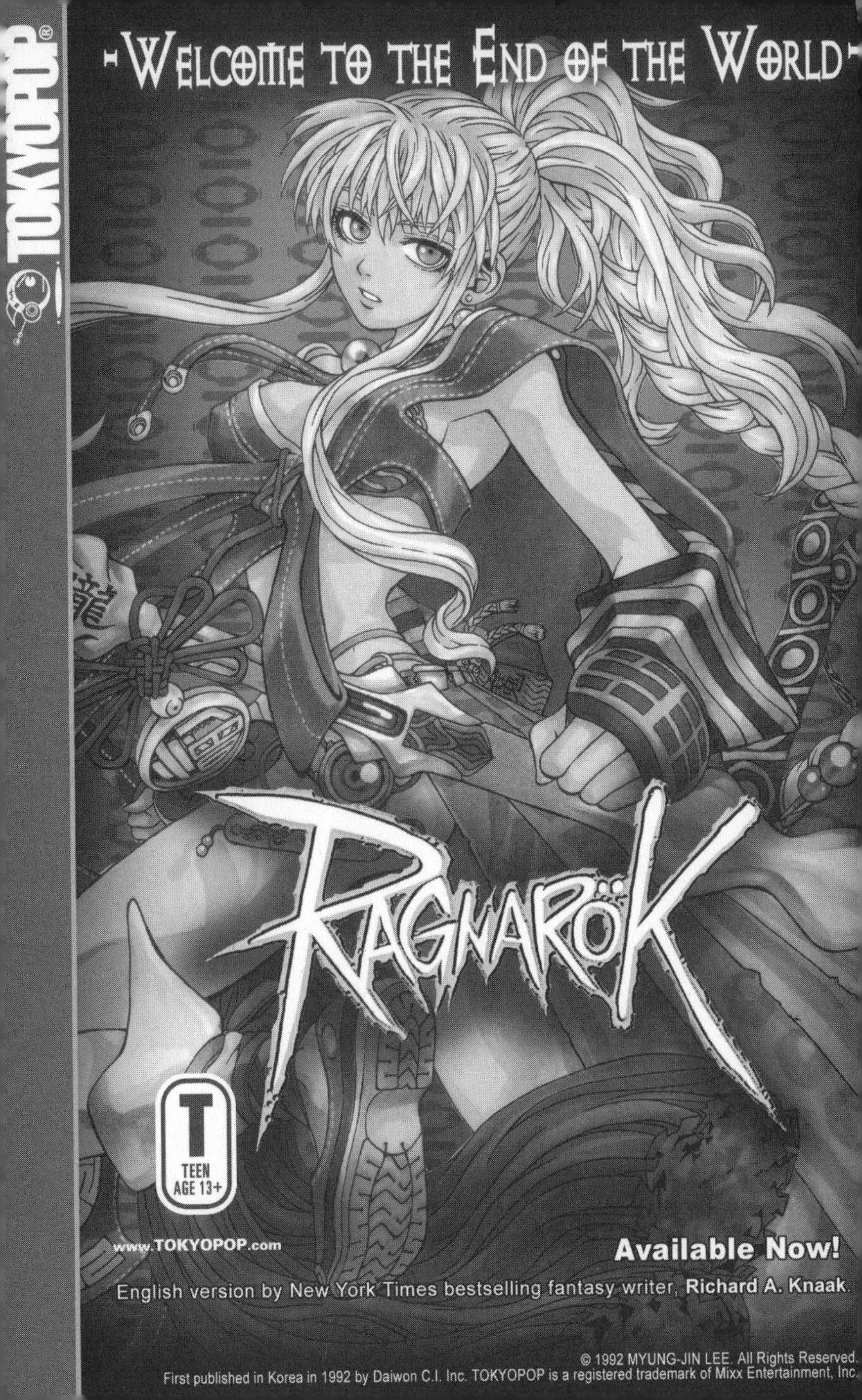
TOKYOPOP
-Welcome to the End of the World-
RAGNARÖK
T
TEEN
AGE 13+
www.TOKYOPOP.com
Available Now!
English version by New York Times bestselling fantasy writer, Richard A. Knaak.
© 1992 MYUNG-JIN LEE. All Rights Reserved.
First published in Korea in 1992 by Daiwon C.I. Inc. TOKYOPOP is a registered trademark of Mixx Entertainment, Inc.

ALSO AVAILABLE FROM TOKYOPOP®

PRINCESS AI
PSYCHIC ACADEMY
RAGNAROK
RAVE MASTER
REALITY CHECK
REBIRTH
REBOUND
REMOTE
RISING STARS OF MANGA
SABER MARIONETTE J
SAILOR MOON
SAINT TAIL
SAIYUKI
SAMURAI DEEPER KYO
SAMURAI GIRL REAL BOUT HIGH SCHOOL
SCRYED
SEIKAI TRILOGY, THE
SGT. FROG
SHAOLIN SISTERS
SHIRAHIME-SYO: SNOW GODDESS TALES
SHUTTERBOX
SKULL MAN, THE
SMUGGLER
SNOW DROP
SORCERER HUNTERS
STONE
SUIKODEN III
SUKI
THREADS OF TIME
TOKYO BABYLON
TOKYO MEW MEW
TRAMPS LIKE US
TREASURE CHESS
UNDER THE GLASS MOON
VAMPIRE GAME
VISION OF ESCAFLOWNE, THE
WARRIORS OF TAO
WILD ACT
WISH
WORLD OF HARTZ
X-DAY
ZODIAC P.I.

NOVELS

CLAMP SCHOOL PARANORMAL INVESTIGATORS
KARMA CLUB
SAILOR MOON
SLAYERS

ART BOOKS

ART OF CARDCAPTOR SAKURA
ART OF MAGIC KNIGHT RAYEARTH, THE
PEACH: MIWA UEDA ILLUSTRATIONS

ANIME GUIDES

COWBOY BEBOP
GUNDAM TECHNICAL MANUALS
SAILOR MOON SCOUT GUIDES

TOKYOPOP KIDS

STRAY SHEEP

CINE-MANGA™

ALADDIN
ASTRO BOY
CARDCAPTORS
CONFESSIONS OF A TEENAGE DRAMA QUEEN
DUEL MASTERS
FAIRLY ODDPARENTS, THE
FAMILY GUY
FINDING NEMO
G.I. JOE SPY TROOPS
JACKIE CHAN ADVENTURES
JIMMY NEUTRON: BOY GENIUS, THE ADVENTURES OF
KIM POSSIBLE
LILO & STITCH
LIZZIE MCGUIRE
LIZZIE MCGUIRE MOVIE, THE
MALCOLM IN THE MIDDLE
POWER RANGERS: NINJA STORM
SHREK 2
SPONGEBOB SQUAREPANTS
SPY KIDS 2
SPY KIDS 3-D: GAME OVER
TEENAGE MUTANT NINJA TURTLES
THAT'S SO RAVEN
TRANSFORMERS: ARMADA
TRANSFORMERS: ENERGON

For more information visit www.TOKYOPOP.com

02.03.04T

ALSO AVAILABLE FROM TOKYOPOP®

MANGA

.HACK//LEGEND OF THE TWILIGHT
@LARGE
ABENOBASHI: MAGICAL SHOPPING ARCADE
A.I. LOVE YOU
AI YORI AOSHI
ANGELIC LAYER
ARM OF KANNON
BABY BIRTH
BATTLE ROYALE
BATTLE VIXENS
BRAIN POWERED
BRIGADOON
B'TX
CANDIDATE FOR GODDESS, THE
CARDCAPTOR SAKURA
CARDCAPTOR SAKURA - MASTER OF THE CLOW
CHOBITS
CHRONICLES OF THE CURSED SWORD
CLAMP SCHOOL DETECTIVES
CLOVER
COMIC PARTY
CONFIDENTIAL CONFESSIONS
CORRECTOR YUI
COWBOY BEBOP
COWBOY BEBOP: SHOOTING STAR
CRAZY LOVE STORY
CRESCENT MOON
CULDCEPT
CYBORG 009
D•N•ANGEL
DEMON DIARY
DEMON ORORON, THE
DEUS VITAE
DIGIMON
DIGIMON TAMERS
DIGIMON ZERO TWO
DOLL
DRAGON HUNTER
DRAGON KNIGHTS
DRAGON VOICE
DREAM SAGA
DUKLYON: CLAMP SCHOOL DEFENDERS
EERIE QUEERIE!
ERICA SAKURAZAWA: COLLECTED WORKS
ET CETERA
ETERNITY
EVIL'S RETURN
FAERIES' LANDING
FAKE
FLCL
FORBIDDEN DANCE
FRUITS BASKET
G GUNDAM
GATEKEEPERS
GETBACKERS

GIRL GOT GAME
GRAVITATION
GTO
GUNDAM BLUE DESTINY
GUNDAM SEED ASTRAY
GUNDAM WING
GUNDAM WING: BATTLEFIELD OF PACIFISTS
GUNDAM WING: ENDLESS WALTZ
GUNDAM WING: THE LAST OUTPOST (G-UNIT)
HANDS OFF!
HAPPY MANIA
HARLEM BEAT
I.N.V.U.
IMMORTAL RAIN
INITIAL D
INSTANT TEEN: JUST ADD NUTS
ISLAND
JING: KING OF BANDITS
JING: KING OF BANDITS - TWILIGHT TALES
JULINE
KARE KANO
KILL ME, KISS ME
KINDAICHI CASE FILES, THE
KING OF HELL
KODOCHA: SANA'S STAGE
LAMENT OF THE LAMB
LEGAL DRUG
LEGEND OF CHUN HYANG, THE
LES BIJOUX
LOVE HINA
LUPIN III
LUPIN III: WORLD'S MOST WANTED
MAGIC KNIGHT RAYEARTH I
MAGIC KNIGHT RAYEARTH II
MAHOROMATIC: AUTOMATIC MAIDEN
MAN OF MANY FACES
MARMALADE BOY
MARS
MARS: HORSE WITH NO NAME
METROID
MINK
MIRACLE GIRLS
MIYUKI-CHAN IN WONDERLAND
MODEL
ONE
ONE I LOVE, THE
PARADISE KISS
PARASYTE
PASSION FRUIT
PEACH GIRL
PEACH GIRL: CHANGE OF HEART
PET SHOP OF HORRORS
PITA-TEN
PLANET LADDER
PLANETES
PRIEST

02.03.04T

STOP!

This is the back of the book.
You wouldn't want to spoil a great ending!

This book is printed "manga-style," in the authentic Japanese right-to-left format. Since none of the artwork has been flipped or altered, readers get to experience the story just as the creator intended. You've been asking for it, so TOKYOPOP® delivered: authentic, hot-off-the-press, and far more fun!

DIRECTIONS

If this is your first time reading manga-style, here's a quick guide to help you understand how it works.

It's easy... just start in the top right panel and follow the numbers. Have fun, and look for more 100% authentic manga from TOKYOPOP®!